The Routledge Concise History of Nineteenth-Century Literature

Nineteenth-century Britain saw the rise of secularism, the development of a modern capitalist economy and multi-party democracy as well as an explosive growth in technological, scientific and medical knowledge. It also witnessed the emergence of a mass literary culture which changed permanently the relationships between writers, readers and publishers.

Focusing on the work of British and Irish authors, *The Routledge Concise History of Nineteenth-Century Literature*:

- considers changes in literary forms, styles and genres, as well as in critical discourses
- examines literary movements such as Romanticism, Pre-Raphaelitism, Aestheticism, Decadence and Symbolism
- considers the work of a wide range of canonical and non-canonical writers
- discusses the impact of gender studies, queer theory, postcolonialism and book history
- contains useful, student-friendly features such as explanatory text boxes, chapter summaries, a detailed glossary and suggestions for further reading.

In their lucid and accessible manner, Josephine M. Guy and Ian Small provide readers with an understanding of the complexity and variety of nineteenth-century literary culture, as well as the historical conditions which produced it.

Josephine M. Guy is Professor of Modern English Literature at the School of English Studies, University of Nottingham.

Ian Small is Professor of English Literature at the Department of English, University of Birmingham.

Routledge Concise Histories of Literature series

The Routledge Concise Histories series offers students and academics alike an interesting and accessible route into the literature of a specific period, genre, place or topic. The books situate the literature within its broader historical, cultural and political context, introducing the key events, movements and theories necessary for a fuller understanding of the writing. They engage readers in debates about the period, genre or region, adding an exciting and challenging element to the reading.

Accessible and engaging, offering suggestions for further reading, explanatory text boxes, bullet-pointed chapter summaries and a glossary of key terms, the Routledge Concise Histories are the ideal starting point for the study of literature.

Available:

The Routledge Concise History of Southeast Asian Writing in English
By Rajeev S. Patke and Philip Holden

Forthcoming:

The Routledge Concise History of Canadian Literature
By Richard J. Lane

The Routledge Concise History of Science Fiction
By Mark Bould and Sherryl Vint

The Routledge Concise History of Nineteenth-Century Literature

Josephine M. Guy and Ian Small

LONDON AND NEW YORK

First edition published 2011
by Routledge
2 Park Square, Milton Park, Abingdon, Oxon OX14 4RN

Simultaneously published in the USA and Canada
by Routledge
270 Madison Avenue, New York, NY 10016

Routledge is an imprint of the Taylor & Francis Group, an informa business

Typeset in Sabon by T&F Books
Printed and bound in Great Britain by TJ International Ltd., Padstow, Cornwall

British Library Cataloguing in Publication Data
A catalogue record for this book is available from the British Library

Library of Congress Cataloging in Publication Data
Guy, Josephine M., 1963–
The Routledge concise history of nineteenth century literature / Josephine Guy and Ian Small.
p. cm.
Includes bibliographical references and index.
1. English literature--19th century--History and criticism. 2. American literature--19th century--History and criticism. I. Small, Ian. II. Title.
PR451.G89 2010
820.9'008--dc22
2010019471

ISBN 13: 978-0-415-48710-8 (hbk)
ISBN 13: 978-0-415-48711-5 (pbk)
ISBN 13: 978-0-203-83941-6 (ebk)

Contents

1 Introduction

What is nineteenth-century literature?

Overview

The division of literary history into a series of distinct chronological periods, of which the nineteenth century can obviously be one, takes place after the events which that history describes. It is therefore retrospective and may seem, to some extent, an arbitrary process, one which begs a number of questions. In terms which are relevant to the present volume, what makes 1800 or 1899 so special that they become respectively a beginning and an end point? What, in terms of the history of *literature*, do they mark the beginning and ending of? Any history has to make the study of the past manageable, and one of the commonest ways of doing so is by dividing it into chronological units. However, we might want to enquire whether events in literary history organise themselves neatly into a chronology, and whether that chronology can conveniently be mapped onto century divisions. As important is the question of defining what those literary 'events' are. Is literary history an account of works, authors, movements or styles? And how do literary events relate to those described in social, economic or political histories? In this chapter we examine briefly some of the general theoretical and methodological problems involved in writing literary history, and explain how the present volume responds to them.

Literary periodisation

We can glimpse the limitations of century divisions for literary historians by examining some of the debates which surround accounts of literary Romanticism in Britain. The origins of Romanticism are usually traced to the last decades of the eighteenth century, but many of its significant literary artefacts were produced in the early years of the nineteenth (certainly for British literary Romanticism). This complication is exacerbated by the untidy details of the genesis of particular literary works and the complexity of their publishing histories. For example, most students of literature would be surprised if, in any account of Romanticism, *The Prelude* by William Wordsworth (1770–1850) were not described as one of that movement's most important works. However, although *The Prelude* began life in 1798–99 as a two-part unpublished poem, it was never made available to a contemporary reading public in that form. It subsequently underwent a long and fairly constant process of revision and enlargement, and was only published in 1850, and in a fourteen-book version which Wordsworth – by then dead – himself never oversaw (even the title of the work was not his). The question for the literary historian who is committed to organising literary history into century divisions is simple: to which of those historical 'periods' does *The Prelude* belong?

The same kind of observation can be made about some of the works and writers associated with literary Modernism: as with Romanticism, it is a literary movement generally thought to straddle a century division. On this occasion, although there is a large measure of agreement that its major works were produced in the first three decades of the twentieth century, its origins are usually traced to the 1890s, or on occasions even earlier. So if we wished to write an account of literary Modernism, how would we deal with those long-lived authors who began writing in one period – in Victoria's reign – but who continued well into another, in this case, well into the Edwardian and Georgian eras. The careers of writers like Thomas Hardy (1840–1928) and W. B. Yeats (1865–1939) again make for untidy period divisions in the sense that, in Hardy's words (written on New Year's Eve, 1900, in his poem 'The Darkling Thrush'), their careers coincided with 'the Century's corpse outleant'. Is Hardy a late Victorian who outlived his time, or a proto-modernist? By the same token, how would we categorise Yeats? Although he suggested, to use his own words, that he and his contemporaries were 'the last Romantics', and although his first volumes of poetry were published in the 1880s, his best work (in the view of most modern critics) did not appear until the First World War.

It was precisely this untidiness which led some literary historians to posit an intervening mini-literary period, termed the 'literature of transition' (and which gave its name to a literary journal, *English Literature in Transition*, founded in 1957 and still in print today), to describe the decades from 1880 to 1920. Other historians identified a shorter transitional moment, that of the 'fin-de-siècle' or 1890s, a decade in which, according to the early twentieth-century critic Holbrook Jackson, people 'were convinced that they were passing not only from one social system to another, but from one morality to another, from one culture to another, and from one religion to a dozen or more' (Jackson 1913: 31). Yet other historians have preferred to make a distinction between what Michael Wheeler terms 'high' Victorian and 'late' Victorian literature, when 'late' Victorian encompasses a time-span from around 1870 to 1901 (Wheeler 1985).

The division of historical periods can have profound consequences for the ways we categorise and value certain authors. For example, in 1888 Mary Ward (1851–1920) published, to considerable contemporary acclaim, what posterity has judged, albeit a little grudgingly, to be her most significant novel, *Robert Elsmere*. Yet, like Thomas Hardy's, her prolific writing career, which encompassed novels, children's fiction and criticism, stretched into the twentieth century, and she was still publishing in the year of her death, 1920. However, Ward almost never appears in histories of either fin-de-siècle or early twentieth-century literature (and today most of her post-1890s works are out of print). Even in histories of nineteenth-century (or late Victorian) literature, she is usually a marginal figure, represented only by one or two novels. The difficulty is that Ward's commitment to literary realism and her conservative politics (she was a leading figure in the Anti-Suffrage League) sit uncomfortably with the formal experimentation and insistent questioning of 'Victorian values' which have often been seen as the most significant features of late nineteenth- and early twentieth-century literary production. Put another way, the values which define Ward's long career, and the consistency with which she adhered to them, make a poor fit with the categories with which historians have typically identified patterns in nineteenth-century literary history. They have tended, that is, to concentrate less on continuity than on identifying moments which mark important changes in literary sensibilities or styles. However, if we were to write a literary history which highlighted the stability of certain canons of literary taste, rather than attempts to challenge their hegemony, then we can imagine a narrative charting a continuous line of development linking the fiction of writers such as George Eliot (1819–80) and Ward to that of later realist novelists such as Arnold Bennett (1867–1931) and John Galsworthy (1867–1933). Just such a re-casting and revaluation of this moment in literary history has been suggested by at least one distinguished critic, John Carey (1992).

It might seem that one way of coming to terms with the dilemmas posed by long careers would be for the historian to focus on works, rather than on the lives of the writers who produced them. Unfortunately, however, we soon run into a similar set of puzzles because individual works, as we have seen in the case of *The Prelude*, may have a long genesis or period of gestation. Moreover, the particular ways in which a work of literature is placed in the public domain are often complex and can cover a long period of time. As we explain in more detail in Chapter 7, the book version of Hardy's novel *Tess of the D'Urbervilles* was first published in 1891, but Hardy continued to revise it through successive editions until the 1920 Wessex Edition. Should we consider *Tess* in relation to the development of twentieth-century prose fiction, and to works like *Women in Love* by D. H. Lawrence (1885–1930), first published in America in 1920 and in Britain in 1921, rather than in relation to late nineteenth-century 'new woman' fiction like *The Woman Who Did* (1895) by Grant Allen (1848–99)? The example of another famous nineteenth-century poet, Gerard Manley Hopkins (1844–89), is equally problematic. Hopkins published almost none of his poetry during his lifetime; on his death he bequeathed his papers to his close friend, the poet and critic Robert Bridges (1844–1930), and it was Bridges who arranged for the selection, editing and publication of Hopkins's poems in 1918, almost thirty years after their author had died. However, a history which places those poems as post-First World War literary productions runs a serious risk of mischaracterising them, and certainly of misunderstanding both the context in which they were written and the culture to which they were a response.

Having noted these fairly basic problems, as well as acknowledging the necessity of making *some* kind of division of the past, we can observe that the period 1800–99 has been chosen because it is judged to possess more of the merits and fewer of the drawbacks of other candidates. The limitation of an obvious competitor – the 'Victorian period' (usually defined as 1832–1901) – is that it presupposes that a logic of literary history can be neatly mapped onto the longevity or otherwise of English or British monarchs (or, to be more precise, of some English or British monarchs, for we have Elizabethan and Jacobean periods, but not a 'Williamite' one). An equally problematic competitor is what some literary historians have termed the 'long nineteenth century', usually seen as beginning with the French Revolution and ending with the outbreak of the First World War in 1914. Here there are two reservations. We might reasonably object that developments in literary culture no more readily map onto the history of wars or revolutions than they do onto the reigns of kings and queens. More pragmatically, such a span of time is too unwieldy to be of much practical use for those interested in the specificities of literary production and literary history: the difficulties of justifying beginning and end dates are not resolved simply by extending them in either direction.

Literature and change: history versus chronology

It does not follow from the decision to divide literary history into centuries either that literary production over the course of any single century was uniform in character or that it changed in consistent ways or at a consistent rate. Nor does it follow that literary historians are in agreement about the events which might comprise such a history. History is not the same as a chronology; to adapt E. M. Forster's famous comment made apropos of the novel, all histories 'tell a story'. To be more precise, literary history may involve the telling of several different kinds of stories, not all of which are compatible with each other. The literary theorist David Perkins puts this point cogently when he argues that 'whatever else they have hoped to accomplish literary historians have sought to represent the past and *to explain it*'. He goes on to elaborate this proposition: 'to represent is to tell how it was and to explain is to state why – why literary works acquired the character they have and why the literary series evolved as it did' (Perkins 1992: 13).

'Series' and 'evolved' are loaded terms. The concept of a 'series' presupposes a set of elements with common properties, or with certain values determined by a common relation. How one defines those properties or that principle of relation will therefore determine which elements – in this case, which literary works – are brought under the historian's scrutiny. Another way to put this is to say that there can be two separate kinds of disagreement among literary historians. First, they can disagree about what it is they are trying to explain (or, in the terms which Perkins uses, how the series is to be defined). So are they writing a history of styles, genres, movements or of literary representations? Second, they can also disagree about the nature of those explanations, or what caused the members of the series to take the particular forms which they did take. For example, should literary histories be contextual in nature, in the sense that they involve reference to the details of the wider culture in which literary works are produced? And if so, which of those contexts – social, economic, technological, religious, political, legal and intellectual – 'matter', and to what extent can their relationship to literary works be said to be a determining one? Alternatively, it might be argued that literary culture has a high degree of autonomy and that changes in literary form can therefore be adequately explained in terms of endogenous 'laws' of literary development. This kind of explanation tends to inform histories of genres when the details of one work need to be understood only in relation to other works in the same genre.

In practice these two sorts of disagreement are closely linked. They usually converge on the question, what is a literary history *for*? And here a further range of possibilities presents itself. Some literary historians examine past literary production in order to identify those works which they perceive to have some relevance and value for the modern reader (although obviously there is room for competing views about which modern readers they have in mind). These historians are seeking to define a 'canon' of nineteenth-century literature, often by challenging the principles underlying the canons defined by earlier historians. Past literary works may be valued for the ways in which they engage with gender roles and sexual or racial identities, these concerns being prominent in the culture of the present day. Or past literary works may be valued for what are perceived to be their formal innovations or stylistic sophistication. Although considerations of a work's politics and its form are not necessarily mutually exclusive tasks, it is none the less the case, as we explain in Chapter 3, that a history of nineteenth-century styles tends to brings different works into view, and will thus result in a different canon, when compared with a history of, say, women's writing. Other historians, however, argue that the purpose of literary history should be documentary rather than evaluative: it should be limited to a description of the reading practices of past cultures and thus be an account of past literary values. In this last view, literary history amounts to writing a history of taste, although there will be differences of opinion about whose tastes, certainly in the nineteenth century, are worthy of the historian's consideration. So would it be the taste of the many thousands of readers who bought the novels of Marie Corelli (1855–1924), most of which are today out of print; or of the few hundred who purchased those by Henry James (1843–1916), nearly all of which are still available in cheap paperbacks?

We can gain an idea of how the various presuppositions made by literary historians produce different sorts of histories of nineteenth-century literary production by considering one specific example, the case of Walter Scott (1771–1832). In the early decades of the nineteenth century Scott was a popular and celebrated writer, his life forming the subject-matter of one of the great biographies of English literature, the *Memoirs of the Life of Sir Walter Scott* (1837–38) by John Gibson Lockhart (1794–1854), Scott's son-in-law. By contrast, today Scott rarely figures on the undergraduate curriculum, his verse and historical romances apparently being out of sympathy with modern interests. For the historian of taste, both Scott's initial high reputation and its dramatic decline demand explanation, one which is generally made in terms of a larger story concerning changing attitudes towards British and Scottish nationalisms and equally far-reaching changes in the narrative strategies employed by nineteenth-century novelists. For the historian concerned with a canon, there is a different problem to address: has Scott been unfairly marginalised? Are there grounds for recuperating his works for modern audiences, perhaps by situating him as the originator of a genre – the historical romance – which continues to find popularity with the general reading public in the work of modern novelists such as Jean Plaidy or Philippa Gregory?

The differences among historians about how to conceive the subject-matter of literary history – the nature of what Perkins calls the 'series' – finds a parallel in attitudes towards that series' evolution. In science there is much debate about the nature and pace of biological evolution, whether it moves in steady incremental ways, or whether there are sudden moments of change, a process which the biologist Stephen J. Gould famously termed 'punctuated equilibrium'. Gould's phrase turns out to be an apt metaphor for the ways in which literary historians have argued that some decades in the nineteenth century possess a greater significance than others in relation to both the nature and pace of change in literary production. The years between the mid-1840s and the mid-1850s have been seen as marking a particularly important moment in the history of the novel, one in which political turmoil in many parts of Europe (including the revolutions of 1848), and social unrest and economic recession in Britain (what used to be called the 'hungry forties'), encouraged British novelists to confront new subject-matter, such as social inequality and class antagonism, as well as the relationship of both of these to the accelerating processes of urbanisation and industrialisation. As we describe in Chapter 3, this new 'seriousness', sometimes seen as an overt politicisation of literature, has been understood as marking a departure from the sensationalism and triviality associated with earlier literary traditions, notably from what have been disparagingly labelled 'silver fork' and 'Newgate' novels. This foregrounding of the mid-1840s to mid-1850s has in turn meant that many novels produced in the 1820s and 1830s have tended to be ignored (and today most remain out of print). As a result, few modern readers are acquainted with the early fiction of Edward Bulwer-Lytton (1803–73), who wrote initially under the name Edward Bulwer, or the works of Mrs Gore (1799–1861) or of William Harrison Ainsworth (1805–82), although all three had a devoted following among nineteenth-century readers and reputations which, at the height of their popularity, rivalled that of Charles Dickens (1812–70).

Other decades which have received what might appear to be a disproportionate amount of critical attention are the 1870s and 1880s: in this case, and as we have hinted above, it has been driven by a concern to locate the moment of transition between so-called 'Victorian values' and the critique of them often understood to signal the experimentation associated with early Modernism. Disagreement among historians over whether it is the 1870s or 1880s which constitute the most crucial transitional decade can be traced to differences in the way they value literary works. So if it is literature's ability to represent gender politics and the ideologies of sexuality which is of interest, then it will generally be the literature of the 1880s which assumes significance, coinciding as it does with the beginnings of the New Woman and Suffragette movements as well as with debates about homosexuality. By contrast, for the historian interested in stylistic innovation, it is the 1870s which represent a crucial turning point, insofar as the arguments associated with the Aesthetic Movement can be seen, as we suggest in Chapter 4, to have paved the way for the kind of formal experimentation which was to find its full expression in Modernism.

Further complications in the way historians map the pace of change are produced by a concern with genre, for genres can seem to develop at quite different rates. As recently as the 1980s, the theatre historian Michael Booth complained that nineteenth-century drama was often dismissed as 'a formless mass of mediocrity, dull and repetitive, lacking literary quality and thematic significance, a vast sea of theatrical trivia and downright badness' (1981: 1–2). Booth went on to suggest that for most historians, nineteenth-century drama did not begin until 'the glorious dawn' of Oscar Wilde (1854–1900) and George Bernard Shaw (1856–1950): in other words, the 1890s was the *only* decade in that entire century in which there was any material worth the attention of the literary or theatre critic. Although (as we will explain in Chapter 2) more recent research, notably in performance studies, has challenged this judgement, Booth's comments none the less stand as a particularly striking example of the disparities which can exist between historians' perceptions of which years or decades saw the most notable or interesting literary 'events' in the nineteenth century.

Literary history and literary theory

For the student of nineteenth-century literary history the diverse, and at times contradictory, ways in which the literature of the period has been discussed may seem confusing. There is, however, a kind of underlying logic to the shifting interests and priorities we have briefly mentioned, in that fashions in literary historiography tend to follow closely in the wake of fashions in literary criticism. It is no accident that histories of nineteenth-century formal developments, which marginalised drama and, to a lesser extent, poetry, coincided with the popularity of formalist criticism and its celebration of linguistic complexity and ambiguity. Likewise, it was the rise to prominence of Marxist criticism in the 1960s and early 1970s which brought about the relative academic neglect of early nineteenth-century fiction (including the works of Jane Austen (1775–1817)) in order to focus attention on the novels of the 1840s and 1850s which, as we noted above, were seen to engage more fully with the inequalities produced by the nineteenth-century class system. The increasing popularity of feminist criticism in the 1970s and 1980s also brought about shifts in the literary historiography of the nineteenth century. As Chapter 6 shows, on the one hand, it brought to notice many 'forgotten' female authors such as Mary Elizabeth

Braddon (1837–1915), Ouida (Marie Louise de la Ramée 1839–1908), Juliana Ewing (1841–85), Sara Grand (1854–1943) and 'Michael Field' (the pen-name of aunt and niece Katharine Bradley (1846–1914) and Edith Cooper (1862–1913)); and on the other, it led to the revaluation of genres in which women had excelled and which (perhaps because of that distinction) had hitherto been overlooked – notably sensation novels and children's fiction.

Similarly the advent of queer theory in the 1980s and 1990s further redrew the map of nineteenth-century literary history, in part by concentrating attention on the last (rather than middle) decades of the century, because of the important legal and cultural debates about gender roles which took place in the 1880s and 1890s. Queer theory also revalued the contributions of individual writers. The most spectacular beneficiary of these changed priorities was probably Oscar Wilde, a writer who represented, until the 1970s, something of an embarrassment to academic critics, but who has since become one of the most widely known nineteenth-century authors. The popularity of postcolonial theory has led to a reassessment of what is meant by 'British' literary history as well as permitting a reappraisal of the work of familiar writers. As we argue in Chapter 6, a seminal study in this respect was Edward Said's *Orientalism* (1978), which alerted readers to an otherwise hidden politics – that of race and empire – which in his view compromised such apparently 'innocent' works as Jane Austen's *Mansfield Park* (1814) or *Jane Eyre* (1847) by Charlotte Brontë (1816–55). It also led to a renewed interrogation of the politics underlying more explicitly orientalist works such as *Don Juan* (1819–24) by George Gordon, 6th Baron, Bryon (1788–1824).

The most recent fashion in literary criticism which has influenced our understanding of nineteenth-century literary historiography has been the project known as 'the history of the book'. Described as 'the golden age of print', the nineteenth century has presented a fertile ground for the thesis of book historians – that bibliography and the study of the materiality of print culture should form a key component in any literary history. This proposition has brought to the forefront of literary history those authors who had a particularly interesting relationship with the publishing industry. They were often women writers of popular fiction whose successful careers coincided with, and testify to, important changes in literary culture, such as the increasing professionalisation of authorship, the growth of mass taste and the impact of technological change upon creativity.

Methodology: history versus histories

It should now be possible to appreciate why this Introduction began with a question – 'What is nineteenth-century literature?'; and why, too, that question does not have any easy or definitive answer. There is no single history of nineteenth-century literature to be written, because there is no consensus about what precisely such a literary history is a history *of*, what its methodologies should be, nor what purpose such a history serves.

However, does the fact that literary history, like most other histories, is contested mean that we can somehow dispense with it? Here the sceptical Perkins has a bracingly terse answer: he acknowledges that while we may not be able to write literary history with 'intellectual conviction', meaning we cannot write a history of nineteenth-century literature which *all* readers will find equally acceptable, none the less literary history 'has an indispensable role in our experience of literature and a broader cultural and social function as well' (1992: 17). In short: most readers feel that they *need* literary history, while simultaneously recognising the provisional nature of any particular account of past literary culture. The present volume aims to respond positively to this paradox: to answer readers' desires for some points of orientation which will permit them to grasp the distinctive nature of nineteenth-century literary production, while at the same time drawing attention to the diverse ways in which the period has been, and can be, mapped. In this respect, the Routledge *Concise History of Nineteenth-Century Literature* is different in conception from most other introductory guides to the period. Readers of this volume will be given neither *the* history of nineteenth-century literature, nor *a* history. Rather, the following chapters will provide different sorts of narratives of the period; moreover, attention will be given to the theoretical assumptions which underpin these narratives in order that readers may appreciate both how and why different histories of nineteenth-century literature have been constructed. While each chapter is designed so that it may be read as a discrete unit, there are also areas of intersection or overlap, as some authors and works are examined and re-examined from different perspectives. When taken together, and while not being, and not aiming to be, exhaustive, Chapters 2–7 attempt to give the reader a sense of the wide variety of literary phenomena and writers to be found in the nineteenth century. Dates of literary works are given for the first published edition (book or periodical) unless otherwise stated; birth and death dates for each author are provided only when they are first mentioned. Given the range of editions of nineteenth-century literary works available to the modern reader – an issue discussed in detail in Chapter 7 – page references for short quotations are cited only when the critical observation refers to a textual variant found in a specific edition. Further details about primary source materials can be found in the 'Guide to primary sources' (see pages 241–244).

All references to secondary sources are given full citations. The body of secondary criticism on nineteenth-century literature is now immense. Throughout the volume references have been given at appropriate points in parentheses to those studies which have been responsible for establishing, or which best exemplify, distinctive ways of thinking about nineteenth-century literary culture; further details can be found in the 'Guide to further reading' (pages 245–49) and 'Works cited' (pages 250–62). Several of the terms used to categorise aspects of nineteenth-century literary culture, terms like 'romantic', 'avant-garde' or 'decadent', are vigorously contested by modern critics. The 'Glossary of terms and contested definitions' (pages 224–40) provides a summary account of these disagreements; fuller discussion can be found in appropriate chapters.

Chapter summary

Chapter 2 begins by providing an overview of those aspects of the historical context which help to explain the differences between the literary culture of the nineteenth century and the cultures of the preceding and succeeding centuries. Initially the focus will be on the distinguishing features of nineteenth-century political, social, economic and intellectual life: that is, on those changes in class, demography and gender relations which accompanied increasing industrialisation, the growth of liberalism and developments in the organisation, structure and authorisation of knowledge, and which presented new challenges and subject-matter for nineteenth-century writers. Chapter 2 will also consider the role of empire and British nationalism, and will describe those changes in epistemology brought about by the rise of what has been termed the 'scientific paradigm', the development of new sciences (such as psychology) as well as changes in religious practices and beliefs. The chapter will then narrow its focus to examine how the processes of industrialisation transformed both the publishing industry and theatrical culture, bringing about fundamental changes in literary taste, as well as in the kinds of literary and dramatic works produced over the course of the century.

Chapter 3 takes as its subject what for many readers is the central purpose of a literary history – that of identifying the principal stylistic or formal developments in a given period. As we have noted, nineteenth-century literary production in Britain has traditionally been seen as dominated by the realist novel; moreover, when compared with, say, French or German literary culture, it has often been viewed as lacking formal innovation. A consequence of this view is that for a significant part of the twentieth century, nineteenth-century poetic, and particularly dramatic, achievements were neglected. Chapter 3 will trace the origin of this way of viewing nineteenth-century literature to the polemic of early twentieth-century Modernist writers, who typically deprecated the achievements of their predecessors in order to highlight their own novelty. It will conclude by examining how recent scholarship in the areas of poetics, performance studies and popular culture has revealed evidence of considerable formal variety and complexity in nineteenth-century literary culture, and has also identified new nineteenth-century literary genres and sub-genres such as life-writing, travel writing, working-class writing, children's literature and, more recently, the literature of 'freakery' and the uncanny – all of which point to an inventiveness and exuberance of literary production formerly obscured by a critical emphasis on the realist novel.

The subject of Chapter 4 is nineteenth-century literary movements. The identification of literary movements is a common way for historians to locate and explain changes in literary sensibilities, although as we will point out, there are several different ways in which they might do this. Chapter 4 concentrates on what we term 'self-identified' movements – those of Pre-Raphaelitism, Aestheticism, Decadence and Symbolism. These are distinguished both from nineteenth-century literary 'schools' on the one hand, and from movements like Impressionism and

Naturalism, on the other. The last two movements originated in France and although they were influential in Britain, they had no exact counterpart in nineteenth-century British literary culture. Chapter 4 will also pay some attention to the concept of avant-gardism, the origins of which are generally located in mid-nineteenth-century French culture.

For many critics the most distinguishing feature of nineteenth-century literature is what may be called its discursive quality; that is, the explicit use of literary forms to address those issues of contemporary intellectual and political concern outlined in Chapter 2, and which included debates about class and franchise reform, science and religion, empire, print culture and gender. Chapter 5 will examine this premise in more detail by investigating what is distinctive about nineteenth-century literature's engagement with social life and civil society compared with the topical referents of earlier works of literature. It will document the various ways in which modern critics have modelled the relationship between nineteenth-century literature and the wider intellectual culture in which it is produced, examining in detail the influence of what has been termed the 'Focauldian turn' on nineteenth-century literary studies, as well as criticisms of that development which have begun to emerge over the past few years.

Among the most significant developments in the academic study of literature has been the advent of gender and postcolonial theory. Chapter 6 will assess the impact of this body of work on the literary historiography of the nineteenth century, examining both new readings of the works of canonical authors (male and female) as well as what are termed 'recovery' projects in which nineteenth-century writers (or sometimes whole genres of writing), hitherto marginalised because of purported gender or racial discrimination, are brought to the attention of modern readers. Chapter 6 will conclude by exploring the politics of nineteenth-century canon formation, describing the role of literature in defining English nationalism, and the relationship between English (or British) literature and the literary culture of European countries, such as France and Germany.

Chapter 7 describes the impact of research into what we earlier called 'the history of the book' on our understanding of the literary culture of the nineteenth century. This body of work has taken as its initial premise the argument that any concept of literature is intrinsically related to the physical objects through which literature is embodied. Chapter 7 will show how the study of these physical artefacts and their relation to contemporary economic, technological and educational systems has led critics to analyse nineteenth-century definitions of literary value in relation to changes in the ways in which books were made, sold and read. Such research in turn has introduced a new terminology for understanding nineteenth-century literature, that of 'consumerism' and 'commodity culture'. The chapter will conclude by examining the problems posed by the fact that nineteenth-century literary works typically exist in multiple textual embodiments, and it will offer readers a brief guide to the ways these embodiments have been treated by modern editors.

Conclusion

- Literary periodisation by century divisions is complicated by authors who enjoy long careers and by literary works with complex publishing histories.
- Changes in literary culture do not map neatly onto changes in social or political culture, nor do they occur at a uniform rate.
- The literary historiography of the nineteenth century can be mapped fairly closely onto the practice of literary criticism, insofar as the advent of new theoretical paradigms in the discipline has tended to redefine the subject-matter of literary history.
- Rather than there being any single history of nineteenth-century literature, it is more appropriate to think of a multiplicity of possible narratives, each of which has different points of emphasis, but which none the less intersect with each other.

2 The contexts of nineteenth-century literature

Overview

Nineteenth-century Britain has been described as the 'first industrial nation' (Mathias 1983). It is the social, political and technological changes brought about over the course of the century by the accelerating processes of industrialisation, including those which effected a revolution in print culture, which are usually invoked to explain the distinctive character of this period of British history. Distinctive, too, was the sheer pace of change: within a single lifetime industry, farming, transport, the domestic home, as well as retailing were transformed. This chapter documents how these rapid and sometimes dramatic developments in nineteenth-century social, economic and intellectual life provided writers with new themes and challenges, as they attempted to come to terms with what later historians would characterise as the beginnings of modernity. We can get a general sense of how different 1890s Britain was from that of, say, the 1830s by briefly comparing the fictional worlds of two well-known novels of the period.

The publication of George Eliot's *Middlemarch* (1871–72) and Oscar Wilde's *The Picture of Dorian Gray* (1890, 1891) are events separated by twenty years; but the novels depict social worlds which are sixty years apart. The setting of Eliot's provincial novel is an English Midlands town in the years leading up to the Great Reform Act of 1832, and it contains what we think of as stereotypically Victorian elements: the valorisation of a rural over a business economy, a paternalistic landowning aristocracy and a clergy whose interests conflict with those of radicals, entrepreneurs and 'new' professionals, such as Dr Lydgate. The novel explicitly celebrates an ethic of restraint, duty and self-denial in which individualism is seen as a form of selfishness. Although it still has any number of recognisably Victorian motifs, Wilde's novel contains some unmistakably modern elements. In contrast to Dorothea, Eliot's heroine, Wilde's characters are not concerned with religion, duty, familial life, nor indeed with any kind of self-restraint; rather, they are driven by a restless pursuit of self-fulfilment. Thoroughly urban, they constantly indulge in new forms of entertainment or distraction in order to 'realise' their personalities: they drink, they smoke and they abuse drugs. Rather than devote themselves to the pursuit of some version of the 'good' life, they become consumers: or, more precisely, in Wilde's novel the fetishising of objects – that is, consumerism – has itself become the most important element of the good life.

Middlemarch and *Dorian Gray* are also materially and formally distinct. Serialised in bi-monthly and later monthly parts over the course of a year, and then published in four volumes, *Middlemarch* is often seen as the quintessential nineteenth-century realist novel: it is long and densely plotted, with a large array of characters and an omniscient narrative voice which presents the psychological development of the protagonists as a form of moral instruction for the reader. *The Picture of Dorian Gray* was first published in both the USA and in Britain in a single number of a family periodical. The story was then lengthened for book publication, but it only amounted to a slender one-volume novel which could be read in a couple of sittings, and in which many of the staple elements of realist fiction, as they are exemplified in *Middlemarch*, are signally absent. The cast of characters is small, there is little by way of character development, and only a rudimentary plot whose closure is highly ambivalent. Much of *Dorian Gray* is devoted to dialogue, and the narrative voice, too, is characterised by extravagant verbal display rather than moralising.

The main task of this chapter will be to map a social and cultural background to the nineteenth century against which the distinctions – formal, material and ideological – between the societies portrayed in Eliot's and Wilde's novels can be understood.

Economics and technology

Two of the most salient features of the social history of Britain during the nineteenth century were its relative domestic political stability (when it is compared with many other European countries and with its own history in the eighteenth century) and the spectacular if uneven increase in the country's prosperity. From the end of the Napoleonic Wars in 1815 to the first decade of the twentieth century Britain was the richest country in Europe (measured in terms of gloss national product per capita), and until 1880 (when the distinction went to the United States of America) the richest country in the world, with an empire that encompassed nearly one quarter of the world's land mass.

Explanations of this economic and political supremacy generally point to a complex set of interdependent processes. Of central importance were the technological innovations that drove industrialisation; in Britain for much of the century technology was more advanced and more widely used than in any other country. This was especially the case in the area of steam power, which transformed farming as well as many aspects of manufacturing, and in the use of iron and steel in buildings and civil and naval engineering. (Charles Dickens's *Dombey and Son* (1846–48) has as a central character the head of a shipping line.) These processes were in turn made possible by an abundant supply of cheap coal, and coal mining itself progressively became a major nineteenth-century industry; by the 1860s it represented an important British export, and by the century's close employed over three-quarters of a million people (Crouzet 1990: 265, 268). Of particular importance for the historian of literary culture is the steam-driven technological revolution of the nineteenth-century printing industry, one which, for the first time, made possible mass literary (as opposed simply to newspaper) publishing. These changes had profound consequences for all kinds of literary writing, including genres such as drama which might not, at first glance, seem to depend on the book trade. From the 1830s onwards mass publishing made popular fiction such a lucrative market for aspiring writers that other kinds of literary production, including the publishing of play-texts (and to a lesser extent, poetry and criticism), no longer seemed as worthwhile, at least in terms of the earnings they offered. But mass publishing also brought new categories of writer into the literary market-place, including women writers who, from the middle decades of the century, figure as prominently as men in the ranks of the highest-paid authors. Perhaps because of these changes, the class and gender politics involved in pursuing a career as a writer become important topics in nineteenth-century literature, notably in the 'novel-in-verse' *Aurora Leigh* (1857) by Elizabeth Barrett Browning (1806–61) and later in the century in *New Grub Street* (1891) by George Gissing (1857–1903), Marie Corelli's *The Sorrows of Satan* (1895) and Sarah Grand's *The Beth Book* (1897).

Technological innovation also brought changes to day-to-day domestic life; the development of gas and later electric light, particularly in the country's big cities, had the consequence of extending the day well into the night. (The night-life permitted by street lighting provided new subjects for late nineteenth-century poets, like Arthur Symons (1865–1945).) Other forms of visual technology, including the development of the kaleidoscope (1815), the daguerreotype and early forms of photography (in the 1820s and 1830s), the phenakistoscope (1832) and stereoscope (1849), the use of magic lanterns and (towards the century's end) the cinematograph and X-ray, flooded nineteenth-century culture with new kinds of images and new ways of troping vision which drew attention simultaneously to an objective and totalising gaze as well as to the subjectivity and contingency of seeing. The consequence for literature, and particularly for literary realism, was a new emphasis on optical and pictorial metaphors, used not only to record the concrete details of the physical world, but as a register of more generalised ways of understanding and perception. Successive advances in telegraphic communication for the first time linked countries and (with the laying of the first successful transatlantic telegraph cable in 1866) continents in real time, thereby transforming communication systems. One consequence was a greater interest in – and in some quarters anxieties about – cultural cosmopolitanism. (The role of communication systems in policing figures strongly in late nineteenth-century crime and detective fiction, and perhaps most famously in *Dracula* (1897) by Bram Stoker (1847–1912).) In the way that it simultaneously provoked both wonder and fear, perhaps the most emblematic of nineteenth-century technological achievements was the steam locomotive. The development of the railways, stimulated in part by the pioneering design of George Stephenson's (1781–1848) award-winning locomotive *Rocket* in 1830 and Isambard Kingdom Brunel's (1806–59) seven-foot-gauge Great Western Railway, brought about profound changes to the British countryside and later in the century made leisure tourism possible. But railways also provoked deep anxieties relating to the dangers (both moral and physical) of travel itself, particularly for women travelling alone. In Gissing's *The Whirlpool* (1897) Alma Rolfe's attempt to assert her independence through an adulterous flirtation is made possible by the suburban railway line. The railway also figures as an omnipresent threat in the stories about the idyllic northern village of Cranford, which were serialised between 1851 and 1853 in *Household Words*, by Elizabeth Gaskell (1810–65); in one notably violent episode, a character is run down by a train. Moreover, it is the failure of an American railway scheme which exposes the fraudulent practices of the corrupt financier Augustus Melmotte in *The Way We Live Now* (1875) by Anthony Trollope (1815–82). More generally, railway crashes were a frequent motif in nineteenth-century melodramas.

Melmotte's occupation highlights a second, and equally significant, element of British economic success: the opportunities produced by capital accumulation. (It is worth noting that the availability of cheap credit played a crucial role in meeting the need for the increased capitalisation of nineteenth-century publishing businesses, and so was as important as any new technology in transforming that industry.) Though treated ambivalently by novelists like Trollope, financial capitalism, made possible by the surpluses accumulated by industrial capitalism, had made Britain the world's leading creditor nation, and as result smaller countries developed in a manner which complemented the British economy – that is, they bought British manufactured goods and in exchange sold to Britain raw materials and primary produce. British dominance in trading relations had also arisen as a consequence of the naval supremacy Britain enjoyed after the Napoleonic Wars; up until the First World War seapower enabled it to control most of the world's major trade routes, and thereby enjoy a near monopoly over many overseas markets. Interestingly, it is the glamour and riches associated with naval life, rather than its politics, which form the backdrop to works such as Jane Austen's posthumously published *Persuasion* (1818), although Gaskell's later *Sylvia's Lovers* (1863), which is also set during the Napoleonic Wars, gives a rather different account of naval life, particularly in its bitter denunciation of the practice of 'pressing' seamen into naval service (by means of what were known colloquially as 'press-gangs').

The growth of the British economy has also been attributed in part to a pattern of reforming and sometimes coercive legislation which contained pressures for social change. A good example is to be found in the way that successive extensions to the franchise were preceded by legislation to control public assembly and the press; much of that legislation (such as the Seditious Societies Act of 1799) was drawn up in an attempt to curtail the activities of radical movements inspired by the 1789 French Revolution. With the exception, then, of the social unrest that marked the first two decades of the nineteenth century (Luddite protests are the subject-matter of Charlotte Brontë's little-read novel *Shirley* (1849)), Britain largely escaped the violent uprisings and their inevitable economic costs which feature so regularly in the history of other European countries, notably its nearest neighbour, France. For these reasons, the second half of the nineteenth century has often been characterised as 'an age of reform', and there are a number of areas where successive parliamentary measures brought about significant changes in living and working conditions. As a consequence the relationship between the individual and state was permanently changed.

Primary among these changes were successive reforms of the legislation which governed working and living conditions: a series of Factory Acts placed limits on the length of the working day and the ability of employers to use child labour (a theme explored by Charles Kingsley (1819–75) in his perennially popular *The Water Babies* (1863)). Parliament also legislated to establish minimum standards for artisans' dwellings, although its motives were based on the misguided assumption that diseases such as cholera were air- rather than water-borne. (These ideas were eventually overturned by the anti-contagionist theory of disease publicised in works such as *Notes on Hospitals* (1859) and *Notes on Nursing* (1860) by Florence Nightingale (1820–1910).) Education was the subject of several Royal Commissions and reforms. Over the course of the century schooling was expanded, partly secularised and, under the direction of the social reformer and politician James Kay-Shuttleworth (1804–77), brought under increasing state regulation through a reformed schools inspectorate and improved teacher training. A growing concern from the 1830s onwards with the education of the working classes eventually led to the landmark 1870 Forster Education Act, which made elementary schooling compulsory for all children from the ages of 5 to 13, and established the first state school system in Britain. However, state provision of education was always controversial, and the fact that the pupil group of state-funded schools prior to 1870 was pauper children meant that it inevitably carried an element of social stigma. Even by the end of the century elementary-school teachers – whose numbers had increased rapidly since 1870 – remained a marginalised and somewhat beleaguered social group, their status largely unrecognised by other professionals. Certainly state education was very far from matching the advantages that accrued to children (mainly male) of the wealthier classes who could afford to attend the fee-paying endowed grammar and the more prestigious public schools, which themselves had undergone reforms in the mid-nineteenth century and which supplied most of the candidates for university education. (The limitations of British state education is a theme explored by Dickens in *Hard Times* (1854) and Thomas Hardy in *Jude the Obscure* (1895), while *Tom Brown's School Days* (1857) by Thomas Hughes (1822–96) is probably the best-known account of life at a public school – in this case Rugby.)

In turn, universities themselves, dominated for most of the century by the ancient institutions of Oxford and Cambridge, were also reformed by a series of measures in the 1850s and 1860s, which in turn gradually professionalised them. Of key importance were the University Test Acts which opened university education to those, such as Catholics, unwilling to subscribe to the

Thirty-Nine Articles of the Anglican faith, hitherto a requirement of university matriculation. The development of provincial universities in England's largest towns began with foundation in 1828 of University College, London (which joined the Anglican King's College in 1836 to become the University of London); in the late decades of the century provincial civic colleges, most of which were concentrated in the more highly populated Midlands and north of England, in cities such as Birmingham, Leeds and Manchester, were granted university status. Also significant in extending the provision of higher education were the establishment of extension lecturing schemes (notably in London) and Mechanics' Institutes. By the 1880s women's colleges had been founded at both Cambridge University (Girton and Newnham) and Oxford (Lady Margaret Hall and Somerville), although those who attended them were prevented from taking full degrees until the twentieth century. (Nineteenth-century prejudices towards the education of women are the subject of *The Princess* (1847) by Alfred Lord Tennyson (1809–92).) The government further restricted what had formerly been seen as an exclusively religious sphere by establishing, through the 1857 Divorce Act, mechanisms for civil divorce; divorce had previously been controlled by canon (i.e. church) law. In the way that it extended to the middle and lower classes what had previously been privileges enjoyed exclusively by the rich, much of this reforming legislation might seem to have possessed a distinctly democratic impetus. However, state intervention into the lives of private individuals was perceived to have another and altogether more sinister element to it, one that also frequently finds expression in the literature of the century: that of social policing and state control.

This ambivalence can be seen particularly clearly in the 1843 New Poor Law (the eligibility test for which was so draconian that many refused to submit to it) and the operation of the Contagious Diseases Acts of the 1860s (which became a method of policing working-class female sexual behaviour). Similar sorts of suspicion are also to be found in debates about franchise reform. During the course of the century there were three main reform bills: 1832, 1867 and 1888. These progressively extended voting rights to most of the adult male population; excluded were women as a group and men who did not own or rent property above a certain rateable value. This link between property and voting rights depended upon the assumption that money, respectability and responsible political judgement were synonymous, and such an assumption seems anything but radical to modern eyes. It is fair to say, then, that the relative political stability of nineteenth-century British society, which has been linked to its economic growth, owed little either to a growing egalitarianism or to the upward social mobility promised by the ideology of 'self-help' proselytised in the middle decades of the century by the work of Samuel Smiles (1812–1904), who was the son of a shopkeeper. Rather the opposite: the division of labour associated with advancing industrialisation led to what were arguably more deeply entrenched social hierarchies, as the middle and lower classes subdivided into a complex range of occupational groups of varying wealth, skills and social status. It has been suggested that competition between these various groups, particularly among skilled artisans and factory workers, hindered the development of a class consciousness and consequently limited effective political activism among labouring groups. And this in turn helps to explain a paradoxical feature of nineteenth-century Britain (one also reflected in much of its literature): that intense anxieties about social and economic inequality did not lead to any fundamental restructuring of British society. Even in the late decades of the century power still tended to reside in the hands of the landed aristocracy, who exercised a disproportionate political influence.

One of the best-known nineteenth-century attempts to describe what modern historians loosely refer to as the British class system is Matthew Arnold's (1822–88) identification in *Culture and Anarchy* (1869) of what he called the 'three great classes of English society': 'our aristocratic, our middle, and our working class'. Finding fault with all these groups, Arnold renamed them more pejoratively as 'the barbarians' (the aristocracy), 'the philistines' (the middle class or bourgeoisie) and 'the populace' (the working classes). An older, but in the nineteenth-century still resonant, description of British social structures was in terms of the 'three estates' of the realm – that is, the nobles, clergy and commoners (to which the historian Thomas Babington Macaulay (1800–59) in his *Historical Essays* (1828) famously added, as a 'fourth estate', the popular press). Nineteenth-century literature generally represents class identity as determined by a combination of money, birth and manners, and somewhat paradoxically the divisions between social classes as both rigid yet requiring systematic policing. As a result, inter-class marriages are usually represented as failures and aspirations for social advancement are frequently the object of condemnation (when involving the working classes) or satire (when they concern lower-middle-class or petit-bourgeois aping of aristocratic life-styles). With the exception of the kind of advancement that comes about through inherited wealth, literary examples of successful or sustained social mobility are relatively rare.

These new kinds of social divisions brought about other tensions, notably between the authority of an expanding professional and administrative class and that of traditional elites (such as the landed gentry), as well as between all of these groups and the entrepreneurs who owed their position to the 'new' money produced by industrialisation – the 'captains of industry', as Thomas Carlyle (1795–1881), one of the early Victorian 'sages', termed them. It is perhaps not surprising, then, that an obsessive concern with status, or more precisely with the relationship between wealth and its origins, and their relation to social position, is prevalent throughout the period. This concern is to be seen in the proliferation of conduct manuals and etiquette books as well as in many literary works, notably those of Trollope (whose semi-autobiographical

The Three Clerks (1857) critiques the English civil service) and William Makepeace Thackeray (1811–63), whose *Vanity Fair* (1847–48) is perhaps the century's most compelling and entertaining satire on social ambition and financial greed. Dickens's *Great Expectations* (1860–61), which is somewhat more forgiving in tone than *Vanity Fair* in that it offers the possibility of redemption, also explores the self-delusions of social ambition, together with the complex nature of gentlemanly behaviour, focused through Pip's humiliating pursuit of the beautiful but disdainful Estella. In *Our Mutual Friend* (1864–65) Dickens provides a further and more ambivalent portrait of contemporary class divisions in his depiction of the role of the working-class Lizzie Hexam in the self-destruction of the passionate but dour school-teacher Bradley Headstone, as well as in the moral reformation of the effete aristocrat Eugene Wrayburn who, although called to the bar, can never actually be bothered to practise.

A further index of the complexity of nineteenth-century attitudes towards social position can be seen in literary representations of two of the oldest professions, medicine and law. Doctors and lawyers offered similar kinds of services for those wealthy enough to be able to afford them, and modern theorists have seen both to be complicit in the processes by which the nineteenth-century body, both individual and social, was disciplined and policed. However, the literary fiction of the time tends to treats these professions in a significantly different way. The lawyer is an omnipresent figure in the plots of many novels; his moral probity is typically discredited and his power resented. By contrast, doctors (that is, physicians, or those responsible for the diagnosis and sometimes also the treatment of disease, rather than surgeons who performed operations on patients), occupy a more ambivalent place. Rarely are they objects either of overt criticism or of romantic interest. Eliot's Lydgate in *Middlemarch* and later Fitzpiers in Hardy's *The Woodlanders* (1887) stand out as exceptions, although it is significant that their lives are represented as only partly successful. The doctor figures in *Frankenstein* (1818) by Mary Shelley (1797–1851) and *The Strange Case of Dr Jekyll and Mr Hyde* (1886) by Robert Louis Stevenson (1850–94) nicely embody this ambivalence: while both, although in different ways, are associated with monstrosity, they remain to a degree sympathetic figures.

The manifest social and economic inequalities in nineteenth-century Britain notwithstanding, historians have often reached for superlatives when trying to sum up its distinctive features. It has been described, as we noted above, as the 'first industrial nation', and thus the first country to develop a recognisably modern economy, one in which sustained and historically rapid growth, coupled with increased productivity, led to real rises in standards of living, even if the comparative gap between rich and poor remained wide throughout the century – so much so that by the end of Victoria's reign between 25 and 30 per cent of the population remained in poverty. Nineteenth-century Britain has also been termed the first 'global superpower', whose ability to project its economic and military power in matters of foreign policy had decisive implications for the whole world (Crouzet 1990). According to one recent historian, through its empire Britain did more to 'promote the free movement of goods, capital and labour' and 'to impose Western norms of law, order and governance around the world' than 'any other organization in history' (Ferguson 2004: xxii). We do not necessarily have to condone such overseas interventions in order to recognise their impact; indeed a number of late nineteenth-century literary works, such as *Heart of Darkness* (1899) by Joseph Conrad (1857–1924) and some of the Anglo-Indian short stories by Rudyard Kipling (1865–1936), registered the achievements of British imperialism with a deep ambivalence.

The 1851 Great Exhibition housed in Joseph Paxton's revolutionary Crystal Palace, a structure built of iron and glass, and intended to showcase to the world the pre-eminence of British manufactured goods, represents an exemplary symbol of the nineteenth-century identification of Britain's civic and national character with its technological and economic success. Visited by some six million people, it inaugurated an era of grand international exhibitions whose legacy survives in modern trade shows. The Exhibition assembled under one roof more than 14,000 exhibitors from around the world and has been interpreted by modern critics as an early example of globalisation, as well as inaugurating a pre-eminently modern way of seeing, one in which the observer-spectator becomes a consumer.

Britain was also the first country to undergo rapid urbanisation, so much so that the townscape of many of the country's major urban centres, such as Birmingham, Glasgow, Manchester and London, remains recognisably Victorian, whether in the form of long rows of Victorian terraces or of spectacular civic buildings such as Sir Charles Barry's (1795–1860) neo-Gothic Houses of Parliament, whose decorations and furniture were designed by Augustus Welby Pugin (1812–52), a leading theorist (along with John Ruskin (1819–1900)) of the Gothic Revival in architecture. (The fashion for 'restoring' ancient buildings in imitation of a notional Gothic style was later vigorously opposed by William Morris (1834–96).) The development of public spaces, particularly urban parks, and of public leisure buildings such as museums, galleries and, later in the century, public libraries, are also key features of nineteenth-century urban development (Chadwick 1996); they came to be recognised as spaces in which middle-class women could enjoy a relative freedom from the strict rules of conduct and chaperonage associated with the domestic home. (However, some of the literature of the time, notably Gissing's *The Odd Women* (1893), registers that liberation ambivalently, viewing public parks as sites of possible sexual impropriety (Nord 1995).) Improvements in infrastructure, such as the building of sewers and the provision of gas and piped water, combined with new transport systems and the conceptualisation and development of the suburb, brought about over the course of the century a transformation in the experience of urban living (Morris and Rogers 1993). And this gave rise to another 'new' phenomenon – the modern cityscape, the pleasures and dangers of which are celebrated in much late nineteenth-century literature, notably in Symbolist and Decadent poetry (for example in *The City of Dreadful Night* (1874) by James Thomson (1834–82)), in the Society Comedy and in some fiction, particularly in the work of Henry James and Oscar Wilde, as well as that of a number of women writers such as Amy Levy (1861–89), who saw city life in terms of the possibilities and opportunities (for education, employment and thus independence) it offered to women (Walkowitz 1992). Particular cities, too, took on, for some writers, a quality that amounted to a distinctive personality, so much so that it is possible to talk of Gaskell's Manchester or Dickens's or Gissing's London(s).

Intellectual and political life

There are also the many British intellectual 'firsts' to consider. Whole areas of knowledge, including medicine, physics, chemistry, biology, geology, economics and mathematics, underwent fundamental and systematic changes in the nineteenth century, with British science often at the forefront of intellectual innovation; in their turn, scientific discoveries both prompted and sustained technological developments in what became a virtuous circle. The prestige of science was underwritten by technologies which 'worked'. The understanding of the body was revolutionised by immunology and germ theory. The latter was wittily exploited in the story which gave its title – *The Stolen Bacillus* (1895) – to an early collection of science fiction by H. G. Wells (1866–1946). It was also transformed by comparative anatomy, embryology and sexology. The use of antiseptics and anaesthetics in the later decades of the century not only revolutionised the possibilities for surgical procedures (including making childbirth safer), they also challenged traditional – and particularly religious – conceptions of pain and suffering, and therefore undermined the link between moral and physical health. In this last view, and indeed in many literary works of the time (notably *Ghosts* (1881) by the Norwegian dramatist Henrik Ibsen (1828–1906) and *La Dame aux camélias* (1852) by the French dramatist Alexandre Dumas, fils (1824–95)), diseases like syphilis and tuberculosis were typically seen as punishments for immoral, and particularly inappropriate sexual, behaviour. In the conclusion of Gaskell's novel *Ruth* (1853), the philandering gentleman Henry Bellingham and his former lover Ruth both contract typhus fever; and the survival of only the former says much about nineteenth-century sexual double standards.

In this context it is also worth noting nineteenth-century attitudes towards what is today termed 'recreational' drug use. The mind-altering effects of opium, cocaine and nitrous oxide (or laughing gas, as it was popularly called) were viewed in some contexts – most famously perhaps in Samuel Taylor Coleridge's (1772–1834) account of the composition of 'Kubla Khan' (1816) or *Confessions of an English Opium Eater* (1822) by Thomas de Quincey

(1785–1859) – as facilitating creativity and providing opportunities for new kinds of aesthetic experiences. More broadly speaking, scientific enquiry also brought about changes in the understanding of mind, consciousness and mental processes. Of these, the most significant centred on the development in the last quarter of the century of psychology as a discipline distinct from philosophy, a process brought about when an earlier tradition of Associationism (most closely identified with the work of the eighteenth-century philosopher David Hartley (1705–57)) combined with early nineteenth-century research into the nervous system to ground the study of mind in brain physiology. One consequence was new ways of understanding perception, including the proposition that aesthetic appreciation had a physiological as much as a moral basis (Rylance 2000). This body of work was especially influential on the writer and critic and (in Britain) most prominent theorist of 'art for art's sake', Walter Pater (1839–94). At the same time, however, it is important to emphasise that the understanding of the mind was also influenced by a number of what are today classified as 'pseudo-sciences', but which held considerable authority during much of the nineteenth century. They included: phrenology, which proposed that intellectual and emotional predispositions could be detected via the surface shape of the skull; physiognomy, which argued that an individual's character could be discerned via the study of facial features and modes of expression; and mesmerism, which claimed to shed new light on the nature of consciousness and will by placing individuals in artificially induced trances (in the late decades of the century, in the hands of the French neurologist Jean-Martin Charcot (1825–93), in whose clinic Sigmund Freud (1856–1939) worked, hypnotism became central to the diagnosis and treatment of various forms of neurosis, including hysteria). These sorts of enquiry proved particularly attractive to novelists, notably to Charlotte Brontë, in part because they offered a set of visual – and thus easily describable – bodily features via which an inner self could be made intelligible through narrative. Moreover, their more sensational aspects could also provide material for populist treatments, such as the best-selling *Trilby* (1894) by George du Maurier (1834–96), in which the tone-deaf eponymous heroine is transformed, through the mesmeric talents of the manipulative Svengali, into a striking operatic singer. In physics, the century saw the emergence of a new understanding of the atomic theory of matter which underlies the periodic table, itself first formulated in the late nineteenth century. There was an equally new theorisation of the forms of energy, particularly in Michael Faraday's (1791–1867) work on electricity and in James Maxwell's (1831–79) on light-waves and electromagnetism. There was also the development of inorganic chemistry and the discovery of set theory in mathematics.

However, from a cultural or social point of view, perhaps the most significant intellectual development was the theory of evolution outlined by Charles Darwin (1809–82) in his *On the Origin of Species* (1859), which transformed conceptions of what it meant to be human, as well as implicitly (and later, and more explicitly, in the 1860 debate between the Bishop of Oxford and Darwin's popularising 'bull-dog' Thomas Huxley (1825–95)) challenging forms of religious authority. The influence of Darwinian evolution on the concept of historical progress was particularly strong on writers like Eliot and Hardy, although they responded to Darwin in quite different ways. New kinds of biblical scholarship, to be seen in the work of figures such as Bishop John William Colenso (1814–83) for which he was excommunicated in 1869, and what was called the German 'higher criticism', together with the influence of Darwin and his followers, helped to fuel a growing tension between religion and science which was in its turn part of a larger movement towards a more secular society, in which traditional forms of religious observance became less central to intellectual and political life. Two of the best-known responses to what is sometimes termed the Victorian 'crisis in faith' are Tennyson's long narrative poem *In Memoriam* (1850) and the short lyric 'Dover Beach' by Matthew Arnold, which was written around 1851 but withheld by Arnold from publication until 1867.

As we have hinted already, it would be a mistake to view the history of nineteenth-century intellectual culture as an inevitable victory of science over religion, or for the forces of rational enquiry over faith, for alongside these technological and scientific advances the nineteenth century (particularly in its later decades) was also witness to a perhaps surprising rise of interest in a variety of supernatural phenomena and practices, including spiritualism, ghost- and fairy-hunting and chiromancy (the nineteenth-century term for palmistry). Works of popular fiction which exploited these interests for comic effect included Oscar Wilde's short stories 'Lord Arthur Savile's Crime' and 'The Canterville Ghost' (both 1887); more serious interest in the topic was represented by the publications of Edward Heron-Allen (1861–1943) on chiromancy and an early collection of short stories entitled *The Celtic Twilight* (1893) by W. B. Yeats, who became heavily involved in his early adulthood in the occult society of the 'Hermetic Order of the Golden Dawn' and Madame Blavatsky's newly formed Theosophical Movement. The Society for Psychical Research (which is still in existence today) was co-founded in 1882 by Frederick Myers (1843–1901), a figure who was none the less well respected in other areas of British intellectual life. It is also worth emphasising that writers who today tend to be associated with the rise of scientific enquiry and empiricism did not necessarily abandon their religious beliefs. A case in point is the geographer Charles Lyell (1797–1875), whose *Principles of Geology* (1830–33) was an important influence on Tennyson's *In Memoriam.* Lyell remained a committed Christian despite the fact that his 'uniformitarian' view of creation, which argued that the entire history of the earth could be understood in terms of causes observable in present-day geology, contested the biblical story of creation by requiring a much expanded time-scale. By the same token, it is also possible to overestimate the decline in importance of religion by concentrating too narrowly on the internal divisions which were viewed as weakening the authority of the Church of England, divisions which include the mid-nineteenth-century debate between the Broad Church Party, who wished to liberalise the Anglican faith, and the Tractarians, who sought the restoration of ritual and the reassertion of the authority of the

Church over that of the state. Evangelicalism and other dissenting religions remained powerful forces throughout the century, so much so that in the 1860s they were cited by Matthew Arnold in *Culture and Anarchy* as undermining social cohesion. Similarly, debates about Jewish assimilation and the rights of Catholics were unlikely to have been given such prominence in the early and middle decades of the century, were it not for the perceived strengths of Jewish and Catholic religious communities.

Setting aside the persistence throughout the century of what can loosely be described as anti-rational beliefs (and indeed the popularity of literary genres like Gothic fiction which drew on them), it is none the less a combination of its intellectual and technological achievements which are generally seen to mark off nineteenth-century Britain, and particularly its later decades, as that historical period in which we can glimpse the beginnings of modernity – that is, of a culture which we recognise as having many elements and concerns in common with our own. It is this quality which partly explains the continued popular appeal of nineteenth-century literature, to be seen in modern television and film adaptations of its fiction. These common concerns include a valorisation of individualism (when that concept is understood in terms of a validation of political, religious, gender and racial difference), which in turn led to a questioning of the role of the state in securing and safeguarding civil liberties, including those afforded to the artist. The nineteenth century saw several prosecutions of writers and publishers for offending public decency, the most famous of which was that in 1888 of Henry Vizetelly (1820–94), the British publisher of the fiction of the French naturalist writer Emile Zola (1840–1902). In addition new legislation in 1843, established in the office of the Lord Chamberlain, brought about a more formal state censorship of drama – that is, of works being performed on a public stage to a paying audience. More generally, there were wide-ranging debates about the rights of women and of religious minorities. It has been argued that the last decades of the century saw the first conceptualisation of homosexuality as an identity rather than a description of sexual acts. These concerns reverberate throughout the literature of the period, and were depicted most often in terms of the fraught relationship between the freedom of the individual and the wider demands of society in general. The *bildungsroman*, a form particularly suited to expressing these concerns, was popular with contemporary novelists and takes as its subject the moral and social development of an individual from childhood to maturity.

Over the course of the nineteenth century the party political landscape was also transformed as the long-standing bipartite opposition between Whig and Tory interests fragmented into more diverse political allegiances which included the growth in the 1860s of liberalism (or the 'new radicalism' as it was termed in the *Fortnightly Review*) and, in the last decades of the century, the emergence of various forms of socialist, anarchist and feminist politics. Alongside reforms to the franchise mentioned earlier, we can see in these processes the seeds of a modern multi-party democracy, as well as the emergence of such quintessentially modern institutions as the British welfare state and its associated bureaucracies.

The British welfare state, based on the concept of publicly financed social welfare, is today popularly identified with the introduction in 1946 of a National Health Service funded through taxation and aiming to provide free medical care at the point of delivery. However, the principle of using public funds raised through taxation to improve social welfare via the provision of services such as education (including free school meals, introduced in 1907), healthcare and sickness and unemployment benefit (the first provision for which was established by the 1911 National Insurance Bill), can be traced back to aspects of late nineteenth-century social policy and legislation. Of particular significance were the systematic investigations into poverty undertaken by late nineteenth-century social reformers; their findings helped to bring about a recognition of the limitations of the Victorian reliance on what was then termed 'voluntaryism' – that is, on charity and philanthropy – to ameliorate social problems.

Given this apparent modernity, it may seem surprising that a consistent topic of interest in nineteenth-century literature is a thoroughgoing distrust of formal political processes and institutions: corrupt politicians (both local and national), venal lawyers, meddling and often incompetent law officers (particularly the detectives of the newly created metropolitan police force), as well as both ineffective bureaucratic structures and the all-too-effective poorhouses and lunatic asylums are frequent targets of criticism or satire for many writers. These concerns typically centre on the coercive nature of the relationship between the individual and various forms of nineteenth-century social control: in the work of Charles Dickens, the latter encompass state bureaucracies such as the Poor Law Officers (satirised in *Oliver Twist* (1837–39)) and Chancery (a division of the High Court) or what Dickens in *Bleak House* (1852–53) calls 'The Circumlocution Office'. Invariably for Dickens, individual fulfilment and therefore happiness is achieved despite, and not because of, such state mechanisms. A writer such as Charles Reade (1814–80), who worked for Dickens, also took as his subject the limitation of a number of forms of state power, particularly as it operated in the penal system and mental asylums. Another of Dickens's friends, Wilkie Collins (1824–89), interrogated what he perceived as the failure of the law to protect individual rights, often those of women. In all of these writers we see a pattern which the modern reader may find surprising: a consistent critique of the role of the Victorian state, particularly in the ways it was perceived to interfere with private and domestic life, as well as a constantly expressed need for the state to reform itself, generally through a limiting of its powers. Put more simply, the success of individual lives in nineteenth-century fiction is typically troped in opposition to the general tendencies of nineteenth-century social institutions, and certainly not as a consequence of them.

In nineteenth-century Britain, as today, the Sovereign was the Head of the State and titular Head of Government. Government consisted of a Parliament comprising an elected House of Commons (or 'Lower House') and a House of Lords (or 'Upper House') whose membership was made up of holders of hereditary peerages, bishops and (from 1876) judicial life peers. Parliament was led by the leader of the political party best able to command a working majority in both Houses; the leader of Parliament – the First Lord of the Treasury, later called the 'Prime Minister' – was therefore not directly elected to this role, and in practice in the nineteenth century might be drawn from the Commons or the Lords. In general terms, this period of history is seen as marking the gradual strengthening of the role of the leader of Parliament (and what later became known as the 'office' of the Prime Minister). Premiers such as Benjamin Disraeli (1804–81) and William Ewart Gladstone (1809–98) systematically cultivated their public profiles. Important, too, was the acceptance, from 1830 onwards, of 'Cabinet' government; the Cabinet is a body of ministers selected by the Prime Minister to carry out the principal executive functions of Parliament. Nineteenth-century literary debates about the legitimacy of contemporary political structures centred on a number of issues. The first concerned the authority of an electoral process which, prior to the Great Reform Bill of 1832, enfranchised less than half a million people. A related anxiety was that of the so-called 'rotten boroughs', or political constituencies in which votes were effectively bought via bribery or patronage, practices which persisted throughout the century despite legislation such as the 1854 Corrupt Practices Act (corrupt elections are a theme in Bulwer-Lytton's *Pelham* (1828) and Trollope's *Doctor Thorne* (1858)). More generally, it was widely recognised that running for Parliament was a costly business, and prospective candidates were therefore required either to possess independent wealth or to have a rich sponsor. A second issue, one which links works as otherwise diverse as William Godwin's (1756–1836) *Caleb Williams* (1794) and George Eliot's *Felix Holt, The Radical* (1866), was a dissatisfaction with the arbitrary power exercised by what was often viewed as a corrupt, decaying and unaccountable aristocracy. Later in the century the focus of resentment became the exclusion of various groups in society, particularly women and the poorest members of the working classes, from the political process.

One area of nineteenth-century life where anxieties about the nature of the institutional structures underpinning civil society were particularly sharply focused was that of crime. The official compiling of crime statistics by the

Home Office, which began in 1810, helped to promote a widespread and long-running series of debates about the nature of the criminal justice system, which encompassed concerns about prison building (for which the most famous proposal is the 'Panopticon' of the political economist Jeremy Bentham (1748–1832)) and prison regimes (such as forced labour and isolation), public executions and methods of policing (for example, the use in the early decades of the century of paid militias – especially for matters of crowd control). With the creation in 1829 of the New Metropolitan Police force, whose membership increased some thirteen-fold over the course of the century, policing gradually became more professionalised and systematic, although modern methods of detection did not extend to all areas of the country until the last quarter of the century, and tensions between parish, county and London detectives – evident in the famous country-house 'Road Hill' murder in 1860 – as well as between all of these instruments of the state and private agents, persisted throughout the century. Moreover, although levels of criminal activity were not necessarily greater in the nineteenth century than in the eighteenth, this heightened concern with policing certainly made crime more visible, and therefore increased anxiety about it. That anxiety in its turn provided fertile material for writers. Nineteenth-century literature from the Newgate novels – which took their subjects and name from the criminal activities recorded in the *Newgate Calendars* (which began publication in 1773 and ended in the 1820s) – onwards can seem to be almost obsessed by the topic (that is, by the concept of transgression, its detection and its punishment).

Charles Dickens's concern with criminality begins in *Oliver Twist* and continued through to *Bleak House*, a novel which featured one of the first fictional police detectives, Inspector Bucket, who was based on a friend of Dickens, an Inspector Field. Although only a minor character, Bucket, like many nineteenth-century fictional portraits of policemen (particularly detectives), is not simply an agent of retributive justice; rather, he acts as a device to bring about narrative closure. Dickens's last novel, *The Mystery of Edwin Drood* (1870), although unfinished, also contains many of the plot devices of the crime or mystery story. Other works of mid-century fiction in which criminality has a useful plot function include Braddon's *The Trail of the Serpent* (1861), which takes a wrongful conviction for murder as its narrative theme. Murder is also central to the sub-plot of *East Lynne* (1861), the best-known novel of Mrs Henry Wood (1814–87). But perhaps the most significant nineteenth-century work to focus on crime and its detection was *The Moonstone* (1868) by Wilkie Collins, enormously popular in its day. Its elaborate plot, which contains many elements that were to become staples of later crime novels, has at its heart the recovery of a jewel (the moonstone) by a police sergeant, whose intrusion into an upper middle-class home is itself represented as a form of transgression. It is also worth noting the frequency with which crime (and particularly murder) was a motif in Robert Browning's (1812–89) poetry; although in works such as 'Porphyria's Lover' (first published as 'Porphyria' in 1836), 'My Last Duchess' (1842) and *The Ring and the Book* (1868–69) – all of which centre on a woman murdered by her husband or lover – it was not the mechanisms of detection that concerned Browning, so much as the opportunity murder offered to explore the relative nature of knowledge and morality.

The ambivalence which attaches to fictional detectives and policemen is a persistent feature of even those works in which crime and its detection is not a central theme. In Elizabeth Gaskell's *North and South* (1854–55) the narrator largely condones the lies of the middle-class heroine, Margaret Hale, which enable her brother to evade the police on his trail (because by returning to England he has broken the terms of his navy service). In Dickens's *Hard Times*, too, a middle-class thief and son of a Member of Parliament – Tom Gradgrind – is aided by family and friends to escape the clutches of the law. Even in Stevenson's *Dr Jekyll and Mr Hyde*, Jekyll's punishment is brought about by his own hand. His loyal friend, Dr Lanyon, who discovers the existence of Hyde, never considers going to the police. Significantly, when detectives do achieve the status of fictional heroes – such as Conan Doyle's (1859–1930) Sherlock Holmes – they are rarely agents of the state; instead they operate independently, often meting out their own forms of justice. Holmes, for example, is consistently represented as solitary, enigmatic and remote (even to his constant companion, the ubiquitous Dr Watson) and also (in his opium addiction and determinedly single status) as an antinomian figure, qualities which are of a piece with his equally singular commitment to the logic of scientific deduction – the linking together of empirical observations to solve an otherwise intractable problem. Conan Doyle's sister was married to another crime writer, E. W. Hornung (1866–1921), who created the character of A. J. Raffles. Raffles, too, operates outside of the criminal justice system: he is a gentleman, excellent sportsman (especially at cricket), also intelligent and enigmatic, particularly to the dull-witted narrator in stories such as 'Gentlemen and Players' (which appeared in *Cassell's* in 1898). However, unlike Holmes, Raffles is also a crook and a rogue, albeit a lovable one who always escapes the clumsy arm of the law. It is not hard to see in the gentlemanly status of Holmes and Raffles, as well as Dr Jekyll, Tom Gradgrind or Frederick Hale, a consistent set of class prejudices at work, in which policing – understood principally in terms of state intervention into private lives – is most consistently resented when it involves intrusions into middle- and upper middle-class homes, that is, into that realm of society which in the nineteenth century had arrogated to itself the role of moral guardian.

Consumerism, print culture and literary taste

In the second half of the century it is possible to see the beginnings of another typically modern phenomenon: what we would call today a consumer or commodity culture, and the consequent growth of a cult of celebrity and the associated industries of advertising and sensationalist journalism. Consumerism has been viewed as bringing in its train what Rachel Bowlby has described as new ways of 'looking' (Bowlby 1985) as well as new modes of representation, such as that of 'spectacle', the function of which is to invest everyday objects with a kind of aura which refigures their consumption as a form of cultural (and so intrinsically valuable) activity. The origins of the 'semiotics of commodity spectacle', as it has been termed, are usually traced to the illuminated methods of display developed for the 1851 Great Exhibition in which manufactured objects were isolated and flooded with light, thereby inviting, from their spectators, a form of aesthetic contemplation (Richards 1991). In this view, the purpose of what can be termed the 'enculturation' of the commodity is to dissociate manufactured goods from their means of production in order to re-present them as autonomous objects of desire for anyone and everyone; advertising is the principal cultural mechanism by which this transformation is achieved.

It is worth noting, however, that some critics have traced the origins of a celebrity culture even further back, to the early decades of the nineteenth century, and the conjunction of a Romantic cult of selfhood with what they view as the growing industrialisation of print culture (Mole 2007). These developments provided the conditions which helped to transform prominent figures, such as Horatio (Lord) Nelson (1758–1805), the Duke of Wellington (1769–1852) and, more controversially perhaps, their antagonist, Napoleon Bonaparte (1769–1821), into 'heroic' personalities, 'owned' by the general public: by the 1830s Napoleon had been so entirely recuperated as a tragic Promethean over-reacher that he appeared in popular songs alongside British heroes, admired by patriots as much as by radicals. Among the first literary figures to exploit – or perhaps to be exploited by – these new 'cultural apparatuses', as Mole terms them, were Byron and Walter Scott: in different ways, the literary reputations of both men were inextricably bound up with a popular interest in their personal lives.

A key site of nineteenth-century consumption is often held to be the modern department store, which developed in Britain in the 1860s. It has been suggested that its characteristic plate-glass windows, and the displays which they made possible, reinvented shopping as a leisure activity. Given such developments, it is significant that in much nineteenth-century fiction, notably that of Eliot, the purchase of domestic goods other than food – that is, a desire to follow the latest fashions in dress or in home furnishings – is typically registered negatively, associated, as with the acquisitive Dodson aunts in *The Mill on the Floss* (1860) and Rosamund Vincy in *Middlemarch*, with female vanity. One of the first such department stores in Britain was Whiteley's in Westbourne Grove, London. In his *My Autobiography and Reminiscences* (1887) the painter William Powell Frith (1819–1909), who had enjoyed considerable popular success with the detailed social panoramas contained in works such as *Ramsgate Sands* (1854) and *Derby Day* (1858), described being asked by its owner to make Whiteley's the subject for his next picture, a commission he declined because he feared that it would associate him too closely with the values of commerce. The dangers of excessive consumption also figure as an important theme in *Goblin Market* (1862) by Christina Rossetti (1830–94); indeed Rossetti's poetry in general, like Eliot's fiction, tends to valorise self-denial and resignation, rather than the indulgence of self associated with a nascent consumer culture. In this respect, one of the most controversial consequences of the identification of subjectivity with consumerism, famously explored, as we noted earlier, in Wilde's *The Picture of Dorian Gray* as well as in much of Henry James's fiction, was the apparent licence of a selfish, even asocial form of individualism, one which contrasted markedly with the alienated self found in earlier Romantic writing, as well as the with the emphasis on duty and social responsibility propagandised by mid nineteenth-century writers like Eliot, Gaskell, Thackeray and Trollope. The tensions between these different notions of selfhood find dramatic expression in *Wuthering Heights* (1847) by Emily Brontë (1818–48). In that novel the heroine's inability to accommodate herself to the kind of bourgeois marriage that is the goal of Jane Austen's heroines, in its turn the result of Cathy's emotionally disastrous identification of self-fulfilment with social status and material comforts, ultimately leads to both her and Heathcliff's annihilation.

This growth of a consumer culture also had irreversible consequences for literary production and thus for the ways in which literary value itself was construed. Over the course of the century methods of book buying changed as the publishing and selling of books became separate, and some writers, such as Dickens or Braddon, developed into literary entrepreneurs in an attempt to control all aspects of their writing, including its publication and marketing. In the process the writer as media personality also took on increasing importance, particularly as publishers saw commercial advantage in exploiting readers' desires to know more about their favourite authors (the nineteenth century witnessed an increased interest in various forms of 'life-writing', including literary biographies). Writers as diverse as the Brontës and, later in the century, Oscar Wilde and Marie Corelli, were all acutely aware of the role that an authorial image played in the formation of a literary reputation. In the last decades of the century, a new profession, that of the literary agent, emerged in order to help sell these new literary 'personalities'; at the very least, their existence testifies to a growing commercial complexity in the relations between writers, readers and publishers, as well as to the new orders of money to be made from writing. By the 1880s and for the first time, it was writers drawn from a wide variety of social backgrounds (which of course contributed to that perceived need for authorial self-fashioning), rather the exceptional few, who were able to earn their living wholly by the pen.

Unsurprisingly, and in conjunction with these developments, we also find anticipations of a recognisably modern unease about a perceived decline in literary standards. One consequence of the transformation of the publishing industry described earlier is that over the course of the nineteenth century judgements about literary taste became the province of different and often competing interest groups, so much so that by the last decades of the century better-off working-class readers formed an important market for literary works. Anxieties about cultural decline were thus typically voiced most urgently by members of that social elite which, in the early decades of the century, had informed virtually every decision about the nature of literary culture, and which by the late decades saw their cultural authority being threatened by what Henry James disparagingly referred to as 'the multitude', and – slightly earlier – Matthew Arnold had called the 'mass of mankind' who were 'always' satisfied with 'very inadequate ideas'. By the 1860s that 'mass' increasingly included womankind as well, and a significant aspect of contemporary anxieties about literary standards centred on the reading habits of women, and what was often perceived as their greater susceptibility to the sensationalism that had come to characterise much popular fiction. That said, and as we argue in more detail in Chapter 7, it needs to be stressed that nineteenth-century literary taste was never simply nor rigidly subject to class (nor indeed gender) divisions, and nor did writers who self-consciously eschewed popular taste, and published only limited editions of their works for a selective readership, necessarily distance themselves from consumerist values (scarcity, after all, commands its own market price). But by the same token, what may appear to be elitist forms of publication – such as the expensive and beautifully printed books from the Kelmscott Press – could be produced by a committed socialist, in this case William Morris.

Furthermore, the boundaries between what can loosely be termed working- and middle-class literature were shifting and were quite porous. So middle-class writers like Thomas Hood (1799–1845), Emily Brontë or Gaskell and, some decades later, Kipling, made explicit use of vernacular language and popular verse forms such as ballads and broadsides, while so-called 'peasant-poets', like John Clare (1793–1864), were often taken up enthusiastically by middle- and upper-class readers. Anthologists such as George Gilfillan (1813–78) produced hard-cover editions of working-class verse aimed at a middle-class readership, while some of the most self-consciously Decadent poetry of the 1890s, by figures like Arthur Symons, drew inspiration from music-hall entertainments. Perhaps the most striking example of this blurring of class boundaries is to be found in the writing of the aristocratic Ernest Jones (1819–68), who abandoned a promising legal career to devote himself to populist politics, producing a quantity of journalism, verse and fiction endorsing the aims of the Chartist movement (activities for which he was imprisoned for two years for sedition).

However, while acknowledging the permeability of class-bound definitions of taste, we should none the less resist the temptation to over-exaggerate the way working-class taste filtered into middle-class culture, for it remains the case that throughout the century most publishing was controlled by middle-class publishers and editors who were highly selective in what they chose to produce, whether they were directing their products to middle- or to working-class audiences. Moreover, many of the cheap works produced for the working classes, particularly in the early and middle decades of the century, were either of the 'improving' kind, to be seen in the material written by the evangelical writer Hannah More (1745–1833) or the publications of the industrious Charles

Knight (1791–1873), producer of cheap encyclopaedias and works with titles like *Library of Entertaining Knowledge* (1825) and *Store of Knowledge* (1842); or they were crudely escapist, as with the infamous 'penny dreadfuls' so despised by the cultural elite and churned out in their thousands by publishers such as G. W. M. Reynolds (1814–79). As a result, indigenous working-class literary traditions, particularly in verse and drama, can be difficult to recover and consequently remain unacknowledged and under-researched in contrast to the attention given to works by middle-class writers (Vicinus 1974 McEthron, Goodridge and Kossick, 2005); an important exception, discussed in Chapter 3, is Chartist poetry (Schwab 1993; Sanders 2009).

Concerns about a decline in literary standards became particularly prominent around the 1880s, when they were viewed as part of a larger cultural 'degeneration' – to use a term which then became fashionable – which in its turn provoked widespread debate about the politics of British (which in practice tended to mean English) nationalism. In the last quarter of the century we see concerted attempts to formalise, via the writing of literary histories, a literary canon, one which embodied what was termed the 'noble English style', and in which Shakespeare became the most prominent figure. By the same token, antiquarian societies in Scotland, Ireland and Wales promoted research into native literatures. These groups saw the identification and preservation of distinctive linguistic, cultural and so also political identities as key resources in their efforts to resist the threat of an English hegemony, and in this way they sought to challenge the basis of that concerted process of nation building which, as Linda Colley has argued, followed the 1801 Act of Union with Ireland (Colley 1992). In Britain's expanding empire, traditions of colonial literature, best exemplified perhaps by new works written in English in British India (particularly poetry), also began to develop.

Nineteenth-century literary genres

Much of the variety that we find in nineteenth-century literature can be attributed to the development of new sub-genres designed to cater to the tastes of new sorts of readers. This was particularly the case in popular forms of writing, which saw the development of detective and sensation fiction, ghost stories, travel writing and various forms of 'self-help' books on topics such as etiquette, home decoration and housekeeping. Educational publishing of many kinds, including children's fiction, which in the early and middle decades of the century was often strongly educational or moralistic in tone, also experienced significant growth.

These changes in the genres of, and tastes for, popular literature had a parallel in the history of the stage. General economic prosperity financed a growth in theatre building, initially in London's rapidly expanding East End in the 1830s and 1840s. Together with the development of more informal venues such as music halls (which were primarily drinking establishments) and penny gaffs, these new theatres were patronised by new kinds of audiences who in turn demanded new sorts of theatrical entertainments. In contrast to the historical and verse dramas by writers such as Percy Bysshe Shelley (1792–1822), Robert Browning or (later) Algernon Charles Swinburne (1837–1909), the tastes of lower middle- and working-class theatre-goers were for genres which relied on visual rather than verbal effects – that is, for melodrama, burlesque and pantomime. It is worth emphasising that working-class audiences were not, in absolute terms, newcomers to the theatre; the hierarchical division of Restoration and eighteenth-century auditoria into differentially priced boxes, pit and gallery presupposed some element of social mixing. However, although a part of that audience was drawn from the working or labouring classes, theatrical culture itself tended to be dominated by aristocratic values. By contrast, what distinguishes the nineteenth-century theatre is the fact that increased urbanisation, particularly in London, produced a concentration of less well-off groups so that they now possessed the critical mass to support their own forms of entertainment. As a result, theatrical culture became more obviously subject to class divisions, and thus more frequently the object of class-based anxieties about taste. So a recurrent preoccupation of the various Parliamentary Select Committees charged with reporting on the state of London's theatres was the class composition of different sorts of theatrical establishments, such as music halls rather than more 'serious' venues such as Drury Lane or Covent Garden. By the same token, in the last quarter of the century many theatrical entrepreneurs, especially those working in London's fashionable West End, saw money as the means by which drama could be revalued to become a respectable or 'high' art form: expensively refurbished or rebuilt auditoria could command higher ticket prices, which in turn attracted the patronage of what were seen as more exclusive and so more discerning audiences.

Alongside the growth of new popular genres, the nineteenth century also saw a significant rise in popularity of traditional forms of writing. Foremost among these was religious publishing, which could encompass sermons and religiously inspired conduct books (such as those by the evangelical writer Sarah Stickney Ellis (1799–1872)), accounts of religious conversions (including familiar Christian works, like the popular *Apologia Pro Vita Sua* (1864) by John Henry Newman (1801–90), as well as a tradition of both Jewish and Christian conversion literature), and the prodigious output of the Religious Tract Society (RTS). Founded in 1799, the RTS began by publishing penny chapbooks, ballads and serials. Later it developed a significant list of children's literature, one which included adventure stories by writers such as George Henty (1832–1902) and, from 1879, the immensely popular *Boy's Own Paper*, which had a circulation of around a quarter of a million (a companion *Girl's Own Paper* was launched in 1880). Perhaps the best-remembered forms of religious literature of the period, alongside works such as Tennyson's *In Memoriam* mentioned earlier, are the devotional sonnets of Christina Rossetti and Gerard Manley Hopkins, as well as novels of religious doubt such as Mary Ward's *Robert Elsmere*. Also important, although often overlooked, are works which focus on the tense relationships between religious groups; they include the anti-Catholic polemic of works such as *Conformity* (1841) and *Falsehood and Truth* (1841) by the evangelical writer Charlotte Elizabeth Tonna (1790–1846) and Charlotte Brontë's *Villette* (1853), or the overt anti-Semitism of *Dr Phillips* (1887) by Julia Frankau (1859–1916) – works which were balanced by the more positive portrayals of British Catholicism and Jewish life found respectively in *Ellen Middleton* (1844) by Lady Georgiana Fullerton (1812–85), 'The Perez Family' (1843) by Grace Aguilar (1816–47) and, arguably, in Eliot's *Daniel Deronda* (1876). Finally, it is perhaps worth noting, too, the notoriety generated by works such as *La Vie de Jésus* (1863) by Ernest Renan (1823–92), which retold, in naturalistic form, the story of Christ, or the survey of Christ's life published anonymously as *Ecce Homo* (1865) by the historian Sir John Seeley (1834–95).

While some genres grew in popularity, others – most conspicuously poetry and criticism – suffered a comparative decline, at least when judged in terms of the numbers of their readers (although there were important exceptions to this trend, such as the popularity of Tennyson's *In Memoriam*). Many late nineteenth-century poets complained about the difficulties they experienced in getting their work into print; critics, too, were aggrieved by the fact that by the 1860s many publishers judged volumes of reprinted essays to be no longer commercially viable. Moreover, at around the same time those who continued to write 'serious' essays for the periodical press – to write what was at the time labelled the 'higher journalism' – also found themselves competing with a new kind of newspaper writing, one more populist in sentiment and sensational in tone and which centred on the short review. That said, and in marked contrast to both the novel and popular theatrical forms, it was poetry which was consistently valued as the highest literary art form (despite, or even perhaps because of, the fact that generally volumes of poetry did not sell particularly well); moreover, attempts to counter the increasing influence of mass taste invariably referred to the ability of poetry to provide a different sort of literary experience from that to be found in either prose fiction or drama. In his 1833 essay 'Thoughts on Poetry and Its Varieties', the British philosopher John Stuart Mill (1806–73) had attempted to describe the unique value of poetry in epistemological and moral terms: simply put, he argued that poetry was 'truth'. This project was expanded in the 1860s by Arnold, who claimed that the status of literature, and particularly poetry, as a form of moral knowledge conferred on it important social functions which were analogous to those formerly predicated of religion.

These debates about the relative value of different literary forms were in their turn part of a larger discussion about the relationships between different sorts of artistic practice. Many commentators on literary topics – including Pater – also wrote extensively on pictorial art, and Pater was one of several critics who invoked the *Laokoon* (1766) by the eighteenth-century German Romantic philosopher, Gotthold Ephraim Lessing (1729–81), to underwrite their views about the superiority of poetry in relation to what Lessing had termed the 'plastic arts' (meaning sculpture and painting). This elevation of the distinctive experience of art, and especially of poetry, found a logical if controversial expression in the 1870s and 1880s in the work of the English Aesthetes (a movement with which, as we noted earlier, Pater was closely associated), and which was popularly characterised by the slogan 'art for art's sake': art, Pater argued in the 'Conclusion' to his controversial 1873 essay collection *Studies in the History of the Renaissance*, 'comes to you professing frankly to give nothing but the highest quality to your moments as they pass, and for those moments' sake'.

Other commentators stressed the continuity between different art forms, to the extent of identifying the experience of one kind of art with that of another. The most important (and indeed widely disseminated) example is to be found in the writings of the art and social critic John Ruskin, who typically interpreted, or 'read', pictorial art for its narrative and often explicitly moral qualities. Such rhetoric appealed in part because of the way technology had made the plastic arts – traditionally the preserve only of wealthy patrons who were able to commission or own paintings and sculptures – more widely accessible to the middle and upper middle classes. This came about both through cheap reproductions (such as the prints produced by the Arundel Society, founded in 1848) and also by improved transport systems, which made famous European centres of art, like Florence, Venice and Paris, hitherto visited principally as part of the eighteenth-century 'grand tour', much less exclusive as the nineteenth century progressed. The opening of public galleries (such as the National Gallery in London, founded in 1824) also played a role in opening access to the plastic arts. In Eliot's *Middlemarch* this form of cultural tourism is represented as an important source of education, not only for the middle classes but also for women (as indeed it had been for Eliot herself). Works such as Dickens's *Little Dorrit* (1855–57) or Henry James's *The Tragic Muse* (1890), however, register the value of such educational tourism more ambivalently.

This growing awareness among the reading public of the importance of the visual imagination was also exploited, although in a different way, by Dante Gabriel Rossetti (1828–82) and Michael Field; both wrote poems inspired by, or in Rossetti's case, to accompany, specific art works. Later, Thomas Hardy attempted to recreate in language the effects of certain kinds of landscape art, particularly that of Joseph Mallord William Turner (1775–1851), whose works became accessible to the public in the National Gallery. Dickens, by contrast, was greatly influenced by the spectacular visual effects of melodrama, his favourite form of theatrical entertainment (the theatrical company of Vincent Crummles is the source of much affectionate comedy in Dickens's *Nicholas Nickleby* (1838–39)). By the same token several nineteenth-century sensation novels, such as Braddon's *Lady Audley's Secret* (1862), were adapted for the stage. In his influential study *Realizations* (1983), Martin Meisel drew attention to what he argued was a common aesthetic, combining narrative with the pictorial in nineteenth-century paintings, literary and dramatic works. Another importance artistic 'alliance' was that which purported to link poetry and music; this connection is most easily discerned in the use by some poets of musical terminology (such as the symphony or the nocturne) for titles of their works, and in the way that composers such as Claude Debussy (1862–1918) used literary terms, such as 'the tone poem', to describe their compositions. Such an intermingling of different art forms found a logical, if extreme, conclusion in some late nineteenth-century Symbolist poems, such as Symons's 'Colour Studies' and 'Mauve, Black and Rose' in his 1897 collection *London Nights*, which attempted to exploit the properties of synaesthesia – an effect or quality which was again summed up in a slogan, this time, 'all the arts are one'.

A common thread in all these discussions about the value of different art forms is the lowly position assigned to contemporary fiction. None the less, it was literary fiction which, as we have suggested earlier, consistently enjoyed the most buoyant market (one which, according to some estimates, presided over the publication of some 50,000–60,000 new titles over the course of the century), and it is the realist novel which has typically been seen as the most significant literary achievement of the period. Prose fiction has continued to dominate literary publishing up to the present day, and its popularity shows little sign of waning. Fiction is also the form which was most obviously affected by nineteenth-century industrialisation, in the sense that it was the transformation of the printing industry by new technology and capital investment which for the first time made the novel accessible to a mass readership. As we have suggested, those same processes also brought about a wider and more general transformation in literary culture itself, one in which the authority of an intellectual (and usually moneyed) elite was no longer taken for granted. In this respect, one way of understanding the impact of industrialisation on nineteenth-century literary production is in terms of the ways in which it helped to undermine hitherto monolithic and totalising concepts of cultural value: by the 1890s, it no longer made sense to talk about a single, unified literary culture in Britain, but rather a number of often competing cultures.

Themes in nineteenth-century literature

A second and less direct way of tracing the impact of industrialisation on nineteenth-century literary production is in terms of the way its consequences for social and civil society provided a new and distinctive range of subjects and themes for contemporary writers. As noted earlier, one of the most important economic preconditions for the rapid development of industrialisation in nineteenth-century Britain was the emergence of new forms of financial capitalism and financial risk management. Although recognised at the time as a prerequisite for an expanding economy – fiduciary (or paper) money was seen as crucial to increasing trade – this kind of wealth creation was none the less always controversial. The bursting of a speculative credit bubble in the 1820s, following the end of the Napoleonic Wars, resulted in a series of bank failures which was followed in later decades by periodic but dramatic collapses of personal fortunes and reputations, most famously perhaps that in 1856 of the businessman, fraudster and former Junior Lord of the Treasury John Sadlier. Such events helped to precipitate a national debate about the value of paper currency relative to bullion (metal money) and thus, inevitably, about the trustworthiness of the Bank of England (which had, ironically, been originally established in the aftermath of an earlier speculative bubble), and so of the nation itself. These anxieties still resonated in the 1870s and 1880s in discussions about bimetallism (or the use of silver as well as gold as a reserve currency), a topic which found its way into such unlikely situations as Wilde's *The Importance of Being Earnest* (1895). For many contemporary commentators on these events, it was the dizzying speed with which fortunes could be lost as well as made, and the agency or otherwise of the individual in such processes, which provoked the greatest unease. Newspapers reporting on Sadlier's frauds typically focused on the plight of his innocent victims, what *The Times*, in a piece which appeared on 10 March 1856, referred to as those 'widows, spinsters, small farmers, traders and clerks' who had entrusted him with their life's savings. The same William Powell Frith who refused to make a department store the subject of art had in 1877–80 produced a series of five narrative paintings with the Hogarthian title *The Race for Wealth*.

In nineteenth-century pre-decimal currency the main units of value were pounds, shillings and pence (abbreviated as *£ s d*); there were 12 pence to a shilling, 20 shillings to a pound, and a guinea represented 21 shillings. In terms of modern coinage, a shilling is equivalent to 5 (new) pence. The inflating of prices and general shifts in commodity values make establishing precise equivalents with modern prices difficult. In the middle decades of the century an average income for a middle-class family was £154 per annum and for a working-class family £58; by contrast, the average upper-class family income was £6,079 (Crouzet 1990: 40). As well as bank notes (the sole issuer of which in England, following the Bank Act of 1844, was the Bank of England), nineteenth-century paper money took a wide variety of recognisably modern forms, some of which could be traded in the market (Crosby 2002). These included: bills of exchange and accommodation (originally used by merchants), promissory notes (a form of personal debt), treasury and exchequer bills (issued by government and redeemable with interest at the end of a set period), bills of lading (used by shipping companies), bills of sale (a form of mortgage on household and personal property), drafts and cheques (drawn on bank deposits), stocks (shares in a company) and bonds (loans made to corporations and governments that paid set interest on a regular basis). Nineteenth-century literature is often remarkably precise about the forms of finance used in particular transactions, as well as about the risks involved.

A less obvious but no less important anxiety concerned the ways in which new types of money-making challenged traditional ideas about the 'natural' relationship between wealth and governance, a relationship enshrined in the ideologies of social paternalism which we find explicitly or implicitly alluded to in a range of early and mid nineteenth-century novels. In Jane Austen's *Emma* (1816) it is the wisdom and experience of the aristocrat Mr Knightley, owner of Donwell Abbey, which restores social order after Emma's disastrous attempts at match-making between the humbly born Harriet Smith and a variety of her social superiors, including the local vicar, Mr Elton. In his early fiction Dickens, too, tends to equate familial with social cohesion and to see the 'good' society dependent on the fundamental benevolence of a patriarch such as the wealthy Mr Brownlow in *Oliver Twist*. This nexus of values is typically troped in terms of the family feast presided over by a figure of male authority, and it is no accident that in *Emma* social tensions reach their height during a picnic outing at Box Hill. By empowering individuals who had traditionally been excluded from political influence, the sudden acquisition of wealth made possible by industrial capitalism threatened the stability of such social hierarchies, both within families and between social classes. Dickens's later novels provide a number of striking registers of these anxieties, notably in the 'dust-heaps' – thought by some to be a euphemism for excrement – which feature in *Our Mutual Friend*; it is these heaps which provide both the metaphorical and actual fortune for the Boffins. In *Our Mutual Friend* we also meet the nouveaux riches Podsnaps, whose extravagant meals no longer represent socially cohesive events, but rather become vulgar exhibitions of the wealth-based nature of class identity.

Similar threats to social order were perceived to derive from those individuals who were completely dispossessed, such as the labouring classes. Changes in traditional work patterns and demography brought about by industrialisation had given this large section of the population a new visibility, particularly in the rapidly expanding urban centres. Where urban infrastructure was unable to keep pace with population movements – typically immigration both from other parts of Britain and from Ireland – the result was poverty: poor housing, poor sewerage and overcrowding. In Manchester, for example, it was estimated that in the 1830s up to 15,000 people were living in dark and airless cellars, a situation graphically documented in Elizabeth Gaskell's *Mary Barton* (1848) and, slightly earlier, in *The Condition of the Working Class in England* (1845) by Karl Marx's friend and principal collaborator, Friedrich Engels (1820–95) (like most of the writings of Marx (1818–83), this work of social criticism was not translated into English until the 1880s). Moreover, such conditions inevitably worsened during periods of economic recession, particularly during the so-called 'hungry forties', when many of the urban labouring classes found themselves suddenly out of work. The typical patterns of development of the larger British cities meant that poor and rich areas tended to exist side by side and it was this proximity, and the fears of contagion that it engendered, which fuelled public anxiety about the living and working conditions of the poorest members of the urban population. A number of Royal Commissions and Parliamentary Select Committees were set up to investigate these problems. The best known were those conducted by Edwin Chadwick (1800–90), particularly his *First Report of the Commissioners for Inquiring into the State of Large Towns of Populous Districts* (1844). Novelists, including the future Tory prime minister Benjamin Disraeli, saw these urgent social problems as a new theme for literary fiction.

This subject-matter gave the novels of the 1840s and 1850s a topicality and political edge which was quite distinct from the middle-class or minor aristocratic and domestic concerns both of Jane Austen and the so-called 'silver fork' novels of the 1820s and 1830s, on the one hand, and the historical romances of Walter Scott and the sensationalist Newgate novels, on the other. William Harrison Ainsworth, the author of the immensely popular and much-pirated *Jack Sheppard* (1839) and *Rookwood* (1834), which had a sub-plot involving the infamous highwayman Dick Turpin, had also been concerned with the activities of an underclass; however, and as we noted earlier, such Newgate fiction worked largely by appealing to a public fascination with crime, the more grisly and sensational the better. By contrast, the declared purpose of more seriously minded mid nineteenth-century novelists – in what has been termed the 'social-problem' or 'industrial' novel – was to attract sympathy for the poor, with a view to ameliorating the conditions which drove them to crime in the first instance. However, modern critics have judged such sympathy to be limited in scope, largely because it is evoked by using familiar domestic tropes underwritten by an equally familiar social paternalism. So it is companionable meals, rather than union activity, that consolidate working-class communities in Gaskell's *Mary Barton*. In that novel's conclusion the possibility of social cohesion is ultimately to be found, just as in Austen's fiction, in the actions of older men (the young hero and heroine having emigrated to Canada), this time in the shape of the reformed patriarch and factory owner Mr Carson and the working-class autodidact Job Legh.

Indeed most mid-century literary representations of working-class activism (certainly by middle-class authors) focused on interrogating the moral competence of the lower classes and their capacity for self-governance, qualities typically judged in relation to alcohol consumption, sexual behaviour and an ability to practise thrift. The need to educate the working classes in the management of their finances was a particular concern of the Unitarian writer Harriet Martineau (1820–76); her *Illustrations of Political Economy* (1832–35), originally serialised in monthly parts, used simply plotted and highly moralised stories as vehicles for economic and financial education; they were immensely popular and sold up to 10,000 copies per month. Largely ignored in middle-class literary fiction were the political rights of the working classes as embodied in the ambitions of the Chartist movement, the most visible and, for many, the most violent, expression of the desire for social change. The issue was whether the working classes had the capacity to vote in any way other than that of what commentators like Arnold perceived as crude self-interest. It is equally significant that, as noted earlier, such competence was defined legally in terms of the ownership of property. This linking of possessions with moral probity and of wealth with political responsibility may in turn explain, at least in part, why criminal behaviour, and particularly its policing and its impact on the middle classes, is, as noted earlier, another recurrent subject in nineteenth-century literary works. Criminality connects the social-problem novels (where the themes of political rights and political activism among the working classes are often entwined with those of drug taking, prostitution, blackmail, theft and murder) with the earlier Newgate novels, the later sensation fiction of the 1850s and 1860s and with the detective fiction of Arthur Conan Doyle in the last decade of the century. In other words, another way of viewing the mid nineteenth-century literary concern with serious social topics, such as class conflict, is in terms of an expression of fear.

That fear, articulated with typical pugnacity by Thomas Carlyle in works such as 'Signs of the Times' (1833) and *Chartism* (1839), took two distinct though related forms. As noted earlier, there was a fear of physiological contagion, that the diseases which were so prevalent in poor areas would spread via what was then called a 'miasma' or bad air to the households of the rich; and there was also a fear of political contagion, that working-class discontent, encouraged by revolutionary actions in Europe (often viewed by mid-century British commentators as simply criminal activities), might coalesce into a potent political force, a possibility which the efforts to form a Grand Consolidated Trades Union in the 1830s and the activities of the Chartist movement briefly threatened to make a reality. Such fear also helps to explain why, unlike the ballads and broadsides published by the Chartists themselves, so much of the fiction of the time, directed as it was to middle-class readers, rarely acknowledges that the poor possess any legitimate political rights. Class conflict is generally resolved by advocating changes to the 'heart' or to the individual rather than to the economy; such resolutions frequently take the form of an exhortation to members of different classes to recognise in each other their common humanity, a recognition typically symbolised via an emblematic reconciliation between a working- and a middle-class character. George Eliot's *Felix Holt*, written just before the Second Reform Act, exhibits a deep distrust of the potential for reasoned and reasonable behaviour among the working classes, while at the same time it satirises a corrupt, feckless and decaying aristocracy: for Eliot, power is to be placed in the hands of the skilled artisan and middle classes, though she obscures the economic basis of their authority by emphasising their intellectual rather than financial resources.

Such conservatism, however, may not only have been the product of political prejudice. Making sense of the ways in which nineteenth-century industrialism was changing the relationship between economics and politics was also made difficult by the body of economic theory which dominated British intellectual culture until the 1870s. Known as 'political economy' and developed from the work of the late eighteenth-century philosopher Adam Smith (1723–90), it appeared to justify nineteenth-century (or, as it was then termed, 'laissez-faire') capitalism by representing the workings of a free market as inevitable, as a kind of 'natural law' which worked in ways which ignored any cost to particular individuals. The strongly moralising rhetoric of so many nineteenth-century literary treatments of wealth may thus be due, in part, to the absence of a readily available coherent economic critique of capitalism. It is worth remembering that the most famous and influential such critique, Karl Marx's *Das Kapital*, the first volume of which was published in 1867, was little known to British readers until, as we noted earlier, the late 1880s and 1890s – at around the same time, that is, when socialism became for the first time an active force in British politics, with the setting up of the Social Democratic Federation in 1881 by Henry Mayers Hyndman (1842–1921) and, a little later, the rival Socialist League by William Morris. The influence of an earlier socialist and industrialist, Robert Owen (1771–1858), who had also advocated communal ownership of property and a society based on co-operation rather than competition, had been limited, largely because his social reforms centred on agrarian societies, and as a result appeared to have little to say about the problems of industrialisation. This lacuna in economic theory may also explain why, in the middle decades of the nineteenth century, literature appeared such a useful resource for exploring issues which other discourses seemed either unable or unwilling to address.

It is also worth stressing that the conservatism of writers like Eliot or Gaskell did not mean that fictional treatments of social issues were uncontroversial, nor that they failed to focus the attention of their middle-class (and mainly female) readership on issues of urgent political concern. Novels like Charles Kingsley's *Alton Locke* (1850) or *Michael Armstrong, The Factory Boy* (1839) by Frances Trollope (1780–1863) helped to raise awareness about the plight of workers in, respectively, the textile and clothing (or 'sweating') industries, a topic which had also been addressed in the immensely popular 'The Song of the Shirt' (1843) by Thomas Hood (1799–1845), and which took the form of an impassioned protest by an overworked seamstress. Concern centred on the high rates of accidents, disease and early mortality which affected those employed in weaving, dying or garment making. However, we should note in passing the emergence, later in the century, of a different set of anxieties centring on dress. As mechanisation, cheap imports and the industrial production of new kinds of synthetic dyes made clothing increasingly cheap, so the purchase of clothes for 'fashion' rather than function became a possibility for a much wider section of the population, including some working-class women. This extension of cultural privilege was perceived as blurring social hierarchies because it enabled individuals from the lower classes to use clothing to represent themselves as belonging to a higher class (Aindow 2009). As with those anxieties about the trustworthiness of fiduciary money, the relationship between who individuals actually were and how they appeared (which in nineteenth-century terms was judged by dress, physiognomy and later, in the 1890s, by the use of cosmetics) was a matter of deep and continuing concern. It informs the elements of deception and disguise in the plots of many sensation novels, notably Collins's *The Woman in White* (1859–60), but perhaps finds its most complex expression in the use of the doppelganger or doubling motif in Stevenson's *The Strange Case of Dr Jekyll and Mr Hyde* and Wilde's *The Picture of Dorian Gray*.

The critique of social class that we see in *Dorian Gray* is a reminder that it is not until the late decades of the century that we find literature being used as a resource to imagine radically alternative social structures – in, for example, the socialist utopias of William Morris's *A Dream of John Ball* (1888) and *News from Nowhere* (1890). Yet even at this point in time, it is a deep pessimism about the possibility of social change which is the dominant note, especially in naturalist-inspired works such as Hardy's *Jude the Obscure* (1895) and Gissing's *Demos* (1886), in which Mr Westlake is a thinly disguised portrait of William Morris. A conspicuous absence from mid nineteenth-century literary culture is a fully developed literature of change or what we might call a revolutionary literature. Although it is possible to see the beginnings of such a literature in the late eighteenth century, particularly in the writings of figures such as William Blake (1757–1827) and William Godwin, it began to stall after the political verse of Percy Bysshe Shelley. As noted earlier, none of this is to deny the significance of traditions of working-class writing, such as that associated with the Chartist movement and the followers of Robert Owen, but merely to observe that the politics of these popular forms – as opposed to their literary devices, which were heavily reliant on melodramatic tropes – did not fundamentally penetrate mainstream culture. The literature of the century, certainly between the 1820s and 1880s, tended to deprecate rather than endorse violent revolutionary change.

Setting aside their relative lack of economic sophistication, nineteenth-century literary works are nevertheless unusually detailed in the attention which they give to financial transactions, and in the consistency with which the making and accumulating of money, typically via investments, wills and inheritances, are used as plot devices. Equally striking is the ambivalence which attaches to money itself. So 'good' – that is, traditionally moral – behaviour is rewarded financially, although the origins of the money involved are often obscure. Jane Austen's heroines are invariably rewarded by marriage into a moneyed family. Similarly, Charlotte Brontë's Jane Eyre is able to marry because of the money that materialises unexpectedly from an inheritance derived from an unexamined colonial trade, as does the money that forms Heathcliff's mysteriously acquired fortune in Emily Brontë's *Wuthering Heights* and that in Austen's *Mansfield Park* (1814). In *Great Expectations* the money which Pip makes himself and which enables him to pay off his creditors and acquire some self-respect also derives from business ventures abroad (though in Egypt rather than the Australia of Magwitch, his criminal benefactor). By contrast, those who *visibly* deal with money, and who appear to take pleasure in the power it brings, like Eliot's Bulstrode in *Middlemarch*, or Dickens's Merdle in *Little Dorrit*, or even the goblins in Christina Rossetti's *Goblin Market*, are not to be trusted: their money-making is assumed to be corrupt.

More acceptable in nineteenth-century literature is money made from 'honest' work, and this could include new forms of manufacturing; such money is acceptable if part of it is devoted to the public good. Philanthropic acts by successful industrialists, such as Titus Salte, and later the Cadbury family, provided important public buildings and amenities, and so, for some writers, they formed the 'acceptable' face of capitalism, because philanthropy permitted the business world to be moralised. The value of philanthropy is a frequent theme in early and mid nineteenth-century literature, particularly (as might be expected) in those works explicitly directed to middle-class audiences: so the factory owner John Thornton in Gaskell's *North and South* is redeemed by the schools and accommodation he agrees to provide for his workers. In Elizabeth Barrett Browning's *Aurora Leigh* it is in part the philanthropic values of Romney Leigh, the suitor of the independently minded heroine, which ultimately makes him acceptable to her (and the implied reader). Later in the century, however, Victorian philanthropy was subject to a greater scrutiny. In the 1880s and 1890s the 'gospel of wealth' proselytised by the American philanthropist Andrew Carnegie received considerable publicity in Britain; not all, however, were as admiring as the Liberal Prime Minister William Gladstone. In Mary Ward's *Marcella* (1894), the aristocratic heroine works for a time as a nurse in the East End of London, employment which she abandons on her marriage to a titled conservative landowner, having rejected a liberal newspaper proprietor. In Oscar Wilde's 'The Soul of Man Under Socialism' (1891) philanthropy was presented less ambivalently – as an exemplary instance of Victorian hypocrisy which perpetuated rather than solved the problem of poverty.

It is also worth noting in passing that money making, as a literary theme, was subject to familiar gender stereotypes. It is typically men who make money, even though they are corrupted by it; and equally typically it is women whose purity is preserved by their innocence from the world of work. When, in late nineteenth-century literature, women do work, there is generally an element of compromise involved; in Gissing's *The Odd Women*, work is seen as an evil made necessary by women's failure in the marriage market, and married women who none the less choose to pursue a career outside the home (as Alma Rolfe does in *The Whirlpool*) suffer physically and psychologically as a consequence. It has been noted that in the late nineteenth-century sub-genre of 'new-woman' fiction, in works such as Sarah Grand's *The Heavenly Twins* (1893) or Grant Allen's *The Woman Who Did* (1895), both of which were immensely popular, the fate of the emancipated heroine is often ambivalently presented: despite her independence, the modern woman rarely thrives. In the sensation novels of Wilkie Collins, money, identity and agency become synonymous terms: loss of an inheritance becomes a literal loss of selfhood, particularly for women. In much nineteenth-century fiction (and later in its drama) the domestic sphere itself, despite its ostensible separation from the public world of work, is nevertheless often represented as just another kind of market-place, in which the most intimate emotional relationships (including marriage and parenthood) are governed by similar systems of exchange – in Thomas Carlyle's famous phrase, by the 'cash-nexus', in which all relations between human beings are understood in terms of money transactions.

Domestic life, then, is seen to be vulnerable to the selfsame anxieties about value as those to be encountered in the economy proper: are lovers, parents or paper money exactly what they represent themselves as being, or are represented to be? Are emotional investments any less risky than financial investments, particularly when emotional transactions have monetary costs? In the denouement of some of Austen's fiction – paradigmatically in *Pride and Prejudice* (1813) – emotional values are confidently assimilated to financial values. However this confidence is largely absent from later nineteenth-century literary works where the basis of 'Modern Love', as George Meredith (1828–1909) termed it in his 1862 sonnet sequence of that title, is more usually presented as a form of exploitation and betrayal, which in some cases amounts to what we would today term domestic abuse: money and emotion are equally untrustworthy. Fiction, poetry and drama all portray marriage as a potential site of domestic violence (both physical and psychological), usually directed against women and children. This disturbing theme links the novels of the Brontës (notably *Wuthering Heights*, and *The Tenant of Wildfell Hall* (1848) by Anne Brontë (1820–49)), with early works by Dickens (such as *Oliver Twist*), sensation fiction (such as Braddon's *Aurora Floyd* (1863) and Collins's *The Woman in White*), as well as Eliot's *Daniel Deronda* and some of Hardy's and James's novels. The abuse of patriarchal power, particularly in the home, was the dark side of social paternalism; moreover, the harsh physical and emotional reality of many marriages, rather than the ideology of domestic bliss to be found in works like John Ruskin's 'Of Queens' Gardens' (1864) and the famous paean to married love, *The Angel in the House* – the first version of which appeared in 1854 – by the Catholic poet Coventry Patmore (1823–96), was daily exposed in the courts and newspapers. Such 'reality' was given robustly unsentimental treatment in George Bernard Shaw's drama *Mrs Warren's Profession*. Published in 1898, but not performed on the nineteenth-century stage, it presented marriage as a form of legalised prostitution – a proposition that completely re-characterises the marital values of an Elizabeth Bennet and Mr Darcy.

Those living in cities, whether from the working or middle classes, were not the only population group with reason to feel ambivalent about nineteenth-century technological change and economic growth. Rural populations also experienced many of the deleterious effects of capitalism; however, because the countryside was less densely populated, rural poverty and suffering were less visible. In much nineteenth-century literature, from the Romantics onwards, rural life is troped in terms of pastoral traditions: it is seen in opposition to, and therefore as a potential escape from, the pressures of urban existence. The most famous examples are to be found in Romantic poetry, particularly in William Wordsworth's 'Michael' (1800) and *The Prelude* and the odes of John Keats (1795–1821). The actuality of rural poverty was of course quite different. In tandem with this use of a reinvigorated pastoral there developed a strong tradition of what might loosely be termed 'natural history' writing, that is, closely observed descriptions of both the flora and fauna of the British countryside as well as the rhythms and traditions of rural life. Following the example of eighteenth-century naturalists such as Gilbert White (1720–93), who wrote about his beloved home village of Selborne, the poet John Clare celebrated in meticulously detailed descriptions the Northamptonshire countryside of his childhood; a little later, Richard Jefferies (1848–87), the son of a Wiltshire farmer, used observations from his 'field notebooks' in works such as *Wild Life in a Southern Country* and *The Amateur Poacher* (both published in 1879). However, this celebration of the particularities of rural life could easily become an unexamined nostalgia for what was represented as a simpler and more innocent way of living; this can be seen in novels by Charles Dickens, Elizabeth Gaskell and George Eliot, or later in the century, in the 'blue remembered hills' of *A Shropshire Lad* (1896) by A. E. Housman (1859–36). At the same time, there were some nineteenth-century writers, most famously Emily Brontë and Thomas Hardy, who were prepared to acknowledge that the beauty of rural life co-existed alongside an inescapable brutality.

This nineteenth-century tendency to romanticise or glamorise things rural, a process which encompasses the valorisation of an untamed nature by Romantic poets, the celebration of the country house and its values in Jane Austen's novels, as well as in Gaskell's Cranford and George Eliot's 'provincial life', can be explained in part by developments in the rural economy. In general terms, and up until the 1870s, the early and mid decades of the nineteenth century saw something of a boom or golden age for British agriculture. The controversial repeal of the Corn Laws in 1846 (which split the Tory Party, keeping it out of power for a generation) had opened the domestic market to competition from overseas. However, it did not lead to the predicted flood of cheap imported corn and the consequent collapse of British agriculture: rather the opposite. Although imports did increase dramatically, corn prices held firm; moreover, levels of animal produce, particularly of beef and of milk, increased significantly. Thus, despite foreign competition, during the middle decades of the century the British agricultural sector maintained strong growth, albeit with different produce capable of being transported to the burgeoning urban markets. This growth was not simply a consequence of increased demand in urban centres; it can also be attributed to a readiness to embrace technology. This receptivity can be seen in the introduction of mechanical threshing machines, which were in use as early as the middle of the century. Such processes inevitably changed traditional patterns of rural labour, especially among the male workforce, some of whose occupations were replaced by machines. Mechanical reapers and threshers were none the less expensive investments for a farmer, and only repaid that outlay over a long period of time, and then on relatively large acreages of land. So although machinery significantly increased productivity, because of this high cost of capital investment (which was in turn necessary to stay competitive) the 'real' incomes of landowners actually fell during this 'golden age' of agriculture.

Although the agricultural workforce was substantially reduced by the 1870s, there was never a rural labour shortage, particularly in the south of the country. This detail explains why, during a period of strong growth, casual farm labourers, of whom there were nearly one and a half million in the 1851 census and who worked hard but irregularly (most would be unemployed over the winter months), consistently formed one of the poorest sections of the British population, a topic addressed by Thomas Hardy in his influential essay 'The Dorsetshire Labourer' (1883). It also explains why there were persistent outbreaks of rural crime – typically poaching, rick burning and the mutilation of farm animals – all of which were caused by rural poverty. In this respect, the main beneficiaries of the farming boom were entrepreneurial tenant farmers; in the fiction of the time, and again particularly in Thomas Hardy's novels of the 1880s, they are typically represented as 'new' men, willing to embrace both technological innovation and, like men of the City, prepared to take financial risks.

In these various ways of depicting rural life and of representing the countryside we can also see a politics at work. For early nineteenth-century writers like Wordsworth and Clare the threat to rural traditions had its origins in the changes in land ownership brought about by events such as the Enclosure Acts. In a famous letter to Charles James Fox, the Whig politician, which is often taken to be a commentary on 'Michael', Wordsworth identified rural depopulation with rural demoralisation; this identification also partly explains the tendency among a number of Romantic writers (and also Emily Brontë in *Wuthering Heights*) to identify political with geographical freedom: the 'free spirit' is metaphorically as well as physically free. By the late decades of the century there are still external threats to rural life, but they are different in nature. In Hardy's novels, as we have noted, it is the newcomers or strangers (such as Alec D'Urberville in *Tess*, or Donald Farfrae in *The Mayor of Casterbridge* (1886)) who threaten to destabilise the economic and social status quo, as they bring with them what are seen as destructive urban values, particularly those of industrial capitalism. In this respect, rural life is often represented in terms of nostalgia for a simpler and more straightforward pre-industrial time.

This tendency to seek answers for present-day social problems in the past, or to use the past to critique the present, has often been explained in terms of a reaction to the increasing pace of change in the nineteenth century – stasis becomes more appealing when change seems inexorable. For many writers, artists and architects this search for stability and simplicity led them to revalue cultural moments in the distant past, particularly those of medieval England and classical Greece and Rome, and in the process to find in these historic cultures traits which often seemed more progressive than features of contemporary life, such as the institutions of Athenian democracy or the forms of co-operation held to underlie medieval Guilds. The most visible elements of this revivalism were to be seen in neo-Gothic architecture. As we noted earlier, this celebration of the buildings of the Middle Ages found its most powerful advocate in John Ruskin, especially in his admiration of Venetian Gothic in *The Stones of Venice* (1851–53). For Ruskin it was not the simply the aesthetics of the buildings of Venice which were to be admired, but also the forms of social organisation which (in his view) permitted their construction in the first place. Ruskin, like William Morris after him, saw works of art as expressions of underlying forms of social life, and in this way art and social criticism became intimately interrelated. Some years later, Ruskin's understanding of the spiritual purity of early Italian art, which he contrasted with the decadence of the High Renaissance, was contested by Vernon Lee (the pen-name of Violet Paget, 1856–1935) in her *Euphorion: Being Studies of the Antique and Medieval in the Renaissance* (1884), which was also a response, in part, to John Addington Symonds's (1840–93) authoritative seven-volume *Renaissance in Italy* (1875–86). However, Lee shared with Ruskin, and many other nineteenth-century writers, a sense that history was embodied in, and therefore could be apprehended via, a sense of place – what she, among others, referred to as the 'genius loci' (the spirit of place) – or through contact with historical objects, such as art works, sarcophagi and buildings (ruined or otherwise) as well as landscapes. A celebration of medieval political, social and cultural values also informed Thomas Carlyle's influential comparison of modern and medieval life contained in *Past and Present* (1843), as well as many of Tennyson's most popular poems, such as his *Idylls of the King* (1842), and William Morris's translations of medieval Icelandic sagas and his *The Defence of Guenevere and Other Poems* (1858). In addition, the poetry and paintings of the Pre-Raphaelites valorised the work of early Italian painters, particularly Giotto, above that of later Renaissance art preferred by institutions such as the Royal Academy and National Gallery. It is worth bearing in mind, however, that this interest in medieval culture, which found a counterpart in historical and philological studies, inevitably involved (like other forms of nostalgia) an element of romanticisation and therefore distortion.

Other historical epochs which held a continuing appeal for nineteenth-century writers and artists were those of classical Greece and Rome. Here the situation is more complex. An appeal to, and celebration of, Greek cultural and Roman civic values are elements in British cultural life that can be traced from the Renaissance, through Augustan literature, to the nineteenth century. It is not the case, then, that nineteenth-century writers 're-discovered' the classical past, although they did uncover a different classical canon (with writers such as Heraclitus and Aristophanes and historians such as Thucydides). More important are the particular values which nineteenth-century writers found in the classical past. In general terms reference to, and the specific use of, classical literary models and myths – in works such as Walter Pater's dense and scholarly novel *Marius the Epicurean* (1885) and poems such as Arnold's 'Empedocles on Etna' (1852) – continued to be one means by which a writer could attempt to identify in advance an elite readership, and a classical education remained throughout the century an upper middle-class educated male preserve, and thus the mark of a gentleman. Ignorance of classical culture, in other words, was consistently used as a way of exposing what was viewed as intellectual pretension. (A famous example is the criticism of Keats's classical learning in works such as *Endymion* (1818), which drew not on first-hand reading, but on text-books such as John Lemprière's *Classical Dictionary*.) At the same time, however, elements of the classical past – notably the values of classical Greek culture, often loosely referred to as 'Hellenism' – could be used to endorse quite different social and moral values. These included, on the one hand, a tradition of civic republicanism identified by scholars such as Benjamin Jowett (1817–93), the enormously influential Master of Balliol College, Oxford and celebrated translator of *The Dialogues of Plato*. But those very same works could also be interpreted, in their discussion of *paiderastia*, by other late nineteenth-century writers, including Oscar Wilde, John Addington Symonds and Edward Carpenter (1844–1929), as an endorsement of what modern commentators have termed homo-social bonding and same-sex desire. Towards the end of the century, *The History of the Decline and Fall of the Roman Empire* (1776–88) by Edward Gibbon (1737–94) became popular among social commentators because, like nineteenth-century versions of the medieval past, it provided a compelling analogy between the classical past and contemporary concerns – as we discuss in more detail in Chapter 4, it offered a model by which the achievements of the British Empire, and a perceived decline in British political and cultural influence, could be measured.

As well as their interest in comparing their own society with classical civilisations, nineteenth-century readers were avid consumers of 'foreignness' of all kinds, whether 'primitive' – to use a term then popular – or modern. Explorers and explorer-scholars, usually with the advantage of independent incomes, catered to an apparently inexhaustible appetite for *exotica* and tales of derring-do with detailed and often highly personal accounts of expeditions to areas such as the Levant (glamorised by Byron in the early decades of the century), Turkey, the Far East, South America and Africa. *Missionary Travels and Researches in South Africa* (1857) by David Livingstone (1813–73) sold more than 70,000 copies within the first few months of publication, but writers such as Charles Darwin with his *Journal* of the Voyage of H.M.S. Beagle (1839), and Richard Burton (1821–90), who published more than forty volumes of travel writings, also enjoyed success with the genre, as did H. Rider Haggard (1856–1925), who moved seamlessly from recounting his own experiences of living in South Africa to the prolific string of adventure stories that brought him fame, beginning with *King Solomon's Mines* (1885) and its African-born explorer-hero and guide to the 'Dark Continent' Allan Quartermain. George Henty wrote similar sorts of tales for a younger audience. In the work of both men, it was the foreign, and often colonial, settings that provided their appeal, along with a narrative that invariably involved the escapades of a clean-cut and clean living man (and his male companions) in an alien land – in, say, Natal or in India – usually in defence of British imperial values and typically climaxing in a spectacular and bloody affray. Even in stories whose settings were less overtly politically loaded, such as *The Coral Island* (1858) by R. M. Ballantyne (1825–94), one of the most popular boy's adventure stories of the century, imperial endeavour was a less than subtle sub-text: the teenage trio's escapades on the Pacific island on which they are shipwrecked, and which involve capture by natives and eventual rescue by an English missionary, allegorise them as civilising colonisers of a savage land.

Other writers could use similar themes but in a more serious and engaged manner. In the 1880s Rudyard Kipling achieved enormous popularity with his *Plain Tales from the Hills* (1888), stories which work by contrasting some of the clichéd ways in which British life in India was understood in Britain and how it appeared to the British in India themselves (how those lives appeared to the colonised of India was, of course, never canvassed). The theme of the imperial adventure as a moral testing ground for the European mind was also employed by Joseph Conrad, again writing at the century's close, when he too used the general framework provided by the simply plotted adventure story. In *Heart of Darkness* and *Lord Jim* (1900) distant lands are not locations where British or European values prove triumphant; they are, by contrast, places where those values, and the individuals who hold them – such as Kurtz and Lord Jim himself – are tested to destruction and found wanting. The early careers of Conrad, Kipling and Rider Haggard overlapped with, and in the case of the last was partly prompted by, the emergence of a number of more specialist studies of 'otherness', in which it is possible to locate the beginnings of the modern discipline of anthropology; these included the multi-volume *Descriptive Sociology* (1873–1934), founded and initially edited by Herbert Spencer (1820–1903), as well as works such as *The Golden Bough* (1890–1915) by Sir James Frazer (1854–1941), the comparative *Man and Woman: A Study of Human Secondary Sexual Characteristics* (1894) by Henry Havelock Ellis (1859–1939) and, most importantly, various anthropological studies by Edward Tylor (1832–1917), such as his *Primitive Culture* (1871), which centred on the proposition that the modern or 'civilised' mind bore 'vestiges' of its past 'savage' state.

Equally popular throughout the century were encounters with cultures which had been made more familiar and accessible by improved rail and steamship travel, predominantly those of Western Europe (particularly Italy) and North America. Moreover, they were often written by authors who had already made their name as poets, novelists or critics, and include works such as Frances Trollope's *Domestic Manners of the Americans* (1832), which was followed by *Paris and the Parisians* (1835), *Vienna and the Austrians* (1838) and *A Visit to Italy* (1842), Harriet Martineau's *Society in America* (1837), Dickens's *American Notes* (1842) and 'Pictures from Italy' (which appeared in the *Daily News* in 1846), Robert Louis Stevenson's *An Inland Voyage* (1878) and *Travels with a Donkey in the Cevennes* (1879), and at the turn of the century George Gissing's *By the Ionian Sea* (1901). As with depictions of the medieval or classical past, nineteenth-century travel literature was never neutral: other cultures were typically held up as a mirror reflecting either British superiority (in, for example, Trollope's and Dickens's offensively condescending accounts of American manners and mores), or (as was often the case with Italy, which was not constituted as a geographical or political entity until unification in 1861) an index of British cultural and artistic inferiority. Moreover, literary works tended to follow these patterns. Whereas for some late eighteenth-century poets and polemicists, like Tom Paine (1737–1809), and slightly later Coleridge and Robert Southey (1774–1843), who devised a utopian scheme for 'Pantisocracy', a commune in New England, America had represented a liberating site of resistance, both geographical and political, from British power, its depiction in much nineteenth-century fiction, from Dickens's *Martin Chuzzlewit* (1843–44) to Wilde's 'The Canterville Ghost', emphasises its status as Britain's inferior, linguistically, artistically and socially, notwithstanding the fact that those same writers' tours of America were prompted by their recognition that the United States was an increasingly important economic market, particularly in its purchase of British cultural products.

This recognition of American wealth also forced an acknowledgement of a vibrancy and 'can-do' quality in American life, which although sometimes represented as naive or vulgar, continued to stand – as it had for some of Paine's generation – as a rebuke to British conservatism and the stultifying power of tradition. Those tensions receive their fullest treatment in the hands of the American expatriate Henry James, for whom America embodied youthful candour and a kind of innocence, as well as vulgarity. Moreover, James often compared American with European (rather than simply British) culture, and in that comparison Europe – and once more particularly Italy – figures as an embodiment of a freedom which can also be demoralising if not corrupting, particularly for men. This sense of Italy as a country of escape and self-realisation, particularly in the area of sexual expression, provided a resource for many contemporary authors. Numerous British expatriate writers, including Symonds and Lee, found Italy, and especially Florence, an environment more conducive than Britain to exploring relationships which could not be accommodated via heterosexual marriage. At the same time, and as James's fiction indicates, that notion of liberation often appears gendered.

One of the best-known uses of Italian culture is perhaps to be found in Eliot's *Middlemarch* where, as we have noted, Dorothea's encounter with Italian art on her honeymoon awakens her to both the possibility of sensual pleasures and the realisation of their absence in her own (British) marriage to Casaubon. The theme had been broached earlier in the character of Caterina Sastri, the daughter of an Italian singer, in Eliot's 'Mr Gilfil's Love-Story' in *Scenes of Clerical Life* (1858). This use of Italy to represent possibilities, both creative and sexual, unavailable in patriarchal Britain in turn looks back to the influential *Corinne, or Italy* (1807) by Mme de Stäel (1766–1817), in which the Anglo-Italian heroine's endeavours to find literary and romantic fulfilment are identified with an oppressed, and explicitly feminised, Italian nation. By contrast, Robert Browning's use of Italy is more ambivalent. Although poems like 'Two in the Campagna' (1855) celebrate the Italian countryside as a site of romantic encounters, with its 'endless fleece | Of feathery grasses everywhere! | Silence and passion, joy and peace, | An everlasting wash of air', other works, like 'Home Thoughts from Abroad' (1845), which begins with the famous lines, 'Oh, to be in England | Now that April's there', speak of a nostalgic sense of loss, in which Mediterranean vibrancy, symbolised in the contrast between England's 'buttercups' and 'this gaudy melon-flower', is mere vulgarity. While dramatic monologues like 'The Bishop Orders His Tomb' (1845) and 'Fra Lippo Lippi' (1855) exploit a familiar and largely conventional troping of the corrupt nature of political and religious life in the Italian Renaissance, albeit in order to point up similar forms of corruption in contemporary British society.

Finally, it is also worth observing that there were some countries, notably France, which served, from the Romantic poets onwards, as a simultaneous register of both the inferiority and superiority of British life: for example, the Paris depicted in Corelli's *Wormwood* (1890) as a den of absinthe-fuelled moral excess (absinthe, the Decadent drink *par excellence* was banned in nineteenth-century Britain) is not recognisable as the same city as that centre of artistic sophistication to which the protagonists of James's *The Tragic Muse* and Du Maurier's *Trilby* escape in order to avoid the stultifying conventions of life in London. Some years earlier, in her *Paris and the Parisians*, Frances Trollope attempted to capture these contradictory qualities in her representation of Paris as excitingly modern in its architecture and social scene (Parisian society was often viewed as less hierarchical than that of Britain), while at the same time possessing an underbelly of violence and squalor, exemplified by the infamous Paris Morgue, which, despite (or perhaps because of) its gruesome contents, was, in the nineteenth century, a site of popular entertainment, drawing crowds of curious onlookers. It is perhaps worth noting in passing, too, that in contrast to Italy, it was French metropolitan life, rather than its countryside, which captured the imagination of British writers, largely because, for much of the nineteenth century (and with the exception of the French Alps and Pyrenees, usually visited only as overnight stops on the journey south from Paris to Lyon and Italy, and some coastal towns), rural and provincial France lacked any particular cultural or geographical attraction. This was partly because information on these aspects of the country was relatively scarce; indeed literary representations of French provincial life, most famously perhaps in the novels of Gustave Flaubert (1821–80) and Honoré de Balzac (1799–1850), tended to emphasise its stultifying tedium. Moreover, despite a railway network which, by 1854, linked most of the major towns to Paris, there was little specialist provision for the traveller – food and accommodation, for example, were often very poor (Rob 2007).

The frequency with which nineteenth-century writers measured themselves against the values of other cultures and societies, both past and present, may seem to undermine that sense of economic, geographical and technological supremacy which the opening of this chapter described. Likewise, the concern in so much of the literature of the period with crime and transgression, both within and beyond the home, also seems to run counter to the common depiction of the century as enjoying an unprecedented degree of domestic political stability. Nineteenth-century literary works rarely speak, or speak unequivocally, to those clichés of progress, equipoise and moral complacency which have popularly characterised the history of this period. However, it is exactly these tensions which explain why many nineteenth-century literary works remain so engaging to modern readers: while registering the distinctiveness of the times in which they were produced – the concerns of works such as *Pride and Prejudice*, or *Middlemarch* or *Tess of the D'Urbervilles* seem quintessentially of their moment – the most rewarding nineteenth-century poems, fictions or dramas are also invariably those which are accompanied by an insistent (and sometimes highly critical) attention to the limitations of the age.

Conclusion

- In the early and middle decades of the nineteenth century the accelerating processes of industrialisation helped to make Britain the most prosperous as well as economically and technologically advanced country in the world, a position which was retained until the last decades of the century.
- Nineteenth-century Britain also witnessed transformations in intellectual and political life, many of which – such as the successive extensions of the franchise – provoked controversy. Over the course of the century tensions grew between the authority of science and that of religion (as well as other non-rational forms of belief). Social reforms, such as those to education and policing, brought about an increasing encroachment of the state into the private lives of citizens, a process which can also be seen in attempts to control literary culture.
- Changes in work patterns and demography brought about new categories of social demarcation and a new self-consciousness about the relationship between wealth, its origins and social status.
- The industrialisation of the nineteenth-century printing industry, a process underpinned by technological advances and new forms of financial capitalism, brought into being for the first time a mass market for literature. New genres and sub-genres developed to cater to the tastes of new kinds of readers; but in the late decades of the century anxieties grew about a perceived decline in literary standards.
- Common preoccupations in nineteenth-century literary works which arise from the transformations brought about in social life over the course of the century include: transgression, its detection and its punishment; the relationship between wealth and governance; and threats to social order.
- Many nineteenth-century writers looked to the past – specifically the medieval and classical past – for solutions to contemporary social problems. They also frequently compared their own culture to varieties of 'foreignness'.

3 Form, style and genre in nineteenth-century literature

Overview

In literary histories written during the early and middle decades of the twentieth century the period from the end of Romanticism to the beginning of literary Modernism – that is, effectively, what is loosely referred to as the 'Victorian' period – rarely attracted attention because of its stylistic or formal innovation. This chapter begins by asking why this occurred, and suggests that part of the answer lies in the influence of the concept of avant-gardism on literary history and the legacy of Modernist readings of Victorian literature. It then outlines alternative ways of conceptualising the relationships between Romanticism and Victorianism, on the one hand, and between Victorianism and Modernism, on the other, before proceeding to a discussion of the main stylistic and generic developments over the course of the century as a whole in, respectively, poetry, fiction, drama and non-fictional prose.

Conceptualising changes in form

There are a number of ways of thinking about formal or stylistic developments within any period of literary history. We may investigate changes which take place within one genre in relation to changes in other genres over the same time-span: for example, how do developments in the genres of fiction in the nineteenth century compare to those which took place in the genres of poetry, drama or critical writing? As we have suggested, and for reasons which will be explained more fully in Chapter 7, nineteenth-century literary publishing, certainly from the 1830s onwards, was dominated by prose fiction, and the achievement of realist novels has often been viewed as the most significant of the period – it has certainly received the most attention from modern critics. A different sort of enquiry would be one which considers the significance of changes in any single genre in a given period relative to that genre's entire history; this would mean assessing the role of nineteenth-century realist fiction within a history of the novel, from its origins (usually traced to the early eighteenth century) to the present day.

Next there is also the possibility of assessing generic developments in British literary culture, in either of the senses defined above, in relation to those taking place in the cultures of other nations. In the nineteenth century comparisons of this sort have most typically been made with French (and sometimes German) literature, and in many cases British writers have been seen as imitators or appropriators of models first developed by their contemporaries on the Continent. In this last line of argument some aspects of English Romanticism, such as the emphasis on poetic genius and celebration of the natural world, have been traced to currents in German literary culture in the 1770s, and particularly to the early philosophical writings of Wolfgang von Goethe (1749–1832) and the lyric poetry of Friedrich von Schiller (1759–1805). In a similar manner, elements of the critique of art's moral utility associated with the English Aesthetic Movement of the 1870s have been found in earlier French writing, notably the Preface to *Mademoiselle de Maupin* (1835) by Théophile Gautier (1811–72). In the late decades of the century (and as we describe more fully in Chapter 4) critics have perceived in Thomas Hardy's and George Gissing's fiction a number of debts to French Naturalism – that is, to the works of writers such as Emile Zola, and in a similar way in the poetry of the 1890s they have detected the influence of Paul Verlaine (1844–96) and Arthur Rimbaud (1854–91). In the same vein of thought the plots and patterns of dialogue found in the tradition of the French 'la pièce bien faite' – or 'well-made play' – associated with the dramatists Victorien Sardou (1831–1908) and Alexandre Dumas fils have been seen as influences on the society comedies of Oscar Wilde, Henry Arthur Jones (1851–1929) and Arthur Wing Pinero (1855–1934).

Whichever of the above approaches to genre is adopted, until relatively recently, it has typically been only isolated examples of stylistic or formal inventiveness which have been noted, such as the development of the dramatic monologue in the work of Robert Browning or Gerard Manley Hopkins's experiments with sprung rhythm. In the case of drama, and as we noted in Chapter 1, for much of the twentieth century it was not unusual for the work of almost the entire period to be dismissed. Such a judgement prompts a simple question: is it really the case that nineteenth-century writers were, on average, less creative or original than their predecessors or successors?

It is tempting to answer this question by looking at changes in the publishing industry which took place over the course of the century: that is, to identify the apparent conventionalism of nineteenth-century literature with the development, described in Chapter 2, of a mass market for literary publishing. In this view, it is the growing commercialisation of literature which explains, in part, the lack of formal experimentation. (In such an argument it would be worth recalling the very small size of the readerships for works such as the *Lyrical Ballads* (1798) compared to, say, Tennyson's *In Memoriam*.) Such an explanation assumes that most writers (and their publishers) were motivated primarily by a desire to make money, and that producing formulaic works whose appeal had already been tested by the market was a more attractive prospect than the uncertainty of literary innovation. Chapter 7 will explore in detail the role of what some literary historians have referred to as a 'capitalist' mode of production in nineteenth-century literary culture and its impact, through factors such as changes in copyright law, on the conceptualisation of literary creativity. For now it is sufficient to observe that there is abundant evidence to suggest that nineteenth-century writers and publishers evinced a marked concern with their readerships, and writers of what were deemed to be controversial works, such as George Moore's *Esther Waters* (1894), experienced difficulty in getting them published as books. Likewise, nineteenth-century critics often castigated as 'obscure' writing which in their view was made inaccessible to a general readership because of its linguistic or syntactic complexity – what, in another context, might be viewed as formal experimentation. Robert Browning's early career, as we explain in more detail later, was marred by just this kind of critical hostility, as was Dante Gabriel Rossetti's later career as a writer. At the same time, however, contemporary critics also deprecated writing which in their view appealed too blatantly to popular taste; and many publishers, including larger houses such as Macmillan, were more than willing to publish works by 'difficult' writers, like Henry James, who they knew would not be commercially viable: James's works, though selling poorly, none the less lent prestige to Macmillan's list. By the same token, the competitive nature of nineteenth-century publishing also meant that new publishers, like Osgood McIlvaine, who brought out the unexpurgated version of Hardy's *Tess of the D'Urbervilles* (1891), were sometimes willing to take more risks than established houses: after all, controversy could also generate sales. Publishing culture, alone, then, cannot account for the apparent lack of formal inventiveness in nineteenth-century literature.

A more productive way of thinking about this problem involves considering how and why histories of forms or styles are written in the first place. Identifying significance in literary history with innovation or originality is a relatively modern concept, one which derives from an aspect of nineteenth-century literary culture itself – specifically the development of avant-gardism in France in the early decades of the century. The metaphor of the avant-garde came first from military usage – it refers to the vanguard or advanced troops of an army – and originated in the political discourses of the French Revolution. Later it was appropriated by artists and writers to designate those who saw themselves as leaders of revolutionary cultural and intellectual opinion. As we argued in Chapter 1, the proposition that it is the innovators in any given period who are important has remained central to the way that literary history is typically constructed, in part because the concept of originality remains deeply embedded in Western notions of artistic creativity. So a common way of establishing the significance of a given work is by providing evidence for its influence on later generations of writers; moreover, judgements about the importance of the subsequent 'influenced' works in their turn tend to hinge on the extent to which they are seen as mere imitations of the original – and thus 'formulaic' – or whether they improve on or modify it. In this respect identifying what is stylistically innovative in a genre at any moment requires a double perspective. Like the avant-garde artist wishing to 'make it new', the historian must both look backwards to see how a genre has changed in relation to what has gone before, and forward to assess the significance of that change for present or future literary works. Put another way, generic 'dead ends' – that is, developments in genres which do not seem to inform later literary works – have rarely received sustained critical attention: avant-garde literary art matters because it is 'ahead of its time', and this simply means that, with the benefit of hindsight, it is judged to have prefigured future developments.

In popular usage the term 'avant-garde' is generally taken to refer to a special kind of militant artistic or literary radicalism which originated in mid nineteenth-century France. However, there is considerable disagreement among historians and theorists of avant-gardism about the precise nature of that radical protest (Guy 1991). For some, the label avant-garde designates artists and writers whose work is noteworthy for its formal or aesthetic innovation; for others, it refers to artists and writers who hold particular political views, and who self-consciously use their art in the service of them. A further area of disagreement centres on the way avant-garde artists define themselves in relation to the past. So while some theorists argue that avant-gardism must involve a complete rejection of all past literary and artistic traditions, others identify avant-gardism with a certain kind of revisionism in which past literary and artistic traditions are invoked in order that they might be transformed or subverted. There is considerable debate too about the cultural conditions which make avant-garde activity possible. In the 1970s a number of commentators argued for the 'death' of the avant-garde on the grounds that avant-gardism had become so successfully co-opted by a modern culture industry that it had itself become a tradition, an avant-garde which had only itself to react against was a contradiction in terms. Regardless of whether avant-gardism is viewed as a historical phenomenon, or as a mode of artistic practice still relevant in today's society, the most significant issue for the student of nineteenth-century literary culture is the virtual absence from most general histories of avant-gardism in Europe of any examples drawn from nineteenth-century British artists and writers: avant-gardism has conventionally been understood to be a Russian and continental flower, with French, German and Italian hybrids, but no British blooms.

A good example of the kinds of judgement produced by this double perspective can be seen in the ambivalence with which twentieth-century critics have approached the poetry of the late 1880s and 1890s, particularly that of Decadent writers. Like their Modernist successors, writers such as Ernest Dowson (1867–1900) and Francis Thompson (1859–1907) took as their subject-matter many of the themes associated with modernity, including an attention to the details of urban life. The attempts in their poetry to aestheticise experiences like cigarette smoking and various forms of intoxication, as well as what were then considered illicit or non-normative sexual activities, such as prostitution, paedophilia and same-sex desire, can still seem provocative to modern readers. Equally innovative and unusual (as we noted in Chapter 2) was a programme of invoking synaesthesic effects, and a concern with capturing moods and images rather than with narrative. However, many Decadent poets articulated these concerns through traditional and, on occasions, self-consciously archaic verse forms and language, as we can see in Dowson's use of the villanelle, or what has been termed Thompson's or Lionel Johnson's (1867–1902) 'Latinised' style. Moreover, this sense of a stylistic belatedness was further emphasised by what the poet W. B Yeats, reflecting on his early career in the posthumously published *Autobiographies* (1955), characterised as a kind of ideological or conceptual retrospection. For Yeats, poets like Dowson and Thompson were 'the last Romantics' – 'last' because in their work the revolutionary rhetoric of Romanticism had been transformed into something like its opposite: a self-indulgent solipsism which indicated a cultural decline rather than a renewal. As the very term suggests, Decadence conjures up a sense of an ending rather than a beginning. Another contemporary voice, Arthur Symons, encapsulated this problem of originality with a further, equally pithy epithet when he wrote in an 1894 review in the *Athenaeum* that Thompson's poetry 'with all its splendour, has the impress of no individuality'. In other words, although there are innovative elements to the poetics of Decadence, Decadent poems have not generally been viewed as formally significant achievements, either in themselves or in terms of their influence on the history of future poetic development. (An exception to this trend, which helped to set in train a revaluation of Decadent poetry, was the work in the 1980s of R. K. R. Thornton (Thornton 1983).)

The tendency to dismiss Decadent experimentation as a stylistic dead end is particularly striking in the polemic of the Decadents' immediate successors, the Modernists, who wished to annex the role of innovators for themselves. Newness requires that there is something old, staid or worn out to reject, and it was the misfortune of many nineteenth-century writers to be troped in just this way in order to set the inventiveness of Modernist writers in starker relief. The best-known (if caricatured) example of this process is to be seen in the attitude to nineteenth-century literary culture exhibited in the work of Lytton Strachey (1880–1932), a famously vituperative Modernist historian. Strachey's *Eminent Victorians* (1918) explicitly set out to define the modernity of his own time, and in so doing it was necessary for him to construct his Victorian predecessors in terms of their difference – that is, in terms of hypocrisy, repression and a stultifying respect for tradition. Virginia Woolf (1882–1941) adopted much the same strategy when, in an influential 1923 essay entitled 'Mr Bennett and Mrs Brown', she criticised as outmoded the nineteenth-century tradition of realist fiction, then to be found in the work of her contemporary Arnold Bennett (1867–1931). Some modernist writers, notably Ezra Pound (1885–1972), did acknowledge the inventiveness of the occasional nineteenth-century writer, particularly Robert Browning; but it was more usual to seek authority in writers from earlier periods of history, such as Elizabethan and Metaphysical poets, or from other cultures – in Pound's case, Chinese and classical writing. Moreover, a tendency to take such Modernist polemic at face value made it possible to construct a history of literary innovation in which most nineteenth-century literature (which in practice was that produced post 1820) was a mere interlude between what were seen as two significant, though different, revolutionary moments: that of Romanticism, which involved a rejection of the Augustan or neo-classical values of early eighteenth-century literary culture, and that of Modernism, which rejected both the subjectivity of Romanticism and the discursive and didactic qualities seen to characterise later nineteenth-century literary traditions. In this respect, we should be aware that literary history, as we suggested in Chapter 1, is always written for a purpose and from a particular point of view; moreover, the concept of the avant-garde is always used evaluatively as well as descriptively.

The legacy of this Modernist reading of nineteenth-century culture has been an enduring one, to the extent that even in the twenty-first century historians often still feel obliged to challenge it directly (Sweet 2001; Wilson 2002). However, an appreciation of the premises upon which that Modernist reading is based suggests how its biases might be questioned. One obvious way of interrogating traditional assumptions about the lack of formal innovation in nineteenth-century literature is to re-examine the basis of the novelty predicated of Modernist or Romantic experimentation. One might, for example, point to a formative relationship between Modernist works and those produced in the late decades of the nineteenth century, and in the process challenge the whole idea that the Modernist aesthetic represents a dramatic break with its immediate past. Good examples of this kind of argument can be seen in the proposition that Imagist poetry, which flourished from around 1910 to 1917, has antecedents in a visual Impressionism that can be traced back to the Decadent emphasis on a poetry of evocation, and – earlier still – to the Pre-Raphaelites' concern with the relationship between the sensuous and symbolic, seen, for example, in Dante Gabriel Rossetti's attempt to evoke emotions (often erotic ones) which resist straightforward linguistic articulation. In a similar way connections have been seen between aspects of the poetics of both W. B. Yeats and T. S. Eliot, on the one hand, and the description by Arthur Hallam (1811–33) of a poetry 'of sensation' made in his 1831 essay 'On Some of the Characteristics of Modern Poetry' (Christ 1984), or between Virginia Woolf's 'stream of consciousness' and the syntactic complexity of Walter Pater's prose (Meisel 1980). More generally, and as we will explain in more detail in Chapter 4, it has been persuasively argued that the preconditions for the formal experimentation associated with Modernism are to be found in the Aesthetic Movement's licensing of non-normative creativity in the 1870s. The Aesthetes' divorce of art from morality allowed for a celebration of the formal rather than the representational and didactic qualities of literary works; as one critic has recently phrased it, it is the very concentration on form which 'makes the transition from aestheticism to modernism' (Leighton 2008: 14). As we noted in Chapter 1, the identification by literary historians of a distinctive period between

Victorianism and Modernism, that of the 'fin-de-siècle' or 'literature of transition', can also be seen as an attempt to revise Modernism's own account of its uniqueness.

A different, though related, strategy of revaluing the formal innovation of nineteenth-century literature has been to disregard the connections with Modernism in favour of focusing on those nineteenth-century works which figure as important models for later literary experiments – to see connections between, say, the work of George Eliot and Ian McEwan's attempts to reinvigorate the realist novel as an arena for ethical debate. Or to see in the subversive wit of Wilde's society comedies a dramatic template for the provocative farces of Joe Orton (1933–67). More generally, it has been noted that the late decades of the twentieth century saw a significant revival of interest in all things Victorian, with several writers of contemporary fiction, including Peter Ackroyd, John Fowles, A. S. Byatt, Peter Carey, Sarah Waters and most recently Will Self, taking direct inspiration from writers such as Dickens, Collins, Tennyson and (again) Wilde (Kaplan 2007). In this kind of argument, nineteenth-century literary genres are valued not so much for their innovatory qualities, but because they provide a resource which can be productively reworked for modern audiences.

Appreciation of nineteenth-century formal experimentation developed through the introduction of new theoretical paradigms into literary studies; seminal readings of Victorian poetry by theorists such as J. Hillis Miller (1963), Isobel Armstrong (1982; 1993) and Angela Leighton (1992), who drew upon some insights of deconstruction, poststructuralism and feminism respectively, argued for a complexity and self-reflexivity that appeared more modern, and therefore more innovative, than had hitherto been appreciated. In this view, it was argued that Victorian poetry engaged with the limitations of its own expressivity – that is, with its status as both a material and a linguistic sign. In a similar way, the application, from the late 1980s, of theories of performance to nineteenth-century dramatic works, particularly to popular genres such as melodrama and pantomime, has disclosed a diversity and vibrancy which traditional literary critical approaches overlooked, as well as a more complex politics. However, it is worth noting that certain types of theoretically informed 're-reading' projects have had something like the opposite effect: as will be noted below (and in more detail in Chapter 5), the application of Marxist and postcolonial theory to some nineteenth-century genres, particularly to the realist novel, have tended to reconfigure its politics as conservative and reactionary, confirming the dominant values of its largely bourgeois readership. In this view, which was common among critics in the 1970s and 1980s, the chief formal value of the realist novel was to be found in the way in which it exhibited the inherently ideological nature of literary works in general.

Finally, it is worth drawing attention to a different and arguably more far-reaching challenge to traditional views about the formulaic nature of much nineteenth-century literature, one which comes from what we referred to in Chapter 1 as textual recovery projects. The last twenty to thirty years has seen the republication of a large number of hitherto forgotten or inaccessible (and generally long out-of-print) nineteenth-century literary works. The impact of this research can been seen most dramatically in the increasing size of modern anthologies of nineteenth-century literature, as editors struggle to do justice to what seems to be an ever-expanding canon: compare, for example, Bernard Richards's 1980 *English Verse 1830–1890* which includes the work of just eighteen poets (of whom two are women), and the selections from some 168 authors in Valentine Cunningham's *The Victorians: An Anthology of Poetry and Poetics*, published in 2000.

In the second edition of his *Longman Companion to Victorian Fiction* John Sutherland notes of this new literary 'wealth': 'the more novels, the more "differences", and the more complex one's sense of the genre and any single item it contains' (Sutherland 2009: x). The 900 novels which he surveys are, however, a mere drop in the ocean of his estimated 50,000–60,000 titles produced during the period. Sutherland's observation can be extended to nineteenth-century literature in general: that far from consolidating our understanding of the period, the sheer volume of works now available is proving to be an obstacle to our ability to generalise about literary culture. More importantly, given the subject-matter of the present chapter, any such widening of the canon jeopardises a critic's ability to describe a coherent history of generic or stylistic change. Nowhere is this more obvious than in recent research into Romanticism: the writers who are now routinely included in what many critics prefer to term 'Romantic period' writing are so many and varied, both ideologically and formally, that it is almost impossible to make meaningful generalisations about Romantic poetry or literature. As a consequence, the term 'Romantic' has for some critics lost any utility as a description. This problem of categorisation also underlies the proliferation in recent years of what are claimed to be new nineteenth-century sub-genres. These include the identification of 'freakery' and 'prison' literature as well as various kinds of 'life' and travel writing (Tromp 2008). Likewise, theatre historians now argue that our understanding of nineteenth-century drama should extend to all kinds of popular theatrical entertainment, such as street and travelling theatre, parades and processions, as well as performances staged in private houses (Davis and Donkin 1999).

The advantage of an expanded canon, and therefore of the literary taxonomies we use to understand it, is that it challenges the biases and alleged simplifications underlying traditional accounts of nineteenth-century generic development. However, we should notice that, when celebrating the variety and eclecticism of Victorian literary forms, historians are effectively invoking a different concept of creativity from that implicit in the idea of an artistic vanguard. They also tend to produce a different sort of literary history, one which concentrates on chronicling or describing genres and styles, rather than attempting to explain putative relationships between them or, more importantly, between them and later works. Ultimately, this tension – between description and evaluation – is not one which can be easily nor adequately resolved, for any coherent narrative of Victorian generic development will necessarily require a degree of selectivity that will in turn invite objections.

What follows, then, is an attempt to negotiate these contradictions by providing an outline narrative of some developments in the genres of fiction, poetry, drama and non-fictional prose, while at the same time drawing attention to the research which has complicated that narrative.

Poetry

The descriptions we most usually encounter in histories of nineteenth-century (and more typically Victorian) poetry are terms such as 'diverse', 'eclectic', 'heterogeneous' and – more positively – a 'cornucopia'; one critic has gone so far as to describe the poetry of this period as resembling a 'Tower of Babel more than a Tower of Ivory' (Richards 1980: xx). In other words, the sheer variety of poetic forms and styles to be found in the period from 1800 to 1899 makes it difficult to isolate either one or a series of dominant poetics, and thus to describe a clear narrative of stylistic change. There certainly is diversity: we find poets writing epics, sonnets, elegies, hymns, various kinds of lyric and narrative poems, as well as working with hybrid forms, such as verse-novels and verse-dramas, and experimenting with blank verse. This in turn is one reason why (with the exception of Romanticism) nineteenth-century poetry has often been relegated to a peripheral role within general histories of literature. What have traditionally been acknowledged as the 'major' achievements of the period – works such as Robert Browning's 'My Last Duchess' (1842), Elizabeth Barrett Browning's *Aurora Leigh*, Alfred Tennyson's *In Memoriam*, Christina Rossetti's *Goblin Market*, Matthew Arnold's 'Dover Beach' or Gerard Manley Hopkins's 'The Windhover' (written in 1877) – seem to have little in common with one another, particularly when they are considered in terms of their formal features, such as their rhythm, diction or metre. Such observations may also explain why a common heuristic way of dividing nineteenth-century poetry is into three uneven phases, with key moments of transition being located only, as we hinted earlier, in the early and late decades of the century. These phases are worth closer examination. Before proceeding, however, it is worth emphasising, and as we discuss more fully below, that this is by no means the only way of understanding poetic developments in the period. For example, Isobel Armstrong's influential study of Victorian (rather than nineteenth-century) poetry categorised works produced from 1830 to 1900 in terms of 'two systems of concentric circles' (a phrase which she borrowed from John Stuart Mill): one concerned 'various strategies for democratic, radical writing' and the other involved the development 'in different forms' of 'a conservative poetry'. Significantly, perhaps, Armstrong acknowledged that her schema necessitated the exclusion of 'much material', a decision which she justified by her ambition to exhibit the 'prolific creativity' of poets who belong 'recognisably to our own cultural situation' while also existing 'in sharp separation from it' (Armstrong 1993: ix).

The first of these three phases, then, spans the opening two decades of the century, and is understood as being informed by various reactions to the poetics of the eighteenth century and the differences between what have traditionally been termed the 'first' and 'second' generation Romantics. As noted in Chapter 1, the careers of many Romantic period writers spanned the century divide, and figures such as Wordsworth, Coleridge, Shelley, Keats, Byron, Clare, Felicia Hemans (1793–1835) and Letitia Landon (1802–38) all published major works in the 1820s and beyond. At the same time, however, critics have noted distinct differences between what have been viewed as the seminal manifestoes of Romantic poetics, such as the 'Prefaces' written by Wordsworth for the second (1800) and subsequent editions of his and Coleridge's *Lyrical Ballads* and Percy Bysshe Shelley's *A Defence of Poetry* (written in 1821, but published posthumously in 1840); and they have also commented on differences between the actual works of Wordsworth and Coleridge, on the one hand, and on the other, those such as Keats's *Endymion* (1818) and *Lamia, Isabella, The Eve of St Agnes, and Other Poems* (1820) and Shelley's *Prometheus Unbound* (1820) and his political response to the Peterloo massacre in 1819, *The Mask of Anarchy* (again published posthumously in 1832). These differences are complex, but broadly speaking they can be understood as centring on a series of doubts about or disillusionment with the moral certainties which underwrote Wordsworth's confident assertion in the 1800 Preface that he (and Coleridge) were engaged in producing 'a class of Poetry ... well adapted to interest man permanently, and not unimportant in the multiplicity, and in the quality of its moral relations'. For Wordsworth, realising the social 'purpose' of poetry, as he termed it, involved choosing 'subjects from common life' and bringing language 'near to the real language of men' (although modern critics have pointed out that his own poetry rarely fulfils these ambitions).

Keats's and Shelley's interest in classical and mythological subjects marks an obvious departure from Wordsworth's ideals; so, too, does their interrogation of the kind of value vouchsafed by the natural world and their distinctive conceptualisations of the role of the imagination. The scepticism in Shelley's 'Mont Blanc' (1817) and 'Hymn to Intellectual Beauty' (1817), in which the beauty invested in nature by the power of the imagination exists in opposition to 'the name of God, and ghosts, and heaven', which are mere 'records of ... vain endeavour', directly challenges the consoling pantheism of Wordsworth's 'Lines Written a few miles above Tintern Abbey' (1798), in which the poet hears in the natural world 'the still, sad music of humanity'. And when in his *A Defence of Poetry* Shelley claimed that 'poetry is indeed something divine', he had in mind a secular, although still exalted, vision of poetry's power, one in which it 'is at the centre and circumference of all knowledge ... [and] is at the same time the root and blossom of all other systems of thought'. It was for this reason that Shelley concluded, in a now famous assertion, that poets are 'the unacknowledged legislators of the world'.

Keats's engagement with Wordsworth's ambitions for poetry took a different form. Although an admirer of Wordsworth's exploration in 'Tintern Abbey' of the 'burden of the mystery', his own conceptualisation of the imagination was that it was an act of 'negative capability' in which the poet's sense of self had to be temporarily suppressed or suspended in order to apprehend the otherness of 'essential beauty' (or truth). This proposition was fundamentally different from Wordsworth's 'egotistical sublime'. More importantly, perhaps, many of Keats's late poems, including works such as the 'La Belle Dame sans Merci' (first published in 1820 in the *Indicator*) and the late odes, register a deep ambivalence about the transcendent power of beauty or, in the words of the 'Ode on a Grecian Urn' (1820), of truth or, indeed, art. The power of Wordsworth's poetry comes from an assiduous moralising of the beauty of the natural world, while that of Keats derives from a recreation of its sensuality, in which an appreciation of physical beauty, often eroticised, is invariably accompanied by an apprehension of its transience. In the words of the 'Ode on Melancholy' (1820), 'She dwells with Beauty – Beauty that must die; | And joy, whose hand is ever at his lips | Bidding adieu; and aching Pleasure nigh, | Turning to poison while the bee-mouth sips.' Moreover, the experience of beauty (and its impermanence) is, as in Shelley's 'Mont Blanc', exclusive to the individual: in the concluding lines of Keats's 'Ode to a Nightingale' (1820): 'Was it a vision, or a waking dream? | Fled is that music – do I wake or sleep?' The interrogative and enigmatic quality of Keats's odes marks them off from the moral and epistemological certainties of some of the earlier Romantics; it may also explain why late nineteenth-century writers (including the Aesthetes) found a model in the visionary qualities of Keats's and Blake's verse, while they tended to react against that of Wordsworth. (It is worth noting, in passing, that this view of Keats was powerfully influential through the twentieth century, and it is only in recent decades that modern critics have begun to see Keats's poetry in terms of its engagement with political and social issues.)

A conventional way of understanding nineteenth-century attitudes towards the first-generation Romantics has been in the terms suggested by Byron and the essayist William Hazlitt (1778–1830): Wordsworth, Coleridge and Robert Southey, although providing inspiration in their youth, had matured into reactionaries – into what Byron termed 'apostates'. An obsession with fame (epitomised by Southey's and later Wordsworth's acceptance of the Poet Laureateship) and a self-regarding parochialism had, in this view, displaced the radical energy of their earlier work, resulting in what Byron saw in the 'Dedication', first published in 1832, to *Don Juan* (1819–24) as a kind of philosophising obscurantism. In reference to works such as Coleridge's *Biographia Literaria* (1817), which attempted to defend Coleridge's and Wordsworth's poetics, Byron caustically commented: 'Explaining metaphysics to the nation; | I wish he would explain his explanation.' Although he was motivated by a variety of personal concerns, Byron's disparagement of the Lake poets, or as he preferred to call them 'the Lakers', and particularly Wordsworth's poetry (such as *The Excursion* (1814)), was not unusual at this time. Shelley and Keats also had reservations about that work, and as late as the 1870s critics such as Matthew Arnold continued to complain about Wordsworth's 'philosophising'. Slightly earlier, Arnold's friend and fellow poet, Arthur Hugh Clough (1816–61), had recommended reducing the seven volumes of Wordsworth's collected works to a mere 'one'. Equally resonant with some of his contemporaries was Byron's demand for what he called a more 'pedestrian' art, like that practised by poets such as George Crabbe (1745–1832). Crabbe's use of the heroic couplet in his detailed and grim portraits of rural Suffolk life in works such as *The Village* (1783) and *The Borough* (1810) had proved more popular with the reading public than anything by Wordsworth or Coleridge. Heroic couplets are also the dominant form of Felicia Hemans's *Records of Women* (1828), another commercial success at this time. (Unlike Byron, Hemans admired Wordsworth, although her 'poetic tales' 'illustrative of the female character, affections and fate' are less Wordsworthian than the posthumously published 'Despondency and Aspiration' (1839) and 'The Rock of Cader Idris' (1822), a work inspired by the landscape of Snowdonia in North Wales.)

The example of Crabbe suggested to Byron the need for a return to the neo-classicism of an earlier age, epitomised in the poetry of eighteenth-century writers such as Alexander Pope (1688–1744). In a much-quoted letter to his publisher John Murray, written in 1817, Byron viewed the Romantic aesthetic which he himself had espoused in the early cantos of *Childe Harold's Pilgrimage* (1812–18) as 'a wrong revolutionary poetical system (or systems) not worth a damn in itself'. A decade or so later saw the writings of many Romantic-period poets, including those of the 'second generation', such as John Clare, fall from favour. Although Clare's *Poems Descriptive of Rural Life and Scenery* (1820) had made him a minor literary celebrity, the volumes which followed it – *The Village Minstrel* (1821) and *The Shepherd's Calendar* (1827) – sold poorly and left him in debt. More in tune with popular taste at this time was the work of Letitia Landon, who, like Hemans, made a good living from her writing. (In the 1820s women poets had become quite fashionable, although some modern historians have accused the publishing industry of exploiting, and ultimately destroying, their talents by encouraging overproduction.) Landon's florid evocations of thwarted desire and jilted love in works such as *The Improvisatrice* (1824) had little in common with the poems of Shelley and Keats, which, by contrast, were not widely appreciated by the contemporary reading public.

The reputation of Keats in particular suffered from attacks made by John Gibson Lockhart (1794–1854) on what he called the 'Cockney School'. Lockhart satirised Keats's lowly social origins and his lack of a classical education; his jibes, which partly provoked Shelley's' elegy 'Adonais' (1821), depressed sales of Keats's works and set the tone for criticism of him until, as noted, the 1880s, when distaste for the populism associated with a developing mass culture permitted a later generation to revalue the idiosyncratic elements of Keats's verse. The death of Keats in 1821 has thus conventionally been viewed as the 'beginning of the end' of Romanticism, a moment which is seen as marking a growing sense of disenchantment with what was perceived as its subjectivist epistemology – that is, a validation of knowledge made principally by reference to personal and felt experience, rather than to social forms of authority. In turn this concern with the self was interpreted as producing an aesthetics of isolation and a consequent alienation of the poet from his or her society – a Romantic mythology which, revalued, re-emerged in the last two decades of the century in the figure of the *poète maudit*, W. B. Yeats's 'tragic generation'.

The second (and more varied) phase of nineteenth-century poetry, which in this general account is seen to have lasted from around 1830 to 1880, is defined in terms of an ambition to counter what the conservative critic William John Courthope (1842–1917) referred to in his 1876 essay on 'Wordsworth and Gray' in the *Quarterly Review* as the 'egotism' and disregard for 'civil life' prevalent in 'modern romantic poetry'. In so doing poets in the middle decades of the century were concerned to attract the attention of a reading public and publishing industry which had become increasingly preoccupied with prose fiction. A concern with sales and readerships figures prominently and regularly in the correspondence of many poets in the middle and late decades of the century, including the Brownings, Matthew Arnold, Dante Gabriel Rossetti and Thomas Hardy; moreover, their complaints were quite distinct from those of their immediate predecessors. Part of the problem, as we noted in Chapter 2, had to do with changes in publishing media. There is some evidence that from the 1830s onwards the periodical press (which had been exploited to such advantage by an earlier generation of poets) was no longer thought to be an appropriate medium for poetry. The specialist literary magazines and reviews which published some of the Romantics had been replaced by cheaper and more accessible newspapers and general-interest magazines, and these were typically viewed, notably by the Brownings, as degrading a 'high' art such as poetry. Equally problematic was the pressure, frequently articulated by contemporary critics, to develop a more discursive, objective and socially engaged poetry; and it is this latter concern which has usually been used as an explanation for the popularity in the middle decades of the century of long narrative poems (which would by their nature be unsuited to occasional magazine publication). These works included classical and what Arnold termed 'domestic' epics, such as Tennyson's *Idylls of the King* (a series of twelve interconnected poems published between 1859 and 1885, with the complete sequence appearing in one volume in 1891) and Coventry Patmore's immensely popular verse sequence *The Angel in the House*; in addition there were sonnet sequences like Dante Gabriel Rossetti's *House of Life* (1881), much of which was written in the 1870s, Elizabeth Barrett Browning's *Sonnets from the Portuguese* (1850) and Meredith's *Modern Love* (1862), as well as 'verse-novels' like Barrett Browning's *Aurora Leigh*. Many of these works self-consciously addressed social concerns, particularly gender roles and the relationship between desire, love and social and moral responsibility – the same concerns, that is, as those which were preoccupying contemporary novelists.

It has been suggested that mid- and late nineteenth-century poetry can be explained, at least in part, in terms of a series of reactions to the perceived limitations of Romantic poetics, particularly the celebration of introspection and solipsism. This account serves to give some coherence to what in fact is a disconcerting variety of poetic practices and theories. The nineteenth century is unusually rich in explicit theorisations of poetics which range from Arthur

Hallam's programme for a 'poetry of sensation' (mentioned earlier), to the classicism of Matthew Arnold. Critical of what he saw as the reflective rather than the expressive character of Wordsworth's verse, Hallam argued for a poetry that would concentrate on 'the simple exertions of eye and ear'. Enabling a transition from the particular and individual to the general and social, such a poetry would, through its grounding in what Hallam saw as physical 'laws' of association, overcome the limitations of Romantic verse without abandoning its expressive and subjective elements. The following lines from Hallam's 'A Scene in Summer' (1834), addressed to his great friend 'Alfred' (that is, Tennyson), with their use of sensual detail to suggest a state of mind, provide a good example of his aesthetic:

before me lies
A lawn of English verdure, smooth and bright,
Mottled with fainter hues of early hay,
Whose fragrance, blended with the rose perfume
From that white flowering bush, invites my sense
To a delicious madness.

Hallam's emphasis on visual and aural detail has some elements in common with the poetics of the Pre-Raphaelites, who also saw themselves (as we argue more fully in Chapter 4) articulating a radically new aesthetic. It took the form of evoking minute sensual details of sight and sound, but especially emotion, in order to suggest feelings which defied easy denotation. A good example can be found in Rossetti's 'Nuptial Sleep', a work first published in 1870 but suppressed in later editions of his poetry; in it precisely observed botanical detail is used to evoke a languid post-coital sensuality:

Their bosoms sundered, with the opening start
Of married flowers to either side outspread
From the knit stem; yet still their mouths, burnt red,
Fawned on each other where they lay apart.

This emphasis on what might loosely be termed an aesthetics of sensation, one which connects Hallam's poetics of the 1830s with those of Rossetti in the 1870s, may also explain the interest of the 1890s poet and critic Richard Le Gallienne (1866–1947) in Hallam's verse: Le Gallienne edited and introduced a new edition of Hallam's *Poems* in 1893.

Arnold, by contrast, saw this aesthetics of experience not as a solution to Romantic solipsism, but as one producing its own problems of poetic expression in the sense that it resulted in a self-serving introspection and a concentration on the quotidian elements of life and thus (in his view) what were merely 'transient feelings and interests'. In the preface to his *Poems* (1853), the argument of which has often been judged to be more significant than the poetry itself, Arnold proposed that poetry should concentrate on 'eternal objects', which he defined as 'excellent' actions which 'most powerfully appeal to the great primary human affections: to those elementary feelings which subsist permanently in the race, and which are independent of time'. Many of Arnold's own works, such as 'Empedocles on Etna' (1852), 'Sohrab and Rustum' (1853) and *Merope: A Tragedy* (1858), took classical or ancient Persian themes as their subjects, and these he viewed as 'nobler' and more 'intense' than those to be derived from modern life and found in works like *The Excursion* or *Childe Harold*. Ironically, perhaps, posterity has tended to prefer Arnold's more personal and self-doubting poems, such as 'Dover Beach', which is arguably his least successful in terms of following his own poetic programme (and which, as we observed above, he published only reluctantly). A further limitation of Arnold's appeal to classical precedence was that the values of 'Hellenism', as Arnold termed it, could be interpreted (as was also noted) in a variety of ways, some of which were directly opposed to Arnold's understanding of what constituted moral excellence.

The celebration of the physical and sensual, to be found in a polymorphous sexuality in the poetry of Algernon Swinburne, for example, invoked a different aspect of ancient Greek culture. A friend of both Dante Gabriel Rossetti and George Meredith, Swinburne's interests were decidedly more modern and Rabelaisian than those of Arnold, and his classical models were the erotic love poetry of Sappho and Catullus, rather than the epics of Homer. In works such as 'Itylus', 'Anactoria' and 'Hermaphroditus', all of which appeared in *Poems and Ballads* (1866), Swinburne celebrated in extravagantly sensual language an erotics centred on rape, prostitution, necrophilia and castration. In 'Anactoria', for example, the poet asks:

> Would I not hurt thee perfectly? not touch
> Thy pores of sense with torture, and make bright
> Thine eyes with bloodlike tears and grievous light?
> Strike pang from pang as note is struck from note,
> Catch the sob's middle music in thy throat,
> Take thy limbs living, and new-mould with these
> A lyre of faultless agonies?

Unsurprisingly, the volume, which was condemned as blasphemous and obscene, was withdrawn by its publisher James Moxon, a decision which provoked Swinburne's impassioned defence of poetic freedom – at least as he understood it – in his 1866 pamphlet *Notes on Poems and Reviews*. In a thinly veiled attack on Tennyson, Swinburne disparaged what he saw as the current fashion for 'the idyllic form', one which, in his view, was suited only to 'domestic and pastoral verse', its 'gentle and maidenly lips ... fit for the sole diet of girls'. England, according to Swinburne, needed a more 'virile' art, one which was 'not truncated and curtailed, but outspoken and full-grown'. Moreover, Swinburne was not the only poet to use classical subjects in what was perceived to be an unacceptably outspoken manner. The later celebration of male beauty in Oscar Wilde's 'Charmides' (1881), which is reminiscent of the work of the American poet Walt Whitman (1819–92), is distinctly homoerotic, while the Sapphic poems in *Long Ago* (1889) by Michael Field, which were inspired by Henry Wharton's 1885 translations of Sappho, are overtly lesbian (Prins 1999).

Another attempt to develop a poetics suited to modern life, one which rejected the appeals of both Romanticism and Classicism as well as the sensualism of Hallam or Rossetti, is to be found in Robert Browning's experiments with diction and form. The publication of *Sordello* in 1840, a long narrative poem in heroic couplets, was initially greeted with incomprehension. Browning's compressed syntax, complex language (which included various neologisms, or newly coined words) and elaborate time-scheme, together with an innovative attempt to combine localised historical and scenic description with metaphysical speculation, baffled contemporary critics who deplored what they saw as his wilful obscurity. In other words, Browning was being criticised for a refusal to connect the personal with the social in the manner that contemporary reviewers demanded. In his later verse, in works such as *Men and Women* (1855) and *Dramatis Personae* (1864), Browning responded to what he termed in his 'Essay on Shelley' (1852) the tensions between the 'subjective' and 'objective' aspects of poetry by developing the form for which he is now best remembered, the dramatic monologue. In it the lyric voice of the poet is displaced onto that of a character. By distancing the poet from the imaginary speaker of the poem Browning was able to foreground the problems of subjectivity, and through the use of irony to explore the expressive power of language as well as its failure. Sceptical, self-deceiving and often vainglorious, the subjects of these monologues appear, in their moral failings, to be thoroughly modern, despite the fact that many are characters drawn from history. Browning's most sophisticated and sustained experiment with the dramatic monologue form appears in his magnum opus *The Ring and the Book* (1868–69). Based on a Roman murder trial, the story is narrated by a succession of speakers, each of whom gives only a partial version of events; the poem can thus be seen to embody a form of epistemological relativism. Tennyson, too, often draws attention to the limitations of the lyric voice, sometimes explicitly – for example, when the speaker in *In Memoriam* confesses that 'words, like nature, half reveal | And half conceal the Soul within' – but also structurally when, like Browning, he attempts to combine lyric and narrative elements. This occurs not only in *In Memoriam*, which T. S. Eliot famously characterised as 'made by putting together lyrics' (the individual lyrics were composed over a period of twenty years), but in works such as *The Princess* and 'Maud' (1855), which were conceived and written over a much shorter period of time.

A concern with the accessibility of poetry, and therefore with the issue of what constitutes acceptable or appropriate poetic diction – one consequence of the demand that poetry should address more social concerns – resonates throughout this second phase of nineteenth-century poetry. However, debates about the language of poetry, or what was sometimes termed the 'noble English style', were particularly intense in the 1860s and 1870s, when the label 'obscure', which had earlier been used to describe Browning's verse, was now applied to that of Swinburne and Rossetti. The target of criticism in the work of both poets was a perceived over-elaboration of language, one associated with that depiction of sensual experience found in works like 'Anactoria'. In a term made famous by the poet and critic Robert Buchanan (1841–1901) in an essay published in 1871 in the conservative *Contemporary Review*, such poetry was viewed as distressingly 'fleshly'. According to Buchanan, its 'hysteric tone and over-loaded style' – which he defined as a use of archaisms to promote 'bad' rhymes, an idiosyncratic and 'affected' accenting of final syllables, and the prevalence of 'burthens' or poetic refrains – had its origins in works such as Tennyson's 'Maud' and 'Vivien' (1859) which for Buchanan marked the limits of acceptable poetic mannerism. (However, later critics were to commend what they judged as an aural mellifluousness of Tennyson's language.) It is worth noting in passing that Buchanan's own language was highly gendered: that excess, whether of emotional or linguistic expression to which he objected, was typically feminised, while the idea of a 'noble English style', which lay behind Buchanan's rhetoric, was characterised as masculine. However, Buchanan was objecting to more than simply a lack of restraint or decorum in the use of language: what disconcerted him was the way in which such 'affluence of words' was used to evoke what he coyly termed the 'secret mysteries of sexual connection', and epithets were carefully chosen 'to convey mere animal sensations'. He had in mind works such as Rossetti's 'Jenny' (1870), a poem about a prostitute which opens with the lines: 'Lazy laughing languid Jenny | Fond of a kiss and fond of a guinea'. In other words, Buchanan saw such poetry as wanting proportion. The sensual pleasures of form – that is, of sound and rhythm – had become ends in themselves, and the natural cadences of English speech had in the process been distorted to resemble those of 'raving madmen'.

The assertion that there was a connection between what Arnold had earlier termed 'clearness and simplicity' of language and moral truth was one widely shared at the time, and has sometimes been used to explain the relative lack of linguistic and prosodic experimentation during this second period. Poets who wished to 'merit the honour accorded to the highest poetry', as the Oxford Professor of Poetry John Campbell Shairp (1819–85) put matters in article on 'English poets' published in 1882 in the *Quarterly Review*, were exhorted to 'cultivate manlier thought and nobler sentiment, expressed in purer and fresher diction, and to make their appeal … to the broader and healthier sympathies of universal man'. The explicit gendering of 'clearness and simplicity' aside, such injunctions may explain why for some poets (notably Tennyson) it is a display of technical virtuosity using traditional forms, to be seen particularly in the handling of complex metre, which is the most striking element in their verse.

The third and last phase in this conventional narrative of nineteenth-century poetry views the final decades of the century as marking a moment of experimentation which anticipates the revolt of twentieth-century Modernist poets.

What is startling about this third stage, however, is (again) the variety of forms to be found in it. It is surprisingly difficult to discern any clear direction to, or pattern in, late nineteenth-century poetics, except for a rejection of the examples of an older generation, such as Tennyson, Arnold or Browning, some of whom were still alive. For the Decadent or 1890s poets, an attention to the fidelity of felt experience – as Walter Pater phrased it his 1883 essay on Dante Gabriel Rossetti (reprinted in *Appreciations*), an ambition to find the 'just transcript of that peculiar phase of soul which [the poet] alone knew, precisely as he knew it' – once again takes precedence over social concerns, leading, as noted above, to an emphasis on the sensual and symbolic. This in turn results in what has been viewed as a new kind of expressive interiority and a concern with image and atmosphere, to be seen in collections such as *In the Dorian Mood* (1896) by Victor Plarr (1863–1929). In 'The Dark Angel' and 'Mystic and Cavalier', both of which were published in *Poems* (1895) by Lionel Johnson, such introspection, despite its explicit Catholic framing, takes the form of a kind of self-loathing despair. 'Mystic and Cavalier', for example, begins with the injunction: 'Go from me: I am one of those, who fall'. A number of Johnson's early poems, along with some by Plarr, were first published in *The Book of the Rhymers' Club* (1892) (a second such collection appeared in 1894). The precise origins of this poetic group are disputed, although its members (several of whom, including W. B. Yeats, were associated with the attempted revival of Irish literary traditions known as the 'Celtic Twilight') were regularly meeting at the Cheshire Cheese public house in Fleet Street in the early 1890s, and they published these two volumes of verse before separating around 1896. Later immortalised by Yeats as 'the tragic generation', the work of the Rhymers has often been taken as a summation of the 1890s, with themes that included city-life, the nature of sin, the meaning of death and an explicit concern with religiosity and artifice.

However, there were other late nineteenth-century poets, notably W. E. Henley (1849–1903), for whom a concern with the self produced opposite effects. Henley's formally innovative *In Hospital* (1888) sequence, based on his own trying experiences as a patient of the pioneering Edinburgh surgeon Joseph Lister, uses blank verse and assonance in the service of an unsentimental and, in its verbal spareness, distinctly modern-sounding realism. The last stanza of 'Interior' is a good example of this style:

> Far footfalls clank.
> The bad burn waits with his head unbandaged.
> My neighbour chokes in the clutch of chloral …
> O a gruesome world!

Also distinct from the Rhymers are the works of the most popular poets of this time, Rudyard Kipling and Henry Newbolt (1862–1938). Kipling, too, aimed for a new sort of realism (one admired, perhaps surprisingly, by Lionel Johnson) by using vernacular verse-forms and language. It is also worth noting that Kipling's diction seems to have captured the idioms of ordinary speech in a manner quite different from the language of Wordsworth's notionally 'common' man. However, many modern readers judge aspects of Kipling's depiction of contemporary soldiering in poems such as 'Fuzzy Wuzzy' and 'Gunga Din' in *Barrack-Room Ballads* (1892) to be offensively racist. Similarly anachronistic to modern eyes is Newbolt's unquestioned celebration of explicitly English (rather than British) patriotism in collections such as *The Island Race* (1898), where in 'Vitai Lampada' the Regiment is urged to remember the (male) sporting values of English public schools and to 'Play up! play up! and play the game'. Another distinctive strand in this third phase of nineteenth-century poetry is represented by the poignant lyricism of Thomas Hardy and A. E. Housman. Housman's *A Shropshire Lad* (1896) and Hardy's *Wessex Poems* (1898) nostalgically evoke the values of a rural England long gone (if indeed it ever existed), although it is often noted that the tone of Hardy's poems is tinged with an irony that is largely absent from the more wistful Housman. These evocations proved to be immensely popular, although they contrast emphatically with the equally popular imperialist values celebrated by Newbolt and Kipling. In Housman's famous lines, the Shropshire countryside represents a lost Eden:

Into my heart an air that kills
From yon far country blows:
What are those blue remembered hills,
What spires, what farms are those?

That is the land of lost content,
I see it shining plain,
The happy highways where I went
And cannot come again.

A similar sense of loss is also to be glimpsed in the title of Hardy's 'The Darkling Thrush', written at the century's end and published in *Poems of the Past and Present* (1901); the adjective 'darkling' recalls both Keats's 'Darkling I listen' in his 'Ode to a Nightingale' and the 'darkling plain' of Arnold's 'Dover Beach'. It thereby recapitulates in miniature the conventional narrative of three phrases of nineteenth-century poetry, those defined by the subjective poetics of Romanticism, their rejection and eventual partial recuperation. Thus the final image of 'The Darkling Thrush' recalls the stoic elements of some of Wordsworth's early verse, although with a sense of radical uncertainty – that 'unaware' 'I' of the final line – that is not a characteristic feature of the earlier poet's work:

That I could think there trembled through
    His happy good-night air

Some blessed Hope, whereof he knew
  And I was unaware.

An obvious but none the less serious limitation to this narrative of nineteenth-century poetic development can be seen in the number and variety of works and poets which it fails to include or explain. Of these, the most problematic is perhaps Gerard Manley Hopkins. Initially influenced by Ruskin and Pater while he was studying at Oxford in the 1860s, the direction of Hopkins's life and poetic career was determined by his conversion to Roman Catholicism, subsequent training as a Jesuit priest and later his appointment as Professor of Greek at the newly established Catholic University College, Dublin. Cut off by his beliefs and profession from the mainstream of literary life in Dublin and London, Hopkins pursued his poetic interests – in the natural world and in his faith – largely in private and certainly apart from the publishing industry. This in turn may help to explain the remarkable individuality of his poetry, which he discussed in a long-running correspondence with his old tutor, R. W. Dixon, his Oxford friend Robert Bridges and his fellow Catholic poet, Coventry Patmore. Among the most distinctive features of Hopkins's poetry are his use of complex compound and often alliterative metaphoric phrases to capture his reactions to the physical world – for example, 'feel-of-primrose hands' in 'The Habit of Perfection' (written in 1866) or 'dappled with damson west', 'lush-kept plush-caped sloe', 'whirlwind-swivellèd snow' and 'The heaven-flung, heart-fleshed, maiden furled | Miracle-in-Mary-of Flame' in 'The Wreck of the Deutschland' (written 1876). Also unique to Hopkins was a personal rhyme scheme which he termed 'sprung rhythm' and which he described in his 'Author's Preface' to *Poems* 1918, as 'the most natural of things … the rhythm of common speech'. Sprung rhythm places stress always on the first syllable of a foot, which may stand alone or else be associated with one to three (and occasionally more) light syllables. Hopkins described sprung rhythm as 'having or being only one nominal rhythm, a mixed or "logaoedic" one, instead of three, but on the other hand in having twice the flexibility of foot, so that any two stresses may either follow one another running or be divided by one, two or three slack syllables'. One feature of sprung rhythm was for the lines to 'rove over', as Hopkins put it – that is for 'the scanning of each line immediately to take up that of the one before, so that if the first has one or more syllables at its end the other must have so many less at the beginning'. Another was the use of what Hopkins called 'hangers' or 'outrides', where one, two or three slack syllables added to a foot did not count in the nominal scanning; they were so called because they 'seem to hang below the line or ride forward and backward from it in another dimension than the line itself'. Hopkins went on to explain that in sprung rhythm 'the scanning runs on without break from the beginning, say, of a stanza to the end and all the stanza is one long strain, though written in lines asunder'. It is precisely this quality which gives to Hopkins's poetry its extraordinary energy as well as the singularity of its rhythms. It also has connections with verse forms that depend principally on stress (such as Old English verse).

A good example of Hopkins's technique is to found in 'Pied Beauty' (written in 1877):

Glory be to God for dappled things –
For skies of couple-colour as a brinded cow;
For rose-moles all in stipple upon trout that swim;
Fresh-firecoal chestnut-falls; finches' wings;
Landscape plotted and pieced – fold, fallow, and plough;
And áll trádes, their gear and tackle and trim.

All things counter, original, spare, strange;
Whatever is fickle, freckled (who knows how?)
With swift, slow; sweet, sour; adazzle, dim;
He fathers-forth whose beauty is past change:
Praise him.

Another powerful, though curiously individual poetic voice, omitted in the narrative just described, is that of Emily Brontë, whose poetry was also largely unknown to nineteenth-century readers. Most of her poems – like those of Hopkins – were not published until the early twentieth century. They share with her better-known novel *Wuthering Heights* a concern with the Yorkshire landscape and articulate a passionate but highly personal theology. Works like 'To Imagination' (which appeared in the 1846 volume *Poems by Currer, Ellis and Acton Bell*) also bear the influence of Romantic poetics, although, unlike Wordsworth and Coleridge, Brontë's 'benignant power' is (like Keats's 'deceiving elf') a 'phantom bliss' which provides only a personal, or a private comfort: 'Sure solacer of human cares, | And sweeter hope when hope despairs!'.

Equally difficult to assimilate to this 'three-phase' history of nineteenth-century poetry are generic curiosities. The best-known of these is the nonsense verse to be found in the work of Edward Lear (1812–88) and Lewis Carroll (the pseudonym of Charles Dodgson (1832–98)) and which, according to some historians, has a lineage that can be traced back to medieval poetry. Less familiar to modern readers is what was termed by contemporary critics the 'Spasmodic' School, the main exponents of which were George Gilfillan, Sydney Dobell (1824–74) and Alexander Smith (?1830–67). The Spasmodics' preferred medium was a kind of unstageable verse drama in which action was completely subordinated to long soliloquies. For their detractors, Spasmodic heroes (typically poets) were self-absorbed to the point of morbidity and the moral (and usually sexual) dilemmas which preoccupied them were considered so bizarre and lurid in their contrivance that they invited only ridicule. The most famous satire on the Spasmodics was *Firmilian: A Spasmodic Tragedy* (1854) by William Edmonstoune Aytoun (1813–65); its effect was completely to undermine their claims to seriousness. However, although works such as Smith's *A Life-Drama* (1853) and Dobell's *Balder* (1854) are today almost entirely forgotten, they retain some interest to the historian because of their perceived formal influence on writers such as Tennyson and both Robert and Elizabeth Barrett Browning, particularly the latter's *Aurora Leigh* (Weinstein 1968; Cronin 2002). It is also worth noting the similarities between the excessively subjectivist aesthetic of the Spasmodics and some of the later preoccupations of the Aesthetic Movement (an issue discussed in more detail in Chapter 4); criticisms of the Spasmodics' self-absorption prefigure reactions to the Aesthetes, notably by satirists such as George du Maurier.

More mainstream than either Spasmodic or nonsense verse, yet also often overlooked, was the widespread nineteenth-century interest in poetry in translation, one which marks a point of continuity with eighteenth-century literary culture (exhibited in, say, Alexander Pope's translations of Homer or imitations of Horace). The work of many of the best-known nineteenth-century poets, including Arnold, both Brownings, Dante Gabriel Rossetti, Morris, Swinburne, Michael Field, as well as Augusta Webster (1837–94), whose translations of Aeschylus's *Prometheus Unbound* (1866) and Euripides's *Medea* (1868) were much admired by contemporary Greek scholars, was informed, at least in part, by experiments in translation. There was, moreover, a lively theoretical debate about the nature and purpose of poetic translation which centred on a discussion about whether the responsibility of the translating poet should be a faithful rendering of the source text, or an attempt to re-create its effects in a modern idiom and for a different culture. Translations of classical works were particularly popular, partly because Roman and Greek literature formed a staple of the public and grammar school and university curricula. These included a translation of the *Iliad* produced by F. W. Newman (one of John Henry Newman's brothers) which provoked a famous controversy with Arnold, which the latter discussed in his Oxford lecture series *On Translating Homer* (1861), as well as William Morris's translation of the *Odyssey* (1886–87). Morris's translations of Icelandic sagas included *Sigurd the Volsung* (1876), and in 1892 he began translating the Old English epic poem *Beowulf*. For women poets, most of whom were denied the privilege of a classical education, the fragments of Sappho were the source of valuable poetic inspiration, if not necessarily providing opportunities for direct translation: not only Michael Field (mentioned above), but earlier poets like Letitia Landon and Felicia Hemans found Sappho an important resource (Reynolds 2003). In addition the nineteenth century saw several renderings of medieval Persian literature; although the most famous is the formally innovative *The Rubaiyat of Omar Khayyam* (1859) by Edward FitzGerald (1809–83), *Poems from the Divan of Hafiz* (1897) by the traveller, archaeologist and Persian scholar Gertrude Bell (1868–1926) is arguably better informed, and certainly more faithful to the idioms of the Persian language. Also numerous were translations of Dante's *Divina Commedia*, of which that by Henry Francis Cary (1772–1844), first published in 1812, was the most influential; perhaps more widely read by students of nineteenth-century poetry is Dante Gabriel Rossetti's translation of Dante's lesser-known *Vita Nuova*. This attraction to translation – and in particular to medieval and classical works – can of course be partly explained by that general interest in the medieval and classical past noted in Chapter 2. Moreover, as with other kinds of engagements with past cultures, some critics have seen in translation a covert political act, one which provided a mechanism by which the expressive power of poetry could be used to interrogate the values of contemporary British culture. Some of the best examples of this strategy can be found in Tennyson's and Morris's re-use of medieval Arthurian legends.

Confronted by such a wide variety of poetic theories, practices and tastes, some literary historians have preferred to categorise nineteenth-century poetry thematically, rather than stylistically, drawing attention to sub-genres of religious, working-class or (more recently) crime verse. Such labels have the advantage of bringing into view new kinds of relationships and alliances, and these in their turn offer new ways of evaluating nineteenth-century poetry. For example, a concern with the poetry of crime has been seen to connect works as formally diverse as street ballads (judged by contemporary middle-class critics to be 'vulgar' in subject and 'lawless' in metre), Edward Robert Bulwer Lytton's (1831–91) verse-drama *Clytemnestra* (1855), which was also ridiculed at the time, as well as the altogether better-received *The Ring and the Book* by Browning and Amy Levy's *Medea* (1884). Viewed as 'murder poems', these works have been read as forms of cultural critique, valuable not for their stylistic features, but for their use of the genre of poetry to expose and interrogate 'the fictions and abstractions of criminal theories, policies, and laws' (O'Brien 2008: 241). The consequences of this kind of historicism, in which literature is valued for its engagement with issues of contemporary intellectual and political concern, will be explored in more detail in Chapter 5.

Thematic categorisations can also permit otherwise anomalous figures, like Hopkins, to be viewed in the context of what are distinctively nineteenth-century intellectual concerns. Thus a self-consciousness about the basis of religious belief, and more particularly an interest in the recovery of biblical figures or types – that is, a typological reading of scripture – has been held to link his poetry with that of John Henry Newman and traditions of Tractarian poetry (little read today), exemplified by the immensely popular *The Christian Year* (1827) by John Keble (1792–1866), as well as works by Christina Rossetti and Tennyson. This narrative in its turn can be juxtaposed with works which are more sceptical and agnostic (a term coined by the nineteenth-century scientist T. H. Huxley). This last treatment of religion traces connections between works such as Shelley's 'Mont Blanc' (1817), Browning's 'Bishop Blougram's Apology' (1855), Clough's unfinished and posthumously published *Dipsychus* (1865), Arnold's 'Dover Beach', James Thomson's 'The City of Dreadful Night' and Hardy's 'Nature's Questioning' (1898) in his *Wessex Poems*. A different reading of nineteenth-century religious poetry might concentrate on the significance of particular modes of religious worship, notably of hymns, a form which became increasingly prominent following the publication in 1861 of the influential *Hymns Ancient and Modern*. It is possible to argue that the widest read, and therefore most socially influential, nineteenth-century poetry was that contained in this collection of hymns, widely used, as it was, by the Church of England well into the second half of the twentieth century. The prosody of these and other hymns (such as John Wesley's 1780 *Collection of Hymns for the Use of the People called Methodists*) has been seen to influence the poetry of Emily Brontë, Tennyson and Hardy, as well as what has been termed 'working-class poetry'; that by Chartists, such as Ernest Jones and Thomas Cooper (1805–92) exploited the social traditions of hymning, and thus its potential as a vehicle for political protest.

The sub-genre of working-class poetry in fact encompassed a variety of forms, of which the most popular was the ballad, often published cheaply on single sheets known, because of the size of the paper used, as 'broadsides'. A further distinctive stylistic feature is the use of regional dialects, to be found in, for example, the Lancashire dialect poems of Edwin Waugh (1817–90) and Stephen Laycock (1826–93), or those of the lowland Scots poet, Janet Hamilton (1795–1873) which challenged the normative appeals made by middle-class metropolitan critics to that 'noble English style' (as had the vernacular idioms of the 'peasant poet' John Clare earlier in the century). A different and less well-known sort of challenge to those linguistic norms came from the Isle-of-Man born, and Oxford educated, T. E. Brown (1830–97), who celebrated Manx themes and the Manx dialect in his *Fo'c'sle Yarns* (1881) and *The Manx Witch and Other Poems* (1889). (It is also worth noting in passing, and as will be discussed more fully in Chapter 6, that there have been other ways of understanding the relationship between regionalism and nineteenth-century poetry which are not centred on dialect: these include Wordsworth's and Coleridge's affiliation to the Lake District, or Crabbe's Suffolk (particularly the coastal town of Aldeburgh), as well as the celebration of the Dorset countryside by Hardy and (a little earlier) by William Barnes (1810–86), and Housman's of the traditions and values of Shropshire.) Language and form aside, a more encompassing definition of working-class poetry concentrates on its radical politics. In this view Chartist poetry can be aligned with that of a variety of other working-class (and often female) activists. These include: Eliza Cook (1818–89), whose several volumes of poetry included 'social-problem' themes such as factory labour; the self-educated servant and campaigner Mary Smith (1822–89), who brought out a collection of her poems in 1863; and the textile worker Ellen Johnston's (?1835–?74) 1867 *Autobiography, Poems and Songs* (Boos 2001).

This foregrounding of regional dialects and political identities suggests yet another possible taxonomy of nineteenth-century poetry, one which attempts to define the poetic traditions of the four nations that then made up Britain, rather than simply England. Of interest here is the difference from Englishness of Irish, Welsh and Scottish poetics, which critics such as Arnold typically assimilated under the umbrella, and usually feminised, term 'Celt' (Davis 1998; Crawford 2000). As will be explained more fully in Chapter 6, one difficulty which this kind of history has to overcome is that many of the best-known Scottish, Welsh and Irish poets – figures such as George MacDonald (1824–1905), J. M. Barrie (1860–1937), Robert Louis Stevenson, and even Oscar Wilde and W. B. Yeats, all of whom have been seen as part of what has been termed a Scottish or Irish diaspora – chose to live and work in England for at least part of their careers, and it was there that they initially found success. By contrast, the comparative obscurity of poets like Jane Hamilton may be due in part to the fact that she spent her entire adult life in the Lanarkshire town of Coatbridge. There is also a related problem of evaluating the authenticity of the representation of national difference: the mythologising of Scottish history in long narrative poems such as Walter Scott's *Marmion* (1808) and *The Lord of the Isles* (1815), which took as their subject-matter the battle of Flodden Field and the chronicles of Robert the Bruce, has often been viewed as peddling a cod or assimilationist view of Scottish identity, one which in turn serves to justify an Anglo-dominated Great Britain by conflating Scottish identity with a primitive and anachronistic Highland culture. Such an argument is given weight by the 'discovery' of Scotland, particularly the Highlands, by an embryonic nineteenth-century English tourist industry, at the head of which was Queen Victoria herself (Davis, Duncan and Sorenson 2004). Success with English readerships did not, however, prevent poetry from articulating national differences. Such explicit political identifications are perhaps most easily seen in Irish writing in English in the last half of the century (the increasing marginalisation of the Irish language following the 1848 famine and the consequent loss of many traditions of native Gaelic music and poetry were lamented by Irish nationalists).

The 'Celtic Twilight' of the 1890s, a movement principally associated with Yeats (who used that term as the title for his 1893 collection of stories designed to illustrate what he saw as a characteristic Irish mysticism), is an element of a longer and more complex affiliation of poetry to Irish nationalism, one which is invariably obscured by a tendency to see the Celtic Twilight as an aspect of English literary traditions, and particularly, as noted above, of English Decadence. That affiliation links the *Irish Melodies* (1808–34) of Thomas Moore (1779–1852) to the poetry of nationalist activists such as the prolific James Clarence Mangan (1803–49) and Jane Wilde (or 'Speranza', 1821–96), both of whom were closely associated with Thomas Davis's (1814–45) 'Young Ireland' newspaper *The Nation*. As might be expected, such poetry advertised its nationalist identity partly in terms of subject-matter, a pattern to be found in Yeats's appropriation of Irish mythology in works such as 'The Wanderings of Oisin' (1889), Mangan's many poems about the Irish famine, including 'Siberia' (1846), and the republican themes of several of Jane Wilde's poems. (It is perhaps worth noting in passing that republicanism was a theme not exclusive to Irish writing; it can also be seen in works such as Swinburne's *A Song of Italy* (1867) and *Songs Before Sunrise* (1871), which express support for Italian independence, and Barrett-Browning's slightly earlier *Casa Guidi Windows* (1851).) However, as neither Mangan nor Yeats spoke Gaelic, their attempt to reinvent a distinctively Irish poetry also depended on capturing the distinctive rhythms of Anglo-Irish speech – which, according to some historians, carry a more even intonation than the characteristic stresses of English prosody – through a reworking of the traditional metres of Gaelic poetry (MacDonagh 1996). A good example of this can be seen in the gently lilting rhythm of the opening lines of Yeats's famous 'The Lake Isle of Innisfree' (1893): 'I will arise and go now, and go to Innisfree, | And a small cabin build there, of clay and wattles made'.

Perhaps more than any other literary medium, the formal and stylistic diversity of nineteenth-century poetry exemplifies the difficulties of reconciling what we have called the descriptive and explanatory demands of literary history: to tell what Perkins termed a coherent 'story' it is necessary to be selective. That selectivity has traditionally been justified on aesthetic grounds: works were excluded because they were judged to be formally and stylistically uninteresting, when 'interesting' was defined in relation to, or anticipating the poetics of, Modernism. A desire to view nineteenth-century poetry in its own terms, and in all its complexity and variability, has considerably expanded this canon, and as a consequence there has been a proliferation of new narratives about styles, forms and themes. Some of these narratives are not easily compatible with each other. Should the early poetry of Yeats be viewed as part of an Irish tradition, as exemplifying that of the final moment of the 'last' Romantics, or as articulating an innovative polyvalent symbolism – simply put, is Yeats an Irish, Decadent or a Symbolist poet? Are the works in Jane Hamilton's posthumous *Poems, Sketches and Essays* (1880) best understood in relation to a tradition of working-class or of Scottish poetry; and within a narrative about poetry and nationalism, how might the critic contrast her use of a Scottish vernacular with Yeats's Anglo-Irish diction? If the focus is narrowed to Hamilton's 'Ballads of Memorie', which celebrates the village life she had known as a child, yet further affinities are suggested, this time with that late nineteenth-century tradition of rural nostalgia usually identified with Hardy and Housman. Given these questions, it might seem that the most significant challenge for future historians of nineteenth-century poetry, is not – as has often been the case in the past – the continuation of 'recovery' projects and thus the expansion of the canon. More pressing, perhaps, is a need to find new frames of reference by which to integrate and explain what is already known: that is, to account for the *totality* of nineteenth-century poetic production.

Fiction

Any historian attempting to summarise the main developments in nineteenth-century prose fiction will be confronted with a dauntingly large body of evidence. Sutherland's estimated total of 50,000–60,000 titles, which we cited earlier, embraces a wide range of fictional media, including three- and one-volume novels, novellas, short stories and prose-poems (the last of which developed in the late decades of the century). It also includes 'improving literature' (such as Harriet Martineau's *Illustrations of Political Economy*) and varieties of children's fiction, which range from the crudely didactic stories associated with evangelical authors in the early decades of the century to the complex fantasies of Lewis Carroll's *Alice in Wonderland* (1865) and *Alice Through the Looking Glass* (1871). And there was also a flourishing trade, throughout the century, in privately published pornographic fiction, some of which appeared in the numerous (and often short-lived) pornographic magazines, such as *The Pearl*, which ran from July 1879 until December 1880, when it was suppressed. Among the best-known of such fiction today are *The Lustful Turk* (1828) and *The Romance of Lust* (1876), both of which were probably authored by William Potter (1805–79), the anonymous *Teleny* (1893) which some modern critics believe was written in part by Oscar Wilde, and the eleven-volume *My Secret Life* by 'Walter' (1888–94). Given such quantity and diversity, any survey of nineteenth-century fiction will inevitably involve being selective in one's attitude towards the evidence – what Sutherland terms literary 'anorexia'. What is at issue, then, is which principle of selection could be adopted, and this in turn is complicated by the need to consider the role of form or style.

Most literary histories propose that nineteenth-century fiction is dominated by the realist (or, as Roland Barthes termed it, 'classic' realist) novel, a form whose moralising tendencies appealed to the interests of its largely bourgeois, and by implication politically conservative and relatively unsophisticated, readership. Associated most closely with mid nineteenth-century writers such as Thackeray, Eliot, Gaskell and Trollope, realism has traditionally been defined in terms of the seriousness of its moral purposes and the attempt to depict a wide contemporary social panorama; more simply, realism describes literary fictions, the devices of which (discussed in more detail below) attempt to represent the world as it 'really' is – that is, in all its complexity and variety. Such aspirations distinguish realism both from Jane Austen's comedies of manners (which tend to concentrate on a single social class) and from the 'silver fork' and 'Newgate' fictions which were also popular in the early decades of the century, and which took their titles from the alleged narrowness of their glamorisation of aristocratic and criminal life-styles respectively. By contrast, the sub-genres associated with nineteenth-century realism disclose a different set of concerns.

They include the 'condition of England', 'industrial' or 'social-problem' novel which focused, as we noted in Chapter 2, on the class conflict that had arisen as result of the industrialisation of parts of the British economy (especially in the Midlands and north of England). The second half of the century also saw several forms of religious fiction: Mary Ward's *Robert Elsmere*, like Thomas Hall Caine's (1853–1931) *The Christian* (1897), centres on a crisis in faith experienced by an Anglican parish priest, whereas her *Helbeck of Bannisdale* (1898) explores the tensions between the Catholicism of its hero and the liberal, Protestant upbringing of the woman with whom he falls in love. John Henry Newman's *Loss and Gain: The Story of a Convert* (1848) is markedly Catholic in its sympathies and sentiments, whereas the less well-known *Paul Faber* (1879) by George MacDonald offers a more straightforward and sentimental tale of Christian redemption centred on a doctor's recovery of his faith. Grace Aguilar's posthumously published *Home Scenes and Heart Studies* (1853) is motivated by concerns with her Jewish faith, as is Amy Levy's rather different portrait of contemporary Jewish life in *Reuben Sachs* (1888). However, perhaps the most singular nineteenth-century novel to deal with matters of faith is Walter Pater's *Marius the Epicurean* (1885), which contrasts various forms of pagan religion in ancient Rome with early Christian practices. The *Chronicles of Carlingford* (1863–76) – the title given to a sequence of novels by Margaret Oliphant (1828–97) which are set in a small country town – also addresses religious themes (in this case the tensions between Anglican and dissenting groups) within another popular fictional sub-genre, the 'regional' or 'provincial' novel, similar examples of which include Gaskell's *Cranford* (1851–53) and Trollope's *Barchester Towers* (1857), both set within what Raymond Williams termed the 'knowable community' of an archetypal mid nineteenth-century rural parish (Williams 1973).

All of these writers had as their ambition a desire, as the dramatist, publisher and journalist Douglas Jerrold (1803–57) put it in an 1845 prospectus to a new shilling magazine, to write fiction 'with a purpose'. That sense of purpose was in turn typically directed towards using literary fiction to debate or advocate social change, usually with regard to areas of social life about which there was significant topical debate, such as contemporary labour relations (including the use of child labour in factories and 'sweat shop' conditions associated with the clothing trade), or religious controversies (provoked, for example, by the Catholic Emancipation Act of 1829 and Oxford Movement, as well as Jewish assimilation), or the destruction of rural communities brought about by encroaching urbanisation, a theme that survives in the oeuvre of Thomas Hardy. Charles Reade, one of the most dogmatic if eccentric of these novelists 'with a purpose', managed to tackle several such themes in a single work; his *Hard Cash* (1863), for example, exposed corruption in both contemporary financial and mental health institutions, although its lurid depiction of nineteenth-century lunatic asylums proved too strong for many readers.

At the other end of the nineteenth century, classic realism has been distinguished from what is viewed as the more experimental and thus proto-modernist 'Impressionism' and complex use of point of view in Henry James's and Joseph Conrad's early fiction, as well as the pessimism characteristic of the novels of Hardy and Gissing. Capturing 'social reality', for these last two authors, typically involves invoking a form of social or environmental determinism – for Gissing the British class system and for Hardy some kind of supernatural force or fate – which is seen to exemplify (as in James's and Conrad's work) a sense of modernity which stands at odds with the emphasis on moral responsibility and individual choice central to realism's depiction of the bourgeois subject. Hardy and Gissing, along with George Moore, were also concerned to test the boundaries of what was considered acceptable subject-matter in representing the 'real' world, especially in the depiction of contemporary sexual mores. In this respect they differed markedly from George Eliot's earlier notions of literary propriety. In an essay on the morality of Goethe's controversial novel *Wilhelm Meister* (1795–96), published in *The Leader* in 1855, Eliot argued that 'no one can maintain that *all* fact is a fit subject for art. The sphere of the artist has its limit somewhere'; she then went on to define those limits as follows:

> The sphere of art extends wherever there is beauty either in form, or thought, or feeling … The tragedian may take for his subject the most hideous passions if they serve as the background for some divine deed of tenderness or heroism, and so the novelist may place before us every aspect of human life where there is some twist of love, or endurance, or helplessness to call forth our best sympathies.

In Eliot's view, the novelist's purpose in depicting what she termed in the same essay 'every aspect of human life', or the 'mixed and erring, and self-deluding' humanity, was to call forth in the reader a capacity for moral judgement. Moreover, actions or lives which did not, in her view, inspire such ethical sympathies, perhaps because they were too wicked, too shabby, or too ordinary – in, for example, Moore's working-class heroine Esther Waters, or Hardy's strangely passive Jude, whose death is precipitated by drink and depression – were no part of literary art as Eliot defined it. This in turn is why Eliot criticised the French novelist Honoré de Balzac, who was an important influence on Hardy, Gissing and Moore, for what she termed 'dragging' the reader through 'scene after scene of unmitigated vice'. Such 'vice' might be 'realistic' in the sense of being an accurate reflection of some aspects of Parisian society, but simply being confronted with it did not, in Eliot's view, extend the moral capacities of the reader; it rather led to what she termed a kind of 'moral nausea'. Another way of putting this might be to suggest that Eliot's notion of 'realism' took the form of a kind of artistic idealism: the role of art, in her view, was to represent human potential, what men and women could be at their best, rather than what they often were and are. (Versions of this debate surfaced later in the century in the reception of French Impressionist art, whose aims were often confused with those of literary realism – a topic addressed in more detail in Chapter 4.) Classic realism, then, has traditionally been distinguished from both early and late nineteenth-century fiction by what can seem a paradoxical combination of high moral purpose and a desire to embrace the rich variety of contemporary social life.

However, to put matters this simply, to equate the mainstream of nineteenth-century fictional development with realism, overlooks the fact that there have been vigorous disputes about what actually constitutes literary realism (that is, about the nature of its formal devices), about its prevalence in the nineteenth century and about how it is to be valued. And these in turn have had implications for how historians shape the canon of nineteenth-century fiction and how they understand the development of nineteenth-century fictional forms. It is worth remembering that throughout the century there were many sub-genres which did not put a premium on the accurate rendering of the minutiae of everyday life and attention to circumstantial detail (held to be staples of realist fiction) and these sub-genres enjoyed sustained popularity. They include Gothic fiction, examples of which can seen at either end of the century in what are perhaps the best-known Gothic novels, *Frankenstein* (1818) by Mary Shelley (1797–1851) and Bram Stoker's *Dracula* (1897), as well as, from the 1870s onwards, ghost stories, fairy-tales (written for both adults and children) and various kinds of romantic and pseudo-scientific fantasies such as H. Rider Haggard's *She* (1887) and *King Solomon's Mines*, Morris's *News from Nowhere* (1888) and H. G. Wells's *The Time Machine* (1895), *The Island of Dr Moreau* (1896) and *The War of the Worlds* (1898). There are also numerous works, such as Emily Brontë's *Wuthering Heights*, which combine elements of non-realistic forms, notably Gothic motifs, with techniques and conventions associated with realism. So Brontë's novel attempts in addition to render accurately local dialects and topography. Dickens's fiction, too, draws on Gothic caricatures, not only in the depiction of foreign villains such as the murderous French maid Hortense in *Bleak House* (1852–53) or Rigaud in *Little Dorrit* (1855–57), but also in the disorientating, squalid and nearly always menacing urban architecture of London, in which characters frequently lose their bearings, morally, socially and geographically. Dickens was also interested in contemporary drama, and in particular in the staging of melodramas which emphasised spectacle over plausibility in plot and characterisation, and this too helps to give many of his novels an exuberance and theatricality at odds with the emphasis on the quotidian or everyday to be found in realism.

The popularity of hybrid genres, such as the historical romance pioneered by Walter Scott with works such as *The Heart of Midlothian* (1818), also testifies to the diverse nature of the nineteenth-century reading public's tastes. It also clearly indicates a distance from the values of modern readers, for relatively few novels in this hybrid genre, with the exception perhaps of Scott's *Ivanhoe* (1819), Dickens's *A Tale of Two Cities* (1859), and Robert Louis Stevenson's *Kidnapped* (1886) and its sequel *Catriona* (1893), which took as their subject the aftermath of the 1745 Jacobite rebellion in Scotland, are read today. In the nineteenth century, however, numerous authors tried their hand at historical fiction, and their efforts at accurately evoking various historical periods were frequently compared. Charles Reade's *The Cloister and the Hearth* (1861) and Eliot's *Romola* (1862–63) are both set in fifteenth-century Europe, but while the former was admired, the latter was widely criticised as worthy but dull. Swinburne, never a writer to mince his words, disparaged *Romola* because of what he termed in a piece published in the *Nineteenth Century* in 1884, 'the wellnigh puerile insufficiency of some of the resources by which the story has to be pushed forward'.

Finally, it is important to acknowledge the enormous success of sensation fiction, a sub-genre which flourished in the middle decades of the century and which was defined, as its name suggests, by features quite the opposite to those associated with realism: that is, by improbable plotting (typically involving bigamy, madness and multiple murders), an obsession with lurid and exaggerated emotional states and a tendency towards caricature. Contemporary critics were particularly critical of the irresponsibly heightened emotions which they assumed such novels evoked in what was a largely female readership. Sensation fiction, in other words, was popularly viewed as offering the opposite reading experience to that education of the ethical sensibilities envisaged by Eliot. That said, it is also worth noting that the line between realism and sensation in individual works was often blurred, and recognised masters of the genre of sensation fiction, like Wilkie Collins, effortlessly combined topical detail, dense plotting and complex casts of characters with improbably melodramatic situations. The narrative structure of *The Woman in White* (1859–60), which comprises written testimony, diary entries and legal evidence, claims for itself a documentary realism; however, in the novel's denouement the plot device which brings the villainous Count Fosco to justice involves the introduction of an obscure Italian secret society which organises his assassination. This difficulty in categorising *The Woman in White* is not an isolated one. As we noted in Chapter 2, Collins's *The Moonstone* is often recognised as the first thoroughgoing example of the nineteenth-century sub-genre of detective fiction which was to flourish in the late decades of the century, and whose origins lay in sensation fiction's obsession with criminality and secrecy, as well as earlier genres such as the Newgate novel, and with works such as Edgar Allan Poe's (1809–49) 'The Murders in the Rue Morgue' (1843) and Eugène Sue's (1804–57) *Les Mystères de Paris* (1842–43). However, sub-plots involving detectives and detection appear in any number of nineteenth-century novels, including Dickens's *Our Mutual Friend* and *Bleak House*, as well as such classic realist works as Trollope's *He Knew He Was Right* (1869), where a husband employs a private detective to gather evidence against his wife, whom he wrongly suspects of adultery. Ironically, that same 'realist' novel also deploys another trope more usually associated with sensation fiction, for the husband's suspicions develop into a pathological monomania which eventually leads to his death.

The proposition that nineteenth-century fiction is dominated by its concern with accurately representing the mundane elements of social life can be disputed on other grounds: a number of the tropes commonly held to demonstrate that concern do not, as some historians have noted, reflect social reality at all. For example, the prevalence of orphans in nineteenth-century fiction – although the trope itself has a long history – might lead one to believe that parentless (and particularly motherless) children were much more common, and thus more visible as objects of social concern, than in earlier centuries. Census data, however, suggests otherwise: nineteenth-century writers of fiction were attracted to the figure of the orphan for literary rather than documentary purposes – they offered a useful and sentimentally loaded device for examining issues of contemporary socialisation. Likewise, non-literary evidence of pre-marital sexual behaviour (such as the numbers of children revealed by parish registers to have been conceived or born outside wedlock) is also markedly different from that found in nineteenth-century realist fiction. In works such as Gaskell's *Ruth* or Dickens's *Oliver Twist* 'fallen women' are aberrations who are treated as social pariahs. Moreover, despite their assiduous efforts at moral rejuvenation – that is, an acknowledgement of guilt and a process of repentance – the sexually compromised reputations of fictional women can only be redeemed by self-sacrifice, and in many cases, by death (Ruth, as we noted in Chapter 2, dies from typhus fever contracted as a result of nursing the father of her illegitimate child and Nancy is killed by Bill Sykes after betraying him to help the innocent Oliver). Later novels which tried to deal more frankly with sexual relationships, such as Reade's *Griffith Gaunt, Or Jealousy* (1866), Sarah Grand's *The Heavenly Twins* (1893), George Moore's *Esther Waters* and Grant Allen's *The Woman Who Did*, although popular with the reading public, were often criticised by reviewers.

It may be tempting to conclude from these examples that, like nineteenth-century poetry, the only secure generalisation to be made about the history of nineteenth-century fiction is that it encompasses wide formal and generic diversity. Such an admission, however, is not particularly helpful to general readers who need some sort of route-map in order to find their way through the sheer quantity of fiction that was produced. Moreover, managing that quantity has traditionally required historians to make value judgements about it, to try to distinguish, as nineteenth-century critics did, what is purportedly good or 'serious' from what is popular but only transient. And here it is significant that many nineteenth-century fictional best-sellers were not in sub-genres where realism, or fidelity to lived experience, was at a premium: the output of Marie Corelli is an exemplary case. The work which first established her uncanny ability to sell, *Barabbas, A Dream of The World's Tragedy* (1893), blithely retold the well-known biblical story by inventing a 'Judith Iscariot' in order to provide the requirements of a romantic love-interest. The extravagant romances of another exceptionally popular author, Ouida, were regularly lampooned for their outlandish plots and comically poor grasp of the social mores of the aristocratic milieu which was often her chosen subject-matter; yet none of Ouida's exaggerations or gaucheries prevented works like *Under Two Flags* (1867) from selling hundreds of thousands, if not millions, of copies. That element of caricature might indeed have been one reason for their success. This association between sensationalism and popularity, which is also a feature of Newgate fiction (William Harrison Ainsworth's *Jack Sheppard* (1839) was much plagiarised), inevitably presented realism as the more intellectually serious or demanding genre, one with pretensions to educate rather than merely to entertain. This in turn helps to explain why, when considering questions of form, it is the devices associated with realist fiction, and particularly the *bildungsroman* or novel of self-development, which, until relatively recently, have preoccupied most modern critics.

Central to the discussion has been the basic claim to verisimilitude held to underpin literary realism, the assumption that the world can be unproblematically or objectively represented by language and that prose fiction can therefore function in part as a type of moral knowledge. At first glance, this ambition for what might be termed a kind of transparency of form may seem to render the genre relatively uninteresting from the point of view of style; to be accepted by the reader as 'true', realist fiction must contrive to disguise its status as an artefact. In this respect, the apparent naivety (or perhaps deceptiveness) of the realist aesthetic stands in sharp contrast to the cynicism about literary representation exhibited in some earlier works of fiction, such as the metafictional experiments found in *Tristram Shandy* (1759–67) by Laurence Sterne (1713–68) or the self-conscious narrators of *Joseph Andrews* (1742) and *Tom Jones* (1749) by Henry Fielding (1707–54). The narrative voice of *Tristram Shandy* constantly reminds the reader that the description the novel offers is a construction, and a partial or flawed one at that; the voice of the narrator in *Tom Jones* advises the reader to treat the work like a meal – something concocted and to be enjoyed at leisure. A questioning of the basis of literary representation, although apparently of little interest to nineteenth-century realists, later re-emerged, although suitably adapted, in the work of modernists such as Joyce and Woolf where a concern with the subjectivity of perception and the provisionality of moral judgements gave rise to experiments with chronology, point of view and the use of free indirect speech or 'stream of consciousness' narration (McCabe 1978, 1985).

It is possible to argue, then, that the nineteenth-century attraction to realism is a kind of interlude in literary history, one which can be explained by reference to a tradition of British philosophical and scientific empiricism. However, viewing realist fiction as an epiphenomenon of larger cultural developments does not really help us to overcome that criticism, made most forcefully by Modernists, of realism's apparent artlessness or lack of formal sophistication. It is worth noting that an early celebration of realist fiction, F. R. Leavis's account of *Middlemarch* in *The Great Tradition* (1948), was made by an appeal to the 'comprehensiveness' of its moral vision, rather than an account of its style (although later critics objected to what they saw as the ideological basis of Leavis's judgement). Another way of putting this problem is to say that discussion of nineteenth-century realist fiction, even while acknowledging the genre's claim to seriousness, has none the less often involved a need to justify it as an object of academic scrutiny. Realist fiction is, after all, rarely considered a difficult 'read' in the manner of, say, Joyce's *Ulysses* (1922) or James's late novel, *The Golden Bowl* (1904), even though details of the contemporary social reality it attempts to depict may be alien to some modern readers.

The most common sort of justification of realism has involved a re-characterisation of its formal devices so that the apparent transparency of representation – that ambition for verisimilitude – is revealed to possess a complexity or a politics which is assumed to have been unrecognised by nineteenth-century readers. When the devices of nineteenth-century realist fiction first began to command sustained critical interest in the 1950s attention was typically drawn to the deftness of the manipulation of plot, characterisation and narrative techniques (including, in Dorothy Van Ghent's view, elaborate symbolic systems) in order to achieve a formal and thematic coherence, what Van Ghent called an aesthetic 'whole' (Van Ghent 1953). However, from the 1960s onwards, that claim for formal coherence became a point of debate with many critics – it was a feature to be interrogated, rather than simply applauded. For example, Marxist critics, whose work dominated discussion of realist fiction in the 1960s and early 1970s, identified it as fundamentally ideological. That is, they viewed the devices of realist fiction, particularly the identification of social reality with a material world and the use of an omniscient narrator to guide the reader's moral judgements, as an attempt to normalise or present as 'natural' the unequal power relations which underlay nineteenth-century capitalist society. To use a term popularised by Catherine Belsey in her appropriation of some of the ideas of the French Marxist philosopher Louis Althusser, realist fiction was seen to 'interpellate' (or as we would now say 'compel' the construction of) readers as bourgeois subjects, and realist fiction was thereby viewed as one of the structures of capitalist society (Althusser called them 'ideological state apparatuses') (Belsey 1980). In this view, the role of the modern critic was to elucidate the textual strategies by which realism perpetuated what was now seen as an illusion of reality, and in the process expose the partial nature of that realist vision and therefore, and most importantly, the politics underlying its claim to verisimilitude. In the case of a writer such as Charlotte Brontë this involved identifying racial prejudices in works such as *Jane Eyre*; in that novel, as in Jane Austen's *Mansfield Park*, sources of colonial wealth, such as the inheritance which enables Jane to marry Rochester and enjoy the proverbial 'happy ever after', are left largely unexamined.

Other critics, influenced by theorists such as Pierre Macheray, drew attention to the difficulties with which realist fiction attempts to 'perform' its 'ideological work', noting that the totalising or omniscient perspective of realism is often undermined by narrative fractures or what came to be popularly known as 'lacunae' (Macheray 1978). As John Lucas had argued earlier in relation to Elizabeth Gaskell's *Mary Barton* (1848), in this view it is, paradoxically, the formal failures of a work, what he saw as an unresolved tension between *Mary Barton*'s documentary realism and its romance plot, which give it value precisely because the novel discloses, despite itself, the limitations of Gaskell's moral solution to what at heart are economic problems to do with inequality of wealth. Lucas argues that the reconciliation between the mill owner, Mr Carson, and the unemployed murderer of his son, John Barton, at the novel's conclusion represents a romanticised appeal to community or a 'brotherhood' of interests, one which serves to disguise the potency of class divisions which early chapters of the novel defined in terms of poverty. Put more simply, there can often be a tension between the formal devices of a realist novel and the ideological work held to be its raison d'être (Lucas 1966).

Similar in approach is criticism inspired by the Russian formalist Mikhail Bakhtin, which concentrates on identifying tensions or contradictions between the realist text's various social 'voices' (what he calls 'heteroglossia') or, in the hands of some critics, between the multiple plots by which it maps what George Eliot referred to as the complex 'web' of social relations that defined nineteenth-century culture (Bakhtin 1981). A good example can be found in the first- and third-person narratives in *Bleak House*, which for many critics work against each other, thus undermining the narrative closure, often thought to be the defining ambition of realism – that moment when form and ideology supposedly cohere. In these sorts of arguments realist fiction becomes formally interesting to the extent that its devices can be seen as 'self-deconstructing', in the sense of betraying their inability to capture the totality of social experience. George Levine has argued that nineteenth-century realist writers were often conscious of the limitations of realism, appropriating realist conventions in order to examine the nature of fictional representation and thus the status of the realist novel itself (Levine 1981). In this view, realist fiction can have metafictional qualities. George Eliot's later novels have provided fertile material for this sort of approach. Several critics have noted how Eliot's recourse to metaphor, a mode of figurative language which David Lodge identified specifically with modernist writing (Lodge 1977), undermines realism's dependence on an objectivity exhibited in the representation (made via the use of metonymy rather than metaphor) of the materiality of social life. Some have gone so far as to claim that the narrative self-consciousness in a work such as *Daniel Deronda* is more appropriately viewed as 'proto-modernist' rather than realist, arguing that Eliot is deliberately drawing attention to, and trying to grapple with, the problems of representation (Newton 1991).

The suggestion that the formal devices of realism can disclose narrative instability and uncertainty (sometimes self-consciously so), contrasts with more recent readings of nineteenth-century fiction which have tended to echo the conclusions of early Marxists. Inspired by the theorisation of power and language offered by the French theorist Michel Foucault, in the late 1980s and 1990s realism was typically interpreted as a form of social discipline. Where earlier writers, like Belsey, had proposed that realist fiction normalised contemporary power relations, it was now suggested that fiction was implicated in actually producing them. Critical enquiry was therefore re-envisaged as the uncovering (or deconstructing) of what were termed the general 'discursive formations' by which power operated, and literary history thereby became assimilated to cultural history. It led to a large body of studies in which nineteenth-century novels were viewed as agents in the construction (and sometimes disruption) of what were called 'regulatory' discourses about issues such as domestic violence, sexual relations, mental health, the management of pain, risk and financial markets, as well as the Victorian criminal justice system and urban sanitation (Armstrong (1987), Miller (1988), Poovey (1988), Sedgwick (1990)).

Much of this criticism is notable for the way that it elides the differences between the literary and non-literary, and between canonical and non-canonical works; it views fiction as part of a larger ideological process to be seen in a range of disparate cultural documents. As a consequence questions about form, style and genre are inevitably marginalised, as the description of discursive formations, which might, for example, involve noting similarities between novels and conduct books, requires issues about textual identity and textual authority to be passed over. In the process, and as we argue more fully in Chapter 5, the sorts of questions which preoccupied earlier critics and literary historians – the problem, for example, of distinguishing what is to be called 'good' fiction from what is popular – simply disappeared. A useful example of these elisions can be seen in Marlene Tromp's revaluation of sensation novels, which she implicates in one of the most serious of nineteenth-century activities: contemporary legislative reform. Noting that her methodology (which combines elements from the work of Foucault and Derrida) 'urges a destabilization of generic boundaries' or 'semiotic drift' between fictional and non-fictional, sensational and realist texts, Tromp goes on to claim, somewhat counterintuitively, that the representation of 'sexual violence' in novels such as Braddon's *Aurora Floyd* (1863) offer a more thoroughgoing kind of truth – a way of 'imagining what might be real' – than that found in 'anti-sensation' fiction by writers like Trollope (Tromp 2000: 8–10). A similar methodology has enabled Elaine Freedgood to examine 'canonical adventure fiction' by writers like Conrad, Kipling and Stevenson alongside contemporary memoirs about ballooning by (the now forgotten) James Glaisher and Henry Coxwell in order to elucidate what she describes as 'a massive, disorganized and highly successful Victorian cultural enterprise: the textual construction of a safe England in a dangerous world' (Freedgood 2000: 1).

More recently, however, some critics have begun to object to what they perceive as the limitations of these Foucauldian projects. What James Eli Adams has termed the 'Foucauldian melodrama' has been viewed as producing repetitive and formulaic accounts of nineteenth-century literary fiction (Adams 2001: 858). Other critics have noted that these projects appear to have little to say about the distinctiveness of the literary and that the selective use of cultural documents (and thus understanding of 'context') gives a limited view of history (Miller 2003). It is also suggested that they tend to construct nineteenth-century readers as simultaneously painfully naive and hopelessly serious. As Anna Maria Jones explains, this mode of critical enquiry seems to rest on a paradox: while it is assumed that 'nothing is outside of discourse' and 'that power invisibly and inexorably penetrates all aspects of social life', the modern critic none the less remains outside such structures, able to infiltrate them in a manner not open to the 'culturally subjugated', 'unconscious subjects' of Victorian Britain (Jones 2007: 4). Interestingly, the same type of objection was made of Belsey's use of Althusser, in the sense that he too failed to explain how the modern critic was exempt from the totalising power of ideological state apparatuses while their nineteenth-century counterparts were not. In essence Lauren Goodlad agrees, but puts the problem slightly differently: she suggests that while we can recognise that all writing is 'socially embedded', those documents which we label as 'literary' none the less seem to 'provide something more' than the 'treatises, journalistic essays, propagandistic tales, and official reports' that are typically read alongside them (Goodlad 2003: x). For Andrew Miller, that 'something more' resides in the 'graphic and enduring' nature of the images to be found in works of literary fiction, in other words in its metaphorical and symbolic structures (Miller 1995: 7) Miller and Goodlad seem to be pointing us to what an earlier generation of critics took for granted as the distinctive character of the literary, as it is exhibited in the specificities of form, style and genre. The difference is that, rather than form being considered for its own sake – in terms of, say, an 'aesthetic' integrity – it is now viewed as enabling fiction to make a privileged contribution to areas of contemporary social debate, a contribution which at the same time may be highly ideological. (In turn this is reminiscent of the tenets of that early Marxist literary criticism associated with figures such as Raymond Williams, which saw in literary works, and especially prose fiction, a special *kind* of historical evidence.)

Despite these disagreements about how precisely form operates in nineteenth-century fiction, about whether it is normalising, or constitutive or disruptive of contemporary ideological structures, it is notable that there has been a marked tendency since the 1960s to view novels and short stories (both realist and non-realist) in terms of their relationship to a perceived social reality, a tendency which will be explored in more detail in Chapter 5 as part of a larger discussion about the relationship between nineteenth-century literature and what is typically called its social 'context'. Here, however, it is worth noting that this concern with context has led to the identification of sub-genres defined in terms of theme, rather than form or style: so historians and critics also recognise categories such as 'socialist' or 'Chartist' fiction (some of which was written by middle-class authors), fictions of Empire, stories of adventure, and so forth. As with nineteenth-century poetry, then, the generic categorisation of fiction is perhaps best viewed as a way of providing alternative frameworks by which different sorts of works can be brought into a productive alignment.

For example, let us take Newman's novel *Callista* (1856). Widely viewed as an allegory of his own anguished conversion to Roman Catholicism, but set in ancient Carthage and recounting the story of the relationship between the Christian Agellius and Greek sculptress Callista (who is eventually martyred for her conversion to Christianity), *Callista* could be viewed as a form of historical romance, comparable perhaps to Corelli's *Barabbas* or to Collins's first novel, *Antonia, Or the Fall of Rome* (1850) which recounts the romance between a Christian heroine and Gothic chieftain in fifth-century Rome, or even the French novelist Gustave Flaubert's *Salammbô* (1862) which is also set in Carthage. Alternatively, *Callista* might be seen as a work of religious fiction, to be read alongside Pater's *Marius*. Similarly generic anomalies, such as the hallucinatory *Private Memoirs and Confessions of a Justified Sinner* (1824) by James Hogg (1770–1835) or Thomas de Quincey's *Confessions of an English Opium Eater*, are both heavily indebted to Gothic traditions, yet their titles explicitly invite comparison with what was (and is) probably the best-known confessional narrative, one widely read in the nineteenth century, the *Confessions* of St Augustine of Hippo (354–430). Finally, acknowledgement should also be given to works which seem to defy classification. One of the most notable (though today, little read) is the posthumously published and partly autobiographical *The Way of All Flesh* (1903) by Samuel Butler (1835–1902). Written in the 1870s and 1880s, it stands as a striking epitaph to the ambition of nineteenth-century fiction writers, as well as to what are popularly termed 'Victorian values'. Its rambling plot, which encompasses dysfunctional patriarchs, fallen women, inter-class marriage, drunkenness, bigamy, imprisonment, inheritance (both financial and biological), as well as a career in the Anglican Church – an option only for the dull or faithless – satirises many of the topoi found in the century's fiction, but with a ferocity that seems to belong to the age of Swift and Johnson, rather than that of Butler's similarly disillusioned contemporaries, Hardy and Gissing.

Before leaving the subject of fiction in this chapter, it is worth briefly mentioning one further way of thinking about form: its relation to publishing culture (a topic that will be explored in more detail in Chapter 7). Literary historians have noted how many of the characteristics of nineteenth-century realist fiction – such as the sheer length of many novels, the complexity of plotting and the bewildering number of fictional characters within any one work – may be explained by the material and economic conditions under which it was produced. All these features have been seen as following directly from the habit of publishing fiction serially (either in general-interest periodicals or in separate monthly instalments) before producing it in book form, as well as the investment of circulating libraries (the main purchasers of hard-back fiction) in the expensive three-volume novel. Knowing that a serialised novel would be consumed over a period of time that could stretch to months rather than weeks meant that the author had to take particular care to sustain the reader's interest, a process which typically involved introducing multiple plot lines with frequent climaxes as well as new and memorable characters. A famous example is Dickens's attempt to revive the revive flagging sales of the serialised *David Copperfield* (1849–50) by bringing back Mr Micawber into the story – in much the same way as writers of modern soap operas revive popular characters. By the same token, filling out the three volumes preferred by the circulating libraries (a system favoured because libraries changed per volume rented, rather than per work) demanded that novels were typically well over 150,000 words long (even if they were not first serialised).

In the early and middle decades of the century publishers were wary of short works, a reluctance which led them into some odd selling arrangements. *Wuthering Heights*, a relatively short novel by nineteenth-century standards, was produced as part of a three-volume set by being bound with the even shorter *Agnes Grey* by Anne Brontë. The decline and ultimate collapse of the circulating libraries' power in the 1880s, combined with the development of new and more specialist literary magazines like *The Strand* (which published Conan Doyle's Sherlock Holmes stories) and *The Yellow Book*, provided a medium in which shorter fictional forms and genres could flourish. These included the novella, the one-volume novel and varieties of short fiction, such as ghost, fairy and detective stories. The development of this last sub-genre was particularly indebted to the growth of cheap literary papers and magazines; Sutherland, for example, notes that it has been estimated that by the mid-1890s 'of the 800 weekly papers in Britain, 240 were carrying some variety of detective story' (Sutherland 2009: 181). In the late decades of the century an increasing number of professional or semi-professional authors found that they could earn a decent living by responding to this new demand for short, plot-driven and so easily consumed fiction; and even authors who had concentrated their attention on three-volume novels, such as George Gissing, eventually adapted to this new market – a situation which Gissing himself describes in his most famous novel, *New Grub Street* (1891). (Ironically Gissing's own very large body of uncollected short fiction has only recently been made available to modern readers.)

The popularity of these new sub-genres thus quickly attracted the attention of serious as well as 'hack' authors, all of whom hoped to make money from what appeared to be a lucrative new literary market (this was especially true in the years following the 1890 Chace Act, which secured copyright agreements with America, thus enabling short stories to be simultaneously syndicated internationally to several magazines). However, it would be a mistake to view nineteenth-century short fiction as wholly defined by, or the product of, commercial imperatives. The examples of French and Russian literature in the last half of the century demonstrated how, in the hands of writers such as Gustave Flaubert, Guy de Maupassant (1850–93), Ivan Turgenev (1818–83) and Anton Chekhov (1860–1904), the short story could become a sophisticated art form, one capable of supporting ambitions as serious as those associated with the realist novel. This in turn helps to explain the pieces collected in *Imaginary Portraits* (1887) by Walter Pater, a writer whose scholarly 'conscience' – to use his own term – led him to disregard the kind of celebrity that came from a popular readership. The volume's stories, which elude simple generic categorisation and include 'Sebastian van Storck' and 'Duke Carl Rosenmold', combined elements of art criticism, biography and fiction; they were defiantly scholarly in their abstruse allusions, long digressions and the subordination of plot and character to their intellectual themes.

The motives of other 'serious' writers of short fiction, such as Henry James or Oscar Wilde, seem to have been more complex, as they attempted to transform the tropes and themes exploited by popular authors while at the same time trying to repeat their commercial success. So in works like James's 'The Turn of the Screw' (1898) the ghost story becomes a vehicle for complex stylistic and psychological experimentation, as well as exploiting the more familiar pleasures of fear and suspense: in that story the reader is left uncertain whether the ghosts seen by the governess are 'real' or fantasies projected by her sexual frustration. Some of Wilde's short stories, such as 'The Canterville Ghost', 'Lord Arthur Savile's Crime' and 'The Fisherman and his Soul' seem to be deliberately 'sending up' or (in the case of the last story, subverting) popular sub-genres by inverting the principles of moral justice on which they traditionally depend: so the Canterville ghost turns out to be comically inept in his attempts to frighten the philistine American Otis family; only by committing murder does Lord Arthur receive the conventional reward of just behaviour, that of a happy marriage; and the fate of the fisherman's soul teaches that spirit is empty when divorced from bodily desire. In stories such as these, distinctions between 'high' and 'low', realistic and sensation, tend once more to become dissolved. Even more prolific practitioners in these genres, like Joseph Sheridan Le Fanu (1814–73) and M. R. James (1862–1936) produced works with a complexity and subtlety that is largely absent from earlier kinds of popular fiction, such as the lurid penny dreadfuls produced in large numbers in the 1840s for a semi-literate working-class audience by writers such as James Malcolm Rymer (Malcolm J. Errym, 1804–84), best remembered today for his Gothic thriller *Varney the Vampyre* (1845–47) and *The String of Pearls* (1846) which inspired the famously gruesome melodrama, *Sweeney Todd, The Demon Barber of Fleet Street*, and the improbably named Thomas Peckett Prest (?1810–59), whose prolific output included plagiarism of works by Dickens and Ainsworth.

Changes in publishing culture, in particular the lowering of the cost of book production, also played an important role in the development of children's fiction in the nineteenth century, in part because it enabled a market to develop which was both large and lucrative enough to attract a wide range of authors. Some, like Juliana Ewing and Hesba Stretton (the pen-name of Sara Smith 1832–1911), specialised in the genre, while others, like Edith Nesbit (1858–1924), whose aspirations initially centred on being a poet, became best known for their writing for children. Women writers were often encouraged by publishers to try their hand at writing for children, particularly when they were beginning their careers (Mary Ward's children's story *Milly and Olly* (1880) preceded her attempts at novel writing); but established authors of adult fiction wrote for children too, their numbers including Hannah More (1745–1833), George MacDonald, Ruskin, Thackeray, Stevenson, Wilde and Kipling. This in turn helped to liberate the genre from the influence of evangelical publishers, such as the Religious Tract Society, which in the early decades of the century tended to favour the production of simple didactic tales, often given out free as Sunday school prizes or used in other educational contexts. An example of this style is the popular *The History of the Robins* (1786) by the prolific Sarah Trimmer (1741–1810). As a consequence, over the course of the century children's fiction became more diverse, necessitating categorisation into a number of sub-genres, many of which stressed the importance of engaging the child's imagination rather than simply instructing her (Bratton 1981). These included fairy-tales and fantasies (the fairy-tales of the brothers Grimm were first published in English translation in 1823), school stories (of which the immensely popular *Tom Brown's School Days* by Thomas Hughes spawned many imitations), tales of adventure (such as Charles Kingsley's *Westward Ho!* (1855) and the prolific G. A. Henty's *With Clive in India* (1884)). Popular too were domestic stories directed, as might be expected, at girls (of which the best known are by Charlotte Yonge (1823–1901) and, later in the century, the industrious Lillie Meade (1844–1914) whose *A World of Girls* (1886) pioneered a sub-genre of girls' school stories).

The growing formal sophistication of children's fiction, exemplified in the linguistic, visual and mathematical puns in Carroll's *Alice* books, had a further consequence: it could lead to confusion about the addressees of so-called 'children's' fiction. Christina Rossetti's collection of fairy-tales *Speaking Likenesses* (1874), although written to take advantage of the Christmas children's market, reads more like a satire on the sub-genre's popularity, one directed towards the adult reader rather than the listening child. Wilde's second collection of fairy-tales *A House of Pomegranates* (1896) also sold poorly, apparently, and if contemporary reviewers are to be believed, because there was a confusion about its intended audience. Aspects of its subject-matter and elaborate verbal style were deemed unsuitable for children. Some of the children's stories written by Laurence Housman (1865–1959), the younger brother of A. E. Housman, are similarly ambiguous (Sumpter 2008). Once again we see that diversity in fictional forms can make generic classification difficult; moreover, that difficulty centres on what by now should also be a familiar issue: the nature of a work's readership. It may be significant that critical discussion of nineteenth-century children's fiction has often focused, like that of adult fiction, on the ideological work such stories perform by, for example, normalising and transmitting (or sometimes subverting) contemporary gender roles and the values of empire (Reynolds 1990; Knoepflmacher 1998; Kutzer 2000). Other critics have identified underlying complexities or sub-texts in children's fiction which in turn are assumed to have been unappreciated by its main addressees. In this view, the genre is valued either as an unwitting expression of the tensions in adult attitudes towards children (such as the adult male's idolisation of a pre-pubescent feminine innocence), or as a safe arena in which to debate ideas that might be controversial in other contexts. Wilde's perennially popular, and superficially quite straightforward, children's tale 'The Selfish Giant' has recently been interpreted as an elaborate and highly charged political allegory about the Irish Land League (Killeen 2007). By the same token, however, those children's stories which are resistant to such sub-textual readings, such as the simplistic moral tales turned out in their hundreds of thousands by the RTS, have been largely ignored, even though they were almost certainly the most widely read children's fiction at the time.

Drama

Rather than the sheer number works which confront the historian of nineteenth-century poetry or fiction, theatre historians for the same period must begin by acknowledging that the evidence with which they have to deal will always be incomplete. There are two distinct reasons for this state of affairs. First, drama is a performance art and the main textual witness of a performance, the play-script, by its very nature can provide only a limited record of what actually happened on the stage on any one night during a play's run. Play-scripts, that is, tell us little about stage machinery or stage business – about the devices by means of which a performance achieves its effects and which include lighting (or its limitations), costume, props or scenery; and they give only a rudimentary indication of how lines should be delivered and the movement of actors on the stage space. They tell us nothing at all about timing, gesture, intonation or expression, nor whether lines in the text were cut, forgotten, or changed, or new ones added or improvised in particular performances. Of course, these problems are not unique to nineteenth-century theatre; they are confronted by all theatre historians studying drama before the age of audio-visual recording equipment. Moreover, historians often have a variety of other documents at their disposal, such as playbills, first-night reviews, theatre- and stage-managers' notebooks, actors' memoirs, and so on, in order to help them reconstruct the experience of contemporary theatre audiences.

The second kind of evidentiary problem, by contrast, *is* specific to the nineteenth century and is potentially more debilitating, for it centres on the ways in which play-scripts, the main source of evidence for performances, were preserved. As we noted in Chapter 2, drama was by no means as popular among aspiring nineteenth-century authors as fiction. The higher sums for the first three-quarters of the century to be earned from novel writing have often been held responsible for circumscribing the development of drama during this period. None the less, it remains the case that over the course of the nineteenth century thousands of new plays were produced. The theatre historian Allardyce Nicoll identified some 20,000 play-titles for the years between 1850 and 1900 alone; in other words, a similar order of numbers to that suggested by Sutherland for fiction. However, the majority of these dramatic works were not preserved in anything like an accessible or durable form because, unlike their eighteenth-century predecessors, or indeed contemporary novelists and poets, most nineteenth-century dramatists did not publish their play-texts in book form.

This state of affairs came about partly because of changes in nineteenth-century copyright legislation. In 1833 the 'Bulwer-Lytton' or 1833 Dramatic Copyright Act granted for the first time to dramatists 'rights of representation'; in simple terms, it enabled them to earn money from the performance of a work, as well as from its publication. A later Act of 1844 formally distinguished between publication and performance rights, in that the mechanisms for registering them – the assignment of copyright – were made separate legal processes. From 1844 assignment of publication copyright did not automatically entail assignment of performance rights. By the same token, the assignment of performance rights could take place in the absence of any published text of a play. Obtaining a performance licence required only that a single text, usually a manuscript, be lodged with the Lord Chamberlain's Examiner of Plays. The 1843 Theatre Regulation Act granted the holder of this office the absolute legal right to forbid the public performance of any play, or any part of it, which was deemed unsuitable (suitability generally being defined in terms of any discussion of the themes of politics and religion). Importantly, what were termed 'licensing copies' often bore only a passing resemblance to what was actually performed on the stage. This separation of performance and publication rights was in turn a response to the absence of international copyright agreements. After 1833 a dramatist who published a play-text ran the risk of losing performance fees from overseas productions of it; in the nineteenth century this effectively meant productions in North America. Over the course of the century North America became an increasingly important overseas market for British cultural goods and its value for British authors steadily increased. It is not surprising, then, that many nineteenth-century dramatists chose to forego publishing royalties in order to protect the potentially much larger fees that might come from overseas performance, which also included English-speaking colonies (later dominions) such as Canada and Australia.

A further reason why many nineteenth-century dramatists did not consider publishing their play-texts was because of the genres which were then in fashion. As we commented in Chapter 2, melodrama, burlesque (which developed out of early nineteenth-century extravaganzas), pantomime and farce were the staples of nineteenth-century theatre repertoires for most of the century; all rely heavily on non-spoken elements, particularly on music, dance, costume, spectacular stage effects, gesture and various forms of physical gags (such as slapstick). So for these genres there was not much actual 'text' – that is, written dialogue – to record. An individual reading such a text would have little idea of the work it became on the stage. The question of what constitutes a dramatic text, or the relationship between the text and the performed work, is always a complex one, but in the nineteenth century the reliance of many popular theatrical genres on non-textual elements of performance makes that relationship particularly elusive. Moreover, there were many performances, such as those in the cheapest form of entertainment, colloquially known as 'penny gaffs', as well as in private dwellings (such as the domestic home), for which no textual record whatsoever was made.

The main textual evidence for works like melodramas and pantomimes consists of either the single licensing copies now held in the Lord Chamberlain's Collection in the British Library (which are often in poor physical condition), or what were termed 'acting editions'. Acting editions were issued by specialist theatrical publishers, usually to capitalise on the interest generated by a play's first London run. Designed for use in the theatre (and particularly for amateur theatricals), they were cheaply produced. There is little evidence to suggest that they were bought in any numbers by the general reading public and today few copies survive outside specialist archives. Printed on flimsy paper in small type, and containing technical information about stage business, they are crudely functional documents. These characteristics of acting editions had a further consequence: they reinforced the marginal status of drama in literary culture in general by emphasising its ephemeral nature. As will be discussed in more detail in Chapter 7, in the nineteenth century the particular material embodiment of a literary work, such as the quality of its printing, paper and binding, was often taken to signify its artistic worth; and this was one reason why established authors like Thomas Hardy placed such a high value on expensive library or 'de luxe' editions of their works. Contemporary drama was rarely judged by nineteenth-century critics to be worthy of the name of literary art at all, a prejudice further underlined by the fact that what were widely considered the 'lowest' forms of literary fiction – Newgate and sensation novels – were often successfully adapted for the stage (examples include

A String of Pearls, mentioned earlier, Mrs Henry Wood's *East Lynne* and Braddon's *Lady Audley's Secret* (1861–62)).

For much of the nineteenth century theatrical publishing was dominated by specialist publishers such as the prolific Thomas Hailes Lacy, who, from 1848 to 1873, published some ninety-nine volumes in his Lacy's Acting Edition of Plays, just one among several series of dramatic works. Cheaply printed on poor-quality paper with small type, and equally cheaply priced (from sixpence to a penny per copy), they were for use by performers, specifically those in provincial and minor theatre companies, as well as by the enthusiastic amateur. A similar series, Duncombe's Acting Editions, produced between 1828 and 1852, has been described by one historian as having been designed 'for those whose grip on literacy was still quite loose' (Eliot 2007: 296). Other publications included Webster's Acting National Drama series, brought out by Chapman and Hall between 1837 and 1850, and Dicks' Standard Plays, an imprint which by 1892 was advertising some 1,200 titles.

The upshot of all these issues for the modern theatre historian is that there is no corpus of reliable nineteenth-century dramatic texts remotely comparable to that which exists for fiction or poetry, certainly for works produced up to 1890. Moreover, the unusual status of the evidence for nineteenth-century drama has played a crucial role in determining the kinds of narratives which historians have used to describe its formal development. Until relatively recently, accounts of drama have tended to use the following kind of argument.

For much of the century theatre was the property of mass audiences, and the forms which most nineteenth-century dramas took – those melodramas, pantomimes, farces and burlesques mentioned above – were appropriate to their principal function as mass entertainment. The basis of their appeal, which can be seen particularly clearly in melodrama, was a reliance on strong or exaggerated emotions (typically centring on intergenerational familial conflicts), stock characters and situations, broad comedy, an exciting plot which provided plenty of opportunities for the staging of spectacular events (such as grisly murders and train crashes, the latter being a particular favourite of melodramas), and a sentimental rewarding of virtue and punishment of vice. The role played by audience taste is well illustrated in the ways in which the sub-genre of farce developed through the century. Eighteenth-century farces typically centre on an age-old carnivalesque comedy of class reversal in which young upper- or middle-class lovers conspire with clever servants to dupe various figures of authority, such as parents and guardians. In the nineteenth century, however, and as Michael Booth argues, farce mutated into a shorter (generally a one- or two-act play), broader and less socially charged form of domestic comedy, one more firmly centred on the lives of the working and servant classes, and often set 'below stairs' – that is, in cellar kitchens or in attics (the latter were typically reserved as accommodation for live-in servants and were also the cheapest form of rented accommodation in boarding houses) (Booth 1991). Thus one of the most popular farces of the time, *Box and Cox* (1847), took as its subject a scheming landlady who rents the same room to a hatter and a printer, for their different patterns of employment – the former works by day, the latter by night – make them unaware of each other's presence until an unexpected holiday leads to a confrontation and fierce territorial dispute which is heightened by the discovery that each is also pledged to marry the same woman. In works such as this, the humour arises from the audience's sense of superiority over the hapless and terrified lower-class characters on stage as they attempt to extricate themselves from increasingly intense, but always trivial, domestic troubles.

There were some exceptions to this general pattern in the early decades of the century, where there are several notable experiments in 'high' genres such as verse and historical dramas as well as imitations of classical plays. These include works written in the Romantic period, such as Shelley's *The Cenci* (1819) and Wordsworth's *The Borderers* (composed in 1796–97 but not published until 1842); and by various women playwrights such as Elizabeth Inchbald (1753–1821), who edited a large collection of old and new plays entitled *The British Theatre* (1806–9) and whose *Lovers' Vows* (1798) adapted from *Das Kind der Liebe* by August von Kotzebue (1761–1819), was the subject of the controversial private theatricals in Austen's *Mansfield Park* (1814). Slightly later there were works like *Ion* (1836) by Thomas Noon Talfourd (1795–1854) and Robert Browning's *The Blot in the 'Scutcheon* (1843). However, few of these 'literary' plays were ever staged publicly, or if so, successfully. Although the 1836 Covent Garden production of *Ion* was something of a triumph, much more usual was the fate of the 1843 Drury Lane staging of *The Blot in the 'Scutcheon*, which ran for only three nights and led to an irreparable breakdown in the relationship between Browning and William Charles Macready (1793–1873), the actor-manager for whom it had been written. These kinds of works therefore had a relatively limited impact on the development of dramatic genres in general, certainly as they were performed.

The main reason underlying the dominance of theatrical forms designed for popular entertainment concerned the burgeoning urban populations brought about by the processes of industrialisation described in Chapter 2. These demographic shifts lay behind two periods of marked expansion in theatre construction: the first began in the late 1820s, a notable area of growth being in the East End of London, the population of which, centred on the expanding East London docks, was mainly working-class. By the 1840s, however, a general economic recession forced many of these 'minor' establishments into bankruptcy and closure, and for two decades theatre building virtually ceased. In order to survive this downturn *all* theatres had to compete fiercely for audiences, generally by lowering prices and, as Michael Booth puts it, 'moving ... firmly in the direction of gratifying popular taste in melodrama, farce and spectacle entertainment' (Booth 1991: 7). Importantly, this process also affected 'major' theatres like Drury Lane and Covent Garden which, until the 1843 Theatre Regulation Act, had viewed themselves as superior to other entertainment venues principally because of the monopoly they had enjoyed on the performance of 'serious' genres like tragedy and because of their ability to attract better-educated and higher-paying audiences. Moreover, even after the economic upturn of the late 1860s had generated a second wave of theatre building and renovation, this time centred in London's West End and catering to a wealthier and predominantly middle-class constituency, establishments like Drury Lane continued to rely in part on the patronage of the lower middle and working classes (the latter group still made up four-fifths of London's population in the 1890s), and could ill afford to ignore their tastes completely. As a consequence, the values embodied in popular theatrical forms continued to influence the development of dramatic genres throughout the century, including those which, from the late 1860s, were directed at the increasingly fashionable West End audiences.

One example of this process can be seen in the development of the musical comedy, of which those written in the last quarter of the century by W. S. Gilbert (1836–1911) to music composed by Arthur Sullivan (1842–1900), and principally for performance at the Savoy theatre, are best known. The use of punning word play, parody and elements of topical humour, as well as elaborate choreography and extravagant costuming, owed much to earlier burlesques and extravaganzas, even though the plots were more complex and the settings more elaborate. *Patience* (1881), for example, satirised the Aesthetic Movement while the target of *Princess Ida* (1884) was Tennyson's pseudo-feminist poem *The Princess*, whose protagonist renounces marriage in order to found a university (though she is courted and eventually won by the son of a neighbouring king). A further example of the continuing influence of popular dramatic traditions can be seen in the sub-genre of the society comedy. A hybrid dramatic form, this time combining elements of traditional melodrama with a new realism in plot and character, it was developed initially by theatrical entrepreneurs such as Tom Robertson (1829–71) in the 1860s, and then by a series of highly successful commercial playwrights. At their most sophisticated, society comedies offered to the new middle-class audiences who were patronising the renovated theatres of London's West End plays which employed witty and urbane dialogue, fashionable settings (typically among the upper middle and aristocratic classes) and intricate plots (the devices of which were often borrowed from French drama). The resulting combination enabled contemporary manners and morals to be aired in a form that combined seriousness of purpose with a general endorsement of the audiences' values. A common theme (also to be found in late nineteenth-century fiction) was the idea of the 'woman with a past', a woman guilty of some form of sexual misdemeanour which, if exposed to public scrutiny, threatened the reputations of herself and family. In addition to Robertson, the most successful exploiters of this new genre were Henry Arthur Jones, who moved from writing largely conventional melodramas such as the enormously popular *The Silver King* (1882) to exploring more contentious contemporary sexual ethics and politics in works like *The Case of Rebellious Susan* (1894) and *Mrs Dane's Defence* (1900); Arthur Wing Pinero, who wrote successful farces as well as plays with more serious social themes such as *The Second Mrs Tanqueray* (1893); and Oscar Wilde, the writer who, with works like *The Importance of Being Earnest*, was responsible more than any other for ensuring that the popularity of the society comedy lasted into the twentieth century (several of his plays were revived in its first decade even though by then they were viewed as 'period' pieces).

Critical debate about this last group of works has generally centred on their politics rather than their form, and the extent to which they merely endorse the values of what are assumed to be their largely middle- and upper-class audiences. Although these plays foreground sexual double standards and gender discrimination, the social transgressors themselves, those women (or occasionally men) with 'pasts', are invariably punished. Usually they are forced into exile (this is the fate of both the 'fast' and repentant women with pasts in Wilde's *Lady Windermere's Fan* (1892), *A Woman of No Importance* (1893) and *An Ideal Husband* (1895)), or they conveniently die. Pinero's Paula Tanqueray kills herself when she realises that knowledge of her past may compromise her husband's and stepdaughter's love for her. In the case of Jones's 'rebellious' Susan, possible transgression is nipped in the bud virtually before it begins, as she is persuaded that the price which women must pay for assuming the same sexual freedom as men is simply too high.

One measure of the conservatism, both formal and ideological, of the commercial theatrical establishment at this time is often taken to be the early career of George Bernard Shaw, whose uncompromising treatment of issues such racketeering in *Widower's Houses* (1892) and prostitution in *Mrs Warren's Profession* meant that he failed to get his early plays publicly staged. He had to resort instead to limited performances at private theatre clubs for which a performance licence was not required, or to single copyright performances. Another yardstick is Continental drama; among dramatists writing for the nineteenth-century British stage there is little that compares with the kind of formal and thematic experimentation found in works by the Swedish August Strindberg (1849–1912) and Norwegian Henrik Ibsen (whose works were performed only at private theatres clubs in Britain) or by the Irish playwright J. M. Synge (1871–1909), whose famous *Riders to the Sea* was performed in 1904 and whose *Playboy of the Western World* caused a riot when it was staged in Dublin's Abbey Theatre in 1907. Comparisons between Synge and a fellow Irishman, Dion Boucicault (1820–90), who enjoyed many successes on the English stage, are particularly striking. Though he was only a generation older than Synge, Boucicault's three Irish dramas, *The Colleen Bawn* (1860), *Arrah-na-Pogue* (1864) and *The Shaugraun* (1874), seem to belong to a completely different theatrical milieu, with their predictable combination of sentimentality, comedy, fast-paced action and stereotyped stage Irish 'characters'. Moreover, even though Boucicault's works were considered dated by the late 1880s, it remains the case that attempts to depart radically from commercially proven formulas were few and far between, and those plays which do aim to startle in the manner of the work of Strindberg, Ibsen or Synge, such as Wilde's symbolist drama *Salome* (1893), partly written while he was in France, generally failed to gain a performance licence.

Finally, it may also be significant that unlike countries such as France (which was seen at the time as possessing a more innovative theatrical culture) Britain did not have a state-sponsored theatre comparable to the Comédie Française, one which might have lessened some of the commercial realities that bore down on playwrights and theatre managers alike. The economic realities of large nineteenth-century theatres, particularly in London, meant that managers could not afford to stage works which risked unpopularity with the audience: nineteenth-century theatre was primarily a business, one which involved substantial economic risk (Davis 2000). There are plenty of examples of spectacular failures, the best-known of which was perhaps George Alexander's production of Henry James's *Guy Domville* at the St James's Theatre in 1895, which left a gap in his repertoire which had to be quickly filled (in the event he persuaded a rival manager to sell him the rights to Wilde's *The Importance of Being Earnest*). That failure also killed off James's ambitions to succeed as a playwright. Arguments for the founding of a national theatre were rehearsed towards the end of the century (by Shaw among others), but they were vigorously resisted (and continued to be so until the 1960s), a situation which stands in sharp contrast to dramatic culture in Ireland. In 1899 similar concerns had led to the founding of the Irish Literary Theatre (later the Irish National Theatre Society) by W. B. Yeats, Lady Augusta Gregory (1852–1932) and Edward Martyn (1859–1923) in order to encourage the development of a more politically informed indigenous drama, a project which, with the 'Celtic Twilight' described above, was part of a larger attempt to establish a native tradition of Irish writing. Initially it was supported by private funds, largely through the patronage of Annie Horniman. Her wealth derived from the tea trade and she provided the new company with a permanent home when she funded the building of the Abbey Theatre in 1904; it was eventually granted a state subsidy in 1925 by the new government of an independent Irish Free State.

The apparent conservatism of the nineteenth-century British theatre, linked as it is to its populism and commercialism, helps to explain why for much of the twentieth century this period has played a marginal role in general histories of the theatre. As noted earlier, histories of form or style tend to put a premium on invention and experimentation; neither of these qualities, however, was particularly important to theatrical success in the nineteenth century. Rather the opposite: as Booth comments, most contemporary drama relied on familiarity and stereotyping, on delivering slight variations on a well-known brand, much like modern soap operas or spaghetti Westerns (Booth 1991: 155). This was a lesson that many dramatists learned early in their careers: it is salutatory to remember that Wilde's run of 'look-alike' West End successes, his four society comedies, was paralleled by a series of failed experiments in tragic genres, including *The Duchess of Padua* (1891) and the incomplete and unpublished *A Florentine Tragedy*, *The Cardinal of Avignon* and *La Sainte Courtisane*. Moreover, where theatrical novelty was demanded, it tended to centre on those areas of production for which there is little reliable record, such as the spectacular stage effects achieved by the ingenuity of nineteenth-century costumiers and set designers, or the pre-eminence of virtuoso individual performers. This last observation also reminds us why it is the work of late nineteenth-century dramatists which (until relatively recently) has dominated critical discussion. A crucial distinction between the careers of Pinero, Jones and Wilde and many of their predecessors lies in the fact that these three authors took advantage of the 1890 Chace Act to publish their main plays – generally those which had enjoyed successful West End runs – as books with literary publishing houses, and so made them accessible for literary evaluation (and eventual reprinting and restaging) in a way that was simply not possible for an unpublished text. W. S. Gilbert was one of the few dramatists before 1890 who was willing to run the risk of copyright infringement by regularly publishing his plays and libretti as books. A consequence of all this is that to contest the conventional narrative of nineteenth-century drama as representing (to repeat Booth's terms) 'a vast sea of theatrical trivia and downright badness' enlightened only by a late 'golden age' of Shaw and Wilde has proved to be a particularly demanding task (Booth 1981: 1–2).

However, in the last two to three decades that process of questioning has begun, in part because archives of play-scripts have been made more accessible through a variety of digitisation projects. As a result, a number of what some theatre historians see as long-held prejudices about nineteenth-century drama are beginning to be challenged. One key area of enquiry has centred on women's involvement in the theatre and the way in which the narrative sketched above excludes or marginalises their achievements in a manner quite distinct from female contributions to poetry or fiction. Feminist theatre historians have noted that although there is evidence that some women did find it difficult to succeed in what was generally a male-dominated world, this does not mean that women had no role at all to play (Scullion 1996; Gardner and Rutherford 1992). The career of the American actress and writer Elizabeth Robins (1862–1952), who came to London in 1888, is probably the best-known exception (Powell 1997). If attention is shifted away from publication as the main measure of a playwright's achievement, then women become more visible. For example, Ellen Donkin has suggested that figures like Eliza Vestris (1797–1856) and Céline Céleste (1810–82) although never writing a word for public consumption, none the less made a major contribution to dramatic authorship in their collaborative participation in the spectacular elements so crucial to the staging of nineteenth-century extravaganzas. In a similar manner Tracy C. Davis has drawn attention to the numbers of women playwrights who 'plied their craft within homes and schools' – in other words, women whose notion of dramatic authorship happened to embrace a more 'inclusive and diverse model of sociability' than their more commercially orientated male contemporaries such as Pinero or Wilde (Davis and Donkin 1999: 19).

More secure evidence for female achievement in the theatre comes from the numbers of women who pursued long and lucrative careers in theatre management, either alone or in partnership with men. Examples include the actress and dancer Sarah Lane (1822–99), popularly known as the 'Queen of Hoxton', who took over the management of the Britannia Theatre in 1871 (a post she held until her death), or the partnership of Squire Bancroft (1841–1926) and his wife, Marie Wilton (1839–1921), who made their names initially through their patronage of Tom Robertson, or the collaboration of Henry Irving (1838–1905) and the actress Ellen Terry (1847–1928), who co-managed the Lyceum Theatre during Irving's tenancy from 1878 to 1902. Other actresses, such as Lily Langtry (1853–1926), became sufficiently eminent to be able to mount their own productions – Langtry's 1890 production of *Antony and Cleopatra* at the Princess's Theatre was noted for its lavishness and expense. The society hostess Lady Archibald Campbell (1846–1923) was viewed as an important pioneer in the production of pastoral plays in England, staging innovative (and sometimes open-air) amateur productions with her 'Pastoral Players'. The involvement of women from a range of social classes in all aspects of the theatre, from composing, to acting, to producing, to theatre management, also helps to give the lie to the impression common in the fiction of the time – from Austen's *Mansfield Park* to James's *The Tragic Muse* – that the theatre was no place for respectable women, and that actresses were little more than prostitutes (Davis 1991). As the century progressed, and as some theatres (certainly in the West End) attracted increasingly wealthy audiences, so the theatrical profession itself began to gain in status (Stephens 1992), and there are examples of male actor-managers, such as George Alexander (1858–1937) or Henry Irving, moving with relative ease within high-society circles, and some actors, notably Lily Langtry and Sarah Bernhardt (1844–1923), became part of what we would now call a celebrity culture, with their lives widely reported in the contemporary press alongside those of royalty (indeed Lily Langtry became the mistress of a future king, Edward VII, a position which gave her status and power, if not real respectability).

A second widely held prejudice, one which has also undergone considerable revision, is the notion that nineteenth-century theatre, as Booth caustically puts it, climbed 'slowly out of a swamp of mob-rule and working-class domination in the earlier part of the century to reach an eminence of profound Victorian decorum and middle-class and fashionable patronage of the theatre' (Booth 1991: 9). Detailed studies of individual theatrical establishments have revealed that throughout the century audiences were considerably more mixed than this schematised opposition would suggest, and that particular auditoria often catered to local populations which in turn could cut across simple class categorisation. Certainly there is evidence that members of the middle and upper classes regularly attended music halls and that West End theatres could in turn attract members of the working classes to their cheaper seats. There is also the complex problem presented by provincial audiences: with the advent of cheap rail fares, all theatres attracted an audience prepared to travel, as well as those from nearby. These details make it very difficult to arrive at secure generalisations about the composition and taste of nineteenth-century theatre audiences, and therefore to assess the politics of particular works. Here some of the most contentious areas of critical debate have centred on what some critics have argued was the subversive potential of dramatic genres, including melodrama, traditionally dismissed for sentimentality or conservatism (Hadley 1995). Recent research into pantomime, for example, has demonstrated that elements of their topical humour could often be sharply satirical, touching on issues of intense local political interest (Sullivan 2011).

A third and related area of research has focused on provincial and regional theatre, notably in Bristol and in Midlands towns, such as Birmingham and Nottingham, in an attempt to overcome the overwhelmingly London-centred bias of much nineteenth-century theatre history (Barker 1974; Foulkes 1994). In a similar manner, other historians have argued for a widening of our concept of theatrical culture to include performances which took place outside conventional theatre buildings, such as portable or booth theatres set up on an ad hoc basis at local fairs by troupes of strolling players, as well as travelling circuses, public lectures, freak shows and various kinds of domestic entertainment. This research draws attention to the considerable variety of nineteenth-century performance art, as well as the need to pay attention to the potential for innovation and experiment *within* established dramatic genres, as theatre managers competed with each other to attract audiences. On the other hand, however, any emphasis on diversity and localism tends inevitably to marginalise questions of form and style, as attention is concentrated on exhibiting the uniqueness of particular theatrical events. And here we can see the tendency of theatre history, like the history of literary fiction, to transform itself into a kind of cultural history in which the main concern is to understand nineteenth-century drama as part of a complex and geographically specific social milieu, rather than to make value judgements about those works which have influenced later theatrical developments or which possess a sustained relevance for modern audiences.

Non-fictional prose

The category of non-fictional prose is something – to use Henry James's phrase – of a 'loose baggy monster', one designed to capture those genres of writing which are judged to have literary merit – that is, in which issues of style and form are foregrounded – but which do not fall into the more familiar genres of poetry, fiction or drama. Of these, the nineteenth-century critical essay has commanded most attention, in part because it was a staple element of the review-based periodical and magazine culture. This culture included titles such as the *Edinburgh Review* (founded in 1802), *Quarterly Review* (founded in 1809), *Blackwood's Edinburgh Magazine* (founded in 1817) and *Westminster*

Review (founded in 1824), and together these made up much nineteenth-century reading matter. Many poets and novelists also wrote essays, using the form to comment not just on literary matters but also on topics like religion, history, philosophy, art, science and contemporary politics. The review or review-essay typically provided an open-ended opportunity to discuss issues beyond the work or event which was ostensibly its occasion; and in the early decades of the century the practice of 'bellelettrism', which centred on the cultivation of a faculty of discrimination in order to distinguish good writing from bad, formed an important part of literary culture. This close connection between essay writing and the medium in which it flourished is significant, because disagreements among modern historians over the nature of periodical culture have played a key role in shaping the canon of non-fictional prose.

Historians have conventionally located the development of the essay in early eighteenth-century literary culture and the growth of the periodical press. For Jürgen Habermas these processes represent a form of democratisation whereby critical debate moved into a newly created 'public sphere' and as a consequence it became a key element in the intellectual freedom popularly associated with the Enlightenment (Habermas 1989). Other critics, however, have drawn attention to an orthodoxy to be found in the essays which formed the backbone of papers like *The Tatler* (1709–11), *The Spectator* (1711–12, revived 1714) and later Samuel Johnson's *The Idler* (which ran from April 1758 to April 1760) and *The Rambler* (March 1750–March 1752), one which aimed to set standards in manners, morals and matters of literary and artistic taste. Such an ambition can be seen, at least in part, as motivated by anxieties about an expanding public sphere in which a dramatic growth in print culture (over the course of the eighteenth century numbers of titles published annually more than doubled, from 21,000 in the 1720s to 56,000 in the 1790s) appeared to be undermining established forms of authority (Raven 1992). In this view, both the critical essay and the medium which fostered it – the literary magazine – are as much forces of reaction as of liberation.

The tensions between these differing views of the periodical press have also informed historians' understanding of nineteenth-century non-fictional prose. For example, some have emphasised the partisan nature of nineteenth-century periodicals (the *Edinburgh Review*, *Quarterly Review*, *Blackwood's Edinburgh Magazine* and *Westminster Review* all had strong party-political affiliations, reinforced by a powerful editorial control), and the consequent inability of individual essayists, who typically wrote anonymously or under pseudonyms, to express their opinions freely. In this practice, the views of the writer were affiliated to those of the title for which they wrote. By the middle decades of the century there is evidence of a growing concern about the politicisation of intellectual debate in the periodical press, to the extent that the *Fortnightly Review*, established in 1865, announced itself as an 'organ for the unbiased expression of many and various minds', an ambition which it argued would be guaranteed by the use of signed articles (a practice subsequently adopted by rival publications such as the *Contemporary Review*, *Nineteenth Century* and

National Review). Historians holding to this view of the periodical press and concerned with the development of critical writing in the nineteenth century typically concentrate on the relatively small number of authors, such as William Hazlitt, Charles Lamb (1775–1834), Thomas Carlyle, John Stuart Mill, Thomas de Quincey, Matthew Arnold, Walter Pater and Oscar Wilde, who collected their critical writings in books and thereby (it is assumed) had the opportunity, through revision, to overcome the censoring hand of the periodical editor, as well as the tendency towards slipshod writing that pressures of time inevitably brought. What matters in this argument is the way in which book publication is alleged to exhibit better the singularity of the critical voice. Reading a collection of essays gives a more concentrated sense of, or places one in a better position to make judgements about, what is peculiar to an author's rhetoric and opinions, and so distinguishes lasting achievement from what is seen as merely occasional and topical.

Discussions of the essays of William Hazlitt, reprinted in volumes such as *The Round Table* (1817) (a collection co-written with Leigh Hunt (1784–1859)), *Lectures on the English Poets* (1818), *Table-Talk* (1821–22) and *The Spirit of the Age* (1825), often comment on their forceful combination of personal commitment (typically to the radical side of an argument) and idiosyncrasy, by which the writer is constructing himself (and in the early decades of the century they were mainly men) as a personality. As Virginia Woolf cogently put it in her essay on Hazlitt in the *Common Reader, Second Series* (1932): 'His essays are emphatically himself. He has no reticence and he has no shame … So thin is the veil of the essay as Hazlitt wore it, his very look comes before us.' Moreover, for Woolf, just as distinctive as his opinions was Hazlitt's style; it captured the reader's attention by means of a combination of twists and turns in the argument and frequent bursts of epigrammatic wit, such as the evocative title of his trenchant denunciation of the forces of reaction, 'Man is a Toad-Eating Animal' (1819). Hazlitt's contemporary, Charles Lamb, was also well known for his critical writing (although he also tried his hand at poetry and drama), and in particular for his *Specimens of English Dramatic Poets* (1808), which championed what were then little-known Elizabethan and Jacobean dramatists, and his regular and pseudonymous contributions to the *London Magazine*, later collected as *Essays of Elia* (1823) and *Last Essays of Elia* (1833). The latter pieces are also notable for their highly wrought, almost quaint style, which Walter Pater later characterised in his essay on Lamb republished in *Appreciations* (1889) as 'delicate, refining, daintily epicurean'. None of these terms is appropriate to describing the no less singular style of the self-taught Thomas Carlyle, which was marked by an outspokenness to rival that of Hazlitt (although from a trenchantly Tory, rather than Radical, point of view). Carlyle's apocalyptic rhetoric, full of neologisms, archaisms and eccentricities of punctuation, today seems almost unreadable. Yet works like *Chartism* (1839), *On Heroes, Hero-Worship and the Heroic in History* (1841), *Past and Present* (1843) and *Latter-day Pamphlets* (1850) earned Carlyle the epithet 'the Sage of Chelsea'. In his biography of Carlyle, which appeared between 1882 and

1884, the historian James Anthony Froude (1818–94) claimed that Carlyle's voice was 'to the young generation of Englishmen like the sound of "ten thousand trumpets" in their ears'.

The note sounded by Matthew Arnold, Carlyle's heir apparent as chief commentator on the country's social ills, was certainly less discordant. His appeal, as Amanda Anderson describes it, was to 'an ideal of temperament or character, whose key attributes bespeak … impartiality, tact, moderation, measure, balance, flexibility, detachment, objectivity, composure' (Anderson 2001: 115). However, other modern critics have complained that Arnold wins his arguments more by force of rhetoric than by logic. In collections such as *Essays in Criticism* (1865) and *Culture and Anarchy*, which, unlike Carlyle's works, are still relatively widely read, we find ourselves in the company of a mind, as Stefan Collini puts it, 'of such balance and sympathy that we come, really without noticing it, to see experience in his terms' (Collini 1988: 1). The major difficulty, however, for many modern critics is that those 'terms' have been judged to be deeply conservative and often contradictory.

Arnold disapproved of all forms of sectarianism, particularly those which he saw to have been promoted by contemporary religious and class interests; of these the most powerfully divisive were those of the Non-Conformists or Dissenters, who defined themselves in terms of their opposition to the Anglican Church, a position which, in Arnold's view, automatically curtailed their ability to make reasoned and reasonable judgements because it meant that their opinions were one-sided. His solution to the social divisions produced by biased judgement, what he described as the forces of 'anarchy', was both normative and elitist. It was the empowering of a secular cultural elite which would naturally discern, and consequently command assent for, 'the best that is thought and known', when the definition of 'best' was a given of his argument. Contrary to the tenor of so much modern political debate, Arnold was generally suspicious of articulations of 'difference', equating regionalism with provincialism and parochialism. An admirer of contemporary French intellectual culture, he was critical of the insular and philistine tendencies of the English (rather than the British) and argued trenchantly for an education that embraced Continental literature and philosophy. For Arnold, wide and what he terms 'disinterested' reading was the most appropriate way to discover that realm of absolute value which would provide a unifying force to counteract the 'centrifugal' tendencies of modern life. This concentration on the forces of cohesion, on what unified a nation, in turn made him oddly untroubled about the potentially coercive powers of the state, and in this his views differed from those expressed by many contemporary novelists, such as Dickens, as well the critic and philosopher John Stuart Mill. Along with many mid-century writers Mill, in *On Liberty* (1861), was deeply concerned about state power, and sought to define the limits of state control in order to protect the liberty of the individual. Mill's ideas in turn can be seen as the beginnings of a concern with the expression of difference which, in a suitably modern form, was taken up by his and Arnold's immediate successors, Walter Pater and Oscar Wilde.

Pater's best-known critical work, *Studies in the History of the Renaissance* (1873), announces its ambitions by contesting the terms of Arnold's most famous critical statement:

> 'To see the object as in itself it really is,' has been justly said to be the aim of all true criticism whatever; and in aesthetic criticism the first step towards seeing one's object as it really is, is to know one's impression as it really is, to discriminate it, to realise it distinctly.

Pater's aesthetic impressionism, which valorises subjectivity and therefore the particularity of experience, transformed Arnold's normative aesthetic into what Pater's detractors viewed as a dangerous form of antinomianism, one likely to provoke exactly the sort of cultural disintegration that Arnold so feared. The hostility which greeted the publication of *The Renaissance* and his fear for his reputation at Oxford led Pater to withdraw the conclusion when he republished it in 1876. In his dialogic essay 'The Critic as Artist', which was revised and reprinted in *Intentions* (1891), Oscar Wilde also took issue with Arnold, although on this occasion turning his predecessor's famous injunction completely on its head by suggesting that:

> The highest criticism, then, is more creative than creation, and the primary aim of the critic is to see the object as in itself it really is not.

For Arnold the 'function of criticism' was to provide the intellectual materials or 'best' ideas with which artists and writers work; for Wilde, criticism became an end in itself, one whose unique value resided (as it seemed to do for Pater) in its capacity to generate an appreciation of variety, rather than delineating essential values. The significance of Pater's and Wilde's reassessment of Arnold will be discussed more fully in Chapter 4 in relation to the Aesthetic Movement. Here it is worth drawing attention to the distinctive rhetoric of both authors, which has also contributed to their critical reputations. Pater's dense, allusive and highly attenuated prose style, in which any final meaning is constantly deferred by a string of qualifying or appositional clauses and sub-clauses, was celebrated at the time, and has since been cited as an important influence on some modernist writers, notably Woolf. His essay 'Style', republished in *Appreciations*, defined 'literary art' as 'the representation of such fact as connected with soul, of a specific personality, in its preferences, its volition and power'. Insofar as the only appropriate measure of good writing was fidelity to personal experience, Pater appeared to oppose those conservative injunctions, cited earlier, concerning a 'noble English style'. Wilde's critical writing, too, is distinctive although for different reasons. What might be termed the Wildean style combines two apparently contradictory qualities: a rambling narrative structure with a tendency towards a self-conscious exhibition of allusions and citations which is interspersed with pithy one-liners (these were often italicised for emphasis when the essays were first published in periodicals). The last habit, however, did not originate with Wilde: his contemporary Augustine Birrell (1850–1933) was also known for his ability to generate memorable epigrams and aphorisms, notably in his first collection of critical essays, *Obiter Dicta* (1884).

That men dominate this list of critical voices is significant. Of course there were women essayists in the nineteenth century; Mary Ward, for example, produced a significant output of non-fictional prose (although it is rarely read today), and so too did Vernon Lee. However it was that group of culturally influential men, often called the Victorian 'sages', who because of their confidence in addressing a wide range of topics virtually colonised the form (Holloway 1953; Orel 1984). Indeed the term 'sage' is so strongly gendered that the *Oxford English Dictionary* defines it as 'a profoundly wise man', and until relatively recently (Morgan 1990; Mermin 1993) this virtually excluded consideration of female contributions to the genre. Excluded too are those many voices who never published their essays as books. Historians such as Laurel Brake and Joanne Shattock, working with assumptions similar to those which underlie Habermas's research, have claimed that the nineteenth-century periodical press possessed a vibrancy and immediacy not present in other kinds of print culture (such as books), and that it is therefore to periodical publications, and particularly critical essays published in journals and magazines, that the historian should turn in order to appreciate fully the variety and complexity of nineteenth-century critical writing. Indeed Brake goes further than this, arguing that the formal development of the essay in the nineteenth century was dependent on periodical rather than book culture (Brake 1994, 2001; Shattock and Wolff 1982). It should be obvious that the historian persuaded by Brake's arguments will have before her a much larger body of evidence to consider, one that may be as daunting in terms of quantity as that confronted by the historian of fiction. For example, it may include the large body of criticism to be found in working-class magazines and journals (Murphy 1994). More particularly it raises questions about how the historian should select evidence, and therefore assess the representative qualities of particular pieces.

A further complicating factor is the attitude of nineteenth-century critics towards their craft. As noted in Chapter 2, anxieties about the growth of a mass reading public and what was seen as a concomitant decline in standards of literary taste recur throughout nineteenth-century culture, and during this period, too, the critical essay itself becomes an important site of debate about literary standards because, as the century progressed, some essayists grew increasingly anxious that their voices were no longer being listened to. Moreover, they typically attributed that decline in authority to the very medium – the periodical press – which in the previous century had been responsible for establishing the popularity of the essay as a form. According to Arnold in *Culture and Anarchy*, the problem was the 'low' standards of taste typically encountered in the 'mass of newspapers' and the inability of the general reading public to appreciate that 'the value of these organs is relative to their being nearer a certain ideal centre of correct information, taste, and intelligence, or farther away from it' (for the purposes of comparison Arnold cited the *Saturday Review* as 'a kind of organ of reason' and the *British Banner* as its opposite). In an 1882 piece entitled 'The Decay of Criticism', published in the *Fortnightly Review*, the otherwise populist writer Grant Allen also complained about the general public's lack of appreciation for critical writing, evidence for which could be found in contemporary publishers' increasing unwillingness to produce books of essays because they were, as the house of Macmillan put it, no longer 'remunerative'. Allen (like Arnold) blamed this falling away of his readership on what he referred to as the 'decadence of newspaper criticism' – that is, a style of popular journalism which had developed over the second half of the century and which he judged to be 'very empirical and hasty in character' and 'absurdly inadequate for anything like real criticism'.

Although some modern critics might view Allen's complaints as little more that a form of intellectual self-justification, the question he raises about the quality of critical writing in the nineteenth century is not quite so easily dismissed, for it rehearses a form of that tension between description and evaluation noted earlier in relation to histories of fiction and drama. Put simply, the historian of nineteenth-century non-fictional prose is confronted with what by now should be a familiar dilemma: should her ambition be to document the variety of critical writing which took place over the course of the century in order to reflect the diversity of intellectual debate; or should she attempt to isolate (and defend) those works whose formal, stylistic and intellectual qualities are judged to possess lasting value. One powerful argument made by historians of periodical culture is that judgements about the originality of the views expressed in critical essays can be skewed if they are viewed in the relative isolation encouraged by book publication. Wilde's essay 'The Soul of Man Under Socialism', which was republished as a book in 1896, is a case in point: when this essay is set against other contemporary periodical articles on the same subject (by authors less well known than Wilde), his paradoxical attempt to combine socialism and individualism appears much less novel. Moreover, the same point holds true for other kinds of comparisons. For example, attention to the nineteenth-century periodical press has also revealed close affinities between popular journalism and the sensational aspects of contemporary fiction writing, and these in turn are a reminder that what might seem to be simply 'escapist' literature was not necessarily as removed from everyday life as we might think.

The critical essay is not the only form of non-fictional prose to have attracted the attention of literary critics and historians. The modern category of 'life-writing', which encompasses biography, autobiography, diaries, memoirs and reminiscences (typically anecdotes of the rich and famous) as well as published letters and travelogues, was also popular in the nineteenth century and formed a significant part of publishing culture (Landow 1979; Fleishman 1983; Peterson 1986; Machann 1994). Moreover, in contrast to the writing of criticism, the contributions of women to these genres (especially what the *Quarterly Review* referred to in 1845 as 'Lady Travellers', who had been newly empowered by improvements in transport) was acknowledged and sometimes celebrated (Sanders 1989). Modern critics can thus make fruitful comparisons between, say, the Africa of David Livingstone and that to be found in *Travels in West Africa* (1897) by Mary Kingsley (1862–1900), or compare Dickens's America with that in *The Englishwoman in America* (1856) and *A Lady's Life in the Rocky Mountains* (1879) by Isabella Bird (1831–1904). Working-class lives, too, occasionally appeared in print, including *Early Days* (1849) by Samuel Bamford (1788–1872). And there are many surviving commonplace books and diaries, such as that kept from 1870 until his death by the Revd Francis Kilvert (1840–79), in which he lovingly described the remote region of the Welsh borders where he lived and worked. Kilvert's record keeping was private and his diaries were never made public in the course of nineteenth century; none the less works like his provide valuable insights into the everyday lives of ordinary individuals drawn from a range of occupations (Burnett 1974, 1982; Vincent 1981; Gagnier 1991).

The rich variety of life-writing in the nineteenth century has also made possible another claim: although none of the genres mentioned above had its origins in nineteenth-century literary culture, it can plausibly be argued that *as a category* life-writing achieved a new significance in this period, and this was for reasons – intellectual, social and cultural – which are unique to the nineteenth century: the development, via a mass reading public, of a substantial market for such writing, and particularly for literary biography. Writers who could generate sales in the tens (and later hundreds) of thousands of copies achieved a cultural prominence that inevitably made them appear exceptional, and this in turn equally inevitably generated an interest, among their readers, in their personal lives. Moreover, publishers themselves were quick to capitalise on this virtuous circle, recognising that a well-written life might not only be a seller in its own right, but also the publicity it generated for its subject could in turn boost sales of his or her works. A case in point is Elizabeth Gaskell's biography of Charlotte Brontë, which helped to create the Brontë myth. Also important in explaining the rise of life-writing in the nineteenth century is the prominence of the ideologies of individualism, most famously propagandised in Samuel Smiles's 'self-help' manuals, which made exemplary lives – especially of writers, artists and statesmen and, for Smiles, engineers like James Watt (1736–1819) and George Stephenson – instructive reading. Historians such as Thomas Carlyle and later Charles Kingsley (in his 1860 inaugural lecture as Professor of Modern History at the University of Cambridge) had also emphasised the role of human agency – or the actions of what Kingsley termed 'great' individuals – in historical causation, and in the process had rejected the proposition, associated with some elements of contemporary French historiography, that social change was governed by abstract laws of development. The success of Macmillan's English Men of Letters edited by John Morley (1838–1923) and the Great Writers Series produced by the Edinburgh publisher Walter Scott are testimony to the strength of this interest in the lives and achievements of what were then considered notable individuals. So, too, is the *Dictionary of National Biography*, set up in

1882 by the publisher George Smith originally under the editorship of Leslie Stephen (1832–1904) (the father of Virginia Woolf) and still available in a revised form today.

The notion of the 'exemplary life' also helps to explain some of the characteristics of what was perhaps the most popular form of life-writing at the time: biography and autobiography. Works such as Newman's *Apologia Pro Vita Sua*, John Stuart Mill's *Autobiography* (1873), Harriet Martineau's *An Autobiographical Memoir* (1877), Ruskin's *Praeterita* (incomplete) and Margaret Oliphant's *Autobiography and Letters* (1899) all recount lives defined by attempts (not always successful) to overcome deep emotional and spiritual struggles. Nineteenth-century biographies, particularly of literary figures, often mapped a similar terrain; the seven-volume *Memoirs of the Life of Sir Walter Scott* by John Gibson Lockhart rewrote Scott's humiliating bankruptcy as a heroic but tragic attempt to regain his honour. The biography of Dickens by his friend and literary executor John Forster (1812–76) was also less than candid (particularly with regard to its subject's sexual life), in order to develop a suitably moralised model of literary endeavour. Froude's life of Carlyle, mentioned earlier, together with the editions he published of Carlyle's *Reminiscences* (1881) and the *Letters and Memorials* (1883) of his wife, Jane Welsh Carlyle (1801–66), provoked considerable controversy because they hinted at a marriage which, emotionally and sexually, was far from perfect.

The overt self-fashioning that characterises these kinds of life-writing, and which also extends to letters and diaries (which were typically heavily edited before being published), means that their value to the modern reader lies less in self-disclosure than in their form – that is, in the methods used in their construction, in the tropes and narrative strategies by which a particular life is given shape, and which can usefully be compared to those found in fictional genres such as the *bildungsroman*. Nineteenth-century critics were not unaware of the contrived nature of genres which purported to be based on fact. The publication in 1874 of *Boswelliana*: *The Commonplace Book of James Boswell* by Charles Rogers (1825–90) revealed to a later generation the extent to which Boswell's *Life of Samuel Johnson* (1791), celebrated by early nineteenth-century critics for its accuracy, was largely the product of artifice and invention. Moreover, when hitherto private documents, such as the love letters of John Keats, did come into the public domain (financial difficulties led the descendants of Fanny Brawne to auction them at Sotheby's in 1886), some lamented personal disclosures as amounting to an unsavoury intrusion of privacy. As Oscar Wilde put it, 'I think they love not art, | Who break the crystal of a poet's heart.' The difficulty was that, once aroused, the general public's appetite for knowledge about the private lives of the great and the good was not easily satisfied, and in the later decades of the century certain kinds of life-writing, particularly literary biography, provoked cultural anxiety, on account of the fact that the lives of some individuals seemed to trade on values uncomfortably close to those associated with what Arnold termed 'low' journalism.

Of course, for figures such as Wilde who thrived on self-publicity, and who often strove to be the architect of their own celebrity, objecting to a contemporary interest in writers' private lives may seem disingenuous. None the less Wilde's comments help to bring to the fore an important distinction between the literary and historical value of life-writing, one which, as has been noted earlier, an attention to questions of form and style helps to clarify. This can be seen most easily perhaps in letters. There is a tradition, which pre-dates the nineteenth century, of the semi-public letter, where apparently private correspondence, such as the letters of Lord Chesterfield (1694–1773) to his son, were perceived on publication to possess a wider social and moral function because of their general educative context. Other forms of correspondence were admired for their 'artfulness' – that they exemplified a fine style. Moreover, it seems clear that some nineteenth-century letter writers habitually preserved their correspondence, and critics, novelists and poets possibly did so with an eye to future publication; or rather, the activity of letter writing may in itself have been, on occasions, a self-conscious and semi-public literary exercise. Letters, such as those by Matthew Arnold, were often read aloud to, or passed around, family members and friends. It is also worth noting that some writers or their descendants, wary of the judgements of posterity, took care to destroy correspondence and diaries: exemplary cases are the personal documents of Jane Austen and Walter Pater. The same holds true for diaries: some kinds of travel writing took the form of diary entries. Keeping a diary or journal, in other words, was not necessarily conceived of as an entirely private enterprise. These observations in turn should make the critic cautious about the evidentiary status of *all* forms of life-writing, published and unpublished, and alert, too, to the possibility that when it is at its most self-consciously literary, nineteenth-century life-writing may also be at its least valuable historically. In other words, and like the reminiscences of modern political figures, nineteenth-century life-writing should perhaps be valued for its qualities of invention.

Conclusion

- With the exception of Romantic-period writing, general literary histories have not usually singled out the nineteenth century for its formal or stylistic innovation – a circumstance which owes much to the influence of Modernist judgements about their literary predecessors.
- The realist novel has often been taken as the dominant literary form in the nineteenth century, with poetic and dramatic genres receiving correspondingly less attention.
- Understanding generic development becomes more complex as the nineteenth-century literary canon expands: in fiction, poetry and non-fictional prose it is often the sheer variety of forms and styles – including the invention of hybrid genres and the blurred relationship between various kinds of sub-genres (such as realist and sensation fiction) – which is most striking.

- The tension between description and evaluation is particularly acute in histories of nineteenth-century form and style, in the sense that the historian must typically choose between, on the one hand, documenting the diversity of literary forms, and on the other, isolating those works whose formal and stylistic features are judged to possess lasting value, or to have influenced future literary works.

4 Nineteenth-century literary movements

Overview

The identification of literary movements is a popular way of marking out significant moments in literary culture; it has the consequence of giving literary history shape and direction. A history of literary movements is, by definition, highly selective; and it begs the question of what sorts of literary practices can be said to constitute a movement? This chapter begins by distinguishing between two basic ways of defining literary movements; it also makes a distinction between literary movements and literary schools. It then proceeds to discuss what are generally agreed to be the four main British literary movements of the nineteenth century: Pre-Raphaelitism, Aestheticism, Decadence and Symbolism. None of these movements was confined solely (nor even principally) to literary culture, and all argued for a strong connection between the literary and visual arts. Moreover, all of them placed a premium on poetry rather than prose, and in this respect they can all be seen, at least in part, as reacting against the taste for popular fiction which, as earlier chapters have observed, had come to dominate literary culture from the 1830s onwards.

Defining literary movements

Literary movements can be broadly categorised in terms of those which are 'self-defined', on the one hand, and those which are the product of definitions or categories devised by later historians, on the other. It is mainly the first kind of movement that will concern us in this chapter; we will concentrate on cases where there is evidence that a particular group of artists and writers publicly identified themselves, or were consistently identified by their contemporaries, as having a distinctive set of literary and artistic ambitions in common. Moreover, that evidence – which might, for example, include a written manifesto – typically points to a more formal declaration (or identification) of collective intent than the kinds of local collaborations often undertaken on an ad hoc basis by individual artists or writers, such as that of Robert Louis Stevenson and W. E. Henley in their jointly authored plays *Deacon Brodie* (1880) and *Admiral Guinea* (1884), or of Wordsworth's and Coleridge's *Lyrical Ballads*. Today, as in the nineteenth century, all four authors are better known for their single-authored works than they are for any of their collaborative projects.

A good example of the second, post-hoc definition of a literary movement, one already encountered in Chapters 1 and 3, is the classification 'Romanticism'. As we noted earlier, the concept of Romanticism, when it is used to mark out a particular moment or period in literary history, was largely an invention – and a continually contested one at that – of twentieth-century literary historians. As early as 1924 Arthur Lovejoy provocatively argued that 'the word "romantic" has come to mean so many things that, by itself, it means nothing' (Lovejoy 1924: 232). Of course as a technical term 'Romanticism' had been in use in literary culture from the eighteenth century onwards, and was most familiar from the writings of the German critic Friedrich von Schlegel (1772–1829), who had described the history of what he termed 'ancient' and 'modern' literature (*Geschichte der alten und neuen Literatur*) in terms of an opposition between Romanticism and Classicism. However, as Kenneth Daley has observed, British writers in the first half of the nineteenth century (in contrast to those in France and Germany) paid relatively little attention to Schlegel's ideas; certainly they never conceived of their *own* literature as Romantic in Schlegel's sense of the term (Daley 2001). 'Romanticism' did not begin to be used with any consistency to define contemporary English literature until the 1870s and 1880s, and even then there was no real agreement over its meaning and application. In the hands of conservative critics like William John Courthope it was identified with a dangerous liberalism, and was used in a largely derogatory sense to refer to what Daley describes as 'an excessive subjectivism, obscure subject matter, indefinite thought, and perverse occupation with style' (ibid.: 5) – qualities which were attributed to the work of contemporary writers like Walter Pater (rather than, say, Coleridge or Keats). Significantly, when Pater tried to deflect such criticism in his 1876 essay 'Romanticism' (later published as the 'Postscript' to *Appreciations* (1889)), he defined it modally, as Schlegel had done; it was not a phenomenon specific to contemporary life, but rather a 'spirit' which 'may be always traceable in excellent art … a product of special epochs … when men come to art and poetry, with a deep thirst for intellectual excitement, after a long ennui, or in reaction against the strain of outward, practical things'. In short, nineteenth-century commentators did not use the term Romanticism to refer to a historically specific literary movement in Britain, nor did they identify it with the same moment in literary history, nor with the same group of writers as subsequent modern critics have done.

A second useful distinction when considering how we might define literary movements is the relationship they have with literary schools, a number of which we have already described in earlier chapters. Nineteenth-century commentators would often identify schools of writing, and this was typically a way of classifying what were perceived as new trends in contemporary literary culture. Examples include the 'Lake School' (a term first used by Francis Jeffrey (1773–1850) in an 1817 review of Coleridge's *Biographia Literaria*, though the existence of such a school was later denied by Thomas de Quincey) and the 'Cockney

School' (used in the conservative *Blackwood's Magazine* also in 1817 to belittle the status and thus the literary ambitions of Leigh Hunt, Keats and William Hazlitt). Later in the century we find the 'Fleshly School' (used in 1871 by Robert Buchanan to criticise the sensuality of the poetry of Dante Gabriel Rossetti and Swinburne) and the 'Spasmodic School' (William Admonstoune Aytoun's term for the emotionally intense though verbose poetry of Sydney Dobell and Alexander Smith). The best-known schools of literary fiction are probably the 'Sensation School' (a term widely used in the 1860s to describe novels and dramas whose lurid plots and concern with extreme psychological states were viewed as a contrivance designed to elicit in their readers and audiences extravagant feelings), and the 'Kailyard School'. (Meaning 'cabbage patch', this term was a dismissive reference to a fashion in the late 1880s and early 1890s for what was viewed as an over-sentimental tradition of vernacular Scottish writing about small-town Scottish life by figures like J. M. Barrie.) Most of these terms were coined to critique and therefore marginalise writers who were understood to be exhibiting too great a difference from what nineteenth-century critics thought to be appropriate taste. To be identified with a particular school of writing, in this respect, was rarely positive; certainly it was quite different from the kind of propagandising 'self-identified' movements alluded to above.

A further, although less firm, distinction between literary schools and movements has to do with their perceived influence. Generally speaking, literary schools were viewed as local and short-lived phenomena; their apparent parochial qualities were often used as a means to marginalise them. However, a literary movement, as the term 'movement' itself suggests, tends to imply a more sustained and broader cultural impact. As we shall see, of the main literary movements which emerged over the course of the nineteenth century, none was limited solely to the sphere of literature, and all made explicit links between verbal and visual culture, particularly between poetry and painting. Moreover, what typically began as a highly specific literary or artistic manifesto linked to a discrete group of writers or artists tended to expand over a period of time into a more general stylistic influence, one whose effects could be perceived in a whole range of cultural media, from furniture to house decoration and clothing.

It is also worth noting that references in the nineteenth century to particular kinds of literary expression do not necessarily provide evidence for the existence of a literary movement. For example, when in 'The Decay of Lying' (1890) Oscar Wilde dismisses the contemporary tendency towards what he terms 'realism' in literary art, he does not have in mind anything so coherent as a literary movement. The writers against whom his speaker, Vivian, directs his satire in that dialogue are, to the modern eye, curiously eclectic, embracing such diverse novelists as Mary Ward (author of the popular religious novel *Robert Elsmere*), Robert Louis Stevenson – Vivian describes *Jekyll and Hyde* as 'like an experiment out of the *Lancet*' – Henry James and H. Rider Haggard. Here, as elsewhere in the dialogue, the force of Vivian's argument depends upon his yoking together of quite different sorts of works. A term like 'Naturalism' functioned in Britain in a similar manner, but with the complicating factor that here its use could be traced back to an actual literary movement, one that originated in France but which had no exact equivalent in Britain. Literary Naturalism was most closely associated with the attempt by the French novelist Emile Zola to apply to fictional representation the objectivity of positivist science, in the belief that human nature was subject to similar kinds of natural law. In practice, this ambition was typically achieved by taking middle- and lower-class lives as the subject-matter of fiction and documenting the minutiae of everyday living, particularly human appetites and instincts. Zola's twenty-volume Rougon-Macquart cycle (1871–93) – which its author described as 'l'histoire naturelle et sociale d'une famille' under France's Second Empire – centred on the actions through several generations of two branches of one family, recounting the ways in which their behaviour, which included drunkenness and sexual promiscuity, was conditioned by environmental and inherited characteristics.

In Britain the work of Zola was controversial, to the extent – as we noted in Chapter 2 – that the publisher of his novels in Britain was prosecuted and imprisoned on charges of obscenity. Zola, however, had his defenders, and of these the most vocal was George Moore, whose own *A Modern Lover* and *Esther Waters* were popularly viewed as 'Zolaesque' in both their subject-matter (premarital sex and illegitimacy) and the frankness with which these topics were treated. Much of Hardy's fiction and some of Gissing's early novels (such as *Workers in the Dawn* (1880), *The Unclassed* (1884), *Demos* (1886) and *The Nether World* (1889)), which are equally unsentimental in their treatment of 'ordinary' life, have also been viewed (by modern critics) as sharing some of the ambitions of Naturalism. However, these similarities both in style and in attitude towards what might constitute appropriate subject-matter for literary art do not on their own permit us to talk of a naturalist movement in late nineteenth-century Britain. Certainly there is little evidence of any *collective* ambition behind the work of Hardy and Gissing (although both men knew each other); and unlike Zola's Rougon-Macquart cycle, Moore's oeuvre is more varied than the label 'naturalist' would suggest – works like *Confessions of a Young Man* (1888) and *Mike Fletcher* (1889) are quite different, formally speaking, from *Esther Waters*.

Like 'Naturalism', the term 'Impressionism' is most familiar from nineteenth-century French culture; in particular it comes from its association with distinctive landscape art, produced by the habit of painting 'en plein-air', by a group of French artists – chiefly Claude Monet (1840–1926), Alfred Sisley (1839–99), Camille Pissarro (1831–1903) and Edgar Degas (1834–1917) – whose ambition was to record accurately the visual world in terms of the effects of light and colour. The first Impressionist exhibition was held in Paris in 1874. However, applications of the term in late nineteenth-century British culture were complicated and varied. In Britain Impressionism was a term used to describe both visual culture and literature; and the term 'impression' could derive from a variety of quite separate discourses, including (in Pater's criticism) that of contemporary psychology. Impressionism in literary culture in Britain was conflated, somewhat confusingly, with both realism and Romanticism (terms which, as we noted earlier, typically referred at this time to modern cultural trends). Wilde, again, provides a useful barometer of the complexity of opinion when, in an introduction to an 1882 collection of poetry by James Rennell Rodd (1858–1941), he talks of 'romantic poetry' as 'essentially the poetry of impressions ... in its choice of situation as opposed to subject; in its dealing with the exceptions rather than with the types of life; in its brief intensity'.

In the introduction to his monograph *The Symbolist Movement in Literature* (1899), Arthur Symons described the effects of literary Impressionism in a similar manner, although (and perhaps oddly to modern eyes) he associated it with 'Realism' and 'the age of material things in literature' when words 'did miracles in the exact representation of everything that visibly existed, exactly as it existed'. As an example, Symons cited the writings of the French Goncourt *frères* (the brothers Edmond and Jules (1822–98, 1830–70)), who transcribed the 'fugitive aspects of a world which existed only as a thing of flat spaces, and angles, and coloured movement'. In the 1880s reviewers consistently ran together Naturalism and Impressionism as terms of censure when they referred to literature and art which took the sordid and the ugly for their subject-matter. For example, an 1893 article by John Alfred Spender (1862–1942) in the *Westminster Gazette,* which Spender edited, discussed at length contemporary attitudes to what he termed the 'repulsive subject' of Degas's *L'Absinthe*. Significantly, neither Wilde nor Symons talks of an Impressionist *movement* in literature in Britain; it is rather that the term 'Impressionism' is used as a marker of a certain style which both associate with modernity. In their own work – in poems such as Wilde's 'Impressions: I. Les Silhouettes, II. La Fuite de la Lune' in *Poems* (1881) and Symons's 'Impression' published in the 1896 edition of his *Silhouettes* – literary Impressionism takes the form of short lyrics which evoke fleeting moods inspired by the colours and sounds of what are often urban landscapes, as well as on occasions (and with Wilde's 'Impressions de Théâtre') distinctive dramatic personalities. It needs to be emphasised, however, that in those same volumes Wilde and Symons also produced poems in quite different forms and genres, such as Wilde's 'Charmides' (also in *Poems* (1881)) and Symons's 'The Lover of the Queen of Sheba' (in *Images of Good and Evil* (1899)).

With these caveats in mind, we can move on to examine what we have suggested are the four main literary movements to have developed in Britain during the course of the nineteenth century: Pre-Raphaelitism, Aestheticism, Decadence and Symbolism. All of these movements occurred in the second half of the century; they coincided with the advent of mass literary publishing and mass taste, as well as a growth of public interest in the arts in general. As we noted in Chapter 2, that interest was largely a product of various government initiatives in art education, such as the founding of the National Gallery (whose new buildings in Trafalgar Square were completed in 1838) and the opening in 1857 of the Victoria and Albert Museum. By the second half of the century Britain had more art schools than any country in Europe, as well as what Bernard Denvir refers to as a 'multitude of institutions destined to improve the taste of adult members of the working classes and other sections of the population' (Denvir 1986: 1). These included Mechanics' Institutes, where influential critics such as John Ruskin and William Morris would often lecture, and which offered classes in architectural and mechanical drawing as well as various pictorial genres, such as life, floral and landscape painting. Popular interest in the arts was further stimulated by organisations like the Arundel Society (founded in 1848 to disseminate, via the new printing method of chromolithography, early Christian art) and a flood of new art magazines, many of which (like the *Art Journal*) attempted to educate their non-specialist readers. This enthusiasm for improving the artistic sensibilities and education of the British population, and particularly those of the middle and lower classes, inevitably made questions of taste central: increasing state sponsorship gave artistic culture a more prominent role in national life, but in the process the values of an artistic establishment – embodied for many in the traditionalism of the Royal Academy – inevitably began to seem normative to those who did not share them. It is in exactly this kind of climate, one where literary and artistic culture is expanding while being simultaneously subject to attempts to control it, that defining literary or artistic 'difference' became important; or rather, such definitions became a matter of *public* interest and debate. The nineteenth-century literary movements which we have referred to were all viewed as 'anti-establishment' in this sense; in some instances they were also criticised as anti-British, as being against the national interest, although 'anti-English' is the phrase most commonly used.

It may also be significant that the main literary works produced by the Pre-Raphaelites, Aesthetes, Decadents and Symbolists were in the genres of poetry and criticism, rather than in prose fiction – they were genres then considered to be a part of minority rather than mass taste. ('Aesthetic' novels like Pater's *Marius the Epicurean* or Moore's *Mike Fletcher* are generically anomalous and formally quite unlike the 'realist' fiction disparaged by Wilde.) It is also relevant that when they argued for an interrelationship between literature and visual media, the Aesthetes and Decadents typically chose examples of pictorial art which were esoteric or exotic; so they drew attention to the work of artists such as Gustave Moreau (1826–98) as well as various kinds of Chinese and Japanese art, all of which were not widely known in Britain. Here again it is tempting to see a self-conscious reaction against mass culture and the homogenising tendencies of mass taste.

A further feature of nineteenth-century literary movements is their tendency to merge into each other. As we will see, contemporary commentators sometimes conflated Pre-Raphaelitism with Aestheticism (to the extent that Dante Gabriel Rossetti was seen to be a member of both movements) and later, Aestheticism with Decadence and Symbolism. Along with this merging of one movement into another it is possible to trace a further, parallel process, one that can loosely be referred to as the 'commodification' of art and literary movements, a topic that will be discussed in more detail in Chapter 7. We noted above that a characteristic that distinguishes a literary movement from a school is the nature of its social impact – the tendency of its ambitions to become dispersed throughout a culture. In the case of Pre-Raphaelitism and Aestheticism this diffusion of ideals took the form of the transference of a particularised aesthetic to a variety of commonplace and mass-produced objects (such as furniture, soft furnishings and dress). In the process, ideas that in their original context may have been viewed as a protest *against* mainstream values became fashionable, absorbed into mass culture and thus trivialised. We can see this trivialisation at work in caricatures of Aesthetes in contemporary magazines like *Punch*; here satire becomes a way of diffusing the seriousness and thus the threat of the Aesthetic Movement's ambitions. As general theorists of the avant-garde have noted, over a period of time avant-garde art tends to be enlisted by the culture industry, in the sense that avant-garde protests eventually become just another commodity in the art market: 'difference', that is, becomes something that can be marketed and so eventually mass produced. The Pre-Raphaelites, Aesthetes, Decadents and Symbolists, although typically beginning their careers in explicit opposition to the mass taste associated with a nascent consumer culture, often ended by becoming deeply implicated in it.

Pre-Raphaelitism

The Pre-Raphaelites have been described as the first official artistic 'opposition' in nineteenth-century Britain. Prior to their campaign, objections to the entrenched authority of the Royal Academy had taken place only at a local and individual level. Led initially by Dante Gabriel Rossetti and the painters John Everett Millais (1829–96) and William Holman Hunt (1827–1910), and later joined by the poet and sculptor Thomas Woolner (1825–92), art critic Frederick Stephens (1828–1907), painter James Collinson (1825–81) and William Michael Rossetti (1829–1919), the brother of Dante Gabriel and the group's official secretary, the Pre-Raphaelites publicly announced their common purpose by attaching to those paintings which they entered for the 1849 Royal Academy Exhibition the gnomic abbreviation 'PRB' (or Pre-Raphaelite Brotherhood). In 1850 they founded *The Germ* as an organ for their ideas; functioning like an avant-garde manifesto, and subtitled *Thoughts Towards Nature in Poetry, Literature and Art* and edited by William Michael Rossetti, it was a commercial failure and ran for only four issues. Broadly speaking, the revolutionary character of Pre-Raphaelitism centred on its commitment to detailed, first-hand observations of the natural world, an aesthetic which the PRB associated with a moral purity and simplicity found (in their view) in the works of the Italian painter Giotto (1266–1337); in so doing they rejected the example of later Italian quattrocento painters such as Raphael (1483–1520) whose work was championed by the Royal Academy (which at the time, and as we noted, represented established opinion). As William Michael Rossetti observed in an 1851 piece entitled 'Pre-Raphaelitism' and published in the *Spectator*, their 'aim is ... truth; and their process ... exactitude of study from nature'.

In practice, early PRB paintings were notable for their bright colours, complex typological symbolism (which though biblical in origin was not simply religious in its connotation) and choice of subjects (which were often taken from the literature of the Middle Ages and were self-consciously archaic). Initially the aims of the PRB were endorsed by the art critic John Ruskin, who had made his reputation through the popularity of *Modern Painters* (the first volumes of which had been published in 1843 and 1846). In letters to *The Times*, Ruskin defended the work of Millais, Hunt and Rossetti, largely because he found in their aesthetic ambitions a corroboration of his own view of art; in private, however, he could be critical of what he viewed as the PRB's technical failings and slipshod execution. In his own 1851 pamphlet *Pre-Raphaelitism*, which was actually more concerned with Turner than with Millais, Hunt or Rossetti, Ruskin gave a sense of the singularity of the PRB's aesthetic when he too attacked what he referred to as the 'Raphaelesque rules' promulgated by the Royal Academy which urged the young painter that 'Nature is full of faults, and that he is to improve her; [and] that Raphael is perfection, and the more he copies Raphael the better, that after much copying of Raphael, he is to try what he can do himself in a Raphaelesque, but yet original manner'.

Behind Ruskin's and the PRB's criticism of accepted canons of artistic taste we can perceive another example of the age-old debate about the roles of realism and idealism in art. In their appeal to 'truth to nature' the members of the PRB were advocating a form of realism – that art should represent the surface phenomena of nature, but only in order to disclose a deeper moral or mystical significance. In this sense, the truth which the PRB aimed at was quite different from the photographic realism commonly associated with the detailed social panoramas of William Powell Frith (which were discussed in Chapter 2). In his 1882 book on Dante Gabriel Rossetti, William Sharp (1855–1904) attempted to define the significance of the Pre-Raphaelites' attention to visual detail when he explained that for them representation was not a matter of providing an image that was 'literally true', but one that 'would yet in another sense *be* true'. Pre-Raphaelite notions of 'truth' also contrasted with the unexpressed assumption behind the Royal Academy's valorisation of later Italian painters: that art should produce an ideal version of, rather than slavishly imitate, the visible forms of the natural world. So although the PRB – like most of their contemporaries – continued to locate the value of pictorial art in the special form of knowledge it vouchsafed to the viewer, they argued that it was only through an accurate delineation of natural forms that such a spiritual truth could be exhibited. For Ruskin, like the PRB, the business of the artist, as he put it in the third volume of *Stones of Venice* (1853), was 'to be a seeing and feeling creature; to be an instrument of such tenderness and sensitiveness, that no shadow, no hue, no line, no instantaneous and evanescent expression of the visible things around him ... shall be left ... unrecorded'. In this emphasis on felt experience

Pre-Raphaelitism also picks up ideas associated with some Romantic-period writers like Wordsworth.

In the late 1850s the Brotherhood effectively dissolved as the careers of its members developed along different paths. Millais, for example, later became a Royal Academician and was appointed the president of that institution in 1896. The influence of the Pre-Raphaelite aesthetic continued to be felt, however, throughout the century in a wide range of artistic and decorative practices. In the late 1850s and 1860s, Pre-Raphaelitism continued to be disseminated in pictorial art through the work of figures like Edward Burne-Jones (1833–98), who had collaborated in 1857 with Rossetti and Morris in their attempt to decorate the new Oxford Union building with fresco painting in the style of early Italian art. A year earlier, Burne-Jones and Morris had founded the 'Oxford Brotherhood', which was modelled on the PRB and which had its own avant-garde journal (financed by Morris), the *Oxford and Cambridge Magazine*. Like *The Germ*, the *Oxford and Cambridge Magazine* published mainly literary material, including poems (such as Dante Gabriel's 'The Burden of Ninevah'), fairy-tales, essays and reviews. Through the firm of Morris, Marshall, Faulkner & Co., Morris later extended Pre-Raphaelite ideas into the area of what were then popularly termed the 'decorative arts' – that is, into the manufacture of marketable products such as stained glass, carpets, furniture, wall-paper, metal-work and ceramics. In his 1877 lecture 'The Decorative Arts', published as a pamphlet in 1878, Morris argued forcefully for the cultural centrality of the decorative arts on the grounds that 'without these arts, our rest would be vacant and uninteresting, our labour mere endurance, mere wearing away of body and mind'. Morris's design principles emphasised (as the initial PRB had done) the importance of organic forms as the basis of pattern design; he also stressed simplicity and function, for which he drew on medieval or traditional English prototypes. Morris's proselytising zeal for an aesthetic as a well as a utilitarian dimension to the design of everyday objects, one driven in later years by his socialist sympathies, helped to inspire institutions such as the Art Worker's Guild (established in 1884) and the Arts and Crafts Exhibition Society (which mounted its first show at the New Gallery in Regent Street in 1888), and thus what has come to be known as the Arts and Crafts Movement.

Of greater significance for literary historians, however, was the attempt to realise Pre-Raphaelite ideas in literature, and especially poetry. Dante Gabriel Rossetti (who often wrote sonnets to accompany his paintings – there are over thirty such 'double' works, where poems are inscribed on frames, on the paintings themselves or sometimes on gold-leaf paper attached to the frame), his sister Christina (who published some of her early poems in *The Germ*), Morris and Swinburne (who became involved with Rossetti's circle in the late 1850s) were all viewed by their contemporaries as followers of a literary programme inspired by Pre-Raphaelitism. 'London to Folkestone', a poem occasioned by a train journey undertaken by Dante Gabriel on his way to France and later published in *The Germ*, provides a good literary example of the Pre-Raphaelite desire to register the immediacy of experience and to record as fully as possible what Ruskin had termed 'visible things'. The poem's opening lines attempt to capture the disorientating effect of seeing a landscape pass by at speed, while at the same time registering details as precise as a single blade of grass:

> A constant keeping past of shaken trees,
> And a bewildering glitter of loose road;
> Banks of bright growth, with single blades atop
> Against white sky; and wires – a constant chain –
> That seem to draw the clouds along with them[.]

(It is perhaps worth noting in passing that in *Dombey and Son* Dickens had given a different account of the railway's impact on the landscape when he described the excavation of the Camden Hill cutting as consisting of 'a hundred thousand shapes and substances of incompleteness, widely mingled out of their places, upside down, burrowing in the earth, aspiring in the air, mouldering in the water, and unintelligible as any dream'.) Rossetti's 'The Woodspurge' (written in 1856, although not published until 1870) places a similar emphasis on the poet as a 'seeing and feeling creature':

> My eyes, wide open, had the run
> Of some ten weeds to fix upon;
> Among those few, out of the sun,
> The woodspurge flowered, three cups in one.

A further characteristic of Pre-Raphaelite poetry, again realised in works by Dante Gabriel, is the iteration of minute sensual details of sight and sound in order to evoke feelings which defy straightforward representation in language. This attempt to 'express the inexpressible' involved attributing to natural images a symbolism which alludes to biblical sources without itself being orthodox in any obvious religious sense. Dante Gabriel's 'The Blessed Damozel' (first published in *The Germ*) exploits the mystical properties of numbers – 'Her blue grave eyes were deeper much | Than deep blue water, even. | She had three lilies in her hands, | And the stars in her hair were seven' – to endow a traditional Christian symbolism of lilies and stars with a more esoteric, though still mystical significance, one which draws the reader's attention to what later critics of Rossetti would term a 'fleshly' aesthetic, here the young woman's 'bosom's pressure' which 'must have made | The bar she leaned on warm, | And the lilies lay as if asleep | Along her bended arm.'

Although he did not hold to any conventional Christian beliefs himself, Dante Gabriel had been brought up in a strongly religious household, one dominated by the Anglo-Catholic faith of his mother and sister Christina. These beliefs influence his art in complex ways (McGann 2000). Their most obvious legacy is to be found in Rossetti's tendency to invest aspects of visible, material life – including, in 'The Blessed Damozel', parts of the female body – with some deeper mystery. Typical in this respect is the poet's response to

'Lady Beauty' in the sonnet 'Soul's Beauty' (published in *The House of Life* (1881)): 'Under the arch of Life, where love and death, | Terror and mystery, guard her shrine, I saw | Beauty enthroned; and though her gaze struck awe, | I drew it in as simply as my breath.' It is worth recalling that in Britain the attraction of Anglo-Catholicism, and thus of Tractarianism (also called the Oxford Movement), lay partly in its concern to preserve the sacred in everyday life; the Tractarians opposed what they perceived as the worldly, sceptical tendencies of a contemporary Protestantism which appeared to be determined to remove from modern life all sense of the awe that accompanied genuine faith. In some of Dante Gabriel's early poetry, this attempt to make the female body simultaneously sexual and sacred can seem like a form of secularised Mariolatry. In his sonnet 'The Girlhood of Mary Virgin', which was written to accompany his 1849 painting of that name, Dante Gabriel again deploys a conventional biblical symbol of purity – the white lily – but in a manner which has distinct erotic overtones: the flower's coming into bloom suggesting a sexual rather than simply moral maturity:

> So held she through her girlhood; as it were
> An angel-watered lily, that near God
> Grows, and is quiet. Till one dawn, at home,
> She woke in her white bed, and had no fear
> At all, – but wept till sunshine, and felt awed;
> Because the fullness of the time was come.

On the surface, 'My Sister's Sleep' (also published in *The Germ*) may seem to be a more conventionally pious poem, insofar as its description of the deathbed of a young woman ends with the clock's first chime at a quarter past midnight ushering in 'Christmas morn', and the consoling refrain: 'Christ's blessing on the newly born'. Yet the status of Margaret's soul is not the main focus of the poem. More striking is the contingent material world which in its very animation impinges on the conventional decorum of a deathbed vigil: attention is drawn away from the dead girl by 'the subtle sound | Of flame, by vents fireshine drove | And reddened', and by the 'ruffled silence spread again | Like water that a pebble stirs', and the mother's knitting needles that 'Met lightly' and her 'silken gown' that 'settled'. In a manner that is recognisably Pre-Raphaelite, Rossetti conveys by a heightened attention to the ordinary details of everyday life a sense of transcendence, but one which is aesthetic rather than religious.

Dante Gabriel's mystification of female sexuality, and his obsession in both his paintings and poetry with depicting a certain kind of female bodily beauty – the buxom, full-lipped 'stunners' with their luxuriant hair, who in practice were paid models, epitomised by Rossetti's plump mistress Fanny Cornforth – can of course be viewed in another light: as a simple objectification of women (Pollock 1988; Psomiades 1997). As Rossetti himself phrases it in 'Jenny' (written in 1856 and published in 1870): 'looking long at you, | The woman almost fades from view. | A cipher of man's changeless sum | Of lust, past, present, and to come, | Is left.' Turning women into art-objects, far from spiritualising them, merely places them in the service of an erotic male fantasy, one which is arguably no less limiting in its view of women than the more orthodox moralising of femininity in works such as Coventry Patmore's 'Angel in the House'. In some of Rossetti's later poems, such as 'The Wine of Circe by Edward Burne Jones' (published in *Poems* (1870)), the female figure is explicitly that of the *femme fatale*: 'Dusk-haired and gold-robed o'er the golden wine | She stoops, wherein, distilled of death and shame, | Sink the black drops.' In the sonnet 'Body's Beauty' (again published in *The House of Life*), images of female beauty formerly used to describe the sacred and the maidenly are applied to the 'shed scent' of Lilith, in some Christian traditions, Adam's first and more obviously sexual consort: her 'soft-shed kisses and soft sleep' are a 'snare', and her 'golden hair' – the 'first gold' – is 'strangling'. In poems such as these we can see connections with Pater's famous word-portrait (in *The Renaissance*) of Leonardo da Vinci's Mona Lisa as 'older than the rocks among which she sits; like the vampire … dead many times'. Likewise, setting Rossetti's 'The Girlhood of Mary Virgin' alongside Ernest Dowson's 'Growth', which was published in *Verses* (1896) and which deploys identical imagery, shows how easily Pre-Raphaelite sensuality could be assimilated into a 'strange' and more self-consciously Decadent aesthetic:

> I watched the glory of her childhood change,
> Half-sorrowful to find the child I knew,
> (Loved long ago in lily-time)
> Become a maid, mysterious and strange …
>
> Till on my doubting soul, the ancient good
> Of her dear childhood in the new disguise
> Dawned, and I hastened to adore
> The glory of her waking maidenhood.

Given the phallocentric nature of Dante Gabriel's and Swinburne's preoccupations, it is unsurprising that in the late 1870s, and as we noted in Chapter 3, the verse of both was labelled 'fleshly', and that label in its turn helped to bring about the popular conflation of Pre-Raphaelitism with Aestheticism. It is also significant that these two movements, along with Decadence, have traditionally been seen to be dominated by men. As Richard Ellmann astutely observed, male writers interested in exploring the range of human desire could be called artists; women with similar interests invited less flattering names. Despite moving in the same circles as her brothers, and despite the fact that seven of her poems were published in *The Germ*, Christina Rossetti was prevented by her sex from becoming a member of the all-male PRB. (So, too, was Lizzie Siddal (1829–62), the lover and eventually the wife of Dante Gabriel.) None the less, Christina's early poetry shares the Pre-Raphaelite preoccupation with the numinous quality of the physical world, and often employs similar imagery: correspondence between Christina and Dante Gabriel reveals that brother and sister often discussed their work, and supported each other in their writing. The exoticism of Christina's 'A Birthday' (published in *Macmillan's Magazine* in 1861) is reminiscent of elements of the iconography of her brother Dante Gabriel's paintings:

> Raise me a dais of silk and down;
>   Hang it with vair and purple dyes;
> Carve it with doves and pomegranates,
>   And peacocks with a hundred eyes;
> Work it in gold and silver grapes,
>   In leaves and silver fleurs-de-lys;
> Because the birthday of my life
>   Is come, my love is come to me.

'Winter Rain' (published in 1862) has the same attentively detailed, sensuous description of the natural world – in lines such as 'Buds will burst their edges, | Strip their wool-coats, glue coats, streaks, | In the woods and hedges' – as that to be found in Dante Gabriel's 'Woodspurge'.

At the same time, however, Christina's sacramentalism was much more conventionally pious than that of her brother, and as result collections such as *Goblin Market and Other Poems* (1862) were thought by contemporary readers and critics to be considerably less controversial than Dante Gabriel's later *Poems* (1870) or the sonnet-sequence *The House of Life* (1881) (Marsh 1994). The spirit of reverie evoked in many of Christina's poems tends to inspire melancholy, rather than awe and rapture, and this in turn was a consequence of her religious belief that the physical world, though a source of natural beauty, was none the less fallen. In 'Another Spring' (published in 1862), an appreciation of the fecund beauty of nature, revealed in phenomena such as 'the leafless pink mezereons', 'chill-veined snowdrops', 'white or azure violet', 'leaf-nested primrose', as well as the 'daylight birds | That build their nests and sing' and 'lusty herds', is accompanied by an insistence on the provisional quality of such experience exhibited in the repeated refrain, 'If I might see another Spring' and summed up in the observation: 'That all my past results in "if"'. Like Keats, the poet's ability to find consolation in the natural world is compromised by a recognition of its impermanence: 'If I might see another Spring | I'd laugh to-day, to-day is brief; | I would not wait for anything: | I'd use to-day that cannot last, | Be glad to-day and sing.'

Poems such as 'A Better Resurrection', 'An Apple Gathering', the interrogative 'Up-hill' and 'What Would I Give?', all of which were written around the same time, articulate a similar sense of rejection or exclusion which, for Christina Rossetti, was a consequence of humanity's fallen nature. So although the poet is recognisably that 'feeling and seeing creature' described by Ruskin, the sensual appreciation of the natural world rarely brings about the kind of eroticised transcendental states described in Dante Gabriel's poetry. In 'A Better

Resurrection' (whose title looks back to a sermon preached by John Donne, and whose themes recall his sonnet 'Batter my heart') the poet's life is described as 'a faded leaf' and 'a frozen thing'; and when in that work the poet asks 'Yet rise it shall – the sap of Spring; | O Jesus, rise in me', the identification of spiritual renewal with that which takes place in the physical world is conventionally religious. In 'What Would I Give?' the response to the question of the title – 'What would I give for a heart of flesh to warm me through, | Instead of this heart of ice-cold whatever I do' – is again thoroughly conventional in its theology: 'not smiles but scalding tears, | To wash the black mark clean, and to thaw the frost of years, | To wash the stain ingrain and to make me clean again.'

In Christina's best-known poem, 'Goblin Market', the combination of a Christian aesthetic of renunciation with a recognisably Pre-Raphaelite sensuality is more complex and ambiguous. Modern opinion has been divided over the interpretation of the significance of the Goblin fruit, 'sweet to tongue and sound to eye', which Lizzie and Laura must try to resist. The indulgent, almost fetishistic enumeration of juicy yet dangerous objects of desire – that is, the 'Bloom-down-cheeked cherries, Swart-headed mulberries | Wild free-born cranberries, | Crab-apples, dewberries, ... Pomegranates full and fine, | Dates and sharp bullaces' – suggests another fruit, that of the tree of knowledge tasted by Eve in the Garden of Eden (Roden 2002). At the same time this kind of sexual temptation has a contemporary economic referent expressed via the language of consumerism (some critics have seen in the poem allusions to Victorian anxieties about widespread food adulteration and corruption (Stern 2003)). Yet Lizzie's sacrificial role as Laura's saviour, in which she enjoins her sister in a parody of the Eucharist to 'Hug me, kiss me, suck my juices | Squeezed from goblin fruits for you, | Goblin pulp and goblin dew. | Eat me, drink me, love me; | Laura, make much of me', complicates the poem's attitude to physicality. At the very least, most critics can agree that 'Goblin Market' represents a more complex interrogation of the assumptions underlying the Victorian idealisation of women than that found in the simple worship of the body by Christina's brother Dante Gabriel.

Aestheticism

Historians have traditionally traced the first consistent references in Britain to 'Aestheticism', or the 'Aesthetic Movement', or 'Art for Art's Sake' to critical discourses in the late 1860s and early 1870s (Johnson 1969, Small 1979). In his 1881 study *The Aesthetic Movement in England*, Aestheticism's first chronicler, Walter Hamilton, described the 'so-called Aesthetic school' as having 'been in existence some years'. The term 'Aesthetic' in Britain apparently derived from the programme for 'aesthetic criticism' set out by Walter Pater in the 'Preface' to his *Studies in the History of the Renaissance* (1873). An earlier version of this piece was published in the *Westminster Review* in 1868 in the form of a review entitled 'Poems by William Morris' (and here again we can see a direct connection between Pre-Raphaelitism and Aestheticism). That programme of aesthetic criticism was generally understood to involve a celebration of the formal properties of a work of art or literature in isolation from its moral content – hence the popular reference to 'art for art's sake', a phrase borrowed from the French 'l'art pour l'art' found in Théophile Gautier's preface to his controversial novel *Mademoiselle de Maupin* (1835), which also argued for the separation of aesthetics from ethics. In this view, Paterian (or English) Aestheticism is an adaptation and development of Gautier's (or French) ideas. However, some critics have noted how Pater (and the English Aesthetes) also drew on indigenous intellectual traditions, and that certain concepts – particularly the proposition that perceptions of beauty were transmitted via an 'impression' of them, and that 'aesthetic' impressions represented a special class of mental phenomena – were borrowed, as we noted above, from contemporary British psychology, particularly the work of popularisers such as Alexander Bain (1818–1903) and James Sully (1842–1923) (Small 1991). However, most historians are in agreement that whatever its origins, English Aestheticism itself represents a distinct cultural phenomenon.

Unlike the PRB there was no clear or self-declared membership of the Aesthetic Movement, although there were certain writers (and occasionally artists) whom late nineteenth-century commentators consistently labelled as 'Aesthetes'. The most important of these were Pater, Swinburne, Wilde, Dante Gabriel Rossetti (although it was only his later poetry – that published in the 1870s and 1880s – which invited this description) and the American painter and polemicist James Abbott McNeill Whistler (1834–1903), who spent most of his productive years in London and Paris. However, in a manner which was reminiscent of Pre-Raphaelitism (with which, as we have noted, it was often confused), Aestheticism was not only nor even principally a literary movement. It was also a social phenomenon, one which was produced in large part by a new emphasis on design and decoration in the middle-class domestic sphere. As Charlotte Gere and Lesley Hoskins argue, an interest in what we now call 'interior design' can be dated to the early decades of the nineteenth century, after which it spread from 'within a cultured and moneyed élite into the prosperous – and increasingly influential – middle classes' (Gere and Hoskins 2000: 35–36). In the late decades of the century such middle-class taste was, as the illustrator and writer Walter Crane (1845–1915) later put it, typically for 'big looking glasses, and machine-made lace curtains, and … furniture … afflicted with curvature of the spine, and dreary lumps of bronze and ormolu … on marble slabs … [and] where every kind of design debauchery is indulged upon carpets, curtains, chintzes and wall papers, and where the antimacassar is made to cover a multitude of sins' (ibid.: 39). 'Aesthetic design' – popularised by Clarence Cook's manual *The House Beautiful* (1878), a phrase which reverberated through literature and wider culture in the 1880s and 1890s – exploited this interest in decoration while simultaneously reacting against it by celebrating simplicity of line, the importance of colour and a harmonisation of decorative principles with selected artistic (and preferably hand-made) artefacts and ornaments. Of particular importance in Aesthetic design was the use of paintings to adorn the walls. When Oscar Wilde lectured on house decoration during his 1882 tour of America he complained about the 'amount of rubbish' cluttering up the domestic home, including 'horrible pictures of historical scenes', and observed how 'our [which was paradoxically the way he habitually referred to things English] Aesthetic Movement has given to the world an increased sense of the value of colour'. Writers and artists associated with the Aesthetic Movement often made their homes and studios, to use another phrase popular at the time, 'palaces of art' – that is, showcases for their artistic principles. Famous aesthetic interiors included: the eighteenth-century home in Cheyne Walk of the poet and artist William Bell Scott (1811–90), which was decorated with Japanese-style friezes and groups of blue and white china about the fireplaces; Whistler's 'White House'; the home of Charles Ricketts (1866–1931) and Charles Shannon (1863–1937), the illustrators of many aesthetic books; as well as Oscar Wilde's Tite Street home, which was decorated according to a scheme laid out by one of the most influential 'aesthetic' designers, E. W. Godwin (1833–86).

Wilde also prescribed that there should be 'no sham imitation of one material in another, such as paper representing marble, or wood painted to resemble stone'. This emphasis on hand-made objects and authentic materials ensured that Aesthetic interiors were not cheap. In practice, indulging Aesthetic taste was restricted to a rich elite living in particular areas of London, such as Chelsea and St John's Wood, as well as the relatively new garden suburb of Bedford Park in Chiswick. Other commentators, such as the artist Lewis Foreman Day (1845–1910) and Charles Eastlake (1836–1906), keeper of the National Gallery and author of the influential *Hints on Household Taste* (1872), were more practical about the relationship between art and machinery; both were prepared to acknowledge that mass-produced furniture did not necessarily work against good design. More generally, Aesthetic taste came to be associated with a cultivated exclusivity and exoticism which in the popular imagination centred on a preference for an eclectic range of objects, such as blue and white china, Chinese lacquer-work, Japonaiserie (the interest in Japanese artefacts dated from the 1851 Great Exhibition and the 'opening up' of Japan to the West in the 1860s) and exotic flowers, chiefly orchids and lilies. The figure of the Aesthete (that is, someone who professed to hold an 'aesthetic' attitude) became recognisable by his whole outlook on life and was a familiar object of ridicule in the popular press. Among the best-known satires on Aestheticism were George Du Maurier's cartoons of the languid Aesthetes 'Jellaby Postlethwaite', 'Maudle' and the 'Aesthetic' Cimabue Brown family in *Punch* in the late 1870s and early 1880s. (Modern critics had traditionally identified Du Maurier's Postlethwaite with the figure of Oscar Wilde, although more recent speculation suggests a number of possible models, including the MP (and later Prime Minister) Arthur James Balfour (1848–1930).) A more recognisably Wildean Aesthete is the figure of Bunthorne in Gilbert and Sullivan's comic opera *Patience*; in this instance Wilde himself went along with this identification when he undertook a lecture tour of America in 1882 organised by the founder of the Savoy Theatre and producer of Gilbert and Sullivan's operas, Richard D'Oyly Carte (1844–1901).)

Evidence of an 'aesthetic attitude' was in turn typically to be found in extravagant dress, a tendency towards social posing and a cultural snobbery; it resulted in the cultivation of the 'beautiful' in a range of objects, often everyday and by no means traditionally defined art-works. Indeed Du Maurier's cartoons show the Aesthete enraptured by a 'six-mark tea-pot', various flowers and wallpaper. By the mid-1880s the figure of the Aesthete was sufficiently recognisable to serve as a subject for serious novelists, most famously perhaps in Henry James's *The Portrait of a Lady* (1881), short story 'The Author of Beltraffio' (1884) and his later *The Tragic Muse*, and of course in Wilde's *The Picture of Dorian Gray*. By the early 1890s, however, Aestheticism as a cultural phenomenon was dated, and consequently Wilde's most famous aesthete, Lord Henry Wotton, is almost a caricature.

In assessing the significance of Aestheticism for literary culture modern critics have tended to begin with Walter Pater, and particularly the influence of what the poet W. B. Yeats remembered Wilde calling his 'golden book', *Studies in the History of the Renaissance*, as well as Pater's novel *Marius the Epicurean*. That influence took two forms: the first, which we described in Chapter 3, was the impact of Pater's prose style. His carefully crafted and grammatically complex sentences, in which meaning seems endlessly deferred by subtle qualification and parenthesis, elevated critical prose to the status of poetry and at a time when the prestige of literary criticism among the general reading public was widely perceived to be decline. (Yeats went so far as to choose a passage of Pater's prose as an example of poetry in the edition of the *Oxford Book of Modern Verse* which he selected in 1936.) In his essay 'The Critic as Artist' (reprinted in *Intentions* in 1891) Oscar Wilde provocatively took Pater's claim about the value of critical writing to its logical conclusion by suggesting that 'the highest Criticism, being the purest form of personal impression, is in its way more creative than creation'. Pater was later celebrated as the greatest living prose stylist writing in English. In the 1870s and early 1880s, however, his prescriptions for style had been viewed more ambivalently. The very complexity which marked its self-conscious 'aesthetic' quality was seen in the hands of other writers as mere affectation – what was termed 'purple prose' – or, on some occasions, as a deliberate obfuscation.

The second and perhaps more important element of Pater's influence was the cultural relativism implicit in his definition of aesthetic criticism. Pater's aesthetic critic, like the heroes in his novel and short stories (in, for example, *Imaginary Portraits*), is defined by his possession of a special sensibility or 'temperament'. Doing little or nothing, the ambition of Pater's hero is to lead a contemplative life, meditating on the nature of experience, particularly on aesthetic experience, which in the subtitle to *Marius* are called 'sensations and ideas', and which, in the concluding sentence to *The Renaissance*, Pater suggests 'give nothing but the highest quality to your moments as they pass, and simply for those moments' sake'. In other words, Pater's definition of aesthetic experience did not work by invoking any abstract literary or artistic standard, one implicit, for example, in Matthew Arnold's recommendation made in 'The Function of Criticism at the Present Time' in *Essays in Criticism* (1865) that critics should always refer to 'the best that is thought or known in the world'. On the contrary, Pater saw taste as 'relative' to the perceiver: the aesthetic critic, by virtue of his special temperament, was enjoined to 'define beauty, not in the most abstract but in the most concrete terms possible, to find not its universal formula, but the formula which expresses most adequately this or that special manifestation of it'. He was to ask 'What is this song or picture, this personality presented in life or in a book, to *me*?' In his 1888 essay 'Style' Pater applied this aesthetic programme to the act of writing itself; here too he argued that the writer's responsibility was only to his own artistic conscience and experiences, to 'the representation of such fact as connected with soul, of a specific personality, in its preferences, its volition and power'. This emphasis on the idiosyncratic in style appeared to some as an abandonment of any form of objective literary standard; equally superfluous was the idea that literature (as Arnold and others had argued) must first and foremost have an ethical function. In this way Aestheticism became associated with what Wilde later called an 'antinomianism' or, more negatively, an anti-social quality.

One of those anti-social qualities was a perception that Paterian Aestheticism endorsed not only an abandoning of critical standards, but also any form of moral regulation. That is, Pater's injunction in the 'Conclusion' to *The Renaissance*, that individuals should strive to 'burn always with this hard, gem-like flame' because 'success in life' was a 'failure to form habits' was interpreted as advocating a simple and therefore dangerous hedonism. The view of the conservative institution, the University of Oxford, in which Pater then worked, and of many contemporary reviewers, was that hedonism, so defined, also involved the possibility of endorsing sexual licence, and more specifically legitimating male–male desire; it is notable that Pater's fictional heroes rarely express any interest in domestic life, nor indeed in women, nor in marriage. In the second edition of *The Renaissance*, published in 1876, Pater omitted the 'Conclusion' for fear, as he later acknowledged in a note to the third (1888) edition, that it 'might possibly mislead some of those young men into whose hands it might fall'. This association between Aestheticism and what was then perceived as a dissident sexuality was reinforced by details of the actual sexual lives of figures associated with the Aesthetic Movement: the sexual lives of Wilde (gaoled in 1895 for gross indecency), Pater (who had been involved in a homosexual scandal which ruined his Oxford career), Swinburne, and to an extent Rossetti, were in direct opposition to those normalised by mainstream culture.

Contemporary disapproval of what was perceived as the anti-social aspects of Aestheticism led to the labelling of Aesthetes as 'morbid' or 'unhealthy' and even, on occasion, as anti-English. Modern critics, however, have viewed the Aesthetic Movement's association of literary and sexual freedom more positively. They have, for example, seen continuities between Aestheticism's concern with style and the formal experimentation found in Modernist writing. (In the semi-autobiographical *Portrait of the Artist as a Young Man* (1914–15) by James Joyce Stephen Dedalus's intellectual and sexual emancipation from the constraints of the Catholic church and life in Dublin are partly troped through a Paterian-sounding endorsement of art, understood as 'the human disposition of sensible or intelligible matter for an esthetic end'.) They have also elaborated more subtle and complex understandings of the sexual politics of Aestheticism (Dellamora 1990; Denisoff 2006). Moreover, this recognition of Aestheticism as a literary or cultural vanguard (rather than, as its contemporary detractors saw it, simply a fad) has in recent years given shape to a question, most neatly posed by Talia Schaffer: 'Who were aesthetic writers, and what texts count as aesthetic?' (Schaffer 2000: 1). As we noted earlier, when literary and cultural historians first began to investigate the Aesthetic Movement in the late 1960s and early 1970s the 'exponents' of Aestheticism, as R. V. Johnson had termed them, were all male (Johnson 1969). By contrast, feminist critics like Schaffer have sought to extend the label Aesthetic to a number of late nineteenth-century women writers, whom she terms the 'forgotten female aesthetes'. To this end, Schaffer has argued for a much 'looser' definition of Aestheticism, in which 'love of children and nature' and the 'employment of epigrams and archaisms for the purpose of camouflaging forbidden topics' become sufficient conditions to group with the familiar Wilde and Pater figures such as Alice Meynell (1847–1922), Rosamund Marriott Watson (who wrote under the pseudonym Graham Thomson, 1860–1911) and E. Nesbit (who, as we noted in Chapter 3, is more usually remembered for her children's fiction, rather than her poetry) (Schaffer 2000: 3–4). A different, but no less provocative re-visioning of the politics of Aestheticism has been offered by Ruth Livesey, who places the 'traditional' aesthetes alongside the work of contemporary socialists such as William Morris (Livesey 2007). Like so much feminist criticism, the larger ambition behind Schaffer's attempt to extend the canon of Aesthetic writers is to refigure our understanding of the role of women in literary history. Schaffer sees the (today) little-read popular novelist Ouida as a pioneer of what she terms the 'aesthetic novel', and thereby an important influence on writers like Wilde and Meredith. Wilde, in this view, merely 'took over' and 'masculinized' a genre which Ouida had developed long before the appearance of *A Rebours* by the French writer Joris-Karl Huysmans (1848–1907), the novel more usually acknowledged as an influence on *Dorian Gray*, and discussed more fully below.

However, it is important to be aware that in identifying a tradition of female Aesthetes Schaffer is applying the term 'Aesthetic' to writers who were not necessarily labelled in this way at the time, and this may be confusing for the modern reader. In Schaffer's schema it is possible for nineteenth-century writers who resisted or opposed the label 'Aesthetic' (as it was used by their contemporaries) to be recuperated into an Aesthetic Movement redefined by criteria developed by modern critics, and in this way we can see how the label 'Aestheticism' is beginning to be used in a manner similar to that of

'Romanticism' – that is, as a modal rather than a historically descriptive definition. A good example of this process can be found in the recent revival of interest in the career of Vernon Lee (the pen-name of Violet Paget) (Zorn 2003; Maxwell and Pulham 2006). The satirical portrait of 'aesthetic London' in Lee's *Miss Brown* (1884) may seem to place her in explicit opposition to the Aesthetes, as do some of her early critical essays. The novel's protagonist, Anne, describes 'being thus constantly made either cross by the touchiness, the morbidness, the disgusting fleshliness, the intolerance of the aesthetes around her, or made to laugh by their affectations, their vanity, their inconstancy, their grotesque manias of wickedness and mysticism'. For some modern critics such polemic aligns Lee with a critical camp which included the conservative writer W. H. Mallock (1849–1923), whose earlier *The New Republic* (1877) had also delivered a withering attack on a number of contemporary literary figures, including Pater (Small 1979). (Pater appears in *The New Republic* in the thin disguise of the character of Mr Rose, whose ambition is to 'follow art for art's sake, beauty for the sake of beauty, love for the sake of love, life for the sake of life'.) More recent critics, however, have re-described Lee's interest in Aestheticism as a form of productive engagement, rather than reactionary critique. In this view, Lee is an important agent in a refiguring and extension of the principles of Aesthetic appreciation, with the result that they embrace a wider range of experiences, including those of women and of the broader reading public (Psomiades and Schaffer, 1999). Lee's comment in *Renaissance Fancies and Studies* (1895) that art should be 'for the sake of life', far from being in conflict with 'art for art's sake', has been interpreted as just another aspect of what has been termed 'aestheticist thinking', insofar as Lee's central preoccupation continues to be, as it was for Pater, that of form (Leighton 2008: 105). In this context it is worth noting Pater's caveat in his 'Style' essay that 'great' art can be distinguished from 'good' art if 'it has something of the soul of humanity in it' and if it 'finds its logical, its architectural place, in the great structure of human life'.

A further way in which recent criticism has complicated earlier understandings of the Aesthetic Movement is in terms of its relationship with consumerism. At first glance it might seem that the association between Aesthetic taste and a cultivated exclusivity – what Lionel Johnson later termed, when talking of Pater's readers, the 'select few' – places the Aesthetic Movement in explicit opposition to the development of mass culture and the commodification of literary value associated with it, a process in which – as we argue more fully in Chapter 7 – aesthetic and economic value are conflated. Certainly it is the case that Pater is careful to distinguish between the ways in which most people might *experience* a mass-produced edition of, say, Shakespeare's *Measure for Measure* and that which is vouchsafed to the aesthetic critic; in Pater's view, it is only the latter's reading experience that can properly be described as 'aesthetic', and in this way the values of art can be held apart from those of the market. Put another way, only the aesthetic critic who is in possession of that special kind of 'temperament' can experience Shakespeare's play *as art*. Wilde and Swinburne, too, are consistently contemptuous of the critical sensibilities of what the former refers to disparagingly as the 'general public', and the latter as mere 'ready readers', and in this contempt they are often viewed as contrasting with figures like Vernon Lee.

However, it is abundantly clear that aesthetic connoisseurship can never be entirely free from market values, for the simple reason that rarity, in a mass market, commands its own price – a circumstance ruthlessly exploited by publishers of aesthetic books, such as the Bodley Head, a firm which (as we also describe in Chapter 7) restricted print runs in order to give an impression of rarity and thus attempt to inflate prices artificially. Here there is more than a suspicion that the cultivated exclusivity of Aestheticism depended for its effects on processes which it appeared most strenuously to disdain. Put another way, Aestheticism only made sense in a culture where, as we noted above, the market had begun to democratise taste by making art available to the many. Given this, it is perhaps ironic that the particular tastes cultivated by individual Aesthetes could in practice be less exclusive than they were prepared to advertise. It has been shown that Wilde (in contrast to Whistler) knew relatively little about some of the art-objects, including the Japanese prints and blue and white china, which he so assiduously promoted as an index of good taste; moreover, he was perfectly willing to exploit the general public's ignorance about art in order to 'sell' a generalised but culturally muddled Orientalism. Even Pater's *carpe diem* philosophy in the 'Conclusion' to *The Renaissance*, in which the aesthetic critic is invited to 'be for ever curiously testing new opinions and courting new impressions', can seem a form of restless consumerism, one in which desire can never be satisfied, and the pursuit of novelty becomes an aesthetic end in itself. In Wilde's *The Picture of Dorian Gray*, Dorian's aesthetic education is nothing *but* consumption, as he moves impatiently, and seemingly without exercising any discrimination, from one experience to the next, immersing himself first in the study of 'perfumes', then 'music', 'jewels', 'embroideries' and 'ecclesiastical vestments', and eventually drug-taking and murder, in a desperate attempt to escape the '*taedium vitae* that comes on those to whom life denies nothing' (Nunokawa 1996). Such an attitude is parodied in Lord Henry Wotton's flippant aside that 'a cigarette is the perfect type of a perfect pleasure. It is exquisite, and it leaves one unsatisfied'. Of course Dorian (like Lord Henry) is also a parody, and arguably a vulgar one at that, of a Paterian aesthete: he has nothing of the fastidious *ascêsis* of Pater's aesthetic heroes which safeguards their intellectual (if not necessarily their moral) integrity. Indeed Dorian's attitude towards art is more properly described as Decadent rather than Aesthetic. As a consequence his moral decline is a reminder of the limitations inherent in Aestheticism's attempted divorce of art from ethics, not the least of which is Aestheticism's reduction of questions of taste to the sum of an individual's experiences. That Aestheticism can lead to a situation where the art-object is ignored also helps to explain why (in contrast to Pre-Raphaelitism) it is much easier (as Du Maurier wittily observed) to delineate an aesthetic 'attitude' than a canon of aesthetic works.

Decadence and Symbolism

Like Aestheticism, Decadence is something of a slippery label, one which had different sorts of meanings in the late nineteenth century, to the extent that some historians prefer to talk of Decadence as a 'discursive field' (MacLeod 2006). Broadly speaking, however, from around the 1860s onwards the adjective 'decadent' was generally used in a derogatory manner to refer to a generalised cultural decay or falling away from artistic standards. To describe a work as decadent was therefore to denigrate it. Decadence as a noun, however, had a more precise referent, although it was not so much to an individual movement (literary or otherwise), as to a particular phase of cultural development. For conservative commentators, Decadence, or 'the Decadence', as it was sometimes termed, described a culture in decline, on this occasion the alleged decay of British culture in the final decades of the century. This anxiety about an imminent breakdown in civilisation had in its turn derived from analogies between contemporary Britain and what the eighteenth-century historian Edward Gibbon had termed 'the decline and fall' of the Roman Empire. For the late Victorians, one particularly troubling and emblematic figure in Rome's decline was the Emperor Nero (who reigned from AD 54 to 68). In this view, Nero's tyranny and brutality, traditionally troped by reference to his ordering of the poisoning of Britannicus, the murder of his mother and the persecution of Christians following the great fire of Rome in AD 64 (which was also often attributed to him), was coupled with a generous patronage of the arts and a personal connoisseurship: Nero was said by nineteenth-century historians to have been particularly skilled in painting and modelling and to have had a statue of the Apollo Belvedere in his villa at Antium. The idea that political corruption and moral depravity could co-exist with a refined artistic sensibility was troubling to a generation brought up on a regime of Ruskin. In volume two of *Modern Painters* Ruskin had famously (though perhaps rather naively) described a great artist as having 'no Evil in his eyes; – only Good, and that which displays good'. In his later lecture *The Queen of the Air* (1869) he had put matters even more unequivocally: 'Great art is the expression of the mind of a great man, and mean art, that of the want of mind of a weak man.' A decadent culture, in this view, was one where the relationship between art and morality, as Ruskin had defined it, had become permanently perverted, or, to use another term popular in the late decades of the century, 'degenerate'. Decadence was therefore a much more threatening phenomenon than either Pre-Raphaelitism or Aestheticism had been, and this in turn helps to explain why contemporary discussions about the Decadence tended towards the apocalyptic – hinted at in popular terms like *fin-de-siècle* and *fin du globe* – rather than the parodic or comedic accounts of Aestheticism.

The concept of degeneration, through which the prospect of cultural decadence was articulated, had its origins in, but was by no means confined to, contemporary evolutionary theory. This idea, associated with the polymath Herbert Spencer, held that a society could easily regress or degenerate, particularly if social policy promoted the survival of those who were then called the 'unfit'. Degeneration was a lens which brought into focus what Daniel Pick has termed 'a kaleidoscope' of cultural anxieties ranging from 'from cretinism, to alcoholism, to syphilis, from peasantry to working class, bourgeoisie to aristocracy, madness to theft, individual to crowd, anarchism to feminism, population decline to population increase' (Pick 1989: 15). What is of interest for the literary historian, however, are the specific anxieties aroused by literary works, and the role attributed to them in the Decadence. Here the most influential theorist of degeneration was the Hungarian writer Max Nordau (1849–1923), who, from 1880, spent most of his life in Paris. Nordau's *Entartung* (first published in 1892 and translated into English as 'Degeneration' in 1895) argued for an explicit connection between the mental health of the nation and the quality of its art and literature. Drawing on the criminal pathology of the Italian writer Cesare Lombroso (1835–1909), Nordau claimed to have identified in contemporary literary and artistic culture a new kind of modern individual whom he termed the 'degenerate', and who was distinguished by a lack of mental discipline and a contempt for conventional customs and morality – characteristics which Nordau attributed to various mental and physical 'stigmata', symptoms, in his view, of an exhausted brain. Nordau also noted the tendency of degenerates to 'consciously and intentionally meet together and found an aesthetic school ... with a title'; 'as a rule', Nordau argued, such activity was the product of 'disease' and analogous to the habit among criminals of uniting in 'bands'.

For commentators such as Nordau, degeneration theory was a way of pathologising and therefore marginalising literary and art works which deviated from, or subverted, what were considered accepted standards of taste. The popular writer Marie Corelli echoed Nordau's prejudices in her best-selling novel *Wormwood*; its sensational attack on bohemian Paris, which Corelli viewed as the origin of all kinds of moral and cultural contamination, was designed to warn 'the English' against the current favour being shown towards 'French habits, French fashions, French books and French fictions'. Although Corelli's Francophobia was extreme, she was not unusual in identifying the first signs of a modern (as opposed to classical) Decadence in French culture. What can usefully be distinguished as 'literary' Decadence (like literary Aestheticism) was (and still is) conventionally traced back to French models, to the poetry of Baudelaire and the figure of the 'poète maudit' epitomised in the life of Paul Verlaine (1844–96), who was imprisoned for shooting his lover and fellow poet, Arthur Rimbaud. The most famous French Decadent work, however, was Huysmans's *A Rebours*, which recounts the experiences of a rich, neurotically sensitive and sexually impotent aristocrat, Des Esseintes, who withdraws from society (which he sees as having been engulfed by 'waves of human mediocrity') into an artificial world of art and reverie in which he concocts increasingly fantastic entertainments for himself in the hope of escaping the monotony of modern life. The novel became infamous for its subject-matter: Des Esseintes's attempt to extend the boundaries of 'normal' experience include his reliving, in a series of lurid hallucinations, former sexual encounters. Also controversial was Huysmans's elaborate and complex metaphorical style. Large sections of the work are devoted to describing the objects Des Esseintes collects – which partly correspond to those admired by Wilde's Dorian Gray and which include fine wines, tapestries, exotic paintings and flowers, sculptures and literary works (often scurrilous, such as Petronius's *Satyricon*) – in his attempt to 'shake off the overpowering tedium which weighed upon him'.

As has been noted, in Britain a work like Wilde's *The Picture of Dorian Gray* was viewed as Decadent (in the sense that this novel was taken as evidence for that perceived cultural decay) in part because of its similarity, stylistically and thematically, to *A Rebours*. This helps to explain why literary Decadence has been conventionally, if rather loosely, described as the 'dark side' of Aestheticism. Literary Decadence, in this view, is a movement of the late 1880s and 1890s which grows out of Aestheticism's concern with the autonomy of art, but which is to be distinguished from it by its emphasis on the bizarre, the exotic, the morbid and the perverse. In Decadence, the aesthetic divorce of art from ethics is translated into a desire to find beauty in what might conventionally be considered ugly experiences. As Ruth Z. Temple describes matters, this involved a preference for 'the city, the man-made, [and] the artificial' and for what is 'sordid or trivial rather than what is obviously beautiful or good' (Temple 1974: 220). More precisely, writers who were viewed as contributing, through their works, to the decadence of contemporary culture tended to view themselves as artistic martyrs who wished to escape from the boredom and trivia of everyday life into an artificially created world of art, one which was typically associated with forms of intoxication induced by drink or drugs. Here we can see a connection of sorts both with the dream-like intensity of some Pre-Raphaelite poetry and with the emphasis in Aestheticism on a life of contemplation rather than action. However, Decadent writing is distinguished from the aims of both these movements by its express ambition to seek transcendence in a form of mental oblivion, one where the poet is completely freed from any connection with Ruskin's 'visible' world, and therefore from all moral or emotional responsibility. We might note in passing the distinction between the role which Pater gives to the exercise of discrimination in aesthetic experience, and the desire in decadent writing for complete surrender to any immediate experience: as Theodore Wratislaw (1871–1933) phrases it in his aptly titled 'Trance' (published in *Caprices* (1893)): 'might we swooning deathwards blend | Our spirits in one perfect kiss!' That process of mental dissociation in turn frees the Decadent writer to explore the full range of experiences and emotions, including those arising from what many late nineteenth-century readers viewed as illicit sexual encounters, typically with individuals on the fringes of society, such as the 'sweet' pleasures of the 'bought red mouth' (as Ernest Dowson terms matters) of street girls and music-hall dancers (who were seen by many as indistinguishable from prostitutes).

Arthur Symons's 'The Absinthe-Drinker' (published in his 1892 collection *Silhouettes*) celebrates the way in which this retreat from an external reality is facilitated by alcohol; the absinthe of the poem's title transports the poet into a timeless present in which moral judgement is indefinitely suspended: 'Gently I wave the visible work away | … The hours are all | Linked in a dance of mere forgetfulness. | I am at peace with God and man | … Rocked on this dreamy and indifferent tide'. Absinthe, or 'the green fairy', a bitter and highly intoxicating aniseed-flavoured liquor distilled in France, was closely associated with Decadence. Dowson described it as 'having the power of the magicians; it can wipe out or renew the past, and annul or foretell the future'. Symons's 'Maquillage' (also published in *Sihouettes*) describes the 'charm of rouge on fragile cheeks, | Pearl-powder, and, about the eyes, | The dark and lustrous Eastern dyes'. Here the pleasure of the artificial – whether it is to do with facial make-up or the street lighting which made late nineteenth-century urban night-life possible – lies in its association with transience and ambiguity: the prostitute's 'fleeting colours are as those | That, from an April sky withdrawn, | Fade in a fragrant mist of tears'. In 'Nora on the Pavement' (published in Symons's *London Nights* (1895)), the ambiguous pleasure at the centre of the poem is explicitly sexual: the 'petulant and bewildered' Nora is a 'Child, and most blithe, and wild as any elf, | And innocently spendthrift of herself, | And guileless and most unbeguiled'. In this poem the valorisation of what is feigned or contrived over what is 'real' involves an arguably (very) male fantasy of what might be termed a 'knowing' purity – that is, the 'voluptuous pretence | Of unacquainted innocence' expertly practised by another of Symons's literary prostitutes, the 'ambiguous child' Bianca in 'Bianca: X. Liber Amoris' (i.e. the 'Book of Love'), also published in *London Nights*.

With themes such as the illicit, night-time pleasures of 'bought' love Decadent literature has moved a long way from the sensual rapture of Pre-Raphaelite poetry. On the other hand, much Decadent literature shares with Pre-Raphaelitism – and particularly the work of Dante Gabriel Rossetti – that same tendency to objectify women. However, with Decadent writers this situation is often more a consequence of a concern with evoking the *experience* of reverie, of what it *feels* like to be emotionally transported, than with delineating the objects which inspire those heightened psychological states (and of course here we see again the connection with, but also the disjunctions from, Aestheticism). Put another way, the Decadent writer's main concern is typically with *himself*, with his own state of mind. One can see the difference by briefly comparing Symons's 'Bianca' with Rossetti's 'Jenny', mentioned earlier. In the latter poem Rossetti at least acknowledges that the 'lazy laughing languid Jenny, | Fond of a kiss and fond of a guinea' might take a different view of her life from that of her poet/client, when he muses: 'With wasteful whims more than enough, | I wonder what you're thinking of … | perhaps you're merely glad | That I'm not drunk or ruffianly | And let you rest upon my knee.' By contrast, Symons's silent 'Bianca' is only ever 'the aching sense of sex'; the poet can only imagine her as a cipher for, or an externalisation of, his own desires, as 'swooning heats of sensual bliss, | Under my hands, under my kiss'.

Although the Decadent writer might yearn for transcendence, often the mental state that preoccupies him is one of weary self-pity or, in some of Lionel Johnson's and Ernest Dowson's poetry, a self-disgust which comes with the realisation, as Dowson puts it in 'Spleen' (published in *Verses* (1896)), that 'I was … tired | Of everything that ever I desired'. The repeated refrain of Dowson's 'Non sum qualis eram bonae sub regno Cynarae' (also published in *Verses*) – 'I was desolate and sick of an old passion' – encapsulates the paradoxical source of this ennui. Despite the Bacchanalian pursuit of 'madder music' and 'stronger wine', the poet's desire can never be satisfied because it is always for something that has already been lost. In 'Amor Profanus' (another work anthologised in *Verses*), the poet dreams of meeting with a past lover, only to realise that the 'old language of the heart | We sought to speak: alas! poor shades! | Over our pallid lips had run | The waters of oblivion, | Which crown all loves of men or maids'. What gives rise to the label 'Decadent' is that a recognition of the inevitability of emotional failure none the less does not prevent the poet's pursuit of transcendence, usually through what would have been perceived as illicit sexual encounters. In Dowson's 'Cease smiling, Dear! a little while be sad' (in *Verses*), the poet laments – in a conventional Keatsian manner – the passing of desire: 'Must we grow old, and leaden-eyed and gray, | And taste no more the wild and passionate | Love sorrows of to-day?' But rather than seek solace in the abstractions of art or beauty – as Keats proposes in the Grecian Urn ode – he wishes instead for a final sexual consummation, one which will bring about the ultimate transcendence through self-annihilation:

> O red pomegranate of thy perfect mouth!
> My lips' life-fruitage, might I taste and die,
> Here in thy garden, where the scented south
> Wind chastens agony;
>
> … dream that we shall lie,
> Red mouth to mouth, entwined, and always hear
> The south wind's melody

Johnson, too, tends to revalue personal failure by turning rejection and loneliness into a kind of death-wish. In the aptly named 'Nihilism' in *Ireland with other poems* (1897) he longs for 'rest! the rest! Only the gloom, | Soft and long gloom! The pausing from all thought! | My life, I cannot taste: the eternal tomb | Brings me peace, which life has never brought'.

It is important to stress that poets like Dowson and Johnson did not explicitly describe themselves as Decadents, nor does this term adequately account for all of their work. (The same might be said of Wilde: his Decadent *The Sphinx* (1894) and popular *The Ballad of Reading Gaol* (1898) were published within five years of each other, but are quite different in tone and subject.) That said, some recent historians, as we noted above, have observed that the styles of writing to which the adjective 'decadent' was applied in late nineteenth-century Britain could be surprisingly varied. Moreover, general uses of the term 'decadent' to describe particular features of literary works pre-date the identification of 'the Decadence' – i.e. that particular moment of cultural decline associated with the late 1880s and 1890s. As a consequence, to define the membership of what Symons, in an 1893 essay, termed the 'Decadent Movement in Literature' is difficult. As a concept 'Decadence' resonates powerfully in late nineteenth-century discourses, but it does not have a very secure referent in British *literary* culture, and cannot easily be identified with a discrete *group* of writers in the manner, say, of Pre-Raphaelitism or even perhaps Aestheticism. Symons himself hinted at the difficulties in pinning down what literary Decadence referred to in his later and more retrospective *The Symbolist Movement in Literature*; he describes how in the late decades of the century 'something which is vaguely called Decadence had come into being'. He tentatively suggests that a movement which 'might be called Decadent *could* but have been a straying aside from the main road of literature'; in terms of its cultural significance, it was but 'half a mock-interlude'.

In recent years the question of who the Decadents were has become as loaded as that which applies to membership of the Aesthetic Movement. Conventionally, Decadence has been viewed as a largely male movement, with its major works confined to poetry: so exemplary Decadent writers include Arthur Symons, Lionel Johnson, Ernest Dowson, Vincent O'Sullivan (1868–1940), Richard Le Gallienne, Oscar Wilde, Lord Alfred Douglas (1870–1945) and Victor Plarr (with Michael Field sometimes included as a token female involvement). However, some critics, particularly feminists, have argued for the centrality both of fiction and of women writers like Olive Schreiner (1855–1920) and George Egerton (pen-name of Mary Chavelita Dunne (1859–1945) (Fox 2006).

Of course Symons's cautious appraisal of a movement with which many would have aligned his own work was not really to do with the vagueness of its ambitions or influence, so much as with his fear of the negative connotations which the label Decadent carried. (It is worth remembering that its most prominent exponent in Britain, Oscar Wilde, had been in prison and was, at the time of Symons's writing, in exile in France and soon to be dead.) Symons noted, for example, how 'it pleased some young men in various countries to call themselves Decadents', but emphasised that the appropriation of such a label was to be understood as a form of youthful rebellion; and he was also dismissive of the idea that these self-proclaimed Decadents constituted a coherent movement. The adjective 'decadent' only made sense, according to Symons, when applied to style, where it designated what he called a 'deformation of language', a kind of writing which was exclusive neither to the late nineteenth century nor indeed to English or French culture (similar deformations were also to be found in works of classical literature). In apparently rejecting the claims of the Decadents, however, Symons merely wished to distinguish their efforts from what he saw as 'something' altogether 'more serious' and which he referred to as 'Symbolism'. The issue, then, was more one of semantics than of ontology – of what a movement was to be called, rather than whether it existed. (Symons had originally thought of entitling *The Symbolist Movement in Literature* as the more loaded *The Decadent Movement in Literature*). Symbolism, according to Symons, was defined in terms of 'an attempt to spiritualise literature, to evade the old bondage of rhetoric, the old bondage of exteriority'; ironically, its membership included many of the self-same writers that had been associated with Decadence – that is, Verlaine, Stéphane Mallarmé (1842–98), Villiers de l'Isle-Adam (1838–89) and Maurice Maeterlinck (1862–1949).

For modern critics and historians, the point at issue is not whether Symons's categorisations are necessarily correct. It is, after all, a matter of judgement as to whether the term 'Symbolist' (rather than Decadent) better captures similarities between the poetry of writers like Mallarmé, Wilde or Symons himself. At least one recent historian, however, has taken his cue from Symons by arguing for a fundamental distinction between the symbolism of earlier nineteenth-century poetry, like that of Romantic-period writers, and the innovative 'polyvalent' symbolism found in later works (Honnighausen 1988). The distinguishing feature of what might more usefully be termed 'Decadent Symbolism' is, as the Irish poet W. B. Yeats suggested, the lack of any secure or single referent for a given symbol. Symbolism is thus used to gesture towards the ineffability of knowledge, and some Decadent symbolism works synaesthesically by evoking the emotional resonance of images – an effect found in, for example, poems such as Wilde's 'Symphony in Yellow' (published in *The Centennial Magazine* in 1899) or Symons's 'Pastel' (in *Silhouettes*). There were also important connections made between literary and pictorial symbolism, and works by artists like Gustave Moreau were readily assimilated to Decadence. Huysmans's Des Esseintes hyperbolically describes Moreau's *Salomé* as 'the symbolic incarnation of undying Lust, the Goddess of immortal Hysteria, the accursed Beauty exalted above all other beauties by the catalepsy that hardens her flesh and steels her muscles, the monstrous Beast, indifferent, irresponsible, insensible, poisoning, like the Helen of ancient myth, everything that approaches her, everything that sees her, everything she touches'.

Symons's concern to redefine himself as a Symbolist rather than a Decadent is perhaps best understood as a powerful testimony to the strategic importance in the late decades of the century of identifying oneself with a literary movement: to place one's work as part of a vanguard was one way of revaluing what in practice could be a depressing combination of critical neglect (or even contempt) and a lack of commercial success. Decadence – and particularly Decadent poetry – in general did not sell. A case in point is Wilde's *The Sphinx*. This elaborately written and expensively produced work, which advertised its exoticism not only in its themes and language but also in the studied extravagance of its printing, illustrations and binding, sold poorly, and probably made a loss for its publisher, the Bodley Head. The same was true of a number of little literary magazines, the most of famous of which were the *Yellow Book* and the *Savoy*, which tended to be associated with Decadent themes. These periodicals marked themselves off from mainstream magazine culture not only by their content, but also by the quality of their printing and design and their serious as well as lavish art work, best seen in the contributions of Aubrey Beardsley (1872–98), the art editor of the *Savoy*.

It should also be noted that, as with Pre-Raphaelitism, Symons's strategy of revaluation was wholly male orientated (his list of Symbolists is entirely male). This does not mean that there were *no* women writing poetry of a kind similar to that produced by Decadents or Symbolists. In her volume *Opals* (1897) Olive Custance (1874–1944), who is perhaps as well known through her disastrous marriage to Lord Alfred Douglas, addressed many stereotypical Decadent themes – such as a yearning for the sexually unattainable – and in a manner which combined an interest in artifice and strangeness with rejection and yearning. The mysteriously resonant 'Twilight', which centres on a 'woman weeping in a silent room | Full of white flowers that moved and made no sound', 'white flowers' which 'were the thoughts men never tell', is typical of her style. Better known than Custance, is the aunt–niece partnership of 'Michael Field'. *Sight and Song* (1892) (which took its inspiration from their visits to the art galleries of Europe) and *Underneath the Bough* (1893) (whose exoticism was hinted at in the title's allusion to *The Rubaiyat of Omar Khayyam*) are both notable for their exploration of the pleasures of an untrammelled (and often explicitly erotic and 'Sapphic') sensuality, but whose marginal status in their time was virtually guaranteed by their tiny print runs – in the case of *Underneath the Bough*, just 150 copies. Yet it is only relatively recently that the female contribution to Decadence is beginning to be appreciated as modern critics, responding to Ellmann's challenge, have begun to develop new terms of reference for understanding the gender politics of the *fin-de-siècle*.

Conclusion

- Literary movements may be 'self-defined' or they may be the product of categories devised by later historians to single out what they consider the most significant developments in past cultures.
- The main self-defined nineteenth-century literary movements all emerged in the second half of the century and all can be seen, at least in part, as reactions against the development of a mass literary culture.
- Self-defined nineteenth-century literary movements tended to valorise poetry over prose, and to place a premium on the relationship between literary and visual culture. Furthermore, none of them was confined only to literature: the influence of Pre-Raphaelitism and Aestheticism in particular could be seen in a wide range of cultural artefacts, from furniture to ceramics and dress.

- In their original formation, Pre-Raphaelitism, Aestheticism, Decadence and Symbolism were strongly gendered: the aesthetic of all four movements tended to centre on male achievement. Modern critics, however, have argued for an appreciation of women's contributions to these movements, although in the process they have sometimes changed the way they are defined, incorporating in them writers who were not necessarily labelled in this way at the time.

5 Nineteenth-century literature and history

Overview

It will be clear, from the argument outlined in Chapter 2, that an important feature of nineteenth-century literature is often assumed to be its qualities of representation, that is, the ways in which literary forms (fiction, poetry and drama) were explicitly used by nineteenth-century writers to engage with a variety of contemporary intellectual, social or political issues. A usual way of framing this engagement of nineteenth-century literature with social life is in terms of the relationship between a literary work and what is loosely called its historical 'context'. Over the past three to four decades interest in the historical contexts of nineteenth-century literature has tended to draw attention to the political or ideological elements of literary works – to what some critics have called the 'ideological work' which they do. That said, there are several ways of defining context, as well as of understanding the relationship between it and a literary work. These differences in their turn have been influenced by a larger philosophical debate about the extent to which all knowledge of the past is relative.

Proponents of relativism argue that the way we construct knowledge of the past is, in part, through literary tropes: in this argument the devices which we associate most commonly with literature – such as metaphor or certain kinds of narrative structures or plots – are also to be found in historical writing, particularly in the nineteenth century (White 1973). Moreover, because literary and historical narratives are constructed in similar ways, so the distinction between fiction and history will always run the risk of being blurred. If we accept that knowledge of the past was (and is) constructed in this manner, and if that process of construction inevitably involves elements of selection and evaluation, then it follows that knowledge of the past can never be objective.

This last proposition has taken a number of forms: at its strongest it involves a scepticism about *all* historical knowledge, one which disables the authority of history itself (or more precisely, it sees history as inherently ideological). Few historians hold trenchantly to this strong view, not least because it presents some intractable logical problems (already hinted at in the discussion of realism in Chapter 3). These problems include the existence of a non-ideological vantage point from which to survey ideology itself, as well as the observation that in order to define a relationship between factual and fictive statements we need to have some means of discriminating between them in the first place. It may be the case that Thomas Carlyle's *History of The French Revolution* (1837) has many similarities with a novel; but it order to be able to distinguish it from Charles Dickens's novel about the same subject, *A Tale of Two Cities* – which most historians and literary critics would want to do – we must already be in possession of concepts of history and fiction quite distinct from each other.

Weaker kinds of historical relativism acknowledge that our understanding of the past will always be incomplete, provisional and value laden, but go on to propose that we can none the less develop mechanisms for judging the adequacy of one historical explanation relative to others. Such mechanisms might involve examining the range, status and consistency of evidence available to the historian, as well as considering the role played by narrative devices in organising this evidence into an explanation of past events. Importantly for the subject of this chapter, these weaker arguments also have ramifications for how we understand the relationship between literature and its historical context. They remind us of the truism that history is constantly being rewritten; so too, therefore, are those events (or contexts) with which literary works allegedly engage. As a consequence, we cannot assume that there are fixed historical events, or unproblematic historical 'facts' about social life, on the one hand, and a literary representation of them, on the other. More to the point, we need to be aware that literary works themselves may be part of that process by which we rewrite the past. To put this another way: a literary work and its context do not exist as conceptually separate entities, as is suggested by the commonly used language of optics – the language, that is, of 'reflection' and 'representation' which presupposes two ontologically separate entities: an object and an image of it. Instead, we might better think about literature and context as existing in a dynamic relationship with each other. Context may be constitutive of literature, in the sense of placing constraints on expressivity; conversely, literature may also be constitutive of context, insofar as literary works themselves, and the formal devices associated with literary expression, may be deeply implicated in the way readers understand the social world around them, and thus also in the ways in which knowledge of the past is constructed.

For all of these reasons defining precisely the way in which literary works and contexts relate to each other can be a surprisingly complicated task. This chapter will attempt to give a sense of that complexity. It will look at how various ways of understanding context bear on our understanding of the politics of nineteenth-century literary works and so, too, the nineteenth-century literary canon. It will do so by focusing on three case studies, each taken from a different decade in the century and involving different genres of writing. It will start, however, by teasing out in more detail the problems involved in the concept of a historical context.

Defining the relationship between literature and context

Broadly speaking, there are two sorts of problems concerning the way in which we understand the contexts of literary works. The first centres on the extent to which the relationship between literature and context can be said to be a determining one. This has implications for the evidentiary status (and so also the value) of literary works in a cultural history. The second problem centres on 'relevance', and this involves determining the kinds of (and limit to) the historical information deemed appropriate to explaining a literary work. One of the longest-established ways of thinking about context is the argument that the attitudes and values found in literary works are informed by the wider intellectual and artistic culture in which they were produced – what used to be labelled a 'history of ideas'. In this view, in order to understand fully the range of reference in a novel such as *Little Dorrit*, the modern reader has also to understand larger debates about prison reform and prison building which took place in the middle decades of the nineteenth century. More particularly, readers need to be aware of the history of the Marshalsea Prison, which features centrally in the novel, and legislation regarding debtors. Additionally readers need to be informed about the bankruptcy of Dickens's own father. Later literary historians – as we noted in Chapter 3 – were concerned to understand the relationship between intellectual and literary culture in terms of power rather than simply of ideas. They sought to isolate those ideas which were so dominant in a culture that they took on the status of an ideology. Influenced by the work of the French philosopher Michel Foucault, historians drew attention to the ways in which a large body or corpus of texts comprised what was termed a 'discourse' or mode of thinking, one which affected many different and apparently unrelated areas of social life. To take the example of incarceration again, Foucault's discussion of nineteenth-century prisons, and particularly his account of the importance of Jeremy Bentham's concept of a panopticon (which permitted, at least in theory, the complete surveillance of all of the inmates of the prison), emphasised its significance as a metaphor in a much more widespread nineteenth-century discourse of social surveillance and policing. In this view, the terms in which *Little Dorrit* describes debt, criminality and transgression are seen to be part of a larger discourse about social discipline or policing: Dickens's novel, then, neither simply reflects, nor is determined by, a particular ideology – rather, it is a constitutive element of it.

The principal significance of this argument – of what has sometimes been termed the 'Foucauldian turn' in nineteenth-century studies – is that the difference between text and context becomes unimportant or is dissolved, and so questions about the extent to which a literary work is determined by its historical context disappear. Furthermore, the concept of discourse enables the historian to align various different kinds of texts (which might, for example, be works to do with economics, medicine, politics, as well as literature) without having to specify any determining relationships between them. Instead priority is given to the manner in which a group of texts, taken as a whole, are evidence for a dominant (or, as it was typically termed, 'hegemonic') mode of thought. We ought to note, however, that side-stepping the question of whether literature is itself determined or is a determining agent does not make it disappear. So there is still a lively debate about whether literary works can disrupt or challenge at least some dominant ideologies, or whether they can be evidence for fractures or discontinuities in those discourses. For example, the popularity of detective fiction in the later decades of the nineteenth century has been explained in terms of its ability to highlight but simultaneously assuage contemporary anxieties about criminal behaviour, and specially threats to domestic life. In this view, the motif of transgression, its detection and punishment can be seen as yet another element of that larger nineteenth-century discourse of surveillance.

At the same time, however, critics have noticed the ambivalent representation of many nineteenth-century detectives. As we noted in Chapter 2, Inspector Bucket in Dickens's *Bleak House* is outside respectable family life, and the most famous nineteenth-century detective, Arthur Conan Doyle's Sherlock Holmes, has a number of anti-social characteristics: he, too, is a loner, he takes drugs and he has a deep strain of misogyny. The 'fracture' that such fiction reveals is that the agents who ensure social cohesion are themselves on the fringes of the society they help to police, a paradox which works to undermine the legitimacy of the discourse of surveillance itself: the agent of justice is himself amoral (a contradiction which persists in much twentieth-century detective fiction). In other words, the question for the critic to resolve is whether detective fiction is normative, insofar as it gives legitimacy to a surveillance society by providing an attractively non-coercive model of social control; or whether it subverts the notion of a surveillance society by depicting its most competent agents operating outside of social convention and (in Holmes's case) often outside of the law.

As we also noted in Chapter 3, in recent years some critics have observed that there is a high price to be paid for assimilating literary identity – that is, the question of what allows a text to be defined as a work of literature – into a generalised notion of discourse. They have also questioned the relevance to nineteenth-century British culture of Foucault's theorisation of power, based as it was on the example of the much more centralised French state (Goodlad 2003). The 'text–context' model of traditional literary historicism was crucially structured on a concept of relevance: non-literary works were only considered to be part of a context if it could be shown that they illuminated or explained some aspect of a literary work. Although there was always significant room for disagreement about which non-literary works 'best' or most fully explained a literary work, none the less there was a broad consensus that relevance had to be established in some manner, usually by providing direct evidence of what was termed 'influence' – evidence, say, of whether an author was known to have read a particular source. Such an assumption underlay John Holloway's criticism of the assertion that Dickens's *Hard Times* was a critique of industrialisation (Holloway 1962). Holloway argued that Dickens's target was much more specific and local: it was publications such as the encyclopaedic *Practical, Theoretical, and Historical Dictionary of Commerce and Commercial Navigation* (1832) and *Descriptive and Statistical Account of the British Empire* (1837) by the mathematician and political economist J. R. McCulloch (1789–1864), and through that work, contemporary debates about appropriate education. By contrast, paying attention to discourse, a process which dissolves the 'text–context' distinction, obviates the need to establish relevance because, as we explained above, all texts become equal evidence for a dominant mode of thought. This strategy has the effect of underwriting a practice in which apparently disparate texts, both literary and non-literary, are read alongside each other without any need to explain why any one class of texts is more important than any other. We need to be aware, then, that disputes about whether literature is itself determined or is a determining agent have at their heart disputes not just about the value of a particular work, but also about the nature (and perhaps the very existence) of literariness itself.

A different way of understanding the contexts of literature, this time underwritten by a less sceptical attitude towards historical enquiry, has been in terms of the history of reading and writing – in other words, in terms of social and material practices rather than ideas, however they are theorised. In relation to the nineteenth century this involves identifying, typically through detailed empirical evidence, which groups in the population were able to read (in the sense of being literate), could afford to read (in the sense of being physically able to acquire books, or afford to buy or borrow them), and which groups had the time and interest to do so (for most of the population the length of the working day and the absence of electric lighting limited the amount of time that could be devoted to reading). The point of drawing attention to these details of social history is to explain not only the attitudes found in nineteenth-century literary works but also their formal properties. This is achieved by making reference to the expectations of readers or addressees, based on the assumption that literature is a social institution made up of writers, publishers and, equally importantly, purchasers of books, and that each of these groups has some agency in defining literary culture. The general objective of this line of research is to correlate changes in the composition of literary readerships over the course of the nineteenth century with changes in literary taste and literary forms.

A third (and most recent) way of understanding context is in terms of the materiality of texts themselves. In this argument texts are considered as physical, embodied and therefore 'made' objects. Whereas the second way of understanding context involved seeing literature as embedded in a variety of social institutions and makes connections between the economics of literary production and literary works, describing the materiality of texts involves considering the changing technology of book production in the nineteenth century and the signifying power of features such as typography, book illustration and design. It suggests, for example, that reading the same text in a periodical and in a cloth-bound and expensively produced book are different sorts of experience, and those differences affect how the text itself is interpreted and valued.

These final two ways of conceptualising the contexts of nineteenth-century literature will be discussed in detail in Chapter 7. The remainder of the present chapter will concentrate on the first understanding of context, exploring the complexities of the relationship between literature and its historical situation by reference to a number of specific but contested examples: the social reference (and thus the politics) of some Romantic period writing, of social-problem novels of the 1840s and 1850s and finally of society comedy in the 1890s. In each case, we will try to show the effect of different ways of defining a historical context on the interpretation and evaluation of particular works.

The contexts of Romanticism

A traditional way of defining Romanticism, one which was responsible for producing the familiar all-male canon of Blake, Wordsworth, Coleridge, Byron, Shelley and Keats, was that popularised by M. H. Abrams in his seminal study *The Mirror and the Lamp* (1953). Abrams located Romanticism within the context of a history of ideas about literary representation. More precisely, and to develop the title of Abrams's study, he defined its distinctiveness in terms of the way eighteenth-century neo-classical mimetic (or imitative) theories of art were superseded by an expressive aesthetic, one in which the value of poetry is held to reside in the uniqueness of the individual poet's 'vision', in his (for Abrams was principally concerned with male poets) ability to articulate that vision, and where the human mind becomes an active agent in the formation of knowledge through a special kind of mental faculty – the faculty that the Romantics called the 'imagination'. It is the operation of the imagination which gives poetry its privileged epistemological status: an ability, as Wordsworth phrases it in 'Tintern Abbey', to 'see into the life of things'. The idealist concept of knowledge which underlies this revolutionary Romantic poetics can also be located in relation to contemporary philosophical debates. Of central importance is the opposition between the rationalism of the English philosopher John Locke (1632–1704), in which the mind is assumed originally to be a *tabula rasa* or blank sheet and in which all knowledge is held to be the product of experience, and the arguments of the German philosopher Immanuel Kant (1724–1804), that there exist transcendental structures within the mind which enable us to make sense of our experiences and which shape our knowledge of the world, while at the same time being themselves beyond the reach of human knowledge. In this view, the radicalism of Romanticism emerges in an opposition not simply to neo-classical ideas about the poet as a craftsman or maker, but also to certain values associated with the Enlightenment, such as the empiricism that had come (and would continue) to dominate contemporary scientific enquiry. In Blake's enigmatic words in *The Marriage of Heaven and Hell* (1790–93): 'Energy is the only life and is from the Body, and Reason is the bound or outward circumference of Energy ... Energy is Eternal Delight.'

Viewed in the context of this literary and philosophical tradition, critical interest tends to focus on the novelty and coherence of the ways in which

Romantic-period writers tried to redefine literary creativity. Put another way, the tradition of relating literature to its time uses context in order to highlight what are essentially formal or aesthetic concerns: philosophical idealism is important only insofar as it illuminates literary themes and tropes. As a consequence, the types of questions that arise are of the following sort: how exactly does the imagination, that source of the poet's visionary power (opposed to what was then called 'fancy') actually 'work'; and how successfully do individual poems articulate it? Can the imagination be both a given of the poetic mind, one which empowers the poet to perceive the general or essential truths of humanity, while at the same time being a faculty which requires stimulus from particular local experiences – typically in Romantic poetry from the natural world – to activate it? The dilemma here is that the origins (and thus the absolute power) of the imagination are on the one hand held to derive from a force *beyond* the individual – as Wordsworth terms matters in 'Tintern Abbey', 'a motion and a spirit that impels | All thinking things, all objects of all thought, | And rolls through all things'. On the other hand, however, this force can only be apprehended through contingent events, especially the vivid but necessarily fugitive and 'animal' (or as Wordsworth terms it in the 'Immortality Ode' (composed between 1802 and 1804)), 'not realised') experiences of childhood. Nature, then, is an external agent that can 'impress | Thoughts of deep seclusion' and in so doing serve to confirm the power of the poet's vision; but at the same time that natural agent – 'the woods | And mountains, and ... all that we behold | From this green earth' – seems to be in part a construction of the poet. As Wordsworth acknowledges in 'Tintern Abbey', 'the mighty world | Of eye and ear' is 'both what they half-create, | And what perceive'. The problem Wordsworth addresses is one of epistemology in general; it has to do with the nature and origins of knowledge, and the status of the poetic imagination.

Wordsworth was not insensible to the limitations of his visionary concept of creativity. However, he tended to be preoccupied with the problems that were consequent upon the loss of the imagination, rather than the possibility that the imagination itself might be subjective, and so partial. As he phrased matters in the opening of the 'Immortality Ode', was he in possession of merely 'common sight', by definition the property of all, or was it 'the visionary gleam', this time the prerogative of only the poet? In that same work Wordsworth eventually finds consolation in identifying the imagination with 'The Soul that rises with us, our life's Star', where the 'Soul' derives its power not from an interaction with the external, material world, but from a Platonic concept of pre-existence which, although only dully and inadequately recollected, none the less shapes the form of that interaction. In the words of the poem, 'Not in entire forgetfulness, | And not in utter nakedness, | But trailing clouds of glory do we come | From God, who is our home'. Paradoxically, then, what distinguishes the Wordsworthian poet is that he is an 'Eye among the blind, | That, deaf and silent, read'st the eternal deep, | Haunted for ever by the eternal mind'. Coleridge, too, was preoccupied by the prospect of losing the power of his imagination. In 'The Eolian Harp', published in *Poetical Works* (1834) (an earlier version was composed in 1795), 'the one life within us and abroad, | Which meets all motion and becomes its soul' is identified with the 'soft floating witchery of sound' made by the 'simplest lute' when it is 'by the desultory breeze caressed!' However, in the later 'Dejection: An Ode' (first published in 1802) the poet is aware only of 'the dull sobbing draught that moans and rakes | Upon the strings of this Eolian lute, | Which better far were mute'.

According to Jerome J. McGann, to concern ourselves with, or to be moved by, such introspection is to come under the sway of what he terms 'Romantic ideology' (McGann 1983). A critical preoccupation with Romanticism's obsessive concern with its own self-representation, and particularly with the ways in which the poet characterises himself, can be at the expense of interrogating attitudes towards what the 'Preface' to the *Lyrical Ballads* called 'common men'. It is thus to ignore what might be a political or ideological element to Romantic aesthetics in favour of focusing on tensions between, say, the visual and aural effects of poetry and the attempt to describe abstract ideas, or on the paradox involved in finding a poetic language adequate to conveying those feelings caused by the failure of the expressive faculty. The culmination of this way of thinking about Romanticism is perhaps to be found in the close scrutiny given by formalist critics to the verbal complexity of Keats's late odes, and particularly the 'Ode on a Grecian Urn'. There the linguistic ambiguity and interrogative structure of the poem are held to enact its central aesthetic paradox, one captured in its gnomic last lines:

> 'Beauty is truth, truth beauty'; that is all
>   Ye know on Earth, and all ye need to know.

Dissatisfied with these sorts of readings of the Romantic canon, later critics expanded the concept of context to include reference to contemporary social and political debates. In this view, what is most striking about Wordsworth's 'eye and ear' in 'Tintern Abbey' is the way in which it effectively depopulates the landscape in which the poem is set, that of the Wye Valley. New historicist critics suggested that the poet's 'vision' causes him to be blind and deaf to certain physical actualities in the scenery that surrounds him, such as the river's busy industries and their impoverished workforce, elements vividly described in *Observations on the River Wye* (1782) by Wordsworth's contemporary, William Gilpin (1724–1804) (Levinson 1986). In the late eighteenth and early nineteenth centuries the River Wye was an important shipping lane for transporting coal and timber from the adjoining Forest of Dean, and its banks were lined with smoke from charcoal furnaces, and not just from the cottages of the peasantry which are the focus of the poet's attention. Gilpin noticed these industrial elements because they detracted from what he saw as the landscape's 'picturesque' qualities – a way of seeing which aimed to re-present the British countryside as a site for aesthetic contemplation (and so leisure tourism) rather than work. To put this observation another way, it can be argued that to concentrate on the intellectual and philosophical rather than the social contexts of

'Tintern Abbey' highlights the novelty of Wordsworth's poetics, but at the expense of diverting attention from what can seem like a reactionary politics – a displacement of human suffering (that produced by social and economic inequalities) onto an aesthetic reverie available at the time only to a privileged few, to those (like Wordsworth) who were sufficiently wealthy to be able to experience the Wye principally as a tourist attraction. The class politics underlying Wordsworth's conceptualisation of Romantic subjectivity can also be glimpsed in his valorisation of childhood: unlike Blake's *Songs of Innocence and Experience* (1789–94), childhood in Wordsworth's poetry is free from the demands of work and the prospect of poverty, and the adult poet's solitary contemplation of nature is similarly removed from the rigours imposed by a life of labour. In this respect there are a number of useful contrasts to be made with the more explicitly political verse of what have been termed 'labouring poets', such as Samuel Bamford and Ebenezer Elliot (1781–1849).

Contextualising Romantic-period literature in terms of its relationship with contemporary political culture is not a just a matter of exposing conservative elements in the poetics of figures such as Wordsworth. Much more compelling has been research which has taken its inspiration from social and cultural historians (e.g. Dickinson 1985; Chase 1988; Worrall 1992; McCalman 1993) to bring to notice the intimate connections between literary production and late eighteenth- and early nineteenth-century radical groups in Britain. It has complicated both dismissive judgements about the politics of the 'first-generation' Romantics – Wordsworth, Coleridge and Southey – as well as what were typically viewed as the apolitical preoccupations of poets like Keats (Roe 2002). In the process, the traditional image of the Romantic poet as an isolated genius set apart from society is replaced by a more politically alert and socially engaged author. More importantly, perhaps, this conceptualisation of context has also led to a prioritising of writers explicitly committed to using poetry in the service of radical causes, with the result that previously marginalised voices are given new emphasis. These voices include figures such as the radical activist, poet and essayist John Thelwall (1764–1834), who was an acquaintance of Wordsworth and Coleridge, as well as John Clare. Seen in this wider political context it is easy to interpret the defiant closing stanza to Clare's 'The Flitting' (1832), an elegiac work which laments his move to Northborough from Helpston, the village of his birth, in terms of its class politics. For Clare the timelessness of the landscape and the fecundity of nature – archetypal Romantic tropes – become a metaphor for the endurance of the down-trodden rural labouring classes:

Time looks on pomp with careless moods
Or killing apathys distain
– So where old marble citys stood
Poor persecuted weeds remain
She feels a love for little things
That very few can feel besides

And still the grass eternal springs
Where castles stood and grandeur died.

If we extend this idea of context still further and take debates about slavery to be one of the dominant political concerns of the time – the political disenfranchisement and economic exploitation of the working classes was often compared to a form of slave labour – then our attention is commanded by yet other hitherto marginalised works, such as Hannah More's 'Slavery: A Poem' and 'A Poem on the Inhumanity of the Slave-Trade' by Ann Yearsley (1756–1806). Yearsley was famously referred to by More – who was her patron (although they later bitterly fell out) – as 'a poor illiterate woman … who sells milk from door to door'. Both poems were published in 1788 as a reaction to a parliamentary bill proposed by William Dolben which would have restricted (although not abolished) the transatlantic slave trade. Significant, too, is the autobiographical *The Interesting Narrative of Olaudah Equiano* (1789); an early example of what have been classified as the sub-genre of 'slave narratives', it went through seventeen editions between 1789 and 1827 (Thomas 2000; Lee 2001). Other slave narratives which provide a useful counterpoint to general discussions of colonial wealth in nineteenth-century literature, include *The Life, History and Unparallelled Sufferings of John Jea, African Preacher of the Gospels* (1814) by John Jea (1773–?) and *The History of Mary Prince, a West Indian Slave* (1831) by the Bermuda-born Mary Prince (1788–?). Prince's narrative was recorded by her amanuensis, the poet and novelist Susannah Strickland (1803–85), who is claimed by some modern critics to have subtly altered the narrative – exaggerating Prince's status as a victim – in order better to appeal to the sympathies of a British readership. Better known at the time than either Jea or Prince was Mary Seacole (1805–81). Jamaican born and a self-taught nurse, she rose to prominence through her work in the Crimea, where she established a hospital for the care of British soldiers; her *Wonderful Adventures of Mary Seacole in Many Lands* appeared in 1857.

That Romantic-period women poets have been seen to have made a particularly significant contribution to anti-slavery literature has been linked to their position in British culture as subjugated 'others'; debarred (like slaves) from participation in political life, they may have had particular reasons for exhibiting sympathy towards the marginalised and dispossessed (Ferguson 1992). A more general scrutiny of the role of gender during this period – yet a further legacy of the desire to broaden the political contexts of Romanticism – has reminded modern readers that, alongside the traditional male Romantic canon, there were numerous women poets, several of whom, like Felicia Hemans and Letitia Landon, were popular, successful and highly valued in their own time (Mellor 1988; Ross 1989; Fay 1998). Some wrote in self-conscious dialogue with what (today) are their better-known male counterparts. 'Poem to Coleridge' (1801) by Mary Robinson (1758–1800) was a tribute to 'Khubla Khan'. Similarly Hemans's 'To Wordsworth' (1828) was inspired by her reading of his *Miscellaneous Poems* (1820), and she later visited him during an 1830 tour of

Scotland and the Lake District. Some modern critics have attempted to isolate what they see as the special qualities of Romantic-period women's writing (Mellor, 1993). It has been suggested, for example, that definitions of Romantic subjectivity to be found in works by Wordsworth, Coleridge and Keats exclude large areas of female experience, especially those of motherhood and domestic life; these, by contrast, are celebrated in works such as Hemans's *Records of Women* (1828). Her 'The Homes of England' (1828) has often been dismissed as sentimental and nostalgic, and it was the subject of a well-known parody by Noel Coward. However, it can appear more politically charged when viewed in the context of the valorisation of female work, and the ways in which it permits a re-visioning of traditional areas of male competence (such as warfare and nation building) in terms of their cost to women and children (Woolfson 2000).

When female agency, and especially female desire, is explicitly addressed by male Romantic-period poets, in works such as Coleridge's unfinished 'Christabel' (1816) or Keats's 'La Belle Dame Sans Merci' (1820), it is often presented as a destructive, unnatural and occasionally a demonic force, of which men are simply victims – a motif which is later picked up in 1890s literature (Dijkstra 1986). In a similar manner Wordsworth's valorisation of childhood, which derives from his own experiences as an orphan, presents the origins of the child's privileged ability to communicate with nature as a consequence of his isolation from all social and familial experience, and particularly from maternal influence. So the child in the opening two books of *The Prelude* (1805) engages in what are frequently solitary activities, for which his parents had hitherto been merely 'props'. As a consequence, nurture and discipline are seen to derive principally from the natural world.

> But I believe
> That Nature, oftentimes, when she would frame
> A favored Being, from his earliest dawn
> Of infancy doth open out the clouds,
> As at the touch of lightning, seeking him
> With gentlest visitation; not the less,
> Thou haply aiming at the self-same end,
> Does it delight her sometimes to employ
> Severer interventions, ministry
> More palpable, and so she dealt with me.

This association between Romanticism and nature has traditionally been contextualised by reference to contemporary theories of the sublime as they were articulated by philosophers such as Edmund Burke (1729–97). Burke's writings, which associated the experience of beauty with smallness and smoothness and that of the 'sublime' with darkness, terror, solitude and emptiness, help to explain how certain kinds of landscapes and geographical features, such as the lakes, rivers and mountains of the Lake District, of North Wales or the Alps, became for some Romantic-period writers a source of spiritual renewal and poetic inspiration, while at the same time provoking regrets about changes in the contemporary rural environment, anxieties which generally take the form of deep misgivings about encroaching industrialisation. One consequence, however, of this philosophical understanding of the Romantic conceptualisation of nature was the marginalisation of a large corpus of Romantic-period writing concerned with other, less native landscapes. So a further political context for re-reading the Romantic canon is suggested by the culture of British imperialism and the discourses of colonialism (Leask 1992; Saree 1992; Richardson and Hofkosh 1996; Fulford and Kitson 1998). From this perspective, the Romantic interest in 'difference' is troped in terms of an opposition not only between nature and the city, and the child and the adult, but also between East and West, to be seen in works such as Southey's *Thalaba* (1801) and *The Curse of Kehama* (1810) or Shelley's *The Revolt of Islam* (1818) (which transposes the French Revolution onto an Oriental setting) and 'Ozymandias' (1818) or, most famously, in De Quincey's *Confessions of an English Opium Eater*.

In this view Romantic poetry is an element, rather than simply a product, of colonial discourse: it plays an important role in the construction of what Edward Said famously termed 'Orientalism' – that Western stereotyping of the East (and particularly Islam and Hinduism) made in order to confirm and consolidate the West's sense of its own superiority as rational and modern (Said 1978, 1993). Consequently the escapist (and often explicitly feminised) images of the East as an exotic and erotic 'other', and so as an alternative source of creativity, to be found in works such as Coleridge's 'Kubla Khan' or Byron's *The Giaour*, can be interpreted politically as a form of cultural imperialism. It is one which cynically exploits (and perhaps commodifies) a contemporary appetite for Oriental subjects which had been fuelled by travellers and writers such as Sir William Jones (1746–94), whose *Poems consisting chiefly of translations from the Asiatic languages* (1772) and *The Moallakat* (1782) introduced many British readers to aspects of Persian culture. In the view of critics like Said, far from being a radical departure from eighteenth-century values, some Romantic poetry is complicit in perpetuating and legitimating earlier colonial ideologies. Moreover, even Romantic poems which appear not to be explicitly concerned with Oriental subjects – such as parts of Wordsworth's *The Excursion* (1814) – can be read in the context of assumptions about the civilising mission of Britishness. However, we should note (and as Chapter 7 will explain) that Said's modelling of East–West cultural relations, as well as his readings of Romantic-period literature, have proved controversial, and some subsequent critics have argued for a greater complexity and ambiguity in Byron's and Coleridge's poems and in the discourses of what is referred to as 'Romantic Orientalism' in general (MacKenzie 1995; Irwin 2006). The extent to which Romantic-period writing is complicit in the ideology of Empire and Imperialism continues to be a contested issue.

As we have seen, different ways of defining context – that is, of expanding the range of ideas or discourses which are perceived to have relevance to literary expression – have permitted different readings of Romanticism, and these in turn have generated what David Perkins calls new 'literary classifications' for understanding this moment of literary history. So we now have a whole range of historicised categories by means of which we can understand the distinctiveness of Romantic-period writing: we can focus on the 'Romantic imagination', the 'Romantic sublime', 'Romantic Orientalism' or the 'Romantic landscape'; alternatively, we might single out the distinctive contribution of 'Romantic women writers' or 'labouring poets' or black writers in Britain. What remains unresolved, however, is whether and how far these different classifications are compatible with one another. For example, read in the context of contemporary gender norms, Felicia Hemans's *Records of Women* can be interpreted as articulating a form of feminism in the sense that Hemans's poems make female experience, and particularly female suffering at the hands of men, a central concern. However, if these same works are read in the context of the discourses of colonialism, Hemans's politics in a poem like the 'The Indian City', the subject of which was adapted from the *Oriental Memoirs* (1813) of James Forbes (1749–1819), take on a more conservative character. On occasions her sensuous language articulates what appears to be a rather stereotypical Orientalism which dissolves the complexity of India's 'difference' into a generalised and familiar exoticism exhibited in that country's flora and fauna:

> Many a graceful Hindu maid
> With the water-vase from the palmy shade
> Came gliding light as the desert's roe.

We might also notice that feminist readings of *Records of Women* as a critique of patriarchal culture assume that poetry retains a partly privileged position which enables it to comment critically or ironically on a dominant ideology, that ideology here being patriarchy. By contrast, the assimilation of 'The Indian City' into the discourses of colonialism tends to undermine such agency, by making the poem express rather than criticise a form of cultural hegemony. So these different conceptions of context not only produce different readings of the poem, but also attribute to it a different status. Yet the text of the poem itself remains unaltered.

We noted in Chapter 4 that periodising or historicising definitions such as Romanticism are often deeply contested. We can now see that this is, in part, a consequence of the variety of historical contexts that have been invoked to explain and interpret what is now more usually termed Romantic-period writing. Finally, we should observe that it might be the case that by drawing attention to such a wide range of styles, forms and themes, these new contexts have deprived the category 'Romanticism' of much of its explanatory power.

The contexts of the social-problem novel

It can be strongly argued that the identification of the mid nineteenth-century fictional sub-genre now known as the 'social-problem' novel would not have occurred in the absence of changes in the ways in which literature was contextualised historically. Considered solely in terms of their formal properties – that is, in terms of features such as plotting, narrative structure, characterisation, the use of figurative language and so forth – the works that came to be categorised as social-problem novels were rarely viewed as possessing any distinctive qualities. It was the general consensus of critics up to the late 1950s that novels such as Elizabeth Gaskell's *Mary Barton* and Benjamin Disraeli's *Sybil, Or the Two Nations* (1845) represented only 'minor' achievements compared with the more formally complex and thematically ambitious *Bleak House* or *Middlemarch*. However, and as we noted in Chapter 2, the growing influence of Marxist criticism in the 1960s provoked an interest in examining literary works in terms of their engagement with social life (rather than simply their formal properties), and this led some literary historians to reassess the value of nineteenth-century fiction in terms of the comprehensiveness of its representation of British society and social structures. The first consequence of this strategy was to give prominence to a group of novels written in the 1840s and 1850s which took as their subject-matter themes which were now viewed as central events in nineteenth-century social history and which had been ignored or marginalised in the class-specific narratives of Jane Austen, the silver fork and Newgate novelists. These themes included industrialisation and its effects on labour relations, social and family life. More particularly, critics like Raymond Williams and John Lucas saw in these mid-century fictions a new set of subjects. One was the sympathetic (rather than merely comical or criminal) treatment of the lives of the urban poor, particularly those who worked in factories in the newly industrialised towns in the north of England, such as Manchester. Another was the attempt to address in fiction the perceived conflicts of interest between this social group and the emerging and (after the 1832 Reform Bill) newly enfranchised middle classes whose wealth typically derived from industry or financial institutions rather than from agriculture or the land (Williams 1963; Lucas 1966).

Measuring the success of these representations of social life demanded a detailed knowledge of their social reference, including the history of contemporary political groups, such as the Chartists, of contemporary labour relations (such as the problems produced by an influx of cheap Irish labour and consequent strikes or 'lock-outs'), of working conditions in factories, of new laws established by various Factory Acts, of trade cycles and of the social and economic conditions behind the depression of the so-called 'hungry forties', as well as knowledge of contemporary urban living conditions (particularly in city slums). This information purported to give the modern reader access to a 'social reality', or to what Williams termed the 'facts of industrialisation', against which they could assess the accuracy or sophistication of the novelist's account of society. Surprisingly, perhaps, critics such as Williams and Lucas made no attempt to disguise what they saw as formal flaws in social-problem novels. They acknowledged that there were weaknesses of characterisation (particularly in the one-dimensional representation of working-class characters) and anomalies of plot (to be seen, for example, in the tensions between the demands of romance and those of documentary realism). They further argued that the conclusions to these novels often felt uncomfortably contrived, and that in order to bring about narrative closure the solutions offered to class conflict were disappointingly sentimental and frequently unconvincing. Such endings were rarely more than a tableau in which working- and middle-class characters recognised in each other a common humanity. In *Mary Barton* a melodramatic encounter between an enfeebled (and soon to be dead) John Barton and his former employer, Mr Carson, is followed by the emigration of the hero and heroine to Canada in search of a better life. In the same author's *North and South* the marriage of Margaret Hale and John Thornton, which at a stroke resolves both the romantic and the class plots, is brought about – as in Brontë's *Jane Eyre* – by an unexpected inheritance, a traditional nineteenth-century literary device that had little relevance to the lives of most individuals of the time (as we noted in Chapter 2, it amounts to a fictional reward for 'good' behaviour).

However, Williams and Lucas went on to suggest that such formal or artistic flaws, far from marring the novels, formed the basis of their claims on our attention. They were the product of an admirable but ultimately failed attempt to confront the complexity of contemporary social relations. The central question for the critic to answer then became how to account for the reasons for that failure. For Lucas, it was fundamentally ideological in origin: a failure of what he termed 'imagination' led authors to fall back on 'stock political attitudes', and these in turn could be attributed to their middle-class self-interest – the novelists' inability, however well-intentioned they might be, to contemplate a form of social organisation in which their own class position and financial privilege would come under scrutiny. In this view, the more striking the formal failure, the more critically interesting the novel becomes, insofar as failure exposes disjunctions in a mid-nineteenth-century liberal bourgeois ideology of social progress achieved through self-improvement. In *Mary Barton* John Barton's absence from the narrative following the rejection of the Chartist petition, and the relocation of the novel's interest from documenting the poverty of the Manchester slums to staging a series of melodramatic performances in a Liverpool courtroom, is seen by Lucas as a form of evasion on Gaskell's part. Her concentration in the second half of the novel on the chequered romance of Mary and Jem, and then the progress of Jem's trial, throws into sharp relief the number of unanswered questions produced by the class antagonism so vividly portrayed in the novel's first half.

In the work of critics like Lucas and Williams we can once again see how the historical contextualisation of a group of novels changes the grounds upon which fiction is to be judged. Formal qualities, so admired by an earlier generation of critics, such as F. R. Leavis or the New Critics, count for little; rather than an aesthetic unity, it is formal incoherence, or more precisely the reasons for its occurrence, which become the most important index of literary value, largely because the point of reading such fiction is assumed to be political or ideological. Subsequent critics of social-problem or industrial fiction attempted to elaborate increasingly sophisticated contextual readings. It was argued that a full appreciation of their representational qualities (and thus, in Lucas's terms, their political integrity) requires the critic or reader to come to terms with the limitations in the ways in which problems produced by nineteenth-century industrial society were understood in their own time. In other words, in this later view, it is not the material processes associated with industrialism which are seen to constitute a relevant historical context – that 'social reality' assumed by Williams and Lucas, but the nineteenth-century ideas and ideologies which those processes gave rise to. However, this change of emphasis still left room for significant disagreements over the value of social-problem novels, and these have their origins in the different ways literary historians conceptualise the relationship between literature and its ideological context.

Historians who understand culture in terms of discourse have suggested that the formal disjunctions in social-problem novels, rather than being the result of individual failures of imagination or of political nerve, as suggested by Lucas and Williams, simply mirror larger ideological disjunctions in the discursive field of which they are an element (Gallagher 1985). That discursive field – comprised of what have been termed the 'discourses of industrialism' – is held to encompass a surprisingly wide range of topoi and concerns, including (in the eyes of some new historicist critics) contemporary debates about the transatlantic slave trade, a market in human labour which has been viewed as industrial in its scope and organisation. As with re-readings of Romantic-period literature, this enlarged context enables the critic to see an association between what Thomas Carlyle bluntly termed the 'nigger question' and the discontents of England's industrial working classes, a project which can in turn refigure our understanding of the politics of mid-century fiction. The value of social-problem novels now lies in the ways in which they foreground the following question: to what extent could the nineteenth-century economy 'afford' to extend to both groups the rights and freedoms, specifically those of political self-determination, enjoyed by wealthier members of society? Moreover, the attempt by middle-class novelists to use the resources of fiction in order to try to give a voice to working-class subjects, and thus to individuate and humanise them (which, we should note, occurs only in domestic and not industrial settings), when viewed in this context can have the effect of making their novels appear more radical.

At the same time, this new context shifts the problem of form from accounting for weaknesses in narrative and plot (what we have described as the tensions between romance and realism), to those in language. In social-problem novels the ambition to render authentic working-class subjectivities is typically achieved by employing different registers for characters from different classes; but in practice the depiction of working-class speech patterns and local dialects can appear to the reader as no more than linguistic tics which serve only to reinforce prejudices about middle-class superiority. Stephen Blackpool's impotent refrain in *Hard Times* – 'It's aw a muddle' – inevitably hands responsibility for resolving class conflict to the more eloquent and better-educated middle classes, for whom life of course is not a 'muddle'. In *Mary Barton* a similar sort of tension can be seen in the contrast between the language of John Barton and that of his daughter Mary. Throughout the novel Mary speaks, somewhat improbably, in standard English, her vocabulary and syntax neatly mirroring that of the omniscient narrator; at the same time John inexplicably retains his unmistakable Mancunian accent and dialect. (It is worth noting in passing that a figure as distinguished as William Gladstone never lost his Liverpudlian accent, so the perception that there was an automatic alignment between speech patterns and moral authority was a fictional device.)

Other critics have seen the origins of the ideological disjunctions in the discourses of industrialism in terms of gender rather than of class or race. Susan Zlotnick identifies tensions between, on the one hand, a male 'repudiation of modernity' (found in the work of Carlyle, Ruskin, Disraeli, Dickens and Arnold) which was fuelled by anxieties over the ways in which women's involvement in the industrial workforce endangered male privilege; and on the other, a willingness on the part of women writers (like Charlotte Brontë, Gaskell, Frances Trollope and Charlotte Elizabeth Tonna) to 'look to the future with hope'. For Zlotnick, the formal properties (and flaws) of social-problem fiction cease to be important. Of greater interest is how this body of fiction helps us to appreciate the centrality of gender rather than simply class in the ways in which nineteenth-century industrialism was configured (Zlotnick 1998). Once again an attention to aspects of the historical context – in Zlotnick's case, the details of nineteenth-century debates about working-class female employment – permits a redescription of the politics of social-problem novels.

A further way of conceptualising the context of social-problem novels, one which is distinct from locating them as part of a generalised 'discourse of industrialism', involves identifying what are argued to be the dominant ways of thinking about problems associated with industrialism – that is, those explanatory paradigms which possessed the greatest social and cultural authority at the time – on the grounds that they may explain, by virtue of their influence or intellectual prestige, the conceptual (rather than simply ideological) limitations we find in nineteenth-century fictional works (Guy 1996). In this kind of argument, a central role is given to the writings of contemporary political economists and social theorists – rather than social reformers – who almost uniformly addressed problems in society (whether of economic inequality, or the behaviour associated with drunkenness) by concentrating on a concept of the individual. For much of the nineteenth century the individual was habitually seen as the basic point of reference for understanding all social issues. This argument proposes a continuity between *Mary Barton*'s use of unrealistic genres such as melodrama and romance (whose plots typically function by subjecting individual characters to a series of trials in which their moral integrity is tested) and its attempted documentary realism (which concentrates, like contemporary statistical enquiry, on enumerating individual facts about poverty rather than explaining it or analysing its social dimensions or causes). Realism, melodrama and romance, far from being incompatible literary forms, are seen to be underwritten by the same framework of 'individualism' that characterises many contemporary non-fictional responses to social problems. In this argument, the point of interest for the modern critic is the extent to which novelists expose, sometimes unwittingly, the limitations of modes of thought derived from individualism.

As we have seen, recent accounts of social-problem novels usefully illustrate the ways in which judgements about a work's formal properties (and therefore its literary value) can depend not only on what the historian defines as a relevant historical context, but also on how the status of literary fiction within a culture is understood. Are social-problem novels elements in a larger 'discourse of industrialism', their value existing in the way in which they help us to understand how that discourse was structured in terms of the politics of gender and class? Or do social-problem novels represent, by virtue of their manipulation of literary devices (which may or may not be compatible with each other), a special kind of response to the problems of contemporary social life, one which can be usefully set against the conclusions of non-fictional social commentary? One of the most recent critical works to address the topic of nineteenth-century fiction's engagement with industrialisation – that is, with urban poverty and class conflict – neatly side-steps these questions by offering a different subject for critical enquiry: what matters in such fiction is not the plausibility (or otherwise) of the representation of industrialism or its discourses; hence the critic need not be concerned with the historical details of the 'social reality' described by Williams. Of greater significance is the 'reality' of the attitudes and emotions betrayed by a novelist's interest in class in the first instance. In this view, the representation of urban poverty continues to be viewed as ideological, but it is argued to be in the service of a rather different project – that of fashioning an appropriate middle-class male identity. The horror of the nineteenth-century urban slum offered itself as a new (and suitably challenging) sphere of activity in which middle-class influence – particularly that of the middle-class male – might be exercised, and therefore as an opportunity for the affirmation of middle-class professional authority. In this line of argument, writing about social problems tells us much more about the politics underlying the process of 'middle-class self-definition' in the nineteenth century than it does about the conditions of the poor (Bivona and Henkle 2006: 4).

The social-problem novel was not the only nineteenth-century fictional form to be concerned with urban poverty and class conflict. Members of the Chartist movement and later early socialist organisations also used literature – both poetry and fiction – as a vehicle for their political views. Of these works, some of the best known are the novels of Margaret Harkness (1854–1923) and Charles Allen Clarke (1863–1935), both of whom wrote under pseudonyms – John Law and Teddy Ashton respectively. In contrast to the mid-century social-problem novels, the analyses of working-class labour in both Harkness's *A City Girl* (1887) and Clarke's

The Knobstick: A Story of Love and Labour (1893) are heavily indebted to Marxist ideas; Clark's later *The Red Flag* (1907) is described by Sutherland as 'the most explicitly communist work of fiction published in Edwardian England' (Sutherland 2009: 127). More contemporary with the social-problem novel was the non-fictional sub-genre of 'slum literature', examples of which include *Sanitary Ramblings: Being Sketches and Illustrations of Bethnal Green* (1848) by Hector Gavin (1815–55), *The Night Side of London* (1861) by J. Ewing Ritchie (1820–98) as well as the better-known *London Labour and the London Poor* by Henry Mayhew (1812–87), which first appeared as a series of articles in 1849 in the *Morning Chronicle*. These works influenced the later 'East-End' novel, the best-known practitioners of which were Arthur Morrison (1863–1945) – particularly his naturalistic *Tales of Mean Streets* (1894) and *A Child of the Jago* (1896) – and Walter Besant (1836–1901) in works like *All Sorts and Conditions of Men* (1882) and *Children of Gibeon* (1886).

The contexts of the society comedy

The sub-genre of the society comedy, which flowered in the 1880s and 1890s, takes its name from a kind of dramatic entertainment developed to cater for the tastes of what was then called 'London Society'. As we noted in Chapter 3, when compared with the works of contemporary European dramatists such as Ibsen and Strindberg, and even those of George Bernard Shaw (whose first plays did not receive a public performance), the society comedy can appear to be both ideologically and formally fairly conservative, and therefore relatively uninteresting in terms of the historical development of drama. The usual explanation of this state of affairs centres on the commercial nature of British theatrical culture (Stephens 1980; 1992). Funded by box office receipts and constrained by the office of the Lord Chamberlain, who had powers of censorship over any play performed for a fee-paying public, neither dramatists nor theatrical producers could afford to offend their West End audiences by staging works which might have been formally too experimental or politically too radical for their tastes. The society comedy's only real claim to novelty thus lies not in invention, but in its synthesis of existing dramatic traditions, particularly that of English melodrama with the French 'pièce bien faite' or 'well-made play' (Powell 1990).

In the late nineteenth-century French theatre was popular with British audiences, and French actresses, such as Sarah Bernhardt (1844–1923), enjoyed considerable popularity on the British stage; there was also a lively British theatrical tourist trade to France, as enthusiastic Francophiles took trips to Paris specifically to enjoy the latest plays (Hemmings 1993). Society comedy took from contemporary French drama an emphasis on witty and urbane dialogue, as well as more sophisticated and complex plotlines which created suspense through surprise disclosures (such as the unexpected delivery of a letter) and by exploiting discrepancies between what is revealed to the audience and what is known to some of the characters on the stage. Many of the themes of French drama also crossed the Channel – particularly the fascination with the lives and sexual mores of the very rich. In society comedy the tensions between the aristocracy and upper middle classes, rather than being exploited for comic effect (as in early Restoration drama's interest in the master–servant relationship), become occasions for acute and often highly personal emotional dilemmas – those crises brought about by the conflict between social duty and 'la voix du sang', or 'the call of blood'. At the same time, however, society comedy continued to rely on a number of devices familiar from the British stage, such as the use of one or a series of melodramatic tableaux to close an act. In this respect, one way of comparing various dramatists' use of the sub-genre is in terms of the sophistication with which they manipulate the traditions which it draws upon. Here we can observe that the repartee in Henry Arthur Jones's *The Case of Rebellious Susan*, though manifestly less melodramatic than in his earlier *The Silver King*, or Arthur Wing Pinero's *The Second Mrs Tanqueray*, none the less lacks the self-conscious brio of Oscar Wilde's plays, particularly *The Importance of Being Earnest*; by the same token, both Jones and Pinero – again in contrast to Wilde – are generally seen as subordinating dialogue to the demands of what is usually a heavily moralised plot.

This sense that Wilde was able to exploit the society comedy in a manner that distinguished him from his contemporaries led some theatre historians and critics in the 1980s to suggested that in the hands of certain dramatists society comedy could be used subversively, although its radical potential came into view only when it was situated more firmly within the specificities of late nineteenth-century British society – that is, within the context of the values and customs of the social class who was both its subject and its main audience. In other words, as with Romantic-period literature and the social-problem novel, it became possible to envisage a revaluation of the society comedy through a more thoroughgoing process of historical contextualisation. This meant understanding more precisely the nature of London Society – that is, its membership, its codes of conduct, the nature of its language and the power of its systems of etiquette.

These lines of research noted the following key issues. During the middle and last years of the nineteenth century, inclusion or exclusion (for example, as a result of divorce or scandal) from the ranks of London Society was serious and could make or mar the careers of the individuals concerned. Social historians generally locate the emergence of London Society in changes in the organisation of status groups in Britain which took place from the 1820s onwards (Davidoff 1973). As the British population grew and as, in the wake of the Napoleonic Wars and increasing industrialisation, Britain became progressively wealthier and ethnically more homogeneous, so the separation of public and private life became socially more important. As a consequence, during the 1830s and 1840s what counted as acceptable social life was systematically codified. This led to

Much historical contextualisation of society comedy concentrates on elaborating for the modern reader the precise details of the social world which is its main subject. However, there has also been a considerable body of research which has concentrated on recovering the performance histories of these works, and which draws attention to the difficulties involved in restaging such topical pieces for modern audiences, whether in the early decades of the twentieth century or in more recent years. Notable modern productions have included those of Wilde's dramas by modern theatre directors like Philip Prowse (for the Glasgow Citizens' Theatre in the mid-1980s) and Sir Peter Hall and Nicholas Hytner in the 1990s.

the development of an elaborate and highly ritualised body of etiquette by means of which social newcomers could be evaluated and their status assessed; they could then be accepted into or excluded from London Society. In simple terms, London Society was an elite made up of the most distinguished figures of the nation – distinguished by political, social and cultural fame – but first and foremost by birth, and then by money. In addition – and most importantly for the themes of society comedy – London Society was self-policing. Like all other status groups, that policing revolved around access to its ranks. During the course of the nineteenth century, London Society developed an elaborate series of social occasions, the rigorously exclusive London Season to which characters in many society comedies of the 1890s – particularly those of Oscar Wilde – refer. Formally, the London Season culminated with the entry of debutantes – eligible, well-connected young women – into Society in order to meet eligible young men of the same social class. (The London Season survived, although in a much less socially important way, until the 1960s.)

These social events included not only private entertainments but also public and semi-public occasions, like the Private Viewing of the Royal Academy and the race meeting at Royal Ascot. The well-regulated life-style which London Society fostered identified those who belonged to it as ladies and gentlemen. To deviate from this life-style (as some of the characters in the plays of the 1890s do) was to relinquish that distinction and place oneself physically as well as morally outside Society. This rigid codification of accepted behaviour regulated domestic life and it also produced an intense feeling of community. The 1890s was London Society's high point; in the early decades of the twentieth century British society became too populous, too disparate and too wealthy to be successfully policed in the ways in which it had been in the preceding half-century. The society comedy, with no real constituency to play to, simply became irrelevant. (Some theatre historians have noted that Edwardian revivals treated the plays of the 1890s as period pieces (Kaplan 1997).)

The significance of this context is that it allows the modern reader to appreciate the political resonance of forms of behaviour, particularly those to do with sexual double standards, which might otherwise appear trivial, dated and simply snobbish. The abundance of etiquette books published in the late decades of the century – which were directed towards both men and women – testifies to the importance of correct manners as a precondition for social acceptance. Manners in their turn were exhibited in a complex variety of ways, including using correct forms of speech and address, observing correct forms of clothing, the appropriateness of the foods one ate and wines one drank, one's possessions, reading habits and so forth. Uncovering the precise social meanings behind such apparently trivial habits as the wearing of a button-hole or the eating of cake has involved looking at publications as varied as *The Illustrated Language of Flowers* (1856), *The Decay of Modern Preaching* (1882) and *Boyle's Fashionable Court & Country Guide, and Town Visiting Directory* (published annually in both January and April in the late nineteenth century) to build up a picture of upper middle-class values and mores. Joseph Donohue's critical edition of *The Importance of Earnest* represents the epitome of this kind of detailed contextualisation; it attempts to give the modern reader access to the same nexus of cultural values as a nineteenth-century audience in order to appreciate the richness of the social nuances of the exchanges in that work (Donohue and Beggren 1995). In so doing it enables the modern reader to distinguish the subtly ironic politics of Wilde's society comedies from the formally very similar, but ideologically more conservative, plays of Pinero and Jones.

As we noted in Chapter 3, the dilemma at the centre of many late nineteenth-century society comedies is that of the woman with a past, or a woman who is sexually compromised, but who is trying to disguise her past in order to gain acceptance into Society (and here acceptance – by way of a good marriage – was the route to economic as well as social success). Once again, examining late nineteenth-century conduct books – works such as *Manners of Modern Society: Being a Book of Etiquette* (1872) and *Manners and Rules of Good Society or Solecisms to Be Avoided* (1888) – helps the modern reader to appreciate the seriousness at that time of women's transgression of contemporary gender norms. Generally speaking, the plots of society comedies function to punish the efforts of these female characters to regain a place in London Society, especially if they involve deception. The social threat posed by the sexually compromised woman is typically removed in the play's denouement, through either death or self-imposed exile. So Elaine Shrimpton, a caricature of the 'new woman' in Jones's *The Case of Rebellious Susan*, criticises that sexual double standard when she tells Sir Richard Kato that: 'We [women] will correct Nature.' Kato then replies: 'By changing your sex? What is it that you ladies want? You are evidently dissatisfied with being women. You cannot wish to be anything so brutal and disgusting as a man. And unfortunately there is no neuter sex in the human species.' The apparent conservatism of Jones's play can be contrasted with a greater sensitivity to the plight of women found in the work of other dramatists, one which can function to undermine the conservative tendencies inherent in society comedy's structure. In *A Woman of No Importance* Wilde allows Mrs Arbuthnot to justify her conduct in appropriately emphatic if melodramatic terms which contrast love with social propriety: 'How could

I repent of my sin when you [her illegitimate son, Gerald], my love, were its fruit! Even now that you are bitter to me I cannot repent. I do not. You are more to me than innocence. I would rather be your mother – oh! much rather! – than have been always pure ... It is my dishonour that has made you so dear to me. ... Child of my shame, be still the child of my shame!' Although this speech is melodramatic in tone, and although it exploits a conservative rhetoric of shame, repentance and sexual disgrace, none the less its emotional power derives from the trumping of these values with an equally conservative, but still powerful celebration of the power of maternal love. Here, then, Wilde uses a conventional dramatic device to expose contradictions in attitudes towards femininity, and it is in ways such as this that we can see the radical or subversive potential in what appears to be a highly conservative form (Worth 1983; Eltis 1996).

The codification of late nineteenth-century gender ideology through conduct and etiquette books was not solely concerned with female behaviour; just as important, at this time, was the defining and policing of appropriate male behaviour through (as with women) dress, manners, sexual behaviour and work (Adams 1995). A further element in the historical contextualisation of society comedy – and particularly those of Wilde – was therefore by reference to the history of homosexuality (a topic discussed in more detail in Chapter 6). Queer theorists, concerned to show how Wilde's plays engaged with contemporary sexual mores governing male (as much as female) behaviour, suggested that his plays employed coded ways of addressing different constituencies in their audiences, and through them confirmed the pleasures to be derived from male–male, rather than male–female, society (Craft 1994). Importantly, those codes could only be detected through a precisely historicised analysis of particular lexical items which contain – in the view of some modern critics – a submerged reference to a gay life-style. One example concerns the alleged sexual reference of the term 'Bunburying' in *The Importance of Being Earnest*. Some critics have pointed to the punning association of 'bun' and 'bum'; another argument was that 'Bunburying' was nineteenth-century British slang for a male brothel; yet others suggest that it was a term for a homosexual pickup (Craft 1990; Mackie 1998). In all of this, the accepted sexual conduct of 1890s London Society – what Adrienne Rich labelled 'compulsory heterosexuality' (Rich 1980) – was contrasted with an altogether more exciting, but necessarily secretive and transgressive, homosexual life-style. In this kind of argument the radicalism of Wilde's use of the society comedy lies in his appropriation of a highly conservative form as vehicle to explore a homoerotic dynamic in London Society.

A rather different way of drawing out the radicalism of Wilde's plays was by contextualising them in relation to debates about English and Irish nationalism (Worth 1978; Cave 1997). This kind of argument stressed the importance to Wilde of the politics of national, rather than sexual, identity in the last years of the nineteenth century. There it is argued that Wilde was at heart a writer who never forgot his Irish origins and his Irish sensibilities. 'Wilde the Irishman' became a shorthand term for describing the motivations behind his ambition to explore and critique the contrasts between what was claimed for the elaborate social and ethical codes of London Society, and what those codes could and often did actually entail. In this view, a concern with local domestic etiquette is seen as possessing powerful national implications, in that to expose the moral hypocrisy of Britain's political and social elite is to undermine British rule both at home and (more importantly) overseas, in colonies like Ireland. In this argument, the textual history of *The Importance of Being Earnest* is central. The manager who first produced that work, George Alexander (1858–1918), bought the copyright of the play. When the play was put into rehearsal, Alexander's dissatisfaction with its four-act structure increased. Sending Wilde (and his lover, Lord Alfred Douglas) away, Alexander set about cutting the play from its original four acts to three, a pattern more familiar in the tradition of nineteenth-century farces. However, it is possible to see in this behaviour a coercive although informal process of censorship at work; the very attempt to suppress aspects of Wilde's play testifies to the acuteness of its critique of British (that is, colonial) authority, one which can be lost to modern audiences insufficiently tuned to the subtle ways in which nineteenth-century power structures were codified and legitimated.

One further way of expanding the historical context of society comedy, which also aims to refigure its politics, has been to relate it to the contemporary fashion industry; the rise of the modern 'fashion show' has been traced to the late decades of the nineteenth century, the same period which also witnessed heated debates about appropriate clothing, both by the Suffragettes and by the Rational Dress Society. In this view London theatre is seen as an element of institutionalised capitalist modes of display in which what we would now call life-style choices are exhibited to an audience as objects of consumer desire (a topic to be discussed in more detail in Chapter 7). Of particular interest is the way in which the elaborate and expensive staging of 1890s society comedies became a vehicle for advertising contemporary fashions in dress (particularly for women) and trends in house decoration. These kinds of plays provided an opportunity for the products of various couturiers and designers to be placed on display, and in this way the social world of the stage and that of the audience merged: contemporary magazines often reviewed characters' dress as if the plays were mere fashion plates (Stowell and Kaplan 1994). In this respect, it can be argued that an appreciation of the intimate ways in which society comedy brought together the worlds of commerce and the theatre permits a more subtle understanding of the tensions – again notably in Wilde's works – between the consumerism endorsed in the production values of this sub-genre and their sometimes subversive sub-texts.

As with accounts of Romantic-period literature and social-problem novels, we can see how the appeal to varieties of contextual information – whether they comprise details about London Society, or late nineteenth-century homosexual sub-cultures, or the politics of Irish nationalism, or the growth of the fashion industry – can work to complicate our interpretation of plays which might otherwise appear relatively straightforward. In the process, society comedy itself can be revalued as a more serious and politically sophisticated dramatic form, at least in the hands of some playwrights. As we noted in Chapter 3, the commercial nature of British theatrical culture meant it was much less well disposed to experimentation than theatre in France. Yet this does not necessarily mean that genres like society drama were inevitably conservative. An attention to its historical context enables the modern critic to distinguish between those plays where the form merely embodied, normalised and endorsed the social values, behaviour and politics of the audience, and those where it could be used for more radical or subversive purposes.

Conclusion

- The relationship between a literary work and its historical context may be understood in a variety of ways, and these have had an impact on how particular nineteenth-century works are interpreted and valued.
- There is considerable disagreement about the kind of historical information that is deemed 'relevant' to understanding nineteenth-century literary works; and there is disagreement too about the extent to which the relationship between literature and context is a determining one.
- The politics of Romantic-period literature have been fundamentally reconfigured as critics have examined a variety of distinct historical contexts, including that of contemporary radical groups, as well as the politics of contemporary gender and race relations.
- Critical debate about the nineteenth-century social-problem novel has tended to centre on its politics, although how these are understood depends upon the nature of the historical context in which they are placed.
- Society comedy has traditionally been viewed as a conservative form which functioned to endorse the values of its mainly middle and upper middle-class audience; however, attention to the precise details of the manners and mores of 'London Society' has enabled critics to distinguish ways in which it could be used radically.

6 Nineteenth-century literature and the politics of sex and nationalism

Overview

The previous chapter describes the manner in which debates about historicism have affected our understanding of the relationship between nineteenth-century literary works and what can loosely be termed their historical contexts. In this chapter we discuss the influence of two other broad areas of theoretical enquiry, gender studies (which encompasses both feminism and queer theory) and postcolonial theory, on the ways in which the literary history of the nineteenth century has been understood. It is beyond the scope of this chapter to provide a comprehensive survey of these theories, which have their own complex histories of development. It is not unusual, for example, for commentators to distinguish between 'American', 'British' and 'French' feminism, or between 'first-', 'second-' and 'third'-wave feminism, and even to talk of a 'post-feminist' criticism. Likewise postcolonial theory embraces several different kinds of paradigms for understanding the relationship between self and other. As we noted in Chapter 2, the model of East–West relations proposed by Edward Said in his pioneering *Orientalism* has been contested and complicated by a range of subsequent theorists. The work of some critics, including Gayatri Spivak's theorisation of the position of the subaltern, Homi Bhabha's concept of cultural hybridity and Mary Louise Pratt's idea of the 'contact zone', has focused on isolating those conditions in which colonised subjects are able to engage with, and so develop strategies of resistance to, the forms of representation that subjugate them (Spivak (1988); Bhabha (1994); Pratt (2009)). Other critics have suggested that there needs to be more sensitivity to the different kinds of political and cultural relations that obtained between Britain and 'Eastern' nations, such those with colonised India, on the one hand, and uncolonised Japan (with whom Britain none the less enjoyed a privileged trade relationship), on the other. Moreover, both gender and postcolonial theory intersect in complex ways in the investigation of the related topic of the formation of identity, and the proposition, perhaps most forcefully articulated by Judith Butler, that identity is constructed in relation to difference, but that the categories through which difference is articulated, whether of race, gender, class or nation, are fundamentally unstable. This occurs, she suggests, partly because they have no reality outside culture, and partly because any act of binary differentiation – whether a distinction between self and other, or between centre and periphery – must necessarily incorporate that which is its opposite (Butler 1990).

Rather than describing the details of these complex theoretical positions, this chapter will restrict itself to the more modest aim of discussing the overall impact of these areas of enquiry on the nineteenth-century literary canon. In the process it will indicate how gender studies and postcolonial theory have brought into sharp focus the question of *why* we read nineteenth-century literature. That question in its turn is part of a larger debate, already alluded to in Chapter 3, about the relationship between what can loosely be termed the 'instrumental' and the 'aesthetic' or formal qualities of literary works, an opposition which also figured in debates about culture which took place in the nineteenth century.

Generally speaking, we can identify two strategies via which gender studies and postcolonial theory have challenged the nineteenth-century literary canon. First, writers hitherto forgotten or marginalised (because, it has been argued, of race or gender prejudice) may be brought to our attention and literary history rewritten to take account of 'their' stories. We have noted an example of this process in Chapter 4 in Talia Schaffer's attempt to recover a history of female Aesthetes. Second, new frames of reference may be proposed for revaluing – or to use a term made popular in the 1980s, 're-reading' – familiar canonical works. In this way Walter Scott's romances can be interpreted as an attempt to provide a view of Scottish identity acceptable to the tastes of English readers, or Charlotte Brontë's fiction can be seen as exhibiting a form of racial prejudice, or Tennyson's *In Memoriam* can be read as a homoerotic work. Occasionally, changing a frame of reference has led to the revaluation of an entire sub-genre, such as that of Gothic fiction so much so that critics now routinely talk of 'male' and 'female' Gothic traditions (Moers 1976; Williams 1995; Ellis 1989; Clery 2000). A complicating factor in assessing how gender and postcolonial theory have affected the construction of the literary canon concerns their relationship with history proper. As Chapters 4 and 5 have hinted, there are often discrepancies between the ways social and cultural historians have talked about events in the nineteenth century and the ways those same events have been discussed by literary historians. So investigations by social historians into social phenomena such as premarital sex, or into the 'invention' of homosexuality in the late decades of the century, or into the mechanisms of British imperialism, have implications for our understanding of the gender and racial politics of nineteenth-century literature. Sometimes they have led to a questioning of widespread assumptions about the 'social reality' with which literature allegedly engages, or which it constructs. A good example of this occurs with the 1890s society comedy, mentioned in Chapter 5. Some critics have seen Oscar Wilde's dandy-aesthetes as subversive, assuming that effeminacy was analogous to homosexuality; however, some historians of sexuality have argued that the dandy is defined principally in class terms, and as a result they have challenged the way literary critics think about the role sexual politics played in the reception of Wilde's works before his trial (Sinfield 1994). In a similar way recent historians of Empire have stressed the complexity and variety of Britain's political, financial and economic relationships with its subject populations, stressing that settlement and the acquisition of land was not the only, nor even arguably the principal, model of colonisation.

Feminism

Throughout the nineteenth century the achievement of women writers was recognised, and the efforts of several were celebrated. Novels by Austen, the Brontës, Gaskell and Eliot were highly praised by their contemporaries. In the early decades of the nineteenth century women poets like Felicia Hemans and Letitia Landon were more popular than some of their male counterparts and, as a category of writers, their contribution to literary culture was valued. The reputations of Christina Rossetti and Elizabeth Barrett Browning rivalled those of their male counterparts; for most of their careers the work of Elizabeth Barrett was more widely read than that of her husband, Robert Browning, and following the deaths of Hemans and Landon in the late 1830s, she became of something of a model for the poetess as a celebrity. Later in the century some of the best-selling novels were written by women, although the fame subsequently enjoyed by figures such as Marie Corelli and Ouida often perplexed male reviewers. A writer like Margaret Oliphant never achieved the public success of the former two women. None the less, in a career of exemplary endeavour in which, as Sutherland puts it, she 'outwrote' Anthony Trollope 'two to one', she managed, following a series of domestic tragedies, to earn enough money to support herself, her own three children (sending her two boys to Eton) as well as three of her widowed brother's children (Sutherland 2009: 481).

One reason for the relatively high visibility (though not always higher reputation) of women writers in the nineteenth century has to do with the large-scale changes in literary culture which were described in Chapter 2. The development of a mass literary market, much of which was made up of middle-class female readers, provided new opportunities for women writers, particularly of fiction, a process reinforced by the growth of periodical literature and the emergence of what have been characterised as a new class of professional writers. The ability of individuals to earn a living from the pen meant that for the first time a career as a writer offered women a degree of economic independence. Successful women writers, especially in the last half of the century, could earn substantial sums: Elizabeth Gaskell, Mary Braddon and Mary Ward were paid sufficient sums for their writing to enable their families to enjoy a high bourgeois life-style. At the same time it is equally true that many women writers continued to be subject to significant prejudice, a process which helped bring about their virtual exclusion from the modern literary canon for the first half of the twentieth century. (Significantly F. R. Leavis included only Austen and Eliot in his 'great tradition' (Leavis 1948).)

Nineteenth-century prejudice operated in a number of ways. The first, and perhaps most disabling, was the assumption that women were suited to writing only about a limited range of topics – typically romance and domestic life. This last category led some publishers to direct the aspiring woman writer towards children's fiction. In this view few women were thought to possess the range of experience necessary to engage with more serious subjects, and many male critics believed that they were intellectually ill equipped as well. In his popular *Enquiry into the Duties of the Female Sex* (1797) the poet and Anglican theologian Thomas Gisborne (1758–1846) gave a long list of what he termed 'studies, pursuits, and occupations, assigned chiefly or entirely to men', reasoning that they demanded 'efforts of a mind endued with the powers of close and comprehensive reasoning, and of intense and continued application, in a degree in which they are not requisite for the discharge of the customary offices of female duty'. They included 'the science of legislation, of jurisprudence, of political economy; the conduct of government in all its executive functions; the abstruse researches or erudition; the inexhaustible depths of philosophy; the acquirements subordinate to navigation; the knowledge indispensable in the wide field of commercial enterprise; the arts of defence, and of attack, by land and by sea'. The qualities of women, by contrast, included 'modesty', 'delicacy' and a 'sympathising sensibility' – in other words, those civilising virtues which made domestic life such an important refuge from what Gisborne termed 'the darkness of uncultivated barbarism'.

Exactly the same male chauvinism reappears thirty years later in Francis Jeffrey's 1829 review of Felicia Hemans's poetry in the *Edinburgh Review* (a periodical Jeffrey had co-founded and which he edited). There he claimed that women 'cannot ... represent naturally the fierce and sullen passions of men – nor their coarser vices – nor even scenes of actual business of contention – and the mixed motives, and strong and faulty characters, by which affairs of the moment are usually conducted on the great theatre of the world'. Jeffrey went on to explain that this failure was due partly to female natures, and partly to their education and upbringing:

> For much of this they are disqualified by the delicacy of their training and habits, and the still more disabling delicacy which pervades their conceptions and feelings; and ... by their actual inexperience ... by their substantial and incurable ignorance of business – of the way in which serious affairs are actually managed – and the true nature of the agents and impulses that give movements and direction to the stronger currents of life. Perhaps they are also incapable of long moral and political investigations, where many complex and indeterminate elements are to be taken into account, and a variety of opposite probabilities to be weighed. ... They rarely succeed in long works, ... their natural training rendering them equally averse to long doubt and long labour.

It was exactly this sort of inveterate sexism – the presumption that woman 'is not intended for the rough business of the world', as the physician John Elliotson (1791–1868) put it in the 1840 edition of his *Human Physiology* – that George Eliot complained about in her essay 'Silly Novels by Lady Novelists' published in 1856 in the *Westminster Review*. (Elliotson was a prominent, if controversial, figure at the time; a member of the Royal College of Physicians and Royal Society, he was also a leading proponent of the less academically respectable 'sciences' of mesmerism and phrenology.) Women, Eliot noted, now had opportunities to develop a literary career but they had paid a high price for that acceptance. Eliot was particularly critical of what she referred to as a contemporary fashion for 'mind and millinery' fiction, writing which was 'frothy, prosy, pious and pedantic', and which bore little relation to 'real life'. In some ways, it might seem that Eliot shared the prejudices of figures like Jeffrey insofar as she, too, was exasperated at what she saw as the triviality and lack of ambition in much contemporary writing by women. It infuriated her that women (that is, the aristocratic 'ladies' of her essay title) were writing about groups in society (such as servants) about whom they knew nothing, and were pretending that they possessed a knowledge of issues such as theology and philosophy of which they were wholly ignorant. For Eliot, these 'lady novelists' seemed to treat writing as a sort of amateur hobby. Eliot, by contrast, was unusually well read for a woman of her time, particularly in Continental (and especially German) philosophy, theology and science. Prior to writing fiction, she had helped to edit, and published articles in, the leading liberal periodical of the day, the *Westminster Review*, as well as a progressive newspaper called *The Leader*. She was acquainted with several prominent intellectuals and men of letters, including the publisher John Chapman, the intellectual polymath Herbert Spencer and, latterly, the already married George Henry Lewes, with whom she lived. Eliot, in other words, was an intelligent, worldly and ambitious woman who wished to make her mark in what was still overwhelmingly a man's world. In this respect, her greatest anger was directed towards the male critics who patronisingly puffed such 'silly novels' while ignoring or condemning what Eliot considered to be women of genuine talent – middle-class women, that is, like Eliot herself or Harriet Martineau.

In her essay Eliot was attempting to open up a debate about what it meant to be a writer and a woman in the middle decades of the nineteenth century, and the conditions which would permit a woman to be considered the intellectual equal of a man. Eliot's point was that novel writing was – or should be – a serious profession, one which required intelligence and education, and that the proliferation of 'silly' lady novelists was effectively damning that profession for all women by suggesting that 'mind and millinery' were the only sorts of theme they were capable of addressing. To be taken seriously as a writer – when serious involved tackling 'long moral and political investigations, where many complex and indeterminate elements are to be taken into account' – meant that one had to be male or at least appear to be male. This was one reason why Eliot (and the Brontës) adopted male pseudonyms, and why Elizabeth Gaskell published her first novel, *Mary Barton*, anonymously.

Of course, there were other strategies women writers could use to combat discrimination; gendered definitions of intellectual ability could also be contested by revaluing the origin of that alleged feminine incapacity – that supposed tendency of women to 'feel' rather than to 'think', women's possession, as Elliotson put it in *Human Physiology*, being 'more acuteness of external sensation, of apprehension, and of emotion, though a smaller range of intelligence and less permanence of impression'. It is worth remembering that these prejudices persisted into the late decades of the century, and found what is perhaps their best-known expression in John Ruskin's 1864 essay 'Of Queen's Gardens', reprinted in his *Sesame and Lilies* (1865). However, it is also worth noting that Ruskin's authority on matters of male–female relationships were compromised by revelations about his personal life which surfaced during his wife's divorce proceedings, the basis of which was Ruskin's failure to consummate the marriage, and his later infatuation with the adolescent Rose La Touche, who was only 11 years old when Ruskin first met her. Writing in the 1880s Amy Levy – who had followed Eliot's career closely and took a professional interest in her fiction (Levy's short novel *Reuben Sachs* is, in part, a response to Eliot's *Daniel Deronda*) – attempted to make this gendered notion of 'feeling' a standard by which *all* literature should be judged, in that she defined a work's literary value in terms its ability to foster a mode of reading which engaged the 'feelings' or sympathy, rather than the intellect alone. Moreover, it was the absence of such a quality in the work of many of her male contemporaries, notably that of Henry James, which formed the basis of Levy's attack on the self-conscious (and in her view, self-interested) 'cleverness' which characterised what she termed in an 1884 essay 'The New School of American Fiction'.

It is not an accident that Eliot and Levy both chose as their battlefield poetry and literary fiction, rather than, say, writing for the stage or literary criticism. As we noted in Chapter 2, for most of the nineteenth century high literary culture did not consider dramatic entertainment to be a serious art form; therefore a career as a dramatist, for either a male or a female writer, offered little cultural prestige, even though it promised considerable sums of money. However, for women there was an additional taint involved in any career associated with the theatre: it was not considered respectable and the association between actresses, 'loose' morals and prostitution was frequently made. While some women did write for the stage and (as we described in Chapter 3) did enjoy successful careers in theatrical institutions, they rarely achieved significant recognition. This may be one reason why the scripting and staging of domestic entertainments offered the best opportunities for an active engagement with drama, even if such performances could have little direct or lasting impact on mainstream theatrical culture. Prejudices operating against women critics were different: literary criticism obviously involved no danger of moral contamination, but like other Victorian high professions, the analytical skills required to be a critic were assumed to be a function of the 'male' mind. Three of the most famous theorists of criticism in the nineteenth century – Matthew Arnold,

Walter Pater and Oscar Wilde – all take for granted that the critical sensibility is male. More importantly, the kind of education – particularly in classics – which was assumed to underlie what Arnold termed 'right' reason, or correct judgement, was also the exclusive property of boys and men, chiefly acquired at a public school.

Also a male possession for most of the century were those institutions of higher education, the Universities of Oxford and Cambridge, and private clubs (such as the Garrick, founded in 1831) where literary networks were forged. Levy, who was the first Jewish woman to study at Newnham College, Cambridge, was acutely aware of the power of these informal institutions and networks both to make and to destroy careers. Her 1888 essay 'Women and Club Life', published in the *Jewish Chronicle*, argued for the need to establish female equivalents; and she proposed the Reading Room of the British Museum library as a forum in which such intellectual comradeship might flourish (that same location is also the chosen haunt of Reardon and Biffen, the impoverished, but aspiring male authors in George Gissing's *New Grub Street* (1891)). None of this meant that women did *not* write critical prose. Nineteenth-century periodicals have many examples of contributions from women on a surprising variety of topics (Onslow 2000).

Harriet Martineau, for example, specialised in writing on the 'male' topic of economics. Anna Jameson (1794–1860) was the author of popular works of travel and art criticism, but she also wrote for publications like the *Atheneaum*, on topics such as female employment in the millinery trade. Women's rights and employment, as well as the contentious issue of domestic violence, was a concern of the activist and campaigner Frances Power Cobbe (1822–1908), whose preferred medium was the newspaper, including the first halfpenny evening paper, the *Echo*. Lady (Florence Caroline) Dixie (1855–1905), the aunt of Oscar Wilde's lover, Lord Alfred Douglas, was a war correspondent for the *Morning Post* during the first Boer War (1880–81). More impressive perhaps was the career of Eliza (Lynn) Linton (1822–98); one of the first salaried women journalists in England, she first found regular employment for three years on the *Morning Chronicle* before moving in 1851 to Paris, where she worked as a foreign correspondent. In the late 1860s she wrote for the *Saturday Review*, where she published a powerful series of anti-feminist articles; her 1891 series entitled 'The Wild Women' continued her robust defence of traditional female occupations, and provoked an angrily dismissive response from the feminist activist Mona Caird (1854–1932), who, in 1888, had written an inflammatory article criticising the institution of marriage for the *Westminster Review*. The prolific Lucy Walford (1845–1915) was the author of a number of novels and short stories, but she was also (from 1889 to 1893) London correspondent for the New York *Critic* (Sutherland 2009: 188, 379, 664).

Few of these names, however, survived to figure in twentieth-century anthologies of critical writing (Buckler 1958; Warner and Hough 1983). Moreover, and as we noted in Chapter 3, those women critics whose names do stand out (in part because of their achievements in other genres) – figures like Mary

Ward, Eliot or Martineau – hardly represent typical cases. We might note that Ward was the granddaughter of Matthew Arnold and her husband, Humphry Ward, was a well-connected Oxford don, and through these family ties she had access to high literary culture, and particularly entry into the literary parties and salons in which writers and publishers often made informal contact with each other. More usual were the experiences of Margaret Oliphant and Vernon Lee (Violet Paget). Although for over forty years Oliphant was a regular contributor to the periodical press, notably to *Blackwood's Edinburgh Magazine*, unlike Eliza Linton she never achieved the status and financial security of a salaried employee. Lee, who was born into wealth and given a cosmopolitan education, consistently complained about her marginalisation from male-dominated literary circles (even though there is evidence from her letters that she was invited to dine with members of London's literary elite). Indeed it was Levy's meeting with Lee in 1886, and her introduction to the artistic circle surrounding Lee in her self-imposed exile in Florence, which seems to have provided a turning point in her career, and which lends weight to her arguments about the necessity of female literary networks.

Today, what are loosely referred to as 'women's magazines' make up one of the most economically significant sectors of the British weekly magazine market and new titles regularly appear. The beginnings of this phenomenon can be traced back to the late decades of the nineteenth century, years which witnessed a proliferation of magazines and periodicals directed specifically to a female readership. Moreover, and like the present day, few of these publications were explicitly feminist – exceptions were *Shafts* and the *Woman's Herald*; rather, the majority exploited traditional stereotypes of feminine behaviour, concentrating on fashion and beauty, society gossip and aspects of domestic management; few lasted longer than a year or two (White 1970). Two examples are worth singling out. The first was the *Victoria Magazine*, founded in 1863 by the feminist publisher Emily Faithful (1856–95); its main function was as a political organ for the women's movement and it ran until 1880. Three years earlier, in 1860, Faithful had founded her Victoria Press which was staffed entirely by women. A less successful, and considerably less polemical, enterprise was Cassell's *Lady's World*; in its 1887 re-launch as the *Woman's World* (with Oscar Wilde as its editor) it attempted to combine serious political articles on topics such as female emancipation and women's involvement in the professions, alongside pieces on travel writing, women's contributions to historical scholarship, as well as works of fiction, poetry and biography by or about women (Ksinan 1998). Despite these lofty ambitions, the magazine still folded, perhaps because there was an insufficiently large number of educated women to form a market for such a publication.

As well as being marginalised by assumptions about women's 'nature', it has been suggested that the print media in which many women chose (or were encouraged) to publish also contributed to their later exclusion from literary history. The reputation of any author who wrote solely or principally for the periodical press was much less likely to survive than that of those who had their work published (or republished) in the more durable form of the single-authored book. Moreover, this was not simply due to the disposable nature of the medium; it was also a consequence of the practice, widespread in the periodical press in the first half of the century, of authorial anonymity. This was particularly so with the lavishly produced and copiously illustrated literary annuals or gift books, such as *The Keepsake* or *The Amulet*, that were popular at Christmas in the early decades of the century. Directed towards 'lady' readers, such publications (which were sometimes edited by women) explicitly traded on their association with feminine culture, to the extent that some male writers (notably Wordsworth) refused, once their reputations were assured, to publish in them, thus perpetuating the medium's association with cultural triviality. The mainly female contributors often had the additional burden of having to serve the interests of the (generally more highly paid) illustrators, for poems and stories were typically commissioned to accompany engravings (and later in the century lithographs and photographs), which in turn were usually of highly conventional subjects. A good example is the contemporary ladies of fashion who featured in *The Book of Beauty*. The demand for thematic coherence, combined with strictly gendered assumptions about what constituted appropriate reading matter for young women, tended to obscure the individual voice (Pulham 2003). It might be thought that the practice, which became more common from the mid-century onwards, of marketing all kinds of literary anthologies solely on the basis of the sex of the contributors – examples include publications such as George Bethune's *The British Female Poets* (1848) and Frederick Rowton's *The Female Poets of Great Britain* (1848) – would have served to foreground female achievement. However, as Linda Peterson has argued, by emphasising female difference, this concretisation in writing of the ideology of separate spheres tended to reinforce the marginalisation of female voices, and seems to have led to their under-representation in more general anthologies such as Alfred Miles's ten-volume *The Poets and Poetry of the Century* (1892–97), which placed women writers in separate volumes and thus isolated them from the main (and male) chronology of poetic development (Peterson 1999).

A major contribution of early feminist criticism, then, has been to alert modern readers to the operation of these nineteenth-century prejudices and to the ways in which they subsequently found their way into twentieth-century critical values. Feminist re-readings of nineteenth-century literary culture, which have resulted in a variety of new anthologies of women's writing – most notably, perhaps, of women's poetry (Reilly 1994; Leighton and Reynolds 1995; Armstrong, Bristow and Sharrock 1996; Blain 2001), but also of women's criticism (Broomfield and Mitchell 1996; Robinson 2003) and drama (Scullion 1996;

Crochunis 2010) – typically aim to highlight the achievements of women who have been marginalised by twentieth-century canon formation. One of the most dramatic examples of this process – already alluded to in Chapter 5 – can be seen in the expansion of the Romantic canon, initially pioneered by the attention given to eighteenth-century women poets by critics such as Roger Lonsdale (Lonsdale 1989). As we have noted, the consideration which is now routinely given to a wide range of early nineteenth-century women poets, novelists, essayists and dramatists poses a challenge to traditional conceptions of what categories like Romanticism mean (Wu 1997; Stabler 2002). A similar kind of revisionism has been undertaken for writing at the end of the nineteenth century: today, students of 1890s 'new woman' literature are encouraged to read alongside Gissing's *The Odd Women*, Hardy's *Jude the Obscure* and Grant Allen's *The Woman Who Did*, novels such as George Egerton's (Mary Chavelita Dunne) *Keynotes* (1893) and Sarah Grand's *The Heavenly Twins* as well as Mona Caird's *The Daughters of Danaus* (1894), *A Yellow Aster* (1894) by Iota (Kathleen Mannington Caffyn, 1853–1926) and *Gallia* (1895) by Ménie Muriel Dowie (1867–1945) (Cunningham 1978; Ardis 1990; Pykett 1992; Richardson and Willis 2001). Recognising the contribution of women writers to this sub-genre of fiction permits us to glimpse a surprising degree of militancy, one which did not detract from their authors' popular reputations: Caird and Dowie, for example, also produced vehemently proto-feminist non-fictional works, such as Dowie's *Women Adventurers* (1893) and Caird's *The Morality of Marriage* (1897). More to the point, perhaps, placing a premium on the political engagement of new woman fiction, rather than on its formal complexity, enables female voices to come to the fore – or rather, it distinguishes women's contribution to this sub-genre from that of their more politically ambivalent male counterparts. And in the process it provides a useful reminder that the nineteenth-century general reading public was more open minded about such material than the largely male critical establishment which made judgements on its behalf.

Recovering forgotten women's voices is rarely a simple matter of finding female equivalents for, or responses to, better-known works by men. Feminist historians have sometimes argued that in the nineteenth century the same literary forms and genres are used differently by men and women, and so recognising women's contribution to literary culture can change the way we understand the history of generic and stylistic development. The best-known example of such an argument is perhaps the proposition, alluded to earlier, that there are separate male and female Gothic traditions (though some women, like Mary Shelley, may on occasion choose to write in a self-consciously 'male' mode). In this view, it is claimed that writers like Anne Radcliffe (1764–1823) use the supernatural paraphernalia of Gothic – which are explained rationally in the course of a work's ending – as a vehicle for exploring the oppressive nature of a patriarchal culture in which women are invariably represented as powerless victims. By contrast, in the work of figures such as Matthew Lewis (1775–1818) and later Coleridge, Keats and Bram Stoker, the Gothic concern with monstrosity articulates male anxieties about female sexual appetite. *Dracula*, for example, has been memorably described as a novel whose central preoccupation is the 'fear of the devouring woman' (Roth 1977). More recent historians, however, have urged caution about seeing forms or genres gendered in this way. A case in point concerns controversies about the 'invention' of the dramatic monologue.

Traditionally, the dramatic monologue has been seen to originate with male poets, usually (and following an influential study by Robert Langbaum (1957)), Robert Browning, and sometimes Tennyson (Tucker 1984). In Langbaum's argument Browning developed the dramatic monologue as a vehicle for psychological exploration, one which could, through the operation of irony, overcome the solipsism associated with the Romantic representations of self by separating the dramatised speaker of the poem from the poet himself. Subsequent accounts of the form by critics like Elizabeth Howe (1996) and W. David Shaw (1999) have followed Langbaum's example and concentrated mainly on male poets, implying that the objectivity of the form, the way it undermines the integrity of the lyric voice, was somehow unsuited to women poets, insofar as they, in contrast to men, wished – as Kate Flint puts it – to 'inhabit the voices, the subject position of others' (Flint, 1996: 166). Or, as Dorothy Mermin suggests, to 'sympathise with their protagonists', rather than to establish an ironic distance from them (Mermin 1986: 75). Does this mean that women had nothing to contribute to what has been viewed, as we argued in Chapter 3, as one of the major formal innovations of the nineteenth century, a form in which questions of gender are often to fore in the unequal power relationship between dramatic speaker and audience, or speaker and subject? The answer to this question depends – as with understandings of Romanticism – upon how one chooses to define the dramatic monologue, and whether Browning's poems, which hinge on the irony of the unintentional revelation, should be seen as exemplary.

Glennis Byron has suggested that if we expand the (male) canon of dramatic monologues to include works by Augusta Webster, Adah Issacs Menken (1835–68), Catherine Dawson (1865–1934), Constance Naden (1858–89), Emily Pfeiffer (1827–90), Amy Levy and May Kendall (Emma Goldsworth 1861–1943), then we can see how the form could also be used for what Bryon terms 'social critique'. That said, Byron is not proposing that there are male (or psychological) and female (or social) versions of the dramatic monologue; she draws attention, for example, to the importance of social critique in works such as Kipling's 'The "Mary Gloster"' (1894). And it is also the case that there are strong elements of social criticism – against religious corruption, for example – in some of Robert Browning's best-known dramatic monologues. Byron's point is rather that looking at dramatic monologues by women enables us to see that 'polemic was a much more important part of the development of the monologue than traditional criticism has allowed'; it 'shows the importance of social critique to the dramatic monologue generally', and this in turn has the effect of 'decentering' Browning, so much so that his monologues become 'representative of only one of the various ways in which the genre's dynamic of self and context was developed' (Byron 2003: 96–97). Put another way, Byron's emphasis on the polemical character of the dramatic monologue, rather than simply its psychological explorations, enables her to define a tradition in which male and female poets play an equally important role.

In a similar vein, Natalie M. Houston compares male and female appropriations of another poetic form, the sonnet, and comes to the perhaps surprising conclusion that 'Victorian sonnet theory, unlike that of the novel, made very few distinctions based on gender'. For Houston there is little formally or thematically to distinguish sonnets by George Meredith and Dante Gabriel Rossetti, on the one hand, from those of Rosamund Marriott Watson and the German-born Mathilde Blind (1841–96), on the other: for all these authors, she argues, the sonnet was simply a 'vehicle for shaping selected observations, whether philosophical or descriptive'. This observation leads Houston to suggest that perhaps we need to rethink our assumptions about the nature of the 'intersections of genre and gender' (Houston 2003: 163–64). Her claim that form may not always be gendered also of course requires a rethinking of the grounds upon which some recovery projects have been justified: why, for example, should we read Watson rather than Rossetti (or vice versa)?

Houston's work – which has itself recently been challenged by Amy Billone, who has made a case for the distinctiveness of nineteenth-century women's appropriation of the sonnet as a form (Billone 2007) – is a useful reminder that there are a number of strands to feminist re-readings of the nineteenth-century canon. The first, which is often biographically inflected, tends to document and explain examples of the absence of female writers from literary history. As we have noted, stress has often been placed on the success which female authors enjoyed in their own time, and on the diversity of their talents. The second, and arguably more problematic, element is concerned with providing appropriate criteria for evaluating these 'forgotten' works. Some of the central issues include: is it possible to identify distinctly female traditions of nineteenth-century writing? That is, should we understand women's writing principally in relation to the achievements of other women (in Elaine Showalter's resonant phrase, in terms of a 'literature of their own' (Showalter 1977))? And how are we to respond to the range of women's writing, and in particular, and as Kathy Psomiades and Talia Schaffer have noted (1999), to what seem to be the traditionally 'feminine' (rather than feminist) preoccupations with topics such as motherhood, fashion, design and gardening found in the work of some authors? A number of prominent and entrepreneurial nineteenth-century women writers – notably Mary Ward and Eliza Linton – held political views which make for uncomfortable reading for some modern feminists: Linton, as we noted, wrote some trenchantly 'anti-feminist' articles, collected as *The Girl of the Period* (1869), while Ward was a vocal spokeswoman for the Anti-Suffrage League (Anderson 1987; Broomfield 2004). If a literary history is obliged to be representative, then how should such 'representativeness' be understood? Early feminist criticism tended to define it politically, although without explaining why gender as a category should take precedence over, say, that of class or race. Perhaps the most debated of these issues is the relationship between gender and form, and whether there is profit in trying to define certain kinds of literary devices, such as the widespread use of omniscient narration in the nineteenth-century realist novel, as 'masculine'.

Finally, it is also worth noting the contribution of feminist criticism to the revaluation of male authors. Some feminists have objected to the way in which a preoccupation with formal and stylistic innovation can blind literary historians to the manner in which canonical works replicate or normalise gender prejudice. Some of Dickens's fiction, for example, has been criticised for allegedly infantilising femininity; for suggesting that the moral agency of women – their ability to civilise men – is dependent upon a child-like (and consequently a sexual) innocence. A good example is provided by Lucie Manette, the 'golden-haired doll' in *A Tale of Two Cities*; described as 'baby, girl, and woman, all in one', she is the means by which the 'moody and morose lounger' Sydney Carton is redeemed, largely because he learns to love her unselfishly (that is, idealistically), eventually sacrificing himself so that she can enjoy a future with another man. In this novel, Dickens's apparent difficulty in acknowledging a mature female sexuality, except in negative terms, can seem like a form of misogyny. More problematic have been feminist responses to aspects of Thomas Hardy's fictional oeuvre. It can be argued that his attempt in works like *Tess of the D'Urbervilles* and *Jude the Obscure* to highlight contemporary double standards in the treatment of female sexuality is evidence of a proto-feminism. But by the same token it can be objected that Hardy's sympathy for the 'fallen' or sexually compromised woman in these novels seems to require that she is wholly unaware of her own sexuality. So while her sexual attractiveness can be laid out in detail before the reader and presented as belonging to 'nature' or a natural order, it cannot be acknowledged by the woman herself. In many of his novels Hardy ascribes to his heroines a degree of vanity. We first meet Bathsheba Everdene in *Far From the Madding Crowd* (1874) looking at herself in a small mirror, and the narrative describes the process by which she is educated into realising that exploiting the passions aroused by her looks is destructive (in her marriage to Sergeant Troy) and that 'real' love is to be found elsewhere, in the worthy but dull Gabriel Oak. We might also think of the way the narrative voice treats what Showalter has termed the 'full-bodied hoggish sensuality' of Arabella in *Jude the Obscure* (Showalter 1996: 178). In these examples, Hardy can be seen to be exhibiting the same kind of anxiety about the relationship between female agency and a fully aware sexuality found in Dickens's fiction.

The alleged 'feminism' of Gissing's late fiction, in works such as *The Odd Women* (first made available to modern readers through the feminist Virago Press) and *The Whirlpool*, has attracted a similar controversy. Although, like Hardy, Gissing was sympathetic towards women who rejected the traditional role of wife and mother, he seems unable in these novels to imagine how any sort of man, even those as self-consciously 'modern' in their views as are

Everard Barfoot and Henry Rolfe, could enjoy a successful relationship with what modern commentators might term a 'career' woman. The point at issue is whether the questioning of gender stereotypes succeeds in transcending the terms by which female achievement was traditionally marginalised. To put this another way, Hardy and Gissing – in some of their works at least – tend to debate gender via a familiar set of oppositions, in which women can be intelligent or sexual but not both, or at least not both at the same time. The central critical question then becomes whether Gissing, and more particularly Hardy, merely *reproduce* (and thereby essentialise) this divide, or whether novels like *Tess* serve to expose it as evidence of the limitations – the confusions and obsessions – of male ways of thinking (Higonnet 1992). For example, it is significant that in *Tess* we are never given access to the heroine's inner consciousness; rather, her story is told to us by others. Is this narrative strategy an attempt to foreground and critique male-centred ways of viewing women; or is it an unthinking reflection of Hardy's own latent misogyny (some critics have noted how the omniscient narrator seems to share the same voyeuristic gaze as the villainous Alec). In many cases the determinedly single status and masculine countenance which tends to characterise the independently minded fictional woman, from Marian Halcombe in Collins's *The Woman in White* to Gissing's tellingly named Rhoda Nunn or even Shaw's Vivie Warren in *Mrs Warren's Profession*, seem to point towards an 'unnaturalness', one which can be seen more strikingly in the works of conservative playwrights of the same time. This unnaturalness simultaneously emasculates men and, through the childlessness of the women concerned, ultimately fails to reproduce itself. According to Showalter, at the heart of some late nineteenth-century male authors' debating of gender is an attempt to recuperate creativity as an essentially masculine attribute by linking it with a productive male (rather than female) sexuality – an assertion of what she provocatively terms a 'phallic literary monopoly' (1996: 180).

Queer theory

A number of social historians, among them Jeffrey Weeks, see the nineteenth century, and particularly its later decades, as marking an important moment in the history of sexuality, one in which the normative concepts of heterosexuality (Rich's concept, noted in Chapter 5, of 'compulsory heterosexuality') and homosexuality emerged in an attempt to survey, categorise and thereby regulate sexual behaviour (Weeks 1977; Rich 1980). In his influential *History of Sexuality* Michel Foucault (1978) pointed to the role played by a nexus Victorian medical and pseudo-scientific discourses in reconfiguring particular kinds of sexual appetites and practices – most notably sodomy – as signifying specific sexual identities which in their turn could be pathologised in terms of an opposition between the normal and the deviant. These included, for Foucault, the classification of the homosexual as a distinct 'type', a process which became most fully visible, according to later historians, in the trials of Oscar Wilde in 1895 (Cohen 1993). Cohen argues that in the reporting of the trials in the local and national press we can see that process of categorisation at work; in it invisible or unnameable sexual acts are identified with that which *is* on display and which *can* be described, in this case the person of Wilde himself. The importance of Wilde's prosecution, in this view, is that it enabled a hegemonic male culture to subordinate as morally degenerate and contemptible what Richard Dellamora identified as 'the new self-consciousness [in the late nineteenth century] of men who desire other men'. Dellamora further argues that scandal was a key process by which sexual identities were articulated at this time. Scandal enabled both 'the reaffirmation of the naturalness of gender norms, of manly men and womanly women, of marriage, of the return of middle-class women to the home, and the primacy of mothering' while at the same time questioning 'the universality of these norms' (Dellamora 1990: 217).

By contrast, more recent historians have disputed the view that Wilde's trial materially changed attitudes towards male–male desire. H. G. Cocks, for example, has documented a long history of prosecutions for sodomy; he also suggests that there is little evidence to support the allegation that the 1890s was, as Dellamora and others have suggested, an especially homophobic decade (Cocks 2003). (This homophobic 'panic' has also been invoked to explain the polemic of some late nineteenth-century feminists where a plea for economic and intellectual independence for women combines with what some modern commentators have viewed as a thoroughly conservative insistence on sexual purity (Showalter 1990).) Other cultural historians, notably Linda Dowling, have pointed to the significance, particularly in earlier decades of the century, of alternative and more affirmative paradigms for understanding male–male desire. In her argument most significant of these is the *paiderastia* of Socratic tradition which both predates and overlaps with the development of the hetero–homosexual binary (Dowling, 1995). There is a lively debate among Wilde scholars about both the terms by which Wilde himself understood his sexuality, and those traditions of understanding sexual love between men most suitable to interpreting the representation of desire in his literary works. More generally, however, and as we have noted in Chapters 4 and 5, social historians have questioned the accuracy of Foucault's account of Victorian sexuality, noting that Victorian medical literature displays a more diverse and at times open-minded range of attitudes towards sexual behaviours than Foucault allowed (Mason 1994; Porter and Hall 1995). Such research in turn points to the need for more subtle and complex theoretical models in order to capture better the tensions and contradictions underlying the representation of same-sex desire in nineteenth-century literature and culture.

Less controversial than this focus on Wilde and on the 1890s is the suggestion that there is a necessary relationship in nineteenth-century discourses about sexuality between the normal and the forbidden. This kind of insight predates queer theory by some decades. In his classic 1966 study *The Other Victorians*, Steven Marcus argues that the late Victorian 'subculture of pornography and the view of sexuality held by the official culture were reversals, mirror images, negative analogies of each other' (Marcus 1966: 283–84). Queer theory, however, helps to articulate an important distinction between scholars of Marcus's generation, on the one hand, and those of Dellamora or Cohen, on the other. For the latter group are not just concerned with the mechanisms by which a dominant culture defines and therefore marginalises sexual difference. Of greater interest are the possibilities for contesting those definitions, as well as for positive representations of outlawed sexual practices and desires. And here literary works, including non-canonical and pornographic novels such as *Teleny* (which some critics believe to have been partly written by Oscar Wilde), are assumed to play a crucial role in the formation of sexual identities in the nineteenth century. Moreover, they may be an element in the configuration of what Eve Kosofsky Sedgwick has termed a 'normative continuum of homo-social desire' – in the means, that is, by which a culture discourages awareness of same-sex relationships, typically by troping them in terms of asymmetrical power relations, often rooted in class, between men and women (Sedgwick 1985). But literature may also contribute to the refashioning of gender norms by exposing, sometimes unwittingly, the instabilities and contradictions in homo-social discourse. One example of this is the manifest tension between bourgeois expectations that a responsible masculinity involves marriage and reproduction, and the formal encouragement of intense male–male bonding through a strictly gendered workplace, particularly among the professions, and all-male educational and leisure institutions such as public schools, private clubs and the armed services. Literary works, in other words, are one arena in which the erotic potential of bonds between men may be safely explored. More controversial, perhaps, has been the way in which queer theory moves beyond the biographical emphasis of some early feminist criticism to enable us to appreciate that all kinds of literary works, including those by apparently 'straight-identified' authors, may participate in debating the articulation of normative sexual identities. Thus what Joseph Bristow terms 'gay-affirmative readers' have not only played a key role in the critical rehabilitation of nineteenth-century gay and lesbian writers (like Wilde, John Addington Symonds, Edward Carpenter (1844–1929), Michael Field and the 'Uranian' poets), but they have also spent much critical energy in unearthing homoerotic sub-texts in the work of more familiar canonical figures, like Gerard Manley Hopkins, in an attempt to delineate a nineteenth-century literary tradition which answers to their interests (Bristow 1997).

In this respect some of the most arresting accounts of nineteenth-century literature by queer theorists are those which invite us to rethink the ways that sexual power relations are exhibited in well-known works, such as Stevenson's *Dr Jekyll and Mr Hyde* or Tennyson's *In Memoriam*. Following Sedgwick's lead (1990), it is now commonplace for the secretive nature of the all-male professional world of Stevenson's novella to be read as a thinly coded response to the anxieties that surrounded the 1885 Criminal Law Amendment Act (or the 'blackmailer's charter', as it was popularly known, because of the way in which its criminalisation of private sexual acts between men required witnesses, who were typically servants). As some readers have noted, the grounds for Jekyll's trust in his male friends are never specified; nor is there any explanation for their reclusive, women-free lives, nor their failure, when suspicions grow about Jekyll's fate, to appeal to external agencies such as the police. In this view, the locked doors (both internal and external) to Jekyll's laboratory, and the 'dark closets' and 'spacious cellar' which Utterson and Jeykll's manservant Poole peer into in their search for the missing doctor, symbolise the mechanisms of a latent homophobia – of a pressing need to keep locked away from public view non-normative sexual appetites. A similar situation occurs in Wilde's *The Picture of Dorian Gray*, a work which more obviously lends itself to the identification of homosexual themes; there too, Dorian, having murdered Basil Hallward, is able to call upon the scientific knowledge of the 'extremely clever young man', Alan Campbell, in the disposal of Hallward's body. Throughout the grisly scene Dorian exhibits a powerful but never fully explained influence over his former friend: certainly Campbell's loyalty and discretion are never in doubt once Dorian reminds him, through 'something' that can only be written on a piece of paper and never articulated, something that is from the secret past that ties them together.

More controversially, perhaps, some of the tensions underlying one of Queen Victoria's favourite poems, *In Memoriam*, have been explained in terms of the nature, rather than simply the intensity, of Tennyson's love for his dead Cambridge friend, Arthur Hugh Hallam – a love which, because it was directed towards another man, could not easily be framed in terms of the conventional elegy. Of course most elegies, including those written in the nineteenth century, have to grapple with contradiction, negotiating the tension between loss and recuperation, and the emotional paradox of both lamenting and celebrating a life that is past, and of being haunted by memory while simultaneously looking positively to the future. However, it has been suggested that Tennyson's inability to come to terms with the overwhelming nature of his grief – he compares himself at various moments in the poem to a lover and a bereaved wife – marks a disjunction between public and private which has its origins in a suspicion of emotional transgression. In this view, trying to find a language appropriate to articulating his feelings for Hallam, Tennyson is unwittingly disclosing a hitherto repressed homoeroticism. Dellamora (1990), for example, makes much of Tennyson's apparently slight revision to Canto XCV of *In Memoriam* (in the earlier 1850 version XCIII) – for some critics the turning point of the poem – where the poet describes a moment of mystic union with his dead friend's ghost. Changing the pronoun from 'his' (that is, Hallam's) living soul to 'the' living soul in the following lines can be seen as a form of self-censorship, making less obviously erotic an image which otherwise might invite inappropriate sexual interpretation:

> So word by word, and line by line,
>   The dead man touch'd me from the past
> And all at once it seem'd at last
>   The living soul was flash'd on mine,

And mine in this was wound, and whirl'd
  About empyreal heights of thought,
  And came on that which is, and caught
The deep pulsations of the world,

Aeonian music measuring out
  The steps of Time –

It is perhaps worth stressing that Dellamora's reading of *In Memoriam* does not necessarily presuppose that Tennyson and Hallam were engaged in a sexual or even an erotic relationship (a suggestion for which most Tennyson scholars and biographers have found no evidence). In other words, such criticism is not a crude attempt at a form of literary 'outing'. None the less, what Christopher Craft terms the 'same gender eroticism' of Tennyson's 'strange manner of address', the invocation to Hallam's ghost to 'descend, touch and enter', as Craft provocatively paraphrases it, has given rise to intense debate (Craft 1994; Nunokawa 1991). A similar case concerns discussions about the sexuality of Henry James, and the suggestion that many of the concerns which dominate his fiction, such as an interest in thwarted love and emotional failure, may have been motivated by what is alleged to be a repression of his own desire for men. The rationale underlying Dellamora's interpretation of *In Memoriam* is simply that it makes the poem's meanings richer, and in so doing releases it from the constraints of a canonical tradition defined in terms of the normative experience of the white heterosexual male. (Of course one of the reasons why Queen Victoria so admired *In Memoriam* was that she saw in it an articulation of her own grief for her husband.)

However, such appropriations of well-known works, regardless of whether they are biographically based, have not been without controversy; moreover, objections to these readings, as Joseph Bristow has noted in relation to Wilde's oeuvre, are not always nor even principally from politically conservative scholars (Bristow 1997). One difficulty centres on their possible anachronism – that they may be imposing on nineteenth-century literature what are quintessentially modern concerns and in this way, Bristow suggests (a propos of Christopher Craft's punning reading of *The Importance of Being Earnest* (Craft 1994)), that nineteenth-century literary texts are 'moulded' into works with a 'fully developed homosexual undercurrent, one that would comply with our post-Stonewall comprehension not only of what it might mean to be *homosexual*, but also what it means to be *gay*' (Bristow 1997: 197–98).

A similar kind of dilemma affects modern interpretations of what have been termed 'romantic friendships' between women. Throughout the century, and particularly in the early decades, affection between young women was actively encouraged, and single gentlewomen often found employment as paid companions to wealthy spinsters. A well-known example which has provoked much speculation from her various biographers is the nature of the relationship between Marie Corelli and her childhood friend and later 'companion' Bertha

Vyver. Biographers have also speculated about the relationship between Vernon Lee and the poet Mary F. Robinson (1857–1944), who for several years travelled with Lee and then lived with her when Lee settled in Italy. Intense female friendships form a common subject-matter in the literature of the time: we might think of the adolescent Jane Eyre's intense relationships while at Lowood School with her fellow pupil, Helen Burns, and her sympathetic teacher, Miss Temple. Yet in a culture in which the existence of lesbianism, as that term is understood today, was barely acknowledged, it is difficult to be certain what these sorts of relationships (real or fictional) involved, except perhaps that they provided socially acceptable roles in which a wide variety of emotional attachments between women could be accommodated.

The hidden nature of same-sex relationships in the nineteenth century produces an obvious problem for the literary historian: that of verifying meanings which had to be coded because the normative nature of nineteenth-century culture rendered them unspeakable. Denying the possibility of the kind of homoerotic sub-texts Dellamora identifies in *In Memoriam*, or lesbian themes in the eroticisation of the relationship between Laura and Lizzie in Christina Rossetti's *Goblin Market*, can be interpreted as a version of the very homophobia which queer theory challenges. At the same time, however, the modern critic cannot evade the question – pertinently put by Cohen – about 'how' precisely 'everyone knows' that a work like *The Picture of Dorian Gray* 'encodes traces of homoerotic desire' while at the same time never 'explicitly violating the norms of heterosexuality' (Cohen 1996: 111). It is worth remembering that on its first publication Wilde's story produced no demands for his or his publisher's prosecution on the grounds of obscenity. Cohen answers his own question by suggesting that it is the way in which *Dorian Gray* problematises representation which lends it value in contemporary controversies about the communication of homoerotic desire. In the view of some commentators, a further and related limitation of queer theory is that it can become programmatic. Peter Rawlings hints at this problem in a review of Eric Haralson's *Henry James and Queer Modernity* (2003) when he complains about the 'weary sense of déjà vu' in encountering yet 'another study of James within a gender and queer theory paradigm' (Rawlings 2004). Perhaps, however, we should view this complaint as testifying simply to the success with which queer theory has permeated modern understandings of the nineteenth-century literary canon. Today it is virtually impossible to find a nineteenth-century literary history which ignores a writer like Wilde, and which ignores, too, the complex connections between writing and sexuality.

Postcolonial theory

Given that the history of nineteenth-century Britain has become so closely identified with British imperialism and the growth of Empire, it is perhaps to be expected that nineteenth-century literature has provided a rich territory for postcolonial theorists. In an age when foreign travel, particularly beyond northern Europe, was expensive and often dangerous, literary works were one of the principal means by which knowledge of other cultures, and Britain's relationship to them, was made accessible. Following Benedict Anderson's emphasis on the role of literary fiction in forging national identities (Anderson 1991), in *Culture and Imperialism* (1993) Edward Said went so far as to argue that it was through narrative, and particularly through the novel, that imperial culture – that is, a justification of imperialism – was constructed. Moreover, such constructions underwrite not just those poems and novels with obvious imperial themes, from Southey's *Thalaba* to Conrad's *Heart of Darkness*; as significant perhaps is the submerged colonial politics to be found in works with apparently more domestic preoccupations. In these cases, Said suggests, imperial ideology is often so normalised that it goes unquestioned and, prior to Said's work, was frequently unnoticed by critics and readers.

In the nineteenth century the British Empire included the Indian subcontinent (and the territories which are now Pakistan, Bangladesh and Sri Lanka) and certain territories of 'white' settlement in Canada, Australia, New Zealand and islands in the South Pacific, as well as South Africa and, later in the century, parts of North and East Africa. Some modern theorists go so far as to describe the nineteenth-century British state as comprising England and three 'internal' colonies of Scotland, Wales and Ireland, and in this way argue that questions about nationalism within the British Isles – that is, what defined Britishness and its relationship with Scottish, Irish and Welsh national identities – are inextricably intertwined with questions of imperialism.

A good example is the apparent blindness of much early and mid-nineteenth-century fiction to the sources of the inherited wealth which so often arrives (in a novel's conclusion) as the reward for virtuous conduct. Writers as varied as Austen, Charlotte Brontë and Dickens, though highly critical of the greed, snobbery and exploitation involved in some forms of domestic wealth creation, can none the less be curiously uncritical of money derived from overseas. In Austen's *Persuasion*, one of the last duties performed by Captain Wentworth is that of 'recovering' for the impoverished Mrs Smith the 'property in the West Indies' of her deceased husband, a mission he accomplishes by 'writing for her, acting for her, and seeing her through all the petty difficulties of the case, with the activity and the exertion of a fearless man and a determined friend'. Such wealth is seen as morally due to Mrs Smith because of the 'services she has rendered' to Wentworth's wife, the novel's heroine, Anne Elliot. What Austen conspicuously fails to mention, and therefore normalises, is the relationship between that property and the institution of slavery, one extensively debated in the early years of the nineteenth century. She is equally silent on the relationship between the meritocratic nature of life in the navy, which the novel favourably opposes to the hypocritical snobbery associated with landed wealth, and one of the navy's roles during the Napoleonic Wars of securing British imperial control of North Atlantic trade routes (the British fleet went so far as to sack Washington in the final moments of the war in order to preserve the status of British interests in North America, that is, of Canada).

Similar paradoxes can be found in *Great Expectations*; at the end of that novel Pip redeems himself from the taint of criminality attached to Magwitch's (Australian) money by taking up a position as a clerk in a merchant shipping office in Egypt. In this way, and like Wentworth, he makes what the narrative voice presents as morally deserved money through participation in the mechanisms of colonial trade: Egypt was politically important to British interests throughout the nineteenth century and became increasingly so from the 1850s onwards because of the strategic value of its location in relation to British trade with India via the Suez Canal, opened in 1870, which culminated in its annexation as a full British colony. Many critics have pointed to Charlotte Brontë's use of Britain's colonial heritage in the figure of the 'mad woman in the attic', the Creole Bertha Mason in *Jane Eyre*. The emphasis on Bertha's physical and emotional differences from Jane – her dark skin, shaggy hair, 'savage face' and unbridled appetites – is uncomfortably similar to the rhetoric of earlier slave traders; similar, too, of course, is the discourse of imprisonment, repression and rebellion that surrounds Bertha's confinement. (That said, and as with readings of the gender politics of some of Hardy's fiction, there is room for disagreement about the narrative self-consciousness of the portrayal of Rochester's first wife, and thus the extent to which Brontë can be said to be either normalising or exposing racial stereotypes (Michie 2006).) Less often commented upon is the role of colonial wealth in *Villette* (1853); in that novel, like Austen's *Persuasion*, Paul Emmanuel's last mission is to sort out business interests in the West Indies – interests, the novel suggests, which may have helped to fund Lucy Snowe's much sought-after independence. Against these examples, it is perhaps worth noting Thackeray's satirical portrait of the corpulent and mendacious Jos Sedley in *Vanity Fair* (Thackeray, we might remember, was born in Calcutta, where his father held a senior position in the Indian civil service). Having enriched himself through his activities as a tax-collector in an Indian backwater – and thereby making himself, in the eyes of the avaricious Becky Sharp, a useful marriage prospect – Jos hardly presents the most flattering portrait of Britain's attempt to 'civilise' India. That said, Thackeray was not above deploying more familiar stereotypes of the alleged untrustworthiness of Indians; in *The Newcomes* (1855), for example, Colonel Newcome (a serving Indian officer) is swindled out of his fortune by a fraudulent Anglo-Indian bank scheme, headed by the crooked financier Rummun Loll.

Where Said gives particular attention to narrative fiction, other postcolonial theorists, such as Mary Louise Pratt, have pointed to the importance of the ideological work undertaken by the sub-genres of nineteenth-century travel and exploration literature in justifying imperial expansion, particularly in Africa and South America. Most such journals and biographies, whether by explorers or missionaries, tell a familiar story, that of the triumph of a defiantly 'British' or – in Charles Kinglsey's historical adventure story, *Westward Ho!* – 'Saxon' spirit over hostile forces and indomitable odds. The rhetoric of 'discovery' underlying such classic accounts as Richard Burton's *Lake Regions of Central Africa* (1860), Pratt suggests, centred on an act of visual colonisation, one which was made 'real' only after the traveller returned home and brought that way of seeing 'into being through texts: a name on a map, a report to the Royal Geographic Society ... a lecture, a travel book'. Language, Pratt argues, is 'charged with making the world' (Pratt 2009: 2000). It is therefore important for the cultural (rather than the literary) historian interested in the mechanisms and institutions of colonialism to investigate all kinds of texts.

In the second half of the century these texts included those of the British periodical press; publications like *The Imperial Gazetteer* (whose India correspondent never visited the country, putting together his reports from research in the British Library), *Punch*, the *Pall Mall Gazette*, *Daily Graphic* and of course *The Times* played a crucial role in the construction and contestation of colonial attitudes, not least because theirs was an arena in which national and imperial discourses, on the one hand, and metropolitan and colonial concerns, on the other, regularly intersected (Codell 2003). Valuable resources, too, are colonial publications, such as the *Calcutta Review*, founded in 1844 by John William Kaye (1814–76), who was employed by the East India Company and later the India Office, and the *Lahore Civil and Military Gazette*, where Kipling was also employed for a time. A further contribution of postcolonial theory, then, is to remind us of the value of interdisciplinarity – of the rewards of reading literary works alongside other forms of nineteenth-century writing, such as contemporary journalism, diaries, notebooks and letters, as well as early anthropological and ethnographic texts (by figures such as Edward Tylor). Robert Knox's (1791–1862) influential and quasi-scientific *The Races of Men* (1850), for example, helped to legitimate racial theories of historical development which consigned the so-called 'dark races' – a category into which Brontë's Bertha Mason would fall – to a position of inevitable inferiority. Interdisciplinarity can also alert us to the importance of the non-fictional works of authors who are better known for their poetry or fiction – a case in point is the diverse oeuvre of Robert Louis Stevenson. Modern readers who know Stevenson largely through *Jekyll and Hyde* are apt to forget that he spent the last years of his life in the South Seas, where he could not avoid becoming engaged with the Western colonisation of those islands (Colley 2004). In these ways, then, literature becomes an element in a larger discursive project, that of defining and legitimating Britishness (or more usually Englishness).

Historians such as Patrick Brantlinger have suggested that imperialism, which he defines quite loosely as the evolution of attitudes about Britain's relationship with the rest of the world, is a pervasive feature of much nineteenth-century writing (Brantlinger 1988). He notes, for example, the flood of responses in poetry, fiction and non-fictional prose, as well as in visual culture, to the 1857 Indian Mutiny (or Indian Rebellion), much of which deployed motifs of spectacle in order to justify British military rule. In the early and middle decades of the century British campaigns against indigenous practices such as suttee – the Hindu prescription that following their husband's death widows should be burned – also helped to justify the colonial project as a civilising mission. One kind of writing which particularly interests Brantlinger is the development in the last decades of the century – at the very moment, that is, when British confidence in its economic ability to sustain an Empire was beginning to be questioned – of a marriage between British adventure fiction and Gothic romance, what he terms 'imperial gothic'. For Brantlinger its most successful practitioners were H. Rider Haggard, Rudyard Kipling and Bram Stoker. He identifies in this sub-genre three main themes, all of which testify to the ways in which literary works could be used to articulate anxieties about the nature of British influence in the rest of the world at the *fin-de-siècle*. They are: the idea of regression or 'going native', which is typically troped by reference to the supernatural or occult (such as the 'inexplicable curses' and 'demonic possession' so common in Kipling's short stories about Anglo-India, a theme which survives into the twentieth century in the works of popular authors such as W. Somerset Maugham (1874–1965)); the invasion of civilisation by 'the forces of barbarism or demonism' (to be seen, for example, in the arrival of Count Dracula at the fishing port of Whitby); and the 'diminution of opportunities for adventure and heroism in the modern world' (a theme exploited by Haggard in his enormously successful Alan Quartermain novels, which began appropriately enough with a search for the mythical 'King Solomon's Diamonds' deep in the African interior.)

While Pratt's and Brantlinger's interest in the ideology of imperialism draws the literary historian's attention to genres which might otherwise be overlooked – those of travel writing, exploration and adventure fiction – Caroline Reitz has suggested that imperialist concerns can also be central to sub-genres we might not immediately associate with Empire, such as that of detective fiction (Reitz 2004). Detective fiction has often been viewed as the opposite to the adventure story, in that it is concerned with policing the 'metropolitan centre', while 'imperial fiction' vouchsafes to British readers an 'exotic … colonial periphery'. By contrast, Reitz argues for an essential continuity between the 'detective who detects crime' and the 'explorer who performs the work of imperial administrators': depending upon local knowledge, both sorts of profession are intelligence-based (ibid.: xvi–xvii). Reitz also reminds us that one of the first detectives to become widely known among the nineteenth-century British reading public resided not in Scotland Yard nor in Baker Street, but rather in British India: William Sleeman, the first superintendent of the Indian Thug Police, was the inspiration for the popular sub-genre of 'Thuggee' narratives which included the best-selling *Confessions of a Thug* (1839) by Captain Philip Meadows Taylor (1808–76). Thugs were Indian gangs of ancient lineage, who were supposedly inspired by the goddess Kali and who specialised in the assassination and robbery of travellers. The secrecy and extreme violence with which they were associated became a byword in these narratives for the threatening 'otherness' of India itself (one which some critics have identified as a sub-theme in Dickens's last novel, *The Mystery of Edwin Drood*). Thus the policing of the Thugs by the British colonial authorities could easily come to stand as a justification for the civilising project of imperialism per se, one in which knowledge of the other becomes the principal means by which it is controlled. For Reitz, this presentation of an authority dependent on local information gathering rather than violence in its turn becomes central to liberal Britain's image of itself, both domestically and in its colonies, as the possessor of superior cultural and political institutions.

It is important to acknowledge that although modern critics and historians are in agreement that nineteenth-century literary works played a crucial role in the construction, and on occasion the interrogation, of the ideology of British imperialism, there is none the less considerable debate about the particular politics of individual works, especially those which appeared in the last quarter of the century. Do the stories in Kipling's *Plain Tales from the Hills* or poems like 'Fuzzy-Wuzzy' in his *Barrack-Room Ballads* merely reinforce racial prejudices about the exoticism and danger of the East (particularly the danger which Indian women, and thus India itself, posed to British men)? Or, does his exposure of the tensions and petty jealousies within Anglo-Indian communities, and the resentment of the civilian population towards the returning British 'Tommy', exhibit a more critical attitude towards Britain's imperial agents? Here there is an interesting contrast to be made with the work of Flora Annie Steel (1847–1929), not well known today but who was referred to at the time as the 'female Rudyard Kipling'. Following her marriage to Henry William Steel, a member of the Indian Civil Service, she went to live in the Punjab, returning to Britain some twenty years later to embark on a career as a novelist, often taking as her subject Anglo-Indian themes, such as the Indian Mutiny in *On the Face of the Waters* (1896), a work which enjoyed considerable success with the reading public (Sutherland 2009: 609).

Argument about a work's colonial ideology often centres on its formal sophistication, and here we confront again the critical problem which, it was suggested, is central to gender theory – that of the relationship between form and politics, and so, too, of the significance of literary works in cultural history. Recent re-readings of Rider Haggard's fiction, for example, have suggested that he was a more accomplished and sophisticated writer than earlier critics had been prepared to acknowledge, and that his ability to synthesise themes and tropes from different writing traditions – including comparative literature, religion and anthropology – made him an innovator in a sub-genre that would later influence the perennially popular action-adventure film (Monsman 2006). Perhaps the most important controversy about form and politics is the one which has centred on Marlowe's encounter with the 'dark continent' in Conrad's *Heart of Darkness*. Conrad's choice of a self-reflexive and unreliable narrator complicates the status of Marlowe's narrative and allows us, Said argues in *Culture and Imperialism*, to draw from the novel two different postcolonial 'visions'. The first conventionally situates the failure of Empire – the inability to 'illuminate' that dark heart of Africa – in terms of a narrative in which 'the colonised world was in some ways ontologically lost to begin with, irredeemable, inexcusably inferior'. Such rhetoric enables the coloniser to concede defeat, but without relinquishing its authority or rectitude. By contrast, the second vision places Marlowe's experience as local to time and place, and in this way is necessarily provisional in its judgements about Africa. That provisionality in turn opens up a space where it is possible, Said suggests, for 'later readers to imagine something other than an Africa carved up into dozens of European colonies' (1993: 79–82). Although the vagueness of that 'something other' may still seem a muted response to the evils of colonialism, its value is thrown into stark relief by comparison with the jingoism of works such as Henry Newbolt's exceptionally popular poetry collection *The Island Race* (1898). The opening poem, 'The Vigil', written on the eve of the Boer War, and later reprinted in *The Times* on the first day of the First World War, exhorts its readers:

> Then let Memory tell thy heart;
> '*England! What thou wert, thou art!*'
> Gird thee with thine ancient might,
> Forth! and God defend the Right!

Newbolt's instinctive identification of Britishness with Englishness – and more particularly of an institutional ethic embodied in English public schools, cricket and school chapel – reminds us that in the nineteenth century questions about nationalism were to do with the relationships between the constituent countries of the United Kingdom, as well as between Britain and the rest of the world. Newbolt's 'Admirals All' constructs a history of naval supremacy, stretching from 'Effingham, Grenville, Raleigh, Drake' to 'Nelson's peerless name'; the fight for a 'kingdom none can take' and 'the realm of the circling sea' is always and only 'for England's sake'. A similar concentration on Englishness (at the expense of recognising the difference of Scottish, Welsh or Irish identities) underwrites much late nineteenth-century literary historiography, such as *A Short History of Modern English Literature* (1898) by Edmund Gosse (1849–1928). Gosse's volume was numbered 'III' in a series of 'Short Histories of the World' which included – at the time of publication – accounts of French, Italian, Spanish, Japanese, Hungarian, American, German and Modern Scandinavian Literature, but no Scottish, Welsh or Irish volumes. Some modern historians have suggested that these sorts of publishing projects (other examples included T. H. Ward's multi-volume *The English Poets* (1880–94) and *English Prose Selections* (1893–97)) were themselves a legacy of one aspect of Victorian racial ideology, of a desire to deploy a literary canon in which the figure of Shakespeare (for Gosse, in his *Short History*, the most 'glorious of English names' (108)) became increasingly central to defending the kind of narrowly defined English nationalism found in Newbolt's verse. Their effect, it has been argued, was to marginalise the kinds of literature which appeared to oppose or contest monolithic notions of Englishness and British culture. Such observations in turn underlie modern attempts to identify, as we noted in

Chapter 2, separate nineteenth-century traditions of Scottish, Irish and Welsh literature, as well as (more recently) literature defined by its regional interests (such as that of the north of England).

However, it is also worth bearing in mind that not all national literary institutions were Anglocentric: a counterpart to the Early English Text Society founded in 1864 was the Scottish Text Society, established in 1882. Moreover, and we noted in Chapter 2, the ideals of English (or British) nationalism were often articulated in relation to European culture; throughout the century, France, Italy and Germany were viewed by certain authors as providing alternative values, the embodiment of a kind of cosmopolitanism, as it were, which countered what Matthew Arnold viewed as the narrow provincialism of the English. Arnold himself wrote widely on contemporary French and German authors, and urged his readers to look beyond their nation's own writers. In the late decades of the century there was a fashion for Russian literature: Dostoevsky (1821–81) and Turgenev had both visited England and many of their works had been translated into English by the early 1890s. We should be cautious, then, about identifying too closely the nationalism of the canons found in late nineteenth-century literary histories with the actual tastes and reading practices of the nineteenth-century reading public. Furthermore, and as Robert Ebbatson has suggested, conceptualising Englishness in terms of its relation to an 'other' will always exhibit some sense of instability and hybridity, because the discussion of Englishness in these terms necessarily brings into play those countries, peoples or landscapes which it is not (Ebbatson 2005). We also need to be aware that reading nineteenth-century literary works as narratives about the formation of colonial and national identities may value them in ways in tension with those produced by other theoretical paradigms. For example, how do we reconcile Wilde's Irishness with his homosexuality and often-expressed identification with things 'English' (including, of course, that quintessentially English institution, the University of Oxford), or Charlotte Brontë's proto-feminism with what can seem, in certain works, to be an unreflecting racism? In this respect, some of the most challenging recent accounts of nineteenth-century literature have been those which attempt to unite the insights of gender and postcolonial theory into the single and more unified paradigm – what has been termed 'homocolonial criticism' (Stape 2004: 340). This burgeoning, but controversial area of nineteenth-century literary studies has led critics to discuss topics such as the influence of race on 'new women' writers (Jusovà 2005) and the relationship between the 'new woman' novel and adventure fiction (Richardson 2006), homo-social relations in Conrad's early fiction (Ruppel 2008) and the sexual and imaginative possibilities which 'cruising' the Pacific offered to Robert Louis Stevenson (Buckton 2007).

Conclusion

- Gender and postcolonial theories challenge modern canon formation by bringing to our attention writers whose careers have been seen to be marginalised because of gender or racial prejudice. In many instances, and particularly with the work of women writers, these 'forgotten' authors were popular and celebrated in their own time. However, the grounds for their contemporary reputations, typically based on assumptions about essential distinctions between male and female natures, can be quite different from those set out by modern critics.

- Recovering lost voices in the nineteenth century has sometimes led to the re-characterisation of entire sub-genres (like Gothic fiction) or literary forms (like the dramatic monologue). However, the extent to which form itself can be said to be gendered remains a complex and contested question. Controversial, too, is the identification of codes or 'sub-texts' by which nineteenth-century literary works are claimed to articulate or engage with sexual identities – such as those concerned with same-sex desire – which a normative culture rendered unspeakable.
- Much postcolonial theory is interdisciplinary in impetus, and recommends the reading of nineteenth-century literary works alongside forms of writing which have been marginalised in conventional literary histories, such as diaries, letters and notebooks. It also brings a renewed attention to popular literary genres and sub-genres, particularly those of adventure fiction and varieties of travel writing. One of its most important legacies, however, has been to alert modern readers to the operation of imperialist ideologies in nineteenth-century literary works not ostensibly concerned with colonialism or Empire. In this way, we can see how nineteenth-century canon formation deployed literary works in the service of a narrowly defined English nationalism.
- The insights of gender and postcolonial theory, when applied to the same works, can produce divergent readings.

7 Nineteenth-century literature and the social production of texts

Overview

At the present time a knowledge of print culture is widely assumed to be an indispensable element of a literary history. This situation derives largely from the influence over the past three decades of two practices within literary studies: the first is termed 'the history of the book' and the second, following the pioneering work of D. F. McKenzie, 'the sociology of texts' (McKenzie, 1986). These areas of enquiry are related and together they challenge both author- and text-centred views of literary history by inviting us to think about literary creativity as the product, at least in part, of material culture and economic forces. What gets to count as literature, in this view, is determined to an extent by how writing is made available for evaluation and this in turn depends upon the processes by which it comes into print. In such an argument any investigation into the nineteenth-century literary canon must begin with an understanding of the mechanisms and institutions of nineteenth-century publishing. That understanding usually involves three distinct kinds of research: an examination of the technology and economics of nineteenth-century publishing, of the power relations which existed in it and of the materiality of nineteenth-century writing or what is termed its 'textual condition'. When taken together these bodies of research show how relationships between writers and publishers, and between writers and readers, were transformed. As a consequence the process of writing itself, and the criteria informing judgements about literary value also, changed. Put more simply, an examination of nineteenth-century publishing culture allows us to see more clearly the relationship between the modern process of canon formation and a history of taste. This chapter will argue that to conceive of a history of nineteenth-century literature in terms of a history of nineteenth-century literary production brings with it some changes as to which writers and which kinds of works are considered important. It will conclude by giving a brief guide to the editorial principles underlying modern editions of nineteenth-century literary works in order to help modern readers understand the status of the variety of texts of any one work available to them.

Nineteenth-century literature and commodity culture

Over the past three to four decades the pioneering work of Richard Altick (1957) has been consolidated and expanded by studies of nineteenth-century print culture. The combined findings of historians such as Allan Dooley (1992), Simon Eliot (1994), John Sutherland (1975, 1995), Clifford Siskin (1998), Alexis Weedon (2003), John Feather (2006) and James Raven (2005) have given the literary historian a wealth of empirical evidence about the changing technology and economics of the production and selling of books during the nineteenth century. There is a growing body of research, too, into the ways in which these changes impacted on reading habits, and so on literary taste (Flint 1993; Jordan and Patten 1995; Brantlinger 1998; Newlyn 2000; St Clair 2004; Hammond 2006; Waller 2006). The nineteenth century witnessed the development for the first time of a mass market for literary works and the cultural entrenchment of what early Marxist historians described as a division between 'high' and 'mass', or 'elite' and 'popular', literature, one which has persisted to the present day. Later Marxist theorists like Norman Feltes concentrated on analysing the power relations underlying what we referred to in Chapter 2 as the nineteenth-century industrialisation of printing, noting how, over the course of the century, literature became increasingly incorporated into a nascent consumer culture, being marketed as if it was just another commodity. In this view, the second half of the nineteenth century is associated with the emergence of what Marxist historians in general and Feltes in particular term a 'late capitalist' mode of production, one in which literary works were traded in new ways. As a consequence their economic and aesthetic value became increasingly conflated so that cheapness and availability was seen to correlate with tastelessness (Feltes 1986, 1993). More precisely, it is claimed that the advent of mass publishing and cheap books made what was previously the exclusive property of a wealthy and well-educated literary elite available for widespread consumption, and as literary works became something that everyone could desire and (in principle) own, so literature itself came to be valued in a manner similar to other sorts of commodities, like sugar or tea. In a phrase made popular by cultural historians, literature became 'commodified', meaning that it was made subject to market evaluations produced by the laws of supply and demand: in the abundance produced by a consumer society, it is the rare object – a work with a restricted readership, one published in a limited, rather than a popular edition, in an expensively bound *édition de luxe*, rather than a 1*s* paperback – which commands the highest price, and so is given the greatest cultural value.

In this argument, the growth in the late decades of the nineteenth century of the rare-book trade and of so-called 'coterie' publishers which specialised in limited print runs are the inevitable corollary of mass literary publishing, as the material embodiment of a given literary work – its physical form – becomes an increasingly important signifier of its aesthetic worth. According to the cultural historian Regenia Gagnier, in the last quarter of the century new modes of evaluation associated with a nascent consumer culture became all-embracing or, to use another Marxist term, hegemonic. Gagnier finds evidence for this process in what she views as a 'convergence' in late nineteenth-century economic and aesthetic discourses, notably in the writings of Walter Pater and the political economist William Stanley Jevons (1835–82). Gagnier's thesis is distinctive because it suggests that around the 1870s a fundamental change occurred in the relationship between the discourses of aesthetics and economics. Historians of eighteenth-century culture tend to see these discourses as articulating competing or opposing definitions of value (Thompson 1996). Martha Woodmansee, for example, argues that the first appearance of theories about the autonomy of art and the disinterested nature of aesthetic experience (what she terms art's 'intrinsic' value, and which she associates with eighteenth-century German philosophy) are attempts to prevent art from being determined by market values (Woodmansee 1994). By contrast, Gagnier has claimed that conceptual similarities in the work of Pater and Jevons represent the emergence of a new form of subjectivity, that of the 'passive consumer' with 'insatiable wants', a phenomenon which came to dominate twentieth-century culture, including literary culture (Gagnier 1992, 2000).

Understanding the late nineteenth-century reader in terms of passive consumption emphasises the role of market forces, rather than 'free' choice, in determining literary value. In a consumer society markets generate profit by creating endlessly disposable objects of desire, in which novelty is set against durability. It is worth remembering that the most fashionable genres of nineteenth-century popular fiction traded on introducing small variations to formulaic plot structures, thus creating what can be seen as a classic consumerist reading experience in which the pleasure of anticipation – of knowing what to expect in, say, a Sherlock Holmes mystery – works to generate an appetite for the next story. In a different but quite compatible study Daniel Lord Smail has described the rise of 'leisure reading' – a process which he suggests has its origins in the eighteenth century but which only becomes widespread in literary culture in the nineteenth – in terms of its 'autotropic' effect. In Smail's view, the experience of reading certain sorts of writing has the capacity, like self-administered drug taking, to alter cognitive patterns (Smail 2008: 157–89). Such an argument suggests that the narrative devices which made popular genres like melodrama and sensation so compellingly exciting for the nineteenth-century reading public may have produced patterns of mental stimulation (or excitation) equivalent in effect to those produced by the addictive properties of other nineteenth-century commodities, such as coffee, alcohol and opiates.

Gagnier's work, although thought provoking, has been disputed, and other historians have placed late nineteenth-century writers like Pater in opposition to emerging consumerist modes of value. It can be argued, for example, that Pater's emphasis on the subjectivity of the critic's response to works of art should be understood as an attempt to *resist* market evaluations because it divorces aesthetic appreciation from a consideration of art objects and therefore avoids conflating the literary value of a work with the material rarity of its textual embodiment (Guy 1999). As we noted in Chapter 4, Pater is careful to point out that although mass publishing enables many people to read a play by Shakespeare, not all of those readers will necessarily experience it as *art*. Likewise, general historians of consumerism, such as Thomas Richards, have pointed out that for most of the century many of the desirable objects created by the new advertising techniques that accompanied a growing consumerism remained beyond the financial reach of much of the population (Richards 1991). At the century's close a significant proportion still lived at or below subsistence level (as revealed in 1889 by the research of Charles Booth (1840–1916) and Seebohm Rowntree (1871–1954)). Consequently, consumerism was by no means a universal phenomenon, and nor were the modes of evaluation and representation, such as that of 'spectacle', that were associated with it. In other words, while there is broad agreement that changes in the nineteenth-century book trade affected ideas of literary value, and that publishers of literary works often manipulated pricing and print runs in order to exploit that association between scarcity and value, there is still considerable debate about the universality of these processes. And there is debate, too, about how individual writers responded to them, and the extent to which, in their own writing practices, they were either complicit with, or resistant to, this alleged commodification of literary value.

The significance of a work's textual embodiment – the material form in which it is made available to the reading public – has also preoccupied textual critics, notably Jerome J. McGann. However, their concern has been less with the signifying value of price and more with the way in which the choice of typeface, page layout, illustrations, bindings, cover design and so forth can also play an intrinsic part in the way a literary work is interpreted and valued (McGann 1991; Frankel 2000, 2009). In this respect what make questions about a work's materiality particularly interesting in the nineteenth century (rather than in earlier periods) are developments which took place in publishing technology. These meant that publishers had a greater variety of affordable techniques at their disposal, especially with regard to illustration. *The Illustrated London News*, launched in 1842, was the first newspaper to specialise in pictorial journalism. Numerous cheap fiction magazines, like *The London Journal* (1845–1912) and Cassell's *Illustrated Family Paper* (1853–67) also made extensive use of engravings, which were thought to increase the appeal of such publications to the semi-literate (a significant market before the 1870 Forster Education Act). This connection between the vividness and immediacy of the visual image and what was argued to be a thoughtless, because passive, process of consumption – a noted feature of railway fiction – inevitably invited critical censure, memorably from John Ruskin. Modern critics, however, have seen subtlety and complexity in the relationships which developed between particular writers and their illustrators – such as that between Dickens and Hablot Browne ('Phiz', 1815–82), or Lewis Carroll and John Tenniel (1820–1914), or Aubrey Beardsley and the editors of *The Yellow Book* and *The Savoy* magazines – with the result that any simple opposition between text and illustration, or between writer and artist, has been questioned (Ray 1976; Muir 1989; Hodnett 1982; Maxwell 2002; Thomas 2004). In the case of some authors, notably Christina Rossetti, it has been suggested that the interplay between verbal and visual texts amounts to the development of a new 'visual-verbal aesthetic' (Kooistra 2002). More generally speaking, what is perhaps most striking about this period is the sheer pervasiveness and, in publications like keepsakes, annuals and beauty books, all of which traded on their visual qualities, the opulence of nineteenth-century illustrated literature, which in turn gave rise to a wide variety of attempted syntheses between the verbal and visual. The practice, widespread until the late decades of the century, of publishing novels serially, in magazines, literary periodicals or in cheap weekly and monthly parts, before they appeared in book form, also meant that much nineteenth-century literature was simultaneously available to the reading public in multiple textual embodiments (Hughes and Lund 1995).

The textual differences between different publications of the same work have implications for the modern critic: many authors used the opportunity of book publication to revise a work previously serialised; the issuing of further book editions, if a work sold well, could mean additional chances to revise. However, as important as these textual variants is the significance of what the French critic Gérard Genette terms the 'paratexual apparatus' – that is, those features which 'surround' and 'extend' the text and thus make it 'present' to the reader (Genette 1997: 1–3). Genette's argument is that it is impossible to conceive of text without some element of paratext, and paratext, as McGann also argues, always has semantic content; that is, how we read the paratext affects how we understand the text. In nineteenth-century literary culture this meant that there was a significant difference between reading a work like *Hard Times* in a hardbound form and reading it in the way in which it first appeared to the public – that is, episodically, in the cheap magazine *Household Words*, where Dickens's text sits alongside advertisements, general-interest articles (on, say, the use of steam technology), as well as essays on politics (such as workers' education) and current affairs. Important, too, is the way in which canon formation may have been informed by subtle prejudices about the values attached to different nineteenth-century textual embodiments – the perception that works which appeared in more disposable forms of publication, like cheap magazines, possessed less merit than those published in books. We have seen an example of this already in Chapter 3, where it was argued that the habit for much of the century of reprinting play-texts only in flimsy acting editions accompanied and perhaps contributed to their marginalisation within literary culture. As we explain in more detail below, much of the extension of the nineteenth-century literary canon (both in drama and in other genres) which has taken place over the last few decades has centred on examining aspects of nineteenth-century print culture previously overlooked by an exclusive concern with books.

Nineteenth-century publishing institutions

In broad outline the story of nineteenth-century print culture is uncontested, and it is one dominated by numbers. James Raven has described how nineteenth-century publishing was transformed by two revolutions (Raven 2005). The first, which began in the late decades of the eighteenth century, was commercial and centred on changes to the financial structures of the book trade and its distribution networks. Together these helped to produce a more competitive market which encouraged entrepreneurial activity and witnessed many new publishing houses, often short-lived small businesses, entering the industry. The most obvious consequence was a steady increase in the numbers of titles published, even though the average number of copies per title printed was at this time still relatively low. For volumes of poetry, verse-drama or critical essays, which were then considered the forms of writing possessing the highest prestige, it might have involved just 300–600 copies. A number of the Romantic poets, notably Coleridge, Southey and Shelley, all began their careers by working with minor, regional bookseller/publishers often associated with radical political movements; none of these poets, however, succeeded in selling many copies of their work with these presses, and they typically moved on to publish with more established (and often metropolitan) houses as their reputations consolidated.

The second publishing revolution was technological and centred on the mechanisation of typesetting and printing. This increased the speed of production, and together with the availability of cheaper raw materials (such as paper) helped to lower the unit costs involved, leading to what Raven terms a transformation in 'printing capacity' (2005: 264). This transformation began with the introduction of steam-driven presses from 1814 and stereotyping from the 1820s onwards; capacity accelerated again in the 1870s with the introduction of rotary printing, hot-metal typesetting and, by the century's close, lithographic and photographic techniques (ibid.: 283). The resulting industrialisation of printing, outlined in Chapter 2, made books much cheaper – over the second half of the century the average real price of books halved. The British population was at the same time becoming more numerous and more prosperous, better educated and, because of changes in work-practices and employment legislation, more interested in reading both as a leisure activity and as a means of self-improvement (we might recall the incidence of working-class autodidacts in nineteenth-century fiction in characters like Gaskell's Job Legh or Dickens's Bradley Headstone).

The principal distinguishing feature of nineteenth-century publishing is thus the development of a mass popular market for books, notably for educational and religious works (sermons were a particularly popular genre), as well as for literary fiction. This category required what Alexis Weedon calls 'considerable "churn"' (Weedon 2003: 92). That is, production was driven by the quantity, rather than quality, of new titles, a situation which in turn encouraged new entrants into the market, as well as exceptional productivity among authors already established. The prolific James Payn (1830–98) published about a hundred novels in his lifetime, as well as collections of critical essays and a volume of poetry. His ability to cater to the tastes of the general reading public also enabled him, as John Sutherland has argued, to 'exercise formidable power as a literary broker and patron' (Sutherland 2009: 500). Payn was variously a co-editor of *Chambers's Edinburgh Journal*, for a time sole editor of the hugely successful *Cornhill Magazine*, as well as a reader of manuscripts for the prestigious publishing house of Smith, Elder (who published among others Charlotte Brontë and Matthew Arnold). Payn's nearest rival in productivity was probably the journalist, war correspondent and popular children's author George Alfred Henty, who was reported to write around 6,000 words a day, eventually producing well over a hundred works for the children's and adult market (Sutherland 2009: 294). Even less obviously populist writers, like Anthony Trollope, can surprise modern readers with their industry; Trollope managed to write some forty-seven novels while simultaneously pursuing a career in the civil service.

The competitive nature of nineteenth-century publishing meant that literary publishing houses varied considerably in size and reputation: moreover, while some are still in existence today (although in a different form), others folded within a few years. Arguably the most prestigious house, and one which recapitulates in miniature the development of literary publishing in general over this period, was that of Alexander (1818–96) and Daniel Macmillan (1813–57). The two brothers, born in humble circumstances and receiving little formal education, built from scratch what became by the century's close an internationally renowned firm, publishing many of the leading writers of the day, and with branches in New York and Bombay. The business began in a modest way in 1843 when the brothers opened a bookshop at 57 Aldersgate Street, London, from where they published a small range of non-fiction titles. A few months later they borrowed heavily in order to buy out a well-established Cambridge bookseller, taking advantage of the local market to expand into academic and literary publishing. In 1846 they absorbed another local firm and began to build a reputation for producing finely made and reasonably priced books. A key element in their success was their ability to attract good writers. Very early on both brothers grasped the importance of placing themselves personally at the centre of social and cultural life, and regular though discrete entertaining of prospective authors remained a crucial and winning element of their business practice. In 1857 a London office was opened in Henrietta Street, Covent Garden, and the firm's main headquarters relocated to London from Cambridge five years later. 1859 saw the launch of the immediately successful *Macmillan's Magazine* (other large publishers, like the Scottish Blackwood and Son, had similar titles – in their case *Blackwoods' Edinburgh Magazine*, popularly known as 'Maga'), and a decade later Macmillan had opened in New York and added children's literature to its list. Under the leadership of Daniel's son, Frederick, the firm led the negotiations which later secured the 1899 Net Book Agreement (Morgan 1943).

The attractions of a literary career in the nineteenth century, particularly for a writer of fiction, are easy to see when one looks at the astonishing rise over the course of the century in numbers of copies printed and, as a consequence, in profits. In the early decades of the century first print runs for an average hard-bound novel were around 1,000 (not much more than for poetry or criticism); those for works by Walter Scott, one of the most popular authors at that time, were still only about ten times this figure. By 1886, however, Robert Louis Stevenson's *Jekyll and Hyde* sold 40,000 copies in just six months, while *The Christian* (1897), by Thomas Hall Caine, was reported to have sold, within a single year, over 150,000 copies (in both Britain and the United States). In the second half of the century the export market for English-language books in Europe, the United States of America and in the expanding British colonial territories became an increasingly important element of the literary market, to the extent that it led (by the century's close) to the establishing of several international copyright agreements, most importantly with the USA (embodied in the 1890 Chace Act). The possibilities offered by foreign publication and translation, as well as by syndication – typically of serialised fiction – meant that late nineteenth-century authors could have multiple contracts, and therefore multiple earnings, for a single work.

Equally important in generating income was the widespread practice of re-printing successful works, both of contemporary fiction and, particularly, of classic literature, in cheap formats, using the larger print runs to compensate for the low profit margins per unit sold. By the mid-1880s, around 60 per cent of books were sold at 3*s* 6*d* or under to non-institutional purchasers, and reprints of some popular novels were available for as little as 1*s*. One factor driving down reprint prices was the popularity from the late 1830s onwards of what was termed 'railway fiction', a market dominated initially by W. H. Smith, the monopoly bookseller at metropolitan stations. Competition from rival firms like George Routledge, who in 1848 established his 'Railway Library', led to writers like Edward Bulwer-Lytton being paid a reputed £20,000 for the lease of all his thirty-five copyrights; while in 1847 Dickens's publisher, Chapman and Hall, produced the first of many cheap reprints of his work (Sutherland 2009: 527). Ironically, however, for much of the century achieving those popular reprint sales, certainly for fiction, required that novelists first had to prove themselves in a much more expensive format, that of the 'three-decker' or three-volume novel. Priced at 31*s* 6*d*, it was sold mainly to institutional purchasers, such as circulating libraries like Mudie or W. H. Smith, who favoured it because it enabled them to make a separate charge for each volume borrowed. The libraries' dominance of the first-edition fiction market gave them enormous power over any writer's career because it was the libraries' tastes which effectively determined the market for cheap reprints – what were advertised as 'popular' editions, issued on thinner paper in smaller print, and with less elaborate bindings. By the late 1880s, however, the conservatism of the circulating libraries, whose main clientele were middle-class women, was generating increasing resentment, most vocally from George Moore, whose 1885 pamphlet

Literature at Nurse, which was prompted by the libraries' refusal to stock his *A Modern Lover* (1883), accused them of exercising a pernicious (although informal) kind of censorship. However it was market forces, rather than polemic, which eventually broke the libraries' monopoly, as publishers began in the late 1880s to issue one-volume novels at the cost of just 6*s*. Moore himself had succeeded in finding a publisher for his next novel, the sexually frank *A Mummer's Wife* (1885) in this format, and boasted in *Literature at Nurse* that within a year it was already in its fourth edition.

Moore's anger at the influence of the libraries was generated in part by the scale of the financial returns which flowed from mid and late nineteenth-century literary publishing. The potential profits from mass readerships meant that it was possible, probably for the first time, for a large body writers, rather than the exceptional individual like Dickens, to earn a decent living wholly by the pen – to become, in effect, literary professionals. Such an opportunity, however, brought in its train new tensions and demands. Some of these were ideological, and centred on the uneasy assimilation of literary creativity to nineteenth-century discourses of professionalism, which were themselves novel, and so relatively unstable. As social historians have noted, the professions, as we understand them today, were largely a Victorian creation (Reader 1966); they brought into being a new class, one whose power resided in its specialist knowledge or cultural capital rather than in the value of its labour, inherited wealth or birth. However, like the concept of the Victorian gentleman, that of the professional was accompanied by larger anxieties about the relationship between qualities which were inborn or innate, on the one hand, and those that could be acquired through education and socialisation, on the other; as Jennifer Ruth puts it, these were also the distinctions between 'ability and effort, intelligence and merit, and being and doing' (Ruth 2006: 3). In terms of writing, professionalism merely gave sharper articulation to an old opposition, that of whether a writer had to be 'born' or whether, by hard work, he could be 'made'.

Other problems which accompanied professionalism, however, were more practical: making a living wholly from writing required new ways of regulating the manufacture and selling of books, as well as a restructuring of the financial relationships between authors and publishers. These included the introduction of more systematic and transparent accounting practices, so that authors could see more clearly the profitability of their work. This was essential when payment was by royalty rather than by subscription or the purchase of a copyright – methods which had been common in the eighteenth century and early decades of the nineteenth century, when print runs were relatively small. The establishment in 1884 of the Society of Authors, the 1899 Net Book Agreement and the emergence around the same time of a new breed of professional, the literary agent (of whom A. P. Watt (1834–1914) and J. B. Pinker (1863–1922) were the most successful), all point to a new formality in author–publisher relations, one driven by the increasing commercialisation of literary production (Gillies 2007). However, perhaps the most important indication that the literary market was changing was, as we have hinted already, reforms in nineteenth-century copyright law.

These reforms, like the process of professionalism of which they were a part, have also been seen as evidence of a change, from the 1830s onwards, in conceptions of literary creativity in which Romantic notions of authorship, centring on the individuality of a writer's genius, were displaced by more mechanical models of composition, where the writer could be viewed as being analogous to the manufacturer (Pettitt 2004).

The ability of both author and publisher to generate income from writing meant that writing had to be viewed as a form of property, and that there had to be protection in law from the theft of it. Modern copyright law begins with the 1709 English Copyright Act (or Act of Anne, as it is sometimes called), which fixed the term of copyright protection for the author of an unpublished book at fourteen years from the date of first publication (or twenty-one years for a book already published). However, in the last decades of the eighteenth century and throughout the first half of the nineteenth the terms of the 1709 Act provoked considerable debate. As we described in Chapter 3, one source of dissatisfaction was the Act's failure to protect the performance rights of authors of contemporary dramatic works, a limitation rectified by the 1833 Dramatic Copyright Act. A second complaint centred on the length of the term of copyright and in the early 1800s Parliament was petitioned to extend it. A measure of success was achieved in the 1814 Copyright Act, which increased the term to twenty-eight years or the author's life (if longer); the subsequent 1842 Copyright Act allowed for an even more generous forty-two years from the date of publication or seven years after the author's death (thus enabling those profits to be passed on to an author's heirs).

One way of understanding these legislative changes is in terms of the increasingly lucrative nineteenth-century reprint market, in its turn a product of expanding readerships. It offered authors the potential to profit from a successful work over a long period of time. Moreover, once long-term copyright protection was secured by the 1842 Act, there was additional encouragement to write exactly the sort of best-seller that might endure; or, to put the case more negatively, for the professional writer earning his living by the pen, copyright security could provide a positive disincentive to producing the kind of experimental fiction that would find only a small readership and generate a limited print run. The 1842 Act included a further provision, one which also gives an interesting insight into the ways in which the mass market was beginning to change literary culture. It exempted from copyright protection what were described as 'short passages' from published literary works 'provided that not more that two such passages from works by the same author are published by the same publisher within five years, and that the source from which such passages are taken is acknowledged' (Mackinnon 1960: 888). In other words, the 1842 Act was attempting to regulate the partial use by one writer of another's work or, as we might define it today, it attempted to draw a line between legitimate borrowing or quotation, on the one hand, and plagiarism, on the other.

Although plagiarism was not a new phenomenon in the nineteenth century, there is evidence that an expanding literary market made it more prominent.

The nineteenth-century professional author was always under pressure to produce copy; moreover the practice, common in the middle decades of the century, of serialising fiction in weekly or monthly parts before publication in book form, meant that a novel was typically being written at the same time that it was being published. It was not uncommon in any one week for an author to be composing chapter 3, revising chapter 2 while correcting proofs for chapter 1. Moreover, few novelists wrote only fiction; many also had other writing commitments, such as writing reviews, commissioned essays and sometimes editorial work for a journal. Such hectic publishing schedules left no time for writer's block, and when inspiration failed, it is perhaps unsurprising that some may have been tempted to 'borrow' material from another writer's work. A further temptation to plagiarise, as Robert Macfarlane has argued, was the dominance in the second half of the nineteenth century of fictional genres – including realism, Naturalism and the sensation novel – which drew inspiration from events in contemporary life. These forms of fiction, in their attempt to seem real, encouraged an 'open interpolation of other textual sources into the novel' (Macfarlane 2007: 130). Zola's *L'Assommoir*, for example, was widely reported to have drawn heavily on Denis Poulot's documentary account of alcoholism among the working classes in *La Sublime* (1870). H. Rider Haggard's *King Solomon's Mines* generated a fierce controversy over its alleged plagiarism of contemporary travel writing, and he was forced to withdraw a poem from his later novel *Jess* (1887) after conceding that it had indeed been written by someone else. Better known perhaps is the fact that chapter 11 of the book version of Oscar Wilde's *The Picture of Dorian Gray* repeats almost word for word long passages from A. C. Church's *Precious Stones Considered in their Scientific and Artistic Relations* (1886) and William Jones's *History and Mystery of Precious Stones* (1880), although contemporary reviewers, distracted perhaps by the novel's controversial themes, did not pick up on this debt (Bristow 2005: 363).

What is of interest for the literary historian is not so much the merit or demerit of individual cases (Haggard, for example, was vigorously defended, as Macfarlane notes, by Andrew Lang, while Wilde's alleged plagiarisms, most notably in his 1881 volume *Poems*, were typically greeted with condescension). More significant is the ways in which the publicity surrounding these cases revealed changing attitudes towards literary creativity. These attitudes were being formed, at least in part, by the way in which the practicalities of professional writing brought about tensions between the concept of literature as property, on the one hand, and on the other, the concept of literature as a form of creation, one which had been made popular (as we noted earlier) by the emphasis of Romantic authors on the imagination and the uniqueness of the authorial voice. Because plagiarism, if proven, entitled the plaintiff to financial compensation (for loss of earnings, or possibly for a compromised reputation), writers accused of it (accusations were often first made in the popular press by professional plagiarism hunters) could rarely allow it to go unchallenged. Significantly, defences against plagiarism, particularly in the later decades of the century, tended to invoke a redefinition of what counted as originality in creative work, rather than a simple denial (by arguing, say, that an alleged theft was unintentional). For the novelist Charles Reade, who, as Macfarlane shows, ruthlessly plundered a variety of literary and non-literary sources for his fiction (including contemporary French drama and Government Blue Books), form was the crucial issue. For Reade, originality resided not in invention per se, but rather in the organisation and re-combination of materials taken from other sources. Similar in spirit is Wilde's definition of plagiarism as a form of literary annexation: in a review he argued that 'it is only the unimaginative who ever invent, the true artist is known by the use he makes of what he annexes, and he annexes everything'. It also made what Wilde termed 'treatment' the only test of originality. This bricolage view of creativity in turn marks an important continuity with some early modernist writing, notably that of T. S. Eliot's *The Waste Land* (1922), and it finds an analogy of a sort in the practice of sampling in contemporary musical culture.

Nineteenth-century literary markets

The growth of a mass market for literature launched many new careers and made successful authors wealthy: the profits from Braddon's *Lady Audley's Secret* reputedly set her 'up for life', as Sutherland puts it, and financed the building by her publisher William Tinsley of an extravagant villa named Audley Lodge (Sutherland 2009: 77). More impressive perhaps is the estate of over £36,000 left by Mrs Henry Wood, who is best known today for her novel *East Lynne*, and who did not begin writing seriously until she was in her fifties (Sutherland 2009: 688; Feather 2006: 137). Contemporary critics and reviewers, however, were often quite ambivalent, if not downright hostile, towards these changes in nineteenth-century print culture. As we noted in Chapter 2, a common source of anxiety centred on issues of quality and the perception that mass taste and mass literary production correlated with a lack of sophistication, or with what we might today term an alleged 'dumbing down' of literary culture. Evidence for that decline typically centred on the weakening, from the 1830s onwards, of the market for volumes of poetry and criticism – those literary genres traditionally held in the highest esteem. It was not that the market for these genres declined in an absolute sense, only that they remained small (and, for some publishers, uneconomic) relative to the dramatic increase in popularity of prose fiction, and more particularly to the new subgenres of sensation, detective and adventure fiction which traded on their entertainment rather than educational value (or, as matters were typically defined in the nineteenth century, their moral value). As Lee Erickson has observed, in the early decades of the century the essay was the 'dominant form of intellectual discourse' (Erickson 1996 :73); yet by 1889 the publisher William Blackwood complained that 'volumes of reprinted ... essays are not remunerative to either publisher or author' (Holland and Hart-Davis 2000: 405n) and evidence from other firms, such as Macmillan, suggests that when such works were retained by a publisher, it was largely for reasons of prestige rather than profit. In his correspondence with Walter Pater over the publication of what would eventually become *Studies in the History of the Renaissance* Alexander Macmillan described feeling 'pleasure and honour' in publishing Pater's 'essays on art subjects'; but he also acknowledged that while he hoped that such a volume might be 'profitable to at least some small extent', he was prepared to bear the costs should 'an unappreciative public leave us with a loss' (Seiler 1999: 67). Such a situation helps to explain Henry James's comparison, also made in 1889, of the contemporary fiction industry with a 'flood' which 'swells and swells, threatening the whole field of letters with submersion'. In fact there were several related concerns at work.

The first was that the growing commercialisation of the book trade – that is, the driving down of unit costs in order to retain competitiveness – meant that the literary market, and therefore also definitions of literary value, were being determined by the purchasing power and relatively unsophisticated tastes of what the poet Algernon Charles Swinburne condescendingly termed 'ready' readers. In an 1883 article in the *Nineteenth Century* Sir Henry Taylor defined this new reading public, enfranchised by educational reforms and an expanding economy, as 'a reading populace – a multitude of readers, who, standing in point of taste and information midway between the learned and the illiterate classes, constitutes the great body of customers for books'. Moreover, the principal problem with this 'populace', as Taylor, James and Swinburne saw it, was its imperviousness to critical advice – or, to put matters more frankly, a resistance to taking on board in the service of self-improvement the views and values of a Taylor, James or Swinburne, members by class and education of the traditional cultural elite. As another contemporary commentator, Grant Allen, complained in an 1882 article in the *Fortnightly Review*, using similar marine metaphors to James's, critics were simply unable to 'stem the tide of public taste'. Allen went on: 'Their authority is only recognised within a small sphere of picked intellects, and does not affect the general current of the popular mind. They have reputations, but they have not influence.' Here was something of a vicious circle: as we observed in Chapter 3, the relative decline in popularity of the critical essay led in turn to a decline in the authority of the critic just at the moment when it appeared that literary critical standards were in most need of reinforcing in order to guard against what Taylor referred to as the reading populace's 'debasing [of] the material of literature'.

Another concern centred on the allegedly corrupting influence of the commercialisation of publishing on authorship itself. The habit of 'booming' or 'puffing' the reputations of young writers before, it was argued, they had properly mastered their craft was seen to compromise literary creativity by encouraging formulaic writing. Objections were made, too, to the more explicit use of advertising and mass-retailing techniques in the literary book trade, as publishers competed to secure customer loyalty. This could take several forms. The most obvious was the development of special series, uniform editions and the use of publisher's lists as a way of branding an author's works with a particular identity, packaging a writer into preconceived categories over which he often had little control. Publishers also became alert to the commercial value of a writer's personality, and the usefulness of selling a book by selling its author, or rather, a carefully cultivated image of its author – a strategy which in its turn was aided by the growth in popularity of literary biography, on the one hand, and the development of new forms of visual media, like photography, on the other (from the late decades of the century there is evidence of writers using posed studio portraits for publicity purposes). Together with the development of literary tourism, where readers were encouraged to make pilgrimages to the homes and landscapes of their favourite writers (notably to the Lake District and the Highlands of Scotland), these practices were viewed by some commentators as inculcating an unhealthy, and on occasion a prurient, interest in authors' private lives, and therefore in reading most works of literature as semi-disguised autobiography (a practice, of course, which we also recognise in our own popular culture).

One modern critic, Allon White, has explained the formal complexity cultivated by late nineteenth-century authors, especially Conrad, Meredith and James, and the resulting obscurity or difficulty of their work, in terms of an attempt to resist such modes of interpretation (White 1981) – to retain, that is, a distinction, insisted upon by Oscar Wilde, between the writer as a private individual and the personality or persona expressed via the work. John Carey has also seen formal complexity as strategic rather than expressive, although he has interpreted the tactic in political terms, seeing in it an anti-democratic desire to make literature impenetrable to a mass readership, and therefore to place it beyond the reach of mass culture (Carey 1992). Other forms of resistance to the development of a mass literary culture, as we noted earlier, can be seen in the emergence in the late decades of the century of what has been termed 'coterie' publishing and the strengthening of the market among collectors for first editions and manuscripts. Eighteen-nineties publishers like the Bodley Head, who worked with artisan printers like the Chiswick Press, as well as William Morris's Kelmscott Press, specialised in expensively priced, finely produced books, usually with restricted print runs (often as low as 300 copies) and directed towards the connoisseur. Trading on the rarity value of their products, these publishing firms exploited the conflation of economic scarcity with literary value, and helped to consolidate the perception, which persisted well into the twentieth century, that there is an inverse relationship between literary value and literary productivity; or rather, the perception that literature which was written merely in order to sell – and this is how much nineteenth-century popular verse and fiction was viewed – ensured that it could never achieve the status of literary art. Such a prejudice underlay the subsequent eclipse of the reputations of many best-selling nineteenth-century writers, such as Edward Bulwer-Lytton, as well as early twentieth-century literary professionals, such as the prolific W. Somerset Maugham.

Of course the modern historian need not take the views of late nineteenth-century commentators about their own literary culture at face value, and many

As well as its reputation for reviving the art of fine printing, nineteenth-century coterie publishing inaugurated what has been described as a 'new era in book design', one reminiscent, in the attempt to harmonise into one aesthetic whole the text, illustrations and bindings, of the illuminated books of William Blake (Seiler 1999: 18). Although this revival is most usually associated with late 1880s and 1890s publishing, and firms such as William Morris's Kelmscott Press, its impetus can be traced back to an earlier moment, specifically, as Seiler argues, to the work of the Pre-Raphaelite poet and painter Dante Gabriel Rossetti. In the early 1860s Rossetti had begun designing book covers both for his own poetry, and that of his sister and brother. Relying on asymmetry and simplicity of line, Rossetti's designs were strikingly different from the conventions of the time (Ball 1985). Equally radical in their design were the covers, title pages and layout of James McNeill Whistler's *The Gentle Art of Making Enemies* (1890), which incorporated Whistler's famous butterfly motif.

of their anxieties about the development of a mass literary culture are open to other interpretations. As we suggested in Chapter 3, the hostility towards Swinburne's 'ready readers' can be seen as simple snobbery; or perhaps an attempt to revalue failure by writers like James who were unable to achieve popular sales. (That James sought to produce work with a more popular appeal, and certainly with a greater commercial value, can be seen in his disastrous attempt to write for the theatre and his experiments, also described in Chapter 3, with popular sub genres, like the ghost story.) It is instructive to learn that the correspondence of many nineteenth-century writers, even those like Matthew Arnold, Dante Gabriel Rossetti or Elizabeth Barrett Browning, writers not necessarily associated with the profit motive, are peppered with anxieties about their sales. Browning, for example, was delighted at the prospect of receiving from a New York periodical the sum of '100 dollars for every single poem', even those 'as short as a sonnet' (Chapman 2007: 80). Studies of the careers of individual writers across the century, from Walter Scott to Charles Dickens, Robert Louis Stevenson and Joseph Conrad, have shown that for many of them writing was, at least in part, a business, one in which the maximising of sales was a central concern (McDonald 1997; Dean 2003). Understanding an author's transactions with his or her publisher can thus shed new light on the nature of literary creativity by revealing the extent to which decisions about what and how to publish were motivated by commercial considerations with which writers themselves were often fully complicit. (On the other hand, there were also writers like George Gissing, whose lack of professionalism in his dealings with his publishers played a significant role in the relative failure of his career as a novelist; he achieved greater success, as we noted in Chapter 3, with short stories and travel writing.)

We should also be alert to an element of possible gender discrimination in the criticism of mass taste. As we observed in Chapter 6, many of the most successful nineteenth-century authors, if success is defined in terms of popularity and sales, were women writers like Felicia Hemans, Mary Elizabeth Braddon, Marie Corelli and Ouida. Yet they were also often among the most disparaged by a largely male critical establishment. While older literary histories tended to ignore the achievements of these women, accepting, apparently, the judgements of their (male) peers, a knowledge of nineteenth-century print culture can provide a new yardstick by which to appreciate their commercial acumen and the success with which they negotiated an industry almost wholly dominated by men. (A case in point is provided in John Sutherland's 1990 biography of Mary Ward, which is dominated by details of Ward's financial transactions with her various publishers.) By the same token, we can also realise that even those writers who appeared to stand aloof from the values of the market, typically, as we noted, by revaluing poor sales as a sign of aesthetic integrity, could rarely afford to ignore the trade completely. Moreover that trade could itself often involve elements of sharp practice. Evidence from publishing historians such as James G. Nelson has shown that firms such as the Bodley Head, which specialised in limited editions, and which promoted material rarity as a signifier of a work's aesthetic value, were not above printing more copies of a work than they actually advertised (Nelson 1971). In a similar way, other publishers attempted to boost flagging sales by advertising as new editions what were in fact rebound pages from an original print run that had failed to sell. Thus, works which might appear to have been popular when judged by the number of editions they ran to, may in practice have been relative failures, commercially speaking.

It is equally important to be aware of the fact that the aggressive selling of literature and authors which late nineteenth-century commentators like James objected to was hardly a new phenomenon. The widespread use of pseudonyms in the early and middle decades of the nineteenth century (by both male and female writers), the use of anonymity and the subsequent cultivation of an authorial mystique by figures such as Walter Scott, as well as the personality cults developed around writers like Byron and, later, Wilde, are all examples of an attempted manipulation of the media – or what has been termed 'marketing the author' – in the service of the selling of literature (Demoor 2004). In this respect the more interesting question for the literary historian is not so much whether nineteenth-century literature becomes implicated in the market and in advertising but, as we noted earlier, the increasing dominance of the new forms of evaluation – the discourses of consumerism, as they are often referred to – brought about by late-capitalist modes of literary production. Cultural historians like Jonathan Freedman (1990) have been concerned to determine the extent to which nineteenth-century authors may be complicit with, or in control of, consumerism, and thus with the ways in which particular literary works, or indeed movements (such as Aestheticism) might resist or critique the commodification of literary value associated with mid- and late-nineteenth-century modes of literary production while at the same time being a part of them. One of the most controversial figures to be subjected to this kind of analysis is Oscar Wilde. He has been viewed as one of the first writers fully to exploit the media – that is, the power of the popular press – in order to fashion a career. Yet modern critics remain divided about whether his work succeeded in 'subverting' the values of a consumer culture, or whether we should rather understand his career to have been made possible by it (Guy and Small 2000; Fortunado 2007). Moreover, these disagreements, as we noted earlier, tend to centre on larger differences in the way historians model the power relations underlying nineteenth-century publishing institutions, as well as their understanding of the pervasiveness in the late decades of the century of the market-orientated theories of value described by Gagnier.

It is also worth noting that relations between author and publisher could vary enormously, with the more successful authors being able to exercise the greatest control over the manner in which their writing was disseminated in print (Dooley 1992). That control existed both in their initial choice of publishing house and in their ability to influence the process by which a manuscript was turned into a book. As we noted earlier, many nineteenth-century authors wrote to publishing schedules which left little time for second thoughts and thus for revision. For the first three-quarters of the century, proof sheets from most printed books came to an author, not as a complete set, but only a few at a time, and these had to be corrected and returned before the next batch arrived. This gave little opportunity for the careful revising of a given work – the exercise of what Walter Pater termed 'labor limae', or the 'labour of the file' – thought necessary for fully developed style. This absence was, moreover, one reason for the widespread disparagement of popular fiction, which was typically written in quantity and to tight deadlines. This speed of production also led to printing errors, as nineteenth-century compositors struggled to interpret the cramped and sometimes barely legible handwriting of the fair-copy manuscripts submitted as printer's copy (typewritten scripts did not come into use until the 1880s and 1890s). A famous example concerns the inconsistent use of names and incorrect positioning of two paragraphs in chapter 59 of Thackeray's *Vanity Fair*, errors which persisted in the first and all succeeding nineteenth-century editions of the novel (Ray 1955: 495–96). However, writers like Tennyson and George Eliot, who combined considerable cultural prestige with reasonably high sales, could use print technology to their advantage, exploiting the various stages of proofing as opportunities for revision. Tennyson, for example, persuaded his publisher to keep type standing so that he could seek advice from his friends. Later in the century, the use of cheap galley proofs for books rather than just newspapers and magazines, gave authors of even popular fiction opportunities for second thoughts, and evidence from surviving manuscript and typescript drafts indicates that figures as prolific as Braddon took more care over their writing than the speed and volume of their productivity might suggest.

The case of Braddon also reminds us of the pitfalls of pigeon-holing nineteenth-century writers simply in terms of an opposition between popular and elitist tastes. In practice, few authors wrote exclusively for one kind of market, nor worked throughout their careers with just one publisher. Braddon wrote three-decker novels for the conservative circulating libraries while contributing stories for the less well-educated readership of such cheap publications as Ward Lock's *Sixpenny Magazine* and Gerald Maxwell's *Halfpenny Journal* (Sutherland 2009: 78). Oscar Wilde, too, secured contracts with a surprising variety of houses, from the respectable David Nutt (who had a reputation for finely produced books aimed at the bibliophile) to Leonard Smithers, whose business included the publication of pornography. Moreover, sales of Wilde's works could vary dramatically, from the few hundred copies of his 1881 *Poems* to the several thousand copies of the (much cheaper) *The Ballad of Reading Gaol* (1898) (Guy and Small 2000: 194–95). A more dramatic case is provided by the West Indian-born writer M. P. Shiel (1865–1947), whose early short stories written in the late 1890s showed him to be an ardent supporter of the artistic ideas associated with the Decadence, but who went on to enjoy a successful career as a writer of popular fiction in the Edwardian period (MacLeod 2006). As we have said, the diversity of output to be found within individual careers suggests that in practice the nineteenth-century literary market evolved in ways more complex than the simple 'mass–elite' binary implies, and that, as with the nineteenth-century theatre, readerships for literary works were not rigidly defined by class or education (Donohue 1988). For example, and as Schaffer notes, popular writers like Ouida could be admired by distinguished arbiters of artistic taste like John Ruskin (Schaffer 2000: 124), while the ascetic Lionel Johnson, as we observed in Chapter 3, could find much to admire in Kipling's best-selling *Barrack-Room Ballads*, poems noted for the immediacy and (to some modern eyes) racism and vulgarity of their vernacular voice.

The very least that can be said for examining nineteenth-century literature from the point of view of publishing culture is that it enables us to appreciate better the variety of ways in which literary works were made available to the reading public, and it is this variety which, as we noted above, has played a crucial role in expanding the nineteenth-century canon. As we observed in Chapter 6, recovery projects which seek to rehabilitate works by forgotten or neglected nineteenth-century writers have often involved investigating forms of print media, such as the periodical press, which traditional literary historians tended to overlook. It was the ambition of most nineteenth-century writers to have works – whether poems, fiction or critical essays – which were first published in magazines or journals reprinted in book form, not least because the book, as a physically durable object, conferred a sense of permanence as well as status. In this publishing hierarchy the expensively bound library, or collected edition, stood at the apex of writerly achievement. Yet there were clearly many authors for whom this ambition went unrealised, with the result that for much of the twentieth century some important aspects of nineteenth-century literary production – principally working-class, Chartist and socialist literature, as well as various forms of critical writing – remained inaccessible and thus unknown to most modern readers. However, and as we discussed in Chapter 3, historians of periodical culture such as Laurel Brake have argued that even where works were republished in book form, it is the periodical version that we should pay attention to, because it was the distinctive conditions of the periodical press which played the greatest role in shaping literary creativity during the course of the nineteenth century (Brake 1994). The most obvious example of such influence, also commented upon in Chapter 3, can be seen in the intricate plotting and inventive characterisation found in the mid nineteenth-century novel; maintaining the reader's interest across a serialisation that might last for a year or more required frequent cliff-hangers, numerous sub-plots and memorable characters. Put another way, it is easy to see why narrative genres which proved popular in the eighteenth century, such as the epistolary novel used by Samuel Richardson (1689–1761) in his *Pamela* (1741) and *Clarissa* (1747–48), quickly fell out of favour in the nineteenth, ill-adapted as they were to serial treatment. But Brake argues that even genres like criticism were shaped by periodical culture, a proposition explored in detail by Jason Camlot, who argues that changes in nineteenth-century theories of rhetoric map those in nineteenth-century publishing. Of particular significance, he argues, is the growth, from the 1830s onwards, of new kinds of literary magazines which resulted in 'new models of the critic and new conceptions of literature' (Camlot 2008: 2).

Editing nineteenth-century literature

Recognising that nineteenth-century literary works typically existed in a wide variety of textual embodiments, in which both text and paratext can differ substantially, brings in its train a number of theoretical and practical problems which have been highlighted by some modern editorial theory. Here the central concern is how modern editors make decisions about which text of a nineteenth-century literary work to print as the copy- or base-text of their editions. It is, after all, via modern editorial practices that the vast majority of modern readers encounter nineteenth-century literary works: we almost never read a nineteenth-century poem, novel, short story, critical essay or indeed a play-script in exactly the material form in which a contemporary reader did, unless of course we are fortunate enough to have access to a copyright or periodical library. Today, as in the nineteenth century, the modern reader is confronted with their own society's proliferation of textual embodiments of nineteenth-century works. These can range from cheap paperbacks with no editorial apparatus, to editions which are aimed at the student reader and provide introductory material, some annotation and usually a prefatory 'note' on the choice of copy-text, to expensive variorum editions (generally bought only by university libraries) which, though providing the fullest annotation and textual apparatus, require the reader to be familiar with the conventions and *sigla* of modern textual editing. Finally, there also exists a wide variety of e-texts, often of dubious textual provenance and textual authority. Price aside, how does the reader choose between these modern editions: do any of them bring us close to the experience of the nineteenth-century reader, and what role should knowledge of that experience play in judgements about literary value? As we shall see, looking closely at modern editors' treatment of the variations between the textual embodiments of nineteenth-century literary works can bring into sharp focus the question with which we began this book, and which is central to the writing of literary history: namely, what do we read nineteenth-century literary works for?

Dramatic works pose a complex set of problems for the modern editor in that he or she is nearly always confronted with the existence of a variety of printed forms of play-texts: in the nineteenth century these may include prompt copies, actors' copies, the licensing copy lodged in the Lord Chamberlain's Office, a limited print run of a work used to establish copyright protection, as well as acting editions published for use by amateur theatrical companies and, later in the century, so-called 'reading texts' (which were not designed for performance at all). Second, the editor must also confront the difficulties posed by trying to recover the numerous non-textual elements of performance, a task which brings into sharp focus the thorny question as to what constitutes 'the text' of a dramatic work, as well as the problem of who constitutes its author.

In making decisions about copy- or base-text modern editors are generally guided by one of several basic editorial principles, and the assumptions underlying them correlate broadly with different ways of conceptualising a literary history – as a history of authors, or of works, or of literature's engagement with social life – which we have discussed in earlier chapters. Editors who give priority to authorial agency, and who identify the integrity of a literary work with an author's control over it, tend to select as copy-text the *first* completed version of a work. In the nineteenth century this will often mean the first book (or sometimes periodical) edition of a novel, poem or critical essay, although on occasions it might also entail using as copy-text a surviving fair-copy manuscript, if the editor judges that the writer had little or no involvement in the process of publication and that his thoughts were 'corrupted' by inappropriate interventions made by a publisher, editor or typesetter. For example, since the 1960s most modern editions of Oscar Wilde's *De Profundis* have reprinted the manuscript of that work which is held in the British Library (and which was first made available for public view in 1962). This is largely because they view the heavily abridged versions of it which were published posthumously in 1905 and 1908 by Wilde's literary executor, Robert Ross (1869–1918), to lack Wilde's authority. (But it is worth noting, in passing, that the most recent edition of that work questions this line of reasoning, suggesting not only that Ross's editorial practice closely follows directions for the part-publication of the manuscript set out by Wilde in a letter to him, but that Ross's text also results in a 'better' literary work, in the sense that it is structurally and stylistically more coherent than Wilde's manuscript (Small 2005: 1–30).) It is worth stressing, too, that the principle of 'first-text' editing, as it is sometimes called, was initially developed in relation to Renaissance literature, where textual variants in scribal and early printed copies, generally made without the original author's knowledge, were viewed as introducing errors into the work (and which were described in a set of loaded terms such as 'foul papers').

Editors who are concerned with the way a literary work develops, and who conceptualise creativity as a teleological process which may involve the intervention of other agents (such as the opinions of editors, professional house readers and even comments from reviewers), are likely to choose as copy-text the *last* version of a published text which an author oversaw in his or her lifetime. So this might mean preferring the text of a library or collected edition, rather that of a first edition or an earlier manuscript. This 'last-text' thesis, however, also has limitations, and they centre on the assumption that creativity is a simple evolutionary process, and that an increase in skill and sophistication correlates with an increase in age, not always a reliable belief. As we noted in Chapter 1, Thomas Hardy spent almost half his life revising the book version of *Tess of the D'Urbervilles*; on every occasion that it was republished he took the opportunity to rework it (and this is true of most of his oeuvre). Initially the process involved restoring passages bowdlerised from the first periodical publication in 1891 in *The Graphic*, but later interventions changed aspects of the characterisation, geography, chronology and dialect. At what point do these obsessive revisions become mere tinkering? More significantly, do Hardy's changing intentions towards his work necessarily result in improvements to it, and is the resulting work still a nineteenth-century novel?

It is worth recalling the example of the large number of nineteenth-century authors, such as Southey, Wordsworth, Swinburne and (to a certain extent) Pater, who became more reactionary, even establishment figures, in later life. And it is significant that modern critics have tended to pay more attention to the works of their youth than of their maturity, often preferring the 1805 thirteen-book *Prelude* to the posthumously published 1850 fourteen-book version (Gill 1984), or the 1873 edition of Pater's *Renaissance* rather than revised versions of 1876, 1888 or 1893, or the library edition of 1910. As regards the many versions of Hardy's *Tess*, modern editors have been divided on the issue of copy-text. While some, such as James Gibson (editor of the 1993 Methuen *Tess*) print as copy-text the 1920 revised Wessex Edition, the last version which Hardy oversaw in his lifetime, others, such as David Skilton (editor of the Penguin *Tess*), have preferred the 1912 Wessex Edition, on the grounds that revisions undertaken after this date 'considerably postdate the composition of the novel as a whole' and 'belong to a different historical period' (Skilton 1979: 498). Skilton's concept of the relationship between the integrity of a work and the length of the period of composition may seem a trifle arbitrary: we could just as well argue that 1912 was a 'different period', culturally, politically and socially, from the 1890s, when the novel was first written, and when Hardy undertook a major series of revisions between the 1892 one-volume edition and

1895 Collected Edition. Skilton's particular editorial decisions have a larger relevance; like many modern editors, he seems to betray an anxiety about conceptualising literary creativity in abstraction from a larger historical context. When authors take the opportunity to revise a work, they rarely do so in a cultural vacuum, and their intentions towards it may change in response to a variety of pressures, not all of which the modern editor (or critic) may judge to be of equal importance. Put another way, modern critics and editors may hold different views about the value of any particular version of a literary work from those of its author; and our views on the way an editor acts on that judgement tell us much about why we read nineteenth-century literature. An attention to the editorial dilemmas which Hardy's oeuvre poses serves to remind us that, as modern readers, we are rarely encountering the same texts of his fiction as our nineteenth-century predecessors, and therefore almost inevitably not encountering precisely the same 'Hardy'. This in turn seems counterintuitive, for he is typically written about by critics as a quintessentially late-Victorian novelist, responding to events of his own time, such as, in *Tess* and *Jude the Obscure*, the figure of the 'new woman'. Moreover, if the modern habit, as we argued in Chapter 6, is to read Tess comparatively, alongside other 'new woman' fiction, then it makes no sense to consult either a 1920 or 1912 text of that work – yet these are exactly the versions of the novel most readily available in popular paperbacks.

It is exactly the kinds of problems associated with what has been called a constantly revising author like Hardy which lead other editors to set aside considerations both of authorial agency and of the integrity of the work in favour of concentrating on that text which had the greatest social impact, when social impact might be defined by numbers of readers (and so popularity), or perhaps by the critical controversy which a particular text of a given work generated. Here we can see a continuity of sorts with those literary historians who see the purpose of a literary history to be that of exhibiting the role of literature in cultural life, rather than singling out the 'best' works in a given period, when 'best' is defined by criteria such as formal complexity or innovation. Interestingly, there are some nineteenth-century literary works where applying the principles of both 'last-text' and 'social-text' editing can seem equally appropriate, a circumstance which in turn usefully alerts us to the complexity of their value for contemporary and modern readers. A good example comes again from Wilde's oeuvre – this time, his well-known novella *The Picture of Dorian Gray*.

As we noted in Chapter 2, in 1890 and 1891 Wilde brought out what were effectively two *Dorian Grays*. The first was a short story of around 50,000 words published in a single number of a family periodical; the second was a one-volume novel of 78,000 words (the greater length of which had been generated by additional material which expanded the work from thirteen to twenty chapters). Which of these texts – the 1890 or 1891 – should a modern editor reproduce as copy or base-text for a work called *The Picture of Dorian Gray*? An editor interested in the cultural impact of Wilde's story would be advised to reprint the 1890 text, since the story which appeared in *Lippincott's Monthly Magazine* reached a relatively wide readership in the late nineteenth century, and it was also responsible for generating the most reviews (including all the most hostile ones); further, it was this version which was used as evidence by the defence in the Queensberry libel case, the first of the three trials in which Wilde was involved in 1895 (Holland 2003). However, Wilde was an author who usually revised when given the opportunity, and we know that he put much effort into preparing the book publication of *The Picture of Dorian Gray*, and that he valued book publication more highly than occasional journalism. Certainly an editor following the principles of 'final-text' editing is likely to prefer the 1891 text on the grounds that it represents Wilde's more mature or considered thoughts about his story; it might also be argued that in the 1891 text, the work known as *The Picture of Dorian Gray* is more fully realised. Most modern paperback editions of the novel follow this last editorial decision, and today there will be many readers of this work who are wholly unaware of the earlier, shorter (and in the view of some modern critics), more explicitly homoerotic and therefore more radical 1890 text.

To complicate matters further, there is evidence that Wilde's motives for revising the 1891 text were mixed. The lengthening of the story was prompted, at least in part, by a simple commercial consideration – the need to persuade readers of the cheap magazine story that it was worth buying the more expensive book (which was six times the price), that in effect they were purchasing a new work, a new kind of reading experience. Wilde's correspondence with his publisher also suggests that the particular way in which he lengthened his story – most of the new material fleshes out the sub-plot involving Sybil Vane's relationship with Dorian – may have been dictated by a need (possibly one perceived more clearly by his publisher than by Wilde himself) to make the story less controversial. On the other hand, that material also contains much new and witty dialogue which in places foreshadows the satire on the British class system that would bring Wilde such success in his later society comedies (*Lady Windermere's Fan* contains a number of lines which first appeared in *The Picture of Dorian Gray*). In other words, the acknowledgment that the 1891 *The Picture of Dorian Gray* may have involved an element of self-censorship does not militate against a critical judgement that it is none the less the better, because more stylistically complex, work. On the other hand, it remains the case that the contemporary critical response to the 1891 book was muted: it received few reviews and sold slowly and poorly in relation to other, similarly priced volumes of fiction. For one modern editor, the only adequate response to this dilemma is to conceive of the periodical and book versions of *Dorian Gray* as two separate works, written for different occasions and with different audiences in mind (Bristow 2005). The problem of choosing between *Dorian Gray*s is thus handed back to the reader, who will be forced to consider the question: what are they reading this work for?

That question is given a concrete answer by the fourth editorial principle, referred to as 'eclectic' editing; in this instance, the editor arrogates to him- or herself an element of authorial responsibility, in that he or she aims to reproduce as copy-text the best possible version of a work, when 'best' is defined in terms of an aesthetic or literary judgement. This kind of editor assumes that the reader is not interested in a work's historical significance or value; nor that she seeks to understand its impact for nineteenth-century readers. In practice, eclectic editing can mean conflating elements of different versions of a work into one text: for example, an editor might begin with the first edition of a work, but 'correct' that text by reinstating manuscript variants which in her view were misinterpreted or omitted by the publisher; she might also substitute variants from later texts – say a second or third edition – if they are judged to represent improvements over the first edition. In this way a text is created which no nineteenth-century reader could have experienced, but which, it is argued, represents the best possible realisation of the work. The significance of this last editorial principle can be more easily appreciated by a concrete example.

One of the best-loved nineteenth-century novels is Emily Brontë's *Wuthering Heights*; yet few modern readers are aware that they are almost certain to be reading a version of the novel which no nineteenth-century reader ever encountered, and which, technically speaking, Emily Brontë herself did not authorise. The motive for publishing *Wuthering Heights* apparently came from Emily's more ambitious and entrepreneurial sister, Charlotte. However, securing a publisher for this unusual work proved to be difficult, and it was eventually brought out by Thomas Cautley Newby (d.1882) under the pseudonym Acton Bell, as part of a three-volume set (the third volume of which was made up of Anne Brontë's *Agnes Gray*). Newby is described by Sutherland as 'without doubt, the most notorious publisher of fiction in the Victorian period' (Sutherland 2009: 466). That notoriety centred on his less-than-honest business practices (he deliberately attributed false authorship to some novels in the anticipation of generating higher sales) and shoddy treatment of writers, many of whom were apparently asked for large advances, which were never repaid, to cover the costs of printing. Like many of his publications, Newby's 1847 edition of *Wuthering Heights* was carelessly and cheaply produced and contains numerous textual oddities (particularly in the spelling, punctuation, which included the frequent use of em-dashes, and paragraphing), and these may have contributed to the novel's poor sales and hostile critical reception. Two years after Emily's death *Wuthering Heights* was republished in a new edition by a different and altogether more respectable publisher, the house of Smith, Elder, who in 1847 had brought out, to great acclaim, Charlotte Brontë's *Jane Eyre*. The second, 1850 edition of *Wuthering Heights* was prepared for the press by Charlotte; moreover, that preparation involved rather more than simply correcting what she claimed were errors in 'orthography' and 'punctuation', which, though marked up on proof sheets, had not been carried through in Newby's text. Charlotte also changed the paragraphing and simplified some of the dialect, apparently in an attempt to make it appear, as she put it her 'Editorial Preface' to the new edition, less 'rude'. In the absence of any surviving manuscript of *Wuthering Heights*, the modern editor is confronted with a dilemma:

does she reprint what Ian Jack terms the transparently 'shoddy' first edition (Jack 1986: xxii), or Charlotte Brontë's tidier version, one which none the less removes some of the idiosyncrasies of Emily's style, and without Emily's authority?

An editor concerned to produce the most widely read version of the novel can simply reprint the 1850 text, noting perhaps that it is partly authored by Charlotte Brontë. However, the editor who is interested in honouring the iconoclastic tendencies of Emily's creation has a more problematic decision. It is worth remembering that the process by which Emily's reputation was eventually recuperated and in which *Wuthering Heights* came to be viewed as a 'classic' centred on perceptions of her stylistic originality and complexity, in comparison to, say, *Jane Eyre*. In the late decades of the nineteenth century, as Emily's reputation increased, so Charlotte's suffered a decline. The 1847 Newby version is undoubtedly closer to Emily's 'original' intentions for her work, yet it also contains obvious errors, although the absence, as we noted, of any surviving manuscript of *Wuthering Heights* means that we cannot distinguish with absolute certainty between errors introduced by the printing process and the idiosyncrasies of Emily's style. A solution of sorts to this dilemma, one taken by the most influential modern version of the novel, the 1976 Clarendon edition (which is also the text reproduced in the popular Oxford World's Classic paperback), is to produce what is in effect an 'eclectic' text. That is, to use the 1847 edition as copy- or base-text, but to then 'correct' it as the modern editor sees fit, a process which means making fine critical judgements about irregularities which are errors introduced by Newby, and those which can stand because they were 'authorial', that is, assumed to have been deliberately contrived for aesthetic effect. The editors of the Clarendon edition, Hilda Marsden and Ian Jack, are thus attempting to create the best *possible* text of *Wuthering Heights* by realising that work in a manner that was allegedly not open to Emily in her own lifetime. Marsden's and Jack's description of their editorial practice – which they describe as being based on a 'careful recension of Newby's edition' – is worth quoting in detail, not least for the number of qualifications it contains:

> We have almost always retained the paragraphing of Newby's edition, and we have usually retained the dashes and exclamation-marks, as well as question-marks after indirect questions. We have had no hesitation in dropping a great many of the commas which pester Newby's text, and we have inserted commas and hyphens where we consider them necessary. Our general aim has been to correct the punctuation and other accidentals where we believe them to be wrong, misleading, irritating, or disconcerting to the reader.
>
> (Marsden and Jack 1976: xxxi–xxxii)

It is ultimately only a matter of 'belief' as to which textual oddities are authorial – that is, originate with Emily – and which are due to printing errors, and this left the way open for later editors to make their own decisions about what to do with Newby's text. Thus the Routledge edition of *Wuthering Heights* edited by Heather Glen (1988), that edited by Linda H. Peterson (1992) for St. Martin's Press and, most recently, the Broadview *Wuthering Heights* edited by Christopher Heywood (2004) offer revisions of the 1847 Newby text which are all different from each other, as well as being different from the text of the Clarendon edition. As a result the modern reader is in the odd position of being able to choose from at least four different versions of the 1847 text of *Wuthering Heights*, none of which, technically speaking, was either authorised by Emily or seen by any nineteenth-century reader.

One way of resolving the problem of how to choose between multiple textual embodiments of a single work is to use the resources of modern computing to display all versions simultaneously, a practice generally referred to as 'hypertext' editing. The ambition of such projects is to make available to the modern reader all known textual variants; in this way each reader becomes his or her own editor. While such editions can have immense scholarly value, they remain impractical for most general reading and teaching purposes, particularly for long works of literature, like many nineteenth-century novels. When faced with a constantly revising author, the general editors of the codex editions of the Cambridge University Press Edition of the works of D. H. Lawrence have argued that most readers still prefer to be provided with a single, stable, authoritative text.

Modern editorial practice is arguably one of the most neglected or misunderstood areas of the discipline of literary studies (it is not often taught, or taught systematically at undergraduate level). Yet Perkins's description of literary history, which we quoted in Chapter 1, that it has 'an indispensable role in our experience of literature and a broader cultural and social function as well' (Perkins 1992, 17), might equally well apply to text-editing. As we have seen, the principles by which modern editors make nineteenth-century works available to us can vary widely. They mean that we may find ourselves reading texts which were not wholly authored by the writer to whom they are commonly attributed, or which may be dated several decades after the period with which we commonly associate their composition and publication. On some occasions, we may find that there exist completely different versions of a work which we thought we knew well. Edward FitzGerald's *The Rubaiyat of Omar Khayyam* went through four editions in his lifetime in which he changed his mind not only about how he translated his Persian sources (which were the various medieval manuscripts, compiled by different hands and of differing authority, attributed to Khayyam), but also about how many quatrains he selected to translate, and how he arranged them. As a result, we cannot refer to any simple idea of what *The Rubaiyat* is – we cannot, that is, identify with confidence the text of just one of those editions with the work and exclude the others. Alternatively, we may discover that a work by a writer whom we commonly think of as Victorian or nineteenth-century (such as Gerard Manley Hopkins) was never made available to a contemporary audience. Of course, if we disconnect literary creativity from a consideration of authors, history and context, then these issues will continue to seem irrelevant to literary appreciation (although it would still be the case that without modern editors there would be many fewer nineteenth-century literary works to read and compare). However, experience suggests that, for most readers, notions of authorial agency and historical specificity remain indispensable elements of their understanding of literary works, and such readers need therefore to be as aware of the complexities of modern text-editing as they are of those of modern literary historiography.

Conclusion

- In examining the relationship between nineteenth-century literary production and print culture, critics have pointed to the importance over this period of changes in the technology and economics of publishing and their impact both on the power relationships between writers, publishers and readers and on a work's material form.
- One of the most controversial aspects of nineteenth-century publishing is its relationship with an emerging commodity culture, and thus the extent to which literary value can be said to be assimilated to the discourses of consumerism.
- There is strong evidence from factors such as developments in copyright law that changes to nineteenth-century publishing practices brought about parallel changes in the ways in which literary creativity was understood, and in particular in the relationship between creativity and originality.
- Individual writers responded to, and were affected by, changes in nineteenth-century publishing culture in different ways: generally speaking, the better-selling or more prestigious authors were able to exercise more control over the process by which their works came into print.
- Most nineteenth-century literary works exist in a number of textual embodiments; however, modern editors may adopt quite different principles for assigning priority to these embodiments, with the result that the modern reader may be presented with several different texts or versions of the same work.

Glossary of terms and contested definitions

Aestheticism Loosely speaking, the term refers to the value placed on beauty, usually divorced from moral, ethical or utilitarian considerations; Aestheticism is also known by the familiar phrase 'art for art's sake'. It is particularly associated with the writings of Walter Pater and his programme for 'aesthetic criticism' set out in his *Studies in the History of the Renaissance* and summed up in that work's final sentence: 'art comes to you proposing frankly to give nothing but the highest quality to your moments as they pass, and simply for those moments' sake'. The most popular proponent of Aestheticism was Oscar Wilde. Modern critics, however, use the term in a number of ways: to refer to the late nineteenth-century 'Aesthetic Movement', which took its cue from Pater; to describe an attitude towards the relationship between art and morality to be found a variety of writers from the 1870s to the early decades of the twentieth century; or to refer to a widespread interest, dating from the 1870s, in the beauty of form, style and decoration in artistic culture, architecture, house decoration, furniture and ceramics.

Avant-garde The term is used to designate artistic innovation or revolution – those writers and artists who are seen to be, and advertise themselves as being, in a cultural vanguard. Avant-gardism is usually considered to be a collective endeavour, involving groups of artists or writers who, by virtue of the aesthetic or political assumptions they have in common, form some kind of ideological community, the existence of which is sometimes publicised by a manifesto. Historians locate the beginnings of avant-garde activity in post-Revolutionary nineteenth-century French artistic culture.

Bildungsroman A sub-genre of fiction, traditionally associated with Johann Wolfgang von Goethe's famous novel *Wilheim Meister*, and which takes as its subject the youth and so the moral and emotional development of a hero or heroine. The definition, certainly when applied to British literary culture, is capacious to the point of fluidity, and has been seen to encompass works as varied as Charlotte Brontë's *Jane Eyre*, Charles Dickens's *David Copperfield*, George Eliot's *Mill on the Floss* and Walter Pater's historical novel *Marius the Epicurean.*

Burlesque A form of light entertainment which developed from extravaganza and flourished in the 1850s and 1860s. As the name implies, burlesque centred on parodying other literary forms, including Italian opera and Shakespearean dramas, and made copious use of ingenious comic paraphrase. (See also *Extravaganza* and *Comic opera*)

Chartism A working-class movement, some of whose leaders were, however, drawn from the professional and business classes. It was active in the 1830s and early 1840s, particularly in the provinces, and its six demands – set out in 'The People's Charter' – included the extension of the franchise to all adult men (but not women), a secret ballot, equal electoral districts, the abolition of property qualifications for MPs, payment for MPs and annual Parliaments. The movement, which in its late phase was influenced by Irish nationalism, was to all intents and purposes a spent force by 1848.

Circulating library These were commercial institutions which made money by making an initial charge for membership and then for every volume borrowed. The best-known and most influential (because of their purchasing power) on matters of literary taste were those established in 1842 by Charles Edward Mudie (and which continued well into the twentieth century) and later, in 1860, by W. H. Smith (whose business also involved book retailing, notably at railway stations). Their power was deeply resented by some authors and was viewed as a kind of informal censorship.

Comic opera The best-known examples of the genre are the Savoy operas of W. S. Gilbert and Arthur Sullivan; initially imported from Europe, this form of musical comedy was closely related to, and eventually supplanted, burlesque.

Commodity culture The term, which describes the kinds of economic exchanges held to underlie Western capitalism, has been applied to late nineteenth-century British culture to refer to the process by which traditional cultural artefacts – such as works of art and literature – come to be traded and valued in a manner similar to other kinds of commodities (in terms, that is, of their market scarcity), as well as to the ways in which ordinary commodities (like sugar or tea, or nowadays motor cars) come to be treated as cultural artefacts – that is, as possessing a symbolic, as well as an exchange value. That said, there is considerable debate among modern literary historians and cultural theorists about both the nature and the pervasiveness in nineteenth-century British society of what has been termed the 'commodification' of literary and artistic value and the concomitant 'enculturation' of the commodity. (See also *Spectacle*)

Copy-text The textual embodiment of a literary work used by editors and publishers to form the basis of a particular edition. Modern editors of nineteenth-century literary works generally choose as copy-text the periodical, the first, or the last book edition of a work.

Darwinism Nineteenth-century understanding of the work of Charles Darwin, and particularly his controversial theory of natural selection outlined in *On The Origin of Species* (1859), was a complex matter, with the result that 'Darwinism' could mean different things to nineteenth-century commentators. For example, not all of those who termed themselves 'Darwinists', or followers of Darwin, necessarily accepted all aspects of his work. So it was possible to agree, as some members of the Church of England did, with his concept of the evolution of species while at the same time rejecting the idea of a common descent. Likewise, Darwin's ideas were often appropriated and applied to aspects of social behaviour and policy with which he had not been directly concerned; most famously, the phrase 'survival of the fittest' was coined not by Darwin but by the social theorist Herbert Spencer, who in the 1860s and 1870s adapted aspects of Darwin's ideas to explain the development of society. In the late decades of the century the term 'social Darwinism', associated with the work of figures like Spencer, became synonymous with a pessimism in which social intervention was seen as pointless and even damaging because, by enabling the 'unfit' to survive, it worked against 'natural' evolutionary processes and ultimately undermined the fitness of the nation.

Decadence Decadence, used as a critical term, originally referred to a French literary and cultural movement which developed from the experimental work of writers such as Paul Verlaine, Stéphane Mallarmé and J.-K. Huysmans. In Britain the term was associated with a number of writers working in the 1890s, the most prominent of whom were Oscar Wilde and Arthur Symons (who was, in his essay 'The Decadent Movement in Literature' published in *Harper's New Monthly Magazine* in 1893, the movement's most cogent theorist). The subjects of Decadent literature were the exotic aspects of sensory experience, abnormal psychological states and forbidden forms of pleasure, especially sexual pleasure. Decadence was also associated with a style of writing which centred on elaborate linguistic constructions and archaic forms, sometimes referred to pejoratively as 'purple prose'. Modern historians have pointed to the range of the term's referents in late nineteenth-century culture, and particularly to its derogatory use to marginalise works which were seen to deviate from normative standards of taste.

Dramatic monologue Conventionally, this poetic sub-genre has been most closely associated with the work of Robert Browning, and its principal characteristic is that it centres on the utterance of a single person, who is not the poet, and who is addressing a silent auditor (or auditors) whose presence can be inferred only from hints in the speaker's address. The precise origins of the dramatic monologue are, however, a matter of dispute; and there is disagreement, too, about some of its defining features.

Edition Modern publishing normally distinguishes an edition from a reprint (or impression). The advertisement of a 'new edition' of a work usually means that substantive textual, rather than merely accidental, changes (such as those to punctuation), have been made to it. However, nineteenth-century publishers often called an edition what was a simple reprint or rebinding of an existing edition, usually as a strategy to boost flagging sales. (See also *Impression*)

Extravaganza Perfected by J. R. Planché, extravaganza was a comic form of theatrical entertainment which flourished in the 1830s and 1840s. Directed towards an educated audience, it made use of witty puns and literary satire; one of the most popular variants was the 'fairy extravaganza', an essential element of nineteenth-century pantomimes, and which combined references to contemporary social and domestic life with fantasy and transformations of characters and scenery which in turn provided opportunities for lavish staging. (See also *Pantomime*)

Fabianism A late nineteenth-century London-based, socialist-leaning, political group whose members included the social reformers Sidney and Beatrice Webb, the writers George Bernard Shaw and H. G. Wells, as well as the later leader of the Labour Party and future Prime Minister, James Ramsay MacDonald. Fabianism advocated a centrally planned economy and labour market to eliminate unemployment and social poverty; in this respect its main political opponent was Liberalism. Fabianism was never a popular movement and its main constituency was a metropolitan intelligentsia. Indeed, it was Keir Hardie, elected to the West Ham constituency in 1892, and who co-founded the Scottish Parliamentary Labour Party (1888) and the Independent Labour Party (1893), who proved more successful in harnessing popular discontent with Liberal policies.

Farce In the nineteenth century a short one- or two-act comic sub-genre which, until the late decades, typically functioned as an afterpiece to the main performance. From the 1840s onwards, farce became less genteel and more focused on domestic settings and lower-class characters, such as servants, tradesmen and journeymen. Its emphasis on low comedy typically involved the intense pressures heaped upon a hapless individual by a series of domestic events over which he or she has no control. By the 1870s, and in order to appeal to what were perceived as the more sophisticated tastes of West End audiences, farces became longer (they now involved three acts) and became the main piece on the bill. In addition, their subject-matter, influenced by the popularity of French farce, became more bourgeois, and typically involved the alleged sexual misdemeanours of otherwise 'respectable' pillars of the establishment.

Gothic novel A fictional sub-genre associated with Horace Walpole, and particularly his *Castle of Otranto, a Gothic Story* (1764); it flourished in the early decades of the nineteenth century. The vogue for Gothic fiction (especially among women writers and readers) was wittily parodied in Jane Austen's *Northanger Abbey*. With its medieval settings, descriptions of gloomy castles complete with subterranean passages, dungeons and ghosts, and emphasis on sensational and supernatural events, the main aim of Gothic fiction was to evoke terror in the reader, typically through recounting a series of mysterious, cruel and generally horrifying experiences. Gothic's preoccupation with the uncanny, macabre and melodramatic, together with its depiction of extreme psychological states and general atmosphere of doom, was influential on a wide range of nineteenth-century British and Irish writers (notably the Brontës), while Gothic novels themselves enjoyed something of a revival in popularity in the late decades of the century, with works such as Bram Stoker's *Dracula*. Modern critics distinguish between various kinds of Gothic traditions and modes, such as 'eighteenth-century' and 'Victorian', 'American' and 'British', 'male' and 'female' Gothic.

Hellenism Generally speaking, the term refers to the active dissemination of the ideals of ancient Greek culture. In the nineteenth century, it was associated with the period between Alexander the Great and the victory by Octavian (later Augustus Caesar, the first emperor of Rome) at Actium and the subsequent capture of the city-state of Alexandria and eventual incorporation of Egypt into the Roman Empire. It was during this period, the so-called 'Hellenistic Age' (c. 336–31 BC), that Greek culture was seen to be most intensely and (insofar as it made possible, in this reading of history, the rise of Christianity) successfully diffused. By contrast, late twentieth-century interpretations of Hellenism tend to centre on the extent to which the process of 'Hellenisation' can be seen as a form of cultural colonisation, and thus a tool of oppression used to marginalise indigenous populations. The term Hellenism is perhaps best known to students of nineteenth-century literary culture from Matthew Arnold's *Culture and Anarchy*, where he uses it to designate a cast of mind associated with creativity and imagination, and which he called 'sweetness and light'. He contrasted Hellenism with what he saw as an opposing cultural force, that of the moralising tendencies of religious thinking, and an emphasis on duty, self-control and earnestness, all of which he termed 'Hebraism'. Modern historians have also identified an intellectual current in nineteenth-century Britain labelled 'Oxford Hellenism', which refers to the value placed on the study of ancient Greek culture as a source of social renewal and a realm of transcendent value alternative to that of Christian theology. This interpretation of classical culture was associated with the reforms in the teaching of ancient Greek at Oxford University undertaken by the powerful head of Balliol College, Professor of Greek, and later vice-chancellor of the university, Benjamin Jowett, and which in turn were an aspect of the general university reforms of the 1850s and 1860s. It was these reforms which placed classical studies in general, and the writings of Plato in particular, at the centre of the prestigious Oxford 'Greats' curriculum, or *Literae humaniores*. In the later decades of the nineteenth century Hellenism became a shorthand way of designating a form of cultural open-mindedness which encompassed a recognition (and for writers such as Oscar Wilde and John Addington Symonds, a celebration) of male–male desire: in this sense, Hellenism operated as a form of homosexual code. (See also *Paiderastia*)

Homo-social The term was popularised by the writings of the queer theorist Eve Kosofsky Sedgwick, who proposed that in Western discourses (including many nineteenth-century literary works) relationships are commonly structured in terms of 'homo-social desire', a concept which is distinct from that of homosexual desire, and which typically functions to proscribe the expression of same-sex relations. Sedgwick argues that many literary works can be read as narratives of homo-social desire, meaning that their overt preoccupation with male–female relationships (evidenced in the marriage plots of so many nineteenth-century fictions) in practice points up the importance of relationships between men (which are not necessarily sexual, although they may be), and who are typically presented as rivals for a woman's love, or may be colleagues, acquaintances or friends. In this argument, women are reduced to mere objects of exchange, and desire itself is seen to be defined and controlled by patriarchal structures which, in the nineteenth century, are also homophobic. The importance of Sedgwick's work was that it enabled critics to appreciate the centrality of homo-social desire (and therefore, in some instances, of a 'closet' homosexuality) to literary works apparently concerned only with 'heterosexual' themes. Put another way, Sedgwick showed how the discourses of heterosexuality – again, notably in nineteenth-century literature – were dependent on what they aimed to exclude, homosexuality. (See also *Queer theory*)

Impression The term usually refers to a reprint – that is, in nineteenth-century terms, one taken from the same plates, and which therefore does not allow for any revision. (See also *Edition*)

Impressionism The term is most closely associated with a movement in late nineteenth-century French pictorial art, and particularly with the work of Claude Monet and Edgar Degas, whose ambition was to record accurately the perception of the visual world in terms of the effects of light and colour. In late nineteenth-century British literary discourses the term had a variety of referents, ranging from an association with Naturalism to a form of critical or aesthetic perception and appreciation. (See also *Aestheticism* and *Naturalism*)

Individualism A term with a number of conflicting meanings in the nineteenth century. When associated with the philosophy of John Stuart Mill, it refers to the valorisation of self-development, and the safeguarding of individual liberties, particularly the freedom of speech. Individualism was also the name given to a short-lived political party which emerged in the late 1880s and was a spent force by 1910. Its members were opposed to most functions of contemporary government, including attempts to regulate labour, education, religion and the arts; through their campaigning arm, the Liberty and Property Defence League, Individualists vigorously defended private property. They saw their main political antagonists to be the various socialist groupings in Britain. In the popular press, the Individualists' anti-statism led to their identification with anarchism. (See also *Socialism*)

Laissez-faire Literally, 'leave to be' or 'leave to do' – colloquially, 'leave alone'. In the early and middle decades of the century the term was identified with the political economy of Adam Smith and David Ricardo, who argued against attempts to regulate the economy; more generally, it referred to what was perceived as anti-interventionist government. In many literary works of the 1840s and 1850s (particularly Dickens's *Hard Times*) the term is pejorative, implying what Thomas Carlyle termed an 'abdication' of responsibility, usually on the part of contemporary political leaders. (See also *Manchester School* and *Political economy*)

Liberalism In the nineteenth century the term is associated with the political and economic writings of John Stuart Mill – who argued for the limitations of state power in the management of the economy and the personal lives of individuals – and the ideology of the Liberal Party, which developed from the majority coalition first formed by Lord Aberdeen in 1852 into an increasingly significant force in British politics, notably under the leadership of William Ewart Gladstone, who headed the first Liberal administration of 1868–74. This was followed by a second Liberal government (1880–85), a coalition government led by Lord Salisbury and which involved the Liberals (1886–92), Gladstone's fourth (minority) Liberal government (1892–94) and the minority Liberal government led by Lord Rosebery (1894–95). Liberal ideology was generally associated with reformist tendencies and the minimisation of state expenditure; it centred on issues such as free trade (including the removal of tariff barriers), religious reform (such as the disestablishment of the Irish Church and repeal of religious tests for Oxford and Cambridge University), land reform (notably in Ireland) and reform to education and the civil service.

Manchester School A mid nineteenth-century group of radical politicians and economists, led by Richard Cobden and John Bright, who advocated free trade and laissez-faire policies in domestic and foreign affairs. They were frequently criticised by Matthew Arnold, particularly in *Culture and Anarchy*.

Melodrama The dominant theatrical form – and arguably the dominant literary and visual aesthetic – for much of the nineteenth century, melodrama enjoyed wide popular appeal. It typically employed domestic (and often working-class) settings, an emphasis on strong emotion (typically conveyed physically, through gesture, bodily movement and facial expression), exciting and suspenseful plots (often involving spectacular events, such as train crashes), clearly delineated 'stock' characters (such as the hero, heroine, villain, comic man, comic woman, good old man, good old woman and so on) and a strongly moralising (and often explicitly sentimental) rewarding of virtue over vice. Typical concerns included the law (with trial scenes and dramatic reprieves being a popular method of heightening suspense), the suffering of women and children and sudden reversals of fortune (often involving the discovery of hitherto secret wills or inheritances). Despite what might appear to be a moral conservatism, melodramatic tropes have been seen by some critics as particularly significant to Victorian radical writing.

Modernism The term is commonly used to describe the artistic experimentation which took place in Europe (and a little later in the United States of America) in the early decades of the twentieth century. The features often identified with literary Modernism, best exemplified in the work of writers such as Virginia Woolf, T. S. Eliot, James Joyce and Ezra Pound, are linguistic complexity, formal novelty and a resistance to the demands of mass culture. In this respect Modernism is popularly seen as marking a radical break with Victorianism. However, literary historians vigorously debate the origins of Modernism, the nature of its relationship with its immediate artistic and literary predecessors, as well as its politics, membership and claims to be free from nineteenth-century commercial values. Today there is so little agreement on any of these topics that the term itself has lost some of its descriptive utility.

Modernity Loosely speaking, the adjective 'modern' refers to the contemporary or present-day, while the noun 'modernity' is invoked to describe those features of social and intellectual life – often popularly traced back to a European post-Enlightenment emphasis on rational enquiry – which are recognised as forming part of Western culture today. However, it is something of a truism to observe that most European societies – certainly from the late Middle Ages or, roughly, the late 1400s onwards – tended to view their own times as representing what is 'modern' or new, and in this sense 'modernity' is perhaps best understood as a relational concept. In the nineteenth century, then, modernity was usually associated with new technology, urbanisation (particularly the growth of the city) and changes in social structures (including the gradual decline in authority of traditional elites, such as the Church and aristocracy, and the rise to prominence of new voices, notably those of the middle classes and, later in the century, the working classes and women). Writers of the time – and here Dickens is an exemplary witness – tend to register the forces of modernity ambivalently, seeing them as a source of marvel and evidence of human progress, while at the same time being deeply threatening. (See also *Modernism*)

Naturalism The term is usually associated with late nineteenth-century French fiction, and particularly the work of Emile Zola, who aimed to employ the objectivity associated with contemporary positivist science to describe the details of day-to-day life, particularly among the middle and working classes. Naturalism has some similarities with realism, with the exception that – in Zola's fiction – there was a strong interest in what were viewed as the sordid elements of life, which were attributed to hereditary or environmental causes, thus leading Naturalism to be associated with social determinism. British writers inspired by French naturalist authors include George Gissing and (in the early years of his career) George Moore. (See also *Impressionism* and *Realism*)

Newgate novel A popular fictional sub-genre which flourished in the 1830s and 1840s and which centred on recounting – often in sensational and gruesome detail – the lives of criminals, with subjects being taken from the Newgate Calendar. The Newgate novel has been seen as an important influence on writers such as Dickens (particularly in *Oliver Twist*) and Thackeray.

New woman fiction A late nineteenth-century fictional sub-genre which took its name from the preoccupation with contemporary debates about the 'new woman' that typically centred on female dress, sexual conduct, employment opportunities and voting rights. Although there were relatively few novels or stories solely concerned with the 'new woman', the character-type – often caricatured in terms of an adoption of traditionally masculine pursuits, like cigarette smoking – was influential on a wide range of both literary and dramatic works.

Orientalism The term, popularised by Edward Said, refers to a binary categorisation between East and West in which the East is troped as the West's inferior and is associated with the feminine, the exotic and strangeness; the West by contrast, is associated with rationality, modernity and the masculine. The discourse of Orientalism thus functions as both justification of, and rationale for, Western colonialism. Although Said's schema has proved influential, it has also been widely criticised as too reductive.

Paiderastia A term used by the ancient Greeks to refer to the sexual pursuit of 'boys' (*paides*) – which in practice meant adolescents (males were by convention viewed as sexually attractive to other males, from puberty to the arrival of a full beard) – by 'men' (*andres*). In some classical accounts of *paiderastia*, particularly in Plato's *Symposium*, the aim of such relationships was claimed to be not adult sexual pleasure, but the spiritual and moral improvement of the boy under the adult's expert tutelage. It was this ambiguous element to the concept of *paiderastia* that, in the late decades of the nineteenth century, permitted the concept of 'Greek love', as it was sometimes termed, to become a coded way of exploring male–male desire, or what Oscar Wilde, quoting the words of his lover Lord Alfred Douglas, termed 'the love that dare not speak its name'. (See also *Sapphic*)

Pantomime Pantomime was a form of popular entertainment that appealed to all classes, and in the provinces the traditional Christmas pantomime was crucial to a theatre's economic survival. The formal structure of the pantomime underwent significant changes over the course of the nineteenth century. These centred on the lengthening of the opening scenes, necessitated by the gradual relegation in importance, from the late 1820s onwards, of the largely wordless comic business of the harlequinade. (The dominance of the harlequinade in the early decades of the century was due in part to the enormous popularity of Joseph Grimaldi, who played the role of Clown.) These opening scenes grew increasingly elaborate as the century progressed and typically included a splendidly staged transformation scene, which in turn set the tone for the basic stage business of mid and late nineteenth-century pantomimes – the comic opposition between the fairy realm of extravaganza and the absurdities and frustrations of everyday domestic life. The fact that the subject-matter of nineteenth-century pantomimes was typically well-known fairy- or folk-tales – such as *Cinderella* or *The Sleeping Beauty* – does not mean that they were apolitical: on the contrary, they were often sharply satirical. Specialist pantomime scriptwriters rewrote familiar stories to provide topical interest designed to appeal to local audiences. (See also *Extravaganza*)

Political economy The term derives from the writings of Adam Smith, particularly his *Wealth of Nations* (1776), which proposed that the market was self-regulating and operated according to its own internal laws or logic, which in turn were based on competition. Smith also argued that the economic sphere constituted the primary explanation of human conduct, thus giving rise to the concept of 'economic man'. In the nineteenth century 'political economy' was used to describe that body of economic theory developed from Smith's work by figures like David Ricardo and John Stuart Mill. Popularly associated with laissez-faire policies, it was criticised by some mid nineteenth-century novelists. (See also *Laissez-faire*)

Postcolonialism Literally, the term denotes the period that follows political decolonisation; more broadly speaking, however, it is used to describe the complex ways in which cultural values and mindsets are informed by a dependence on, and a resistance to, colonial institutions and practices. Postcolonial criticism is typically premised on the argument that Western concepts of selfhood, loosely referred to as 'humanism', are defined through an essentialising language of race, in which racial 'others' (colonised subjects) stand in opposition to the humanity of a homogeneous (and white) race (colonisers). In this respect, a central project of postcolonial criticism is the deconstruction of Western discourses of colonialism – in which nineteenth-century literary works have been seen to play a crucial role – based on oppositions defined in terms of race, colour and ethnic origin.

Pre-Raphaelite As an adjective, the term describes literary and art works (and also furniture, wallpapers, soft furnishings and ceramics) that possess features associated with the literary and visual aesthetic of the mid nineteenth-century

Pre-Raphaelite Brotherhood. These included: an emphasis on natural forms and 'truth to nature'; the use of bright colours; and archaic or medieval subjects.

Prose poem Short pieces of descriptive writing that exploit poetic devices, such as figurative language and rhythm, but without the use of conventional stanzaic structures or metrical patterns. The form originated in the early eighteenth-century in France, where it was championed by writers such as Montesquieu and Jean-Jacques Rousseau and, in the nineteenth century, by Chateaubriand and Baudelaire. Among the best-known examples in English are William Blake's prose-poem *The Marriage of Heaven and Hell* and Oscar Wilde's six 'poems in prose' published in the *Fortnightly Review* in July 1894, works which take as their inspiration biblical subjects.

Queer theory A central preoccupation of queer theory has been to show how the categories by which desire, and therefore sexual identities, are defined, are not fixed. In nineteenth-century literary studies, queer theory is associated with new ways of reading apparently 'straight' texts (by authors such as Tennyson and Stevenson) as well as bringing to notice writing and writers concerned with exploring the nature of homoerotic desire.

Radicalism A protean term which changes its meanings over the course of the nineteenth century. In the early decades, the adjective 'radical' – often used in a derogatory manner – tended to be applied to those who were seen to be sympathising with the principles behind the French Revolution, and consequently opposed to the British legal and political establishment. Confusingly, however, it also encompassed so-called 'philosophical radicals' like Jeremy Bentham and his disciples, or 'Benthamites' (as they were known), who, although opposing the French Revolution, none the less were vigorous advocates of reform to the law and prisons. By the 1830s and into the middle decades of the century, the term 'radical' designated those groups (like the Chartists) and individuals (liked the 'radical' MP John Bright) agitating for political reform of Parliament (including a reform of the electoral system through the extension of the franchise). In the 1860s a series of articles in the *Fortnightly Review*, termed the 'New Radicalism', came to be identified with Liberalism. (See also *Individualism*)

Realism The term realism derives from mid nineteenth-century French literary and artistic culture, where it was used to describe the works of Honoré de Balzac, Gustave Flaubert and the painter Gustave Courbet; it designated an attempt to represent the world 'as it is', or a commitment to verisimilitude in art. In this respect it was often contrasted with the idealism of an earlier generation. In the work of Courbet, who has been seen to have been directly inspired by the 1848 French Revolution, realism also implied a radical politics – a programme to document the lives of the poor and underclasses in French society. More generally, however, and certainly in nineteenth-century British literary culture, realism describes a mode of literary representation, rather than a specific politics, one which concentrates on documenting the details of everyday life and which uses a number of devices, such as an omniscient (and often strongly moralising) narrative voice, to disguise the artefactual or contrived nature of fiction. Exemplary British realist novelists include George Eliot and Anthony Trollope. It is worth bearing in mind, however, that there is no clear divide between realist and non-realist fiction in nineteenth-century Britain, and critics continue to debate the precise features and functions of realist texts. (See also *Naturalism* and *Sensation fiction*)

Romanticism The term is popularly used today to designate a period of literary history – lasting roughly from 1789 to 1832 – which has been associated with aesthetic and political radicalism, and which involved significant developments in the literary cultures of European countries as well as in the United States. Beyond this loose period designation, there is much debate about the features which characterise what is usually referred to as 'Romantic-period' writing (as opposed to the earlier literary-critical term, the 'Romantic Movement'). By contrast, in nineteenth-century critical discourses 'romanticism' was often a derogatory term, referring to literary works which were 'fanciful' or lightweight, or over subjective.

Sapphic An adjective taken from the seventh-century BC lyric poet Sappho (only fragments of whose poetry have survived); in post-classical times Sappho was often described as a 'lover of women', and her poetry was seen as articulating a female homoeroticism. In the nineteenth century 'Sapphic' desire could thus designate female homosexuality, or 'lesbianism' – a nineteenth-century term which in its turn took its name from the island of Lesbos, from where Sappho also came.

Sensation fiction The term describes a sub-genre of popular fiction which flourished in the middle decades of the century, particularly the 1860s, and which was characterised by an emphasis on 'sensational' events, and its encouragement in its readers of heightened emotion. Deriving its subject-matter and some elements of its style from popular journalism, sensation fiction typically centred on domestic crime (notably bigamy), arson, murder and insanity, and tended to subordinate characterisation to the demands of plot.

Serial publication The serialisation of nineteenth-century fiction – that is, publication in monthly and quarterly instalments – began in the 1830s and quickly became widespread through the success of family orientated periodicals and magazines (sometimes referred as 'serials') such as *Bentley's Miscellany* (which began in 1837) and the *Cornhill Magazine* (launched in 1860). Also significant were the launch of cheap weekly papers, such as Chambers's *Edinburgh Journal* (in 1832) and Dickens's *Household Words* and *All The Year Round* (in the 1840s), which helped to make literary fiction available to a wide reading public, a process which culminated in highly popular late nineteenth-century publications such as the *Strand Magazine* and the *Graphic*.

Silver fork novel A fictional sub-genre which flourished from the 1820s to the 1840s and which centred on the depiction of fashionable aristocratic life-styles, and which was directed towards middle-class readers wishing to ape the manner of that social class.

Socialism Broadly speaking, socialism refers to a political system that advocates the common ownership of property, means of production and distribution; today it is closely identified with Marxist thought. However, its history and its origins, which are usually located in early nineteenth-century French social theory, are complex. Although the nineteenth century, and particularly its late decades, are traditionally associated with the rise of socialism in Britain, there was no single socialist party or movement, and those who called themselves 'socialist' often held widely differing views, particularly with regard to the role of the state and the nature and pace of social change. The earliest British socialist is usually thought to be the industrialist Robert Owen, although his followers, or 'Owenites', had little long-term impact on British political culture; more influential in this respect were the late nineteenth-century Social Democratic Federation (founded by H. M. Hyndman) and Socialist League (founded by William Morris). (See also *Fabianism*)

Social-problem novel A sub-genre of nineteenth-century fiction – also sometimes referred to as 'industrial' or 'condition of England' novels – which flourished in the 1840s and 1850s and took as its subject the social inequality and economic hardship associated with contemporary processes of urbanisation and industrialisation. The works which comprise this sub-genre, as well as its politics, have been the subject of much critical debate.

Society comedy Also sometimes referred to as the 'society play', 'society comedy' was a hybrid genre that developed in the late decades of the century in order to appeal to the wealthy clientele then patronising the refurbished and newly fashionable West End theatres. Involving an amalgamation of elements of British melodramatic traditions with those of the French well-made play, society comedy offered settings in a fashionable, and often aristocratic, milieu which provided an opportunity to explore the relationship between manners and morals. A frequent theme was the attempt by outsiders or parvenus to gain entry into polite society; its appeal lay partly in the glamour of the life-styles depicted and partly in the topical nature of its concerns, which often centred on sexual double standards, unhappy marriages and the threat – to those transgressors against society's strict moral codes – of social disgrace and ostracism. (See also *Melodrama* and *Well-made play*)

Spasmodic A mid nineteenth-century literary school which enjoyed only a brief moment of popularity, and which today is largely forgotten. Its most characteristic works were long verse-dramas, marked by an emphasis on psychological extremes and the use of extravagant imagery.

Spectacle Generally speaking, the term is used to describe the growing importance of visual images in nineteenth-century culture, which in turn has been attributed, in part, to developments in optics and various forms of visual technology. Spectacle influenced many aspects of literary and artistic culture, although it is most closely associated with the theatre and the visual effects which figured prominently in the staging of many nineteenth-century melodramas. Famous non-literary examples of nineteenth-century 'spectacular' entertainments included: the 1851 Great Exhibition, Madame Tussaud's wax-work 'Chamber of Horrors', the Egyptian Hall, Piccadilly (which in 1845 'exhibited' a group of 'South African Bushmen'), panoramas (popular in the 1850s) and various events – including balloon flights, firework displays and huge orchestral concerts – staged in Victorian pleasure gardens. Spectacle has also been seen to have formed a key element in the development of advertising techniques and the modern department store, with its characteristic plate-glass windows, as well as a whole variety of street entertainments, from travelling circuses and menageries, to freak shows and parades. More narrowly, spectacle defines a particular mode of looking, one associated with the birth of a new kind of subjective observer. An early theoriser of this mode of looking was the French poet Charles Baudelaire in his concept of the *flâneur*; later in the century, spectacle defines a mode of looking associated with the passive consumer of modern capitalism. In this last case, the function of 'spectacular' modes of vision, of which the keynotes are light and movement, is to divorce commodities from their mode of production and refigure them as objects of desire. (See also *Commodity culture*)

Suffragette A term given to those women in the late nineteenth century who campaigned for women's right to vote – or the 'suffrage'. In 1897 Mrs Millicent Fawcett's Union of Women's Suffrage Societies brought together a number of like-minded campaigning organisations; its activities were later superseded by the Women's Social and Political Union, founded in 1903 by the Pankhursts, which encouraged violence against property and politicians, as well as the use of hunger strikes by those of its members imprisoned for their activities.

Symbolist The term was coined in the late decades of the nineteenth century by Arthur Symons to describe what he saw as a new kind of symbolism originating in the work of French poets, such as Théophile Gautier, Charles Baudelaire and Stéphane Mallarmé. He saw their language distinguished by its polyvalent character – that is, by the plurality of a symbol's referents. In Britain and Ireland, the term is associated with a number of 'minor' 1890s poets as well as the early poetry of the Irish writer W. B. Yeats.

Thirty-Nine Articles, The Articles defining the doctrine of the Anglican Church approved in 1563 (and based on the forty-two articles drafted by Thomas Cranmer during the reign of Edward VI). In 1571 a Subscription Act required beneficed clergy to assent to them. In the nineteenth century, and until the University Test Acts, subscribing to the Thirty-Nine Articles was a precondition for university matriculation; they were also a bone of contention for the Tractarians, who questioned their compatibility with Roman Catholicism. For much of the century the label could be used as a shorthand description of members of the Anglican faith. (See also *Tractarian Movement*)

Three-decker novel The term derived from the practice, widespread from the 1820s until the 1890s, of publishing new fiction in the form of three octavo volumes, each priced at 10*s* 6*d*, thus making the cost of a whole novel an exorbitant 31*s* 6*d*. The format of these novels, which were almost exclusively purchased by commercial circulating libraries, has been held responsible for the length and prolixity of much Victorian fiction. The three-decker novel disappeared in the 1890s, when the circulating libraries stopped purchasing them, and was replaced by the cheaper one-volume novel, typically priced at 6*s*.

Tory Historically the term 'Tory' designated members of the political party which opposed the exclusion from power of the Duke of York (later James II). In the early decades of the nineteenth century the Tory Party was generally viewed as supporting the established order of monarchy and Church, as well as being hostile to reform (especially the 1832 Reform Bill, which was supported by the Whigs). Attempts to reform the Tory Party in the 1840s by those hostile to its then leader, Sir Robert Peel, were led by the charismatic Benjamin Disraeli and his 'Young England' lobby. None the less, for much of the middle decades of the century the Tory Party was excluded from power, losing six elections between 1847 and 1868. Able to command sufficient support only for minority governments, the Tories enjoyed but brief periods of office during this time, as the various parties in the coalition – Whigs, Liberals or Radicals – would inevitably fall out, forcing an election in which the Tories would be defeated. The fortunes of the party improved in the 1870s when Disraeli, after briefly succeeding Lord Derby as Prime Minister in 1868, headed a second Tory (or, as it was now termed, 'Conservative') government from 1874 to 1880. (See also *Young England* and *Whig*)

Tractarian Movement Also known as the 'Oxford Movement', a body of thought and doctrine associated with a group of Anglican theologians, principally in Oxford, which was critical of what were seen as the prevalent latitudinarian tendencies of the Church of England, and argued for the reinstatement of ritual and the reassertion of the power of church over state authority. Its main proponents were John Keble, John Henry Newman and R. H. Froude, whose series of publications, *Tracts for the Times* (1833), gave the movement its name. It inspired a tradition of 'Tractarian' poetry, whose popularity outlived the movement itself.

Utilitarianism A body of thought, deriving from the work of seventeenth- and mid eighteenth-century philosophers such as Thomas Hobbes and David Hume, and popularised in the nineteenth century by Jeremy Bentham and the philosophical radicals; it became widely known through the succinct formula, 'the greatest happiness of the greatest number'. An emphasis on quantitative rather than qualitative modes of assessing value led to the widespread criticism of utilitarianism and utilitarian ways of thinking by many novelists and poets, from Charles Dickens to Oscar Wilde. (See also *Radicalism*)

Verse-drama A dramatic sub-genre, more popular in the early decades of the century, which, as the term implies, was written entirely in verse. It was deliberately 'literary' in character and was thus was rarely intended for performance.

Well-made play The well-made play, or 'la pièce bien faite', was a dramatic genre that originated in mid nineteenth-century France; among its most influential practitioners as regards British theatrical culture were Victorien Sardou and Alexandre Dumas (fils). As the phrase itself implies, the defining characteristics of the genre included complex plotting, typically involving the careful feeding of information to the audience and surprising revelations through the delivery of letters or telegrams. These helped enable an act to close on a moment of emotional climax. The well-made play also tended to value high standards of urbane, witty dialogue. The sexual misdemeanours which provided the motivation for many French well-made plays became less explicit in their British counterparts; adultery, for example, was likely to be translated into the socially less transgressive activity of flirting. (See also *Society comedy*)

Whig For the first half of the century, the main political opposition to the Tory Party, and associated with reform, particularly the 1832 Reform Bill. More generally, the adjective 'Whig' or 'Whiggism' – exemplified in the work of the historian Thomas Babington Macaulay – has come to designate a gradualist view of historical and political development, one which combines an idealisation of continuity with a faith in progress, and which contrasts both with revolutionary ideas of social change proposed by Marxist socialism and with the reverence for tradition popularly associated with Toryism. (See also *Tory*)

Young England A Tory political reform group of the early 1840s, sometimes also called 'One Nation' Toryism, most closely associated with Benjamin

Disraeli and his trilogy of 'Young England' novels – *Coningsby* (1844), *Sybil* (1845) and *Tancred* (1847) – which were written to promote the group's ideas. These centred on a nostalgic mixture of neo-feudal models of power and high Anglicanism. As a political force, the Young England Party lost much of its impetus in 1845, when Disraeli apparently betrayed the cause by voting against an increased grant to the Irish Catholic Church in Maynooth.

Young Ireland A name used to refer to an Irish nationalist movement which agitated for the repeal of the 1801 Act of Union between Great Britain and Ireland. It was led by the poet and journalist Thomas Davis; its main organ of publicity was its national newspaper, *The Nation*, founded in 1842, and for which the poet James Clarence Mangan worked. The Young Ireland Movement led the Irish Rebellion of 1848, and by its association with a romantic view of Irish nationalism became an important influence on later nineteenth-century Irish writing, particularly that of 'Speranza' (Lady Jane Wilde) and, later still, W. B. Yeats, who both took Irish nationalist concerns as one of their main subjects.

Guide to primary sources

Poetry

The most comprehensive general anthologies of nineteenth-century poetry and poetics are as follows.

Collins, Thomas and Vivienne Rundel (eds) (1999) *The Broadview Anthology of Victorian Poetry and Poetic Theory*, Peterborough, Ontario: Broadview Press.
Cunningham, Valentine (ed.) (2000) *The Victorians: An Anthology of Poetry and Poetics*, Oxford: Blackwell.
Karlin, Daniel (ed.) (1997) *Penguin Book of Victorian Verse*, Harmondsworth: Penguin.
Ricks, Christopher (ed.) (1990) *The New Oxford Book of Victorian Verse*, Oxford: Oxford University Press.
Wu, Duncan (ed.) (2006) *Romanticism: An Anthology*, 3rd edn, Oxford: Blackwell.

These are usefully supplemented by anthologies which concentrate on women's poetry, as listed below.

Armstrong, Isobel and Joseph Bristow with Cath Sharrock (eds) (1996) *Nineteenth-Century Women Poets: An Oxford Anthology*, Oxford: Clarendon Press.
Blain, Virginia (ed.) (2001) *Victorian Women Poets: A New Annotated Anthology*, Harlow: Longman.
Leighton, Angela and Margaret Reynolds (eds) (1995) *Victorian Women Poets: An Anthology*, Oxford: Blackwell.
Reilly, Catherine (ed.) (1994) *Winged Words: Victorian Women's Poetry and Verse*, London: Enitharmon Press.
Wu, Duncan (ed.) (2003) *Women Romantic Poets*, Oxford: Blackwell.

Information about nineteenth-century women poets can also be found in the relevant volumes of the *Dictionary of Literary Biography*.

William B. Thesing (ed.) (1999) *Dictionary of Literary Biography*, Vol. 199, *Victorian Women Poets*, Detroit, London: Gale Group.
William B. Thesing (ed.) (2001) *Dictionary of Literary Biography*, Vol. 240, *Late Nineteenth- and Early Twentieth-Century British Women Poets*, Detroit, London: Gale Group.

A further useful resource is the Woodstock facsimile reprints (which contain brief but informative biographical and bibliographical introductions); the following two series are particularly relevant for students of nineteenth-century literary history.

Small, Ian and R. K. R. Thornton (eds) *Decadents, Symbolists, Anti-Decadents: Poetry of the 1890s*, Oxford: Woodstock Books.

Wordsworth, Jonathan (ed.) *Revolution and Romanticism, 1789–1834*, Oxford: Woodstock Books.

Examples of working-class and Chartist poetry can be found in the following anthologies.

Hollingworth, Brian (ed.) (1977) *Songs of the People: Lancashire Dialect Poetry of the Industrial Revolution*, Manchester: Manchester University Press.

Maidment, Brian (ed.) (1987) *The Poorhouse Fugitives: Self-Taught Poets and Poetry in Victorian Britain*, Manchester: Carcanet.

McEathron, Scott, John Goodridge and Kaye Kossick (eds) (2005) *Nineteenth-Century English Labouring-Class Poets, 1801–1900*, 3 vols, London: Pickering and Chatto.

Schneckner, Peter (ed.) (1989) *An Anthology of Chartist Poetry: Poetry of the British Working Class, 1830s–1850s*, New York: Oxford University Press.

Fiction

As described in Chapter 7, reprints of nineteenth-century fiction are available from a number of publishers and the range of available titles increases year by year. Those produced by Methuen, Oxford World's Classics and Penguin have useful introductions, detailed explanatory notes and guides to secondary reading. The editions of Broadview Press include additional contextual material as appendices. Some of the less well-known works can be found in the open-access, ongoing Gutenberg archive, www.gutenberg.org. The most comprehensive and user-friendly guide to the enormous variety of nineteenth-century fiction is: Sutherland, John (2009) *The Longman Companion to Victorian Fiction*, London: Pearson Education. Sutherland's volume contains entries for 900 authors and plot synopses for 560 novels; in addition, there are entries for those magazines and periodicals which carried fiction. The following anthologies contain generous samples of short fiction from the period.

Cox, Michael (ed.) (1992) *Victorian Tales of Mystery and Detection: An Oxford Anthology*, Oxford: Oxford University Press.

——and R. A. Gilbert (1991) *Victorian Ghost Stories: An Oxford Anthology*, Oxford: Oxford University Press.

Denisoff, Dennis (ed.) (2004) *The Broadview Anthology of Victorian Short Stories*, Peterborough, Ontario: Broadview Press.

Jump, Harriet Devine (ed.) (1998) *Nineteenth-Century Short Stories by Women: A Routledge Anthology*, London and New York: Routledge.

Zipes, Jack (ed.) (1989) *Fairy Tales: The Revolt of the Fairies and Elves*, London and New York: Routledge.

Drama

Students of nineteenth-century drama are poorly served compared to those of poetry and fiction. Most nineteenth-century dramatic works remain out of print; of those modern editions of single works which are available, the best are published by Methuen and the 'New Mermaids' imprint of A. & C. Black and W. W. Norton. The work of scholars such as Michael Booth and George Rowell in the 1960s and 1970s was invaluable in providing modern readers with anthologies of nineteenth-century dramatic works. In recent years, these have been supplemented by a variety of web-based publishing projects (such as the Victorian Plays Project) as well as further codex editions (notably by Broadview).

Bailey, J. O. (ed.) (1966) *British Plays of the Nineteenth Century*, New York: Odyssey Press.

Booth, Michael R. (ed.) (1969–76) *English Plays of the Nineteenth Century*, 5 vols, Oxford: Clarendon Press.

——(ed.) (1964) *Hiss the Villain*, London: Eyre & Spottiswoode.

Cox, Jeffrey N. and Michael Gamer (eds) (2003), *The Broadview Anthology of Romantic Drama*, Peterborough, Ontario: Broadview Press.

Crochunis, Thomas C. (ed.) (2010) *The Broadview Anthology of British Women Playwrights, 1777–1843*, Peterborough, Ontario: Broadview Press.

Rowell, George (ed.) (1972) *Nineteenth Century Plays*, 2nd edn, Oxford: Oxford University Press.

——(1968) *Late Victorian Plays, 1890–1914*, Oxford: Oxford University Press.

Scullion, Adrienne (ed.) (1996) *Female Playwrights of the Nineteenth Century*, London: J. M. Dent.

Wells, Stanley (ed.) (1977–78), *Nineteenth-Century Shakespeare Burlesques*, London: Diploma Press.

——(1982–87) *British and American Playwrights 1750–1920*, 9 vols, Cambridge: Cam bridge University Press.

Reference works with useful bibliographical information include the following.

Booth, Michael R. (1965), *English Melodrama*, London: Jenkins.

——Richard Southern, Frederick Marker, Lise-Lone Marker and Robertson Davies (eds) (1975), *The Revels History of Drama in English, vol. VI, 1750–1880*, London: Methuen.

Hunt, Hugh, Kenneth Richards and John Russell Taylor (eds) *The Revels History of Drama in English, vol. VII, 1880 to the present day*, London: Methuen.

Jackson, Russell (ed.) (1989) *Victorian Theatre*, London: A. & C. Black.

Nicoll, Allardyce (1930) *A History of Early Nineteenth-Century Drama, 1800–1850*, 2 vols, Cambridge: Cambridge University Press.

——(1946) *A History of Late Nineteenth-Century Drama, 1850–1900*, 2 vols, Cambridge: Cambridge University Press.

George Rowell (1978), *The Victorian Theatre*, 2nd edn, Cambridge: Cambridge University Press.

Senelick, Laurence, David F. Cheshire and Ulrich Schneider (eds) (1981) *British Music Hall 1840–1923: A Bibliography and Guide to Sources*, Hamden, CT: Archon Books.

Criticism / Non-fictional prose

The *Wellesley Index to Victorian Periodicals* (available in both codex and online versions) is an invaluable tool for researching the most important source of nineteenth-century critical writing – the numerous periodicals and magazines published over the course of the century. The volumes in the Routledge Critical Heritage series bring together the principal contemporary reviews of the literary works of selected (and usually canonical) nineteenth-century authors; the Casebook Series published by Macmillan provides similar information, although the emphasis in these volumes is on providing a sample of critical opinion from publication to the present day. The following anthologies give an indication of the range of critical material produced at the time.

Beetham, Margaret and Kay Boardman (eds) (2001) *Victorian Women's Magazines: An Anthology*, Manchester: Manchester University Press.

Bromwich, David (ed.) (1987) *Romantic Critical Essays*, Cambridge, Cambridge University Press.

Broomfield, Andrea and Sally Mitchell (eds) (1996) *Prose by Victorian Women*, New York: Garland.

King, Andrew and John Punkett (eds) (2005) *Victorian Print Media: A Reader*, Oxford: Oxford University Press.

Mundhenk, Rosemary J. and LuAnn McCracken Fletcher (eds) (1999) *Victorian Prose: An Anthology*, New York: Columbia University Press.

Small, Ian (ed.) (1979) *The Aesthetes: A Sourcebook*, London: Routledge and Kegan Paul.

Robinson, Solveig C. (ed.) (2003) *A Serious Occupation: Literary Criticism by Victorian Women*, Peterborough, Ontario: Broadview Press.

Stanford, Derek (ed.) (1971) *Writing of the 'Nineties*, London: Dent.

Warner, Eric and Graham Hough (eds) (1983) *Strangeness and Beauty: An Anthology of Aesthetic Criticism*, 2 vols, Cambridge: Cambridge University Press.

Anthologies of life-writing include the two listed here.

Burnett, John (ed.) (1982) *Destiny Obscure: Autobiographies of Childhood, Education and Family from the 1820s to the 1920s*, London: Allen Lane.

——(ed.) (1974) *The Annals of Labour: Autobiographies of British Working-Class People, 1820–1920*, Bloomington, IN: Indiana University Press.

Also useful as a research resource is the following.

Burnett, John, David Vincent and David Mayall (eds) (1984–89) *The Autobiography of the Working Class: An Annotated Critical Bibliography*, 3 vols, New York: New York University Press.

Guide to further reading

The contexts of nineteenth-century literature

Details about the contexts of nineteenth-century literature are available from general historical studies which describe the major social, intellectual, political and cultural developments in the century as they relate to literary works (it is usual to find separate volumes devoted to Romantic-period and Victorian literature). Examples include the following.

Gilmour, Robin (1993) *The Victorian Period: The Intellectual and Cultural Context of English Literature, 1830–1890*, Harlow: Longman.

Jarvis, Robin (2004) *The Romantic Period: The Intellectual and Cultural Context of English Literature*, Harlow: Longman.

Such volumes are usefully read alongside general historical studies of the period, such as these two.

Daunton, M. J. (1995) *Progress and Poverty: An Economic and Social History of Britain, 1700–1850*, Oxford: Oxford University Press.

McCord, Norman (1991) *British History 1815–1906*, Oxford: Oxford University Press.

There are also a number of useful anthologies of essays examining various aspects of nineteenth-century culture as they relate to the literature of the period.

Curren, Stuart (ed.) (1993) *The Cambridge Companion to British Romanticism*, Cambridge: Cambridge University Press.

McCalman, Iain (ed.) (1999) *An Oxford Companion to the Romantic Age: British Culture 1776–1832*, Oxford: Oxford University Press.

O'Gorman, Francis (ed.) (2005) *A Concise Companion to the Victorian Novel*, Oxford: Blackwell.

Shattock, Joanne (ed.) (2010) *The Cambridge Companion to English Literature: 1830–1914*, Cambridge: Cambridge University Press.

Tucker, Herbert F. (ed.) (1999) *A Companion to Victorian Literature and Culture*, Malden, MA: Blackwell.

Form, style and genre

There are many individual studies devoted to the treatment of formal developments in nineteenth-century poetry, the novel, drama and criticism respectively; examples are given below. It is also worth drawing attention to Leighton, Angela (2008) *On Form*, Oxford: Oxford University Press, which argues for the emergence in the last quarter of the nineteenth century of a critical discourse prioritising form and style as the basis of literary appreciation.

Armstrong, Isobel (1993) *Victorian Poetry: Poetry, Poetics, and Politics*, London: Routledge.

Bodenheimer, Rosemary (1988) *The Politics of Story in Victorian Fiction*, Ithaca, NY and London: Cornell University Press.

Booth, Michael R. (1991) *Theatre in the Victorian Age*, Cambridge: Cambridge University Press.

Cox, Jeffrey (1987) *In the Shadows of Romance: Romantic Tragic Drama in England, Germany and France*, Athens, OH: Ohio University Press.

Curran, Stuart (1986) *Poetic Form and British Romanticism*, Oxford: Oxford University Press.

Garrett, Peter (1980) *The Victorian Multi-Plot Novel: Studies in Dialogical Form*, New Haven and London: Yale University Press.

Gross, John (1969) *The Rise and Fall of the Man of Letters* (1996), New York and London: Macmillan.

Jenkins, Anthony (1991) *The Making of Victorian Drama*, Cambridge: Cambridge University Press.

Levine, George (1981) *The Realistic Imagination: English Fiction from Frankenstein to Lady Chatterley*, Chicago: University of Chicago Press.

——and William Madden (eds) (1968) *The Art of Victorian Prose*, New York: Oxford University Press.

Miller, D. A. (1981) *Narrative and its Discontents: Problems of Closure in the Traditional Novel*, Princeton, NJ: Princeton University Press.

Richardson, Alan (1988) *A Mental Theater: Poetic Drama and Consciousness in the Romantic Age*, University Park, PA: Pennsylvania State University Press.

Wellek, R. (1965) *A History of Modern Criticism, 1750–1950*, vols 3–4, New Haven, CT: Yale University Press.

Wolfson, Susan (1997) *Formal Charges: The Shaping of Poetry in British Romanticism*, Stanford, CA: Stanford University Press.

Nineteenth-century literary movements

There are several general studies of Pre-Raphaelitism, Aestheticism, Decadence and Symbolism, as well as studies focusing on the careers of particularly prominent members of these movements. Below are examples of influential general studies.

Hilton, Timothy (1970) *The Pre-Raphaelites*, New York: Oxford University Press.

Honnighausen, Lothar (1988) *The Symbolist Tradition in English Literature*, condensed and trans. Gisele Honnighausen, Cambridge: Cambridge University Press.

Hunt, John Dixon (1986) *The Pre-Raphaelite Imagination, 1848–1900*, London: Routledge and Kegan Paul.
Johnson, R. V. (1969) *Aestheticism*, London: Methuen.
Lang, Cecil Y. (1975) *The Pre-Raphaelites and their Circle*, 2nd edn, Chicago: University of Chicago Press.
MacLeod, Kirsten (2006) *Fictions of British Decadence, High Art, Popular Writing and the Fin de Siècle*, New York: Palgrave.
Schaffer, Talia (2000) *The Forgotten Female Aesthetes*, Charlottesville and London, University Press of Virginia.
Small, Ian (ed.) (1979) *The Aesthetes*, London: Routledge and Kegan Paul.

Gender and sexuality in nineteenth-century literature

Arguably the most useful place to begin any examination of the many accounts of the gender politics of nineteenth-century literature is with the body of theory which has informed such studies. Although queer theory and gender studies represent a large field in their own right, there are some useful introductions, including these.

Felski, Rita (2003) *Literature After Feminism*, Chicago: Chicago University Press.
Hall, Donald E. (2003) *Queer Theories*, Basingstoke: Palgrave Macmillan.
Moi, Toril (1985) *Sexual/Textual Politics: Feminist Literary Theory*, London: Routledge.
Sullivan, Nikki (2001), *A Critical Introduction to Queer Theory*, Edinburgh: Edinburgh University Press.

Helpful too are general introductions to the theorisation of desire in works such as these.

Bristow, Joseph (1997) *Sexuality*, London: Routledge.
Colebrook, Claire (2004) *Gender*, Houndmills: Palgrave.
Nye, Robert (1999) *Sexuality*, Oxford: Oxford University Press.

Below are examples of studies concerned with the general history of nineteenth-century sex and gender, followed by works examining the specific relevance of these concepts and ideas to nineteenth-century literature.

Gay, Peter (1984–86) *The Bourgeois Experience: Victoria to Freud*, 2 vols, Oxford: Oxford University Press.
Mason, Michael (1994a) *The Making of Victorian Sexuality*, Oxford: Oxford University Press.
——(1994b) *The Making of Victorian Sexual Attitudes*, Oxford: Oxford University Press.
Porter, Roy and Leslie Hall (1995) *The Facts of Life: The Creation of Sexual Knowledge in Britain, 1650–1950*, London: Yale University Press.

Adams, James Eli (1995) *Dandies and Desert Saints: Styles of Victorian Masculinity*, Ithaca, NY and London: Cornell University Press.
Craft, Christopher (1994) *Another Kind of Love: Male Homosexual Desire in English Discourse, 1850–1920*, London: University of California Press.

Dellamora, Richard (1990) *Masculine Desire: The Sexual Politics of Victorian Aestheticism*, Chapel Hill, NC: University of North Carolina Press.
Dowling, Linda (1995) *Hellenism and Homosexuality in Victorian Oxford*, Ithaca, NY: Cornell University Press.
Fay, Elizabeth (1998) *A Feminist Introduction to Romanticism*, Oxford: Blackwell.
Gilbert, Sandra and Susan Gubar (1979) *The Madwoman in the Attic: The Woman Writer and the Nineteenth-Century Literary Imagination*, New Haven and London: Yale University Press.
Laqueur, Thomas and Catherine Gallagher (eds) (1987) *Sexuality and the Social Body in the Nineteenth Century*, Berkeley, CA: University of California Press.
Mellor, Anne K. (ed.) (1988) *Romanticism and Feminism*, Bloomington, IN: Indiana University Press.
Sinfield, Alan (1994) *The Wilde Century: Effeminacy, Oscar Wilde and the Queer Moment*, London: Cassell.
Sussman, Herbert (1995) *Victorian Masculinities: Manhood and Masculine Poetics in Early Victorian Literature and Art*, Cambridge: Cambridge University Press.

Race and nation in nineteenth-century literature

Most studies of race and nation in nineteenth-century literature are informed by a complex (and to some extent) contested body of theoretical literature. Seminal texts in this theoretical debate, as noted in Chapter 6, include Anderson, Benedict (1991) *Imagined Communities*, Princeton NJ: Princeton University Press (on the origin and spread of nationalism) and Said, Edward (1978) *Orientalism*, London: Pantheon Books (on the nature of colonial and imperial ideology). Important subsequent engagements with these ideas are to be found in works such as the four listed.

Bhabha, Homi (1994) *The Location of Culture*, London: Routledge.
Pratt, Mary Louise (1992, 2009) *Imperial Eyes*, London: Routledge.
Spivak, Gayatri (1987) *In Other Worlds*, London: Routledge.
Young, Robert (1995) *Colonial Desire: Hybridity in Theory, Culture and Race*, London: Routledge.

There are also many excellent introductory guides to, and general collections of essays on, postcolonial theory, including the ones below.

Ashcroft, Bill, Gareth Griffiths and Helen Tiffin (2006) (eds) *The Post-Colonial Studies Reader*, 2nd edn, London: Routledge.
Edwards, Justin (2008) *Postcolonial Literature*, Houndmills: Palgrave.
Harrison, Nicholas (2003) *Postcolonial Criticism: History, Theory and the Work of Fiction*, Cambridge: Polity Press.
Loomba, Anna (1998) *Colonialism/Postcolonialism*, London: Routledge.

As with general accounts of the contexts of nineteenth-century literature, there are few single-volume discussions of race or nationalism in relation to literary works that cover the entire century; rather, most studies focus on these topics as they relate to either Romantic-period or Victorian writing. Below are some examples of useful introductory studies, general historical overviews and essay collections.

Bayly, C. A. (1989) *Imperial Meridian: The British Empire and the World 1780–1830*, London: Longman.

Bivona, Daniel (1990) *Desire and Contradiction: Imperial Visions and Domestic Debates in Victorian Literature*, Manchester: Manchester University Press.

Brantlinger, Patrick (1988) *Rule of Darkness, British Literature and Imperialism: 1830–1914*, Ithaca, NY: Cornell University Press.

Colley, Linda (1992) *Britons: Forging the Nation, 1701–1837*, New Haven, CT: Yale University Press.

Koebner, Richard and Helmut Dan Schmidt (1965) *Imperialism: The Story and Significance of a Political World, 1840–1960*, Cambridge: Cambridge University Press.

Leask, Nigel (1992) *British Romantic Writers and the East: Anxieties of Empire*, Cambridge: Cambridge University Press.

Richardson, Alan and Sonia Hofkosh (1996) (eds) *Romanticism, Race, and Imperial Culture, 1780–1834*, Stanford: Stanford University Press.

Nineteenth-century publishing culture

As we described in Chapter 7, studies of nineteenth-century publishing culture are numerous and diverse, and tend to concentrate either on documenting the changing economics and/or technology of the nineteenth-century book trade; or describing its impact on writers, readers and issues of literary taste. In addition, there are numbers of more specialist studies devoted to topics such as the impact of changes in copyright law (Seville, Catherine (1990) *Literary Copyright Reform in Early Victorian England*, Cambridge: Cambridge University Press), the growth of literacy and its impact on literary culture (Brantlinger, Patrick (1998) *The Reading Lesson: The Threat of Mass Literacy in Nineteenth-Century British Fiction*, Bloomington, IN: Indiana University Press), or the development of literary agents (Gillies, Mary Ann (2007) *The Professional Literary Agent in Britain, 1880 1920*, Toronto: University of Toronto Press). Below are examples of useful general overviews of nineteenth-century publishing.

Erickson, Lee (1996) *The Economy of Literary Form: English Literature and the Industrialization of Publishing: 1800–1850*, Baltimore and London: Johns Hopkins University Press.

Feather, John (2006) *A History of British Publishing*, 2nd edn, London and New York: Routledge.

Jordan, John O. and Robert L. Patten (eds) (1995) *Literature in the Marketplace: Nineteenth-Century British Publishing and the Circulation of Books*, Cambridge: Cambridge University Press.

St Clair, William (2004) *The Reading Nation in the Romantic Period*, Cambridge: Cambridge University Press.

Weedon, Alexis (2003) *Victorian Publishing: The Economics of Book Production for a Mass Market, 1836–1916*, Aldershot: Ashgate.

Works cited

Abrams, M. H. (1953) *The Mirror and the Lamp*, New York: Norton.

Adams, James Eli (2001) 'Recent Studies in the Nineteenth Century', *Studies in English Literature 1500–1900*, 41, 4: 827–79.

——(1995) *Dandies and Desert Saints: Styles of Victorian Masculinity*, Ithaca, NY and London: Cornell University Press.

Aindow, Rosy (2009) *Clothing and Identity in Turn of the Century Urban Britain*, Aldershot: Ashgate.

Altick, R. D. (1957) *The English Common Reader: A Social History of the Mass Reading Public*, Chicago: University of Chicago Press.

Anderson, Amanda (2001) *The Powers of Distance: Cosmopolitanism and the Cultivation of Detachment*, Princeton, NJ: Princeton University Press.

Anderson, Benedict (1991) *Imagined Communities: Reflections on the Origins and Spread of Nationalism*, rev. edn, London: Verso.

Anderson, Nancy Fix (1987) *Women Against Women in Victorian England: A Life of Eliza Lynn Linton*, Bloomington, IN: Indiana University Press.

Ardis, Ann L. (1990) *New Women, New Novels: Feminism and Early Modernism*, New Brunswick: Rutgers University Press.

Armstrong, Isobel (1993) *Victorian Poetry: Poetry, Poetics, and Politics*, London: Routledge.

——(1982) *Language as Living Form in Nineteenth-Century Poetry*, Brighton: Harvester.

——Joseph Bristow with Cath Sharrock (eds) (1996) *Nineteenth-Century Women Poets: An Anthology*, Oxford: Clarendon Press.

Armstrong, Nancy (1987) *Desire and Domestic Fiction*, Oxford: Oxford University Press.

Bakhtin, Mikhail (1981) *The Dialogic Imagination: Four Essays*, M. Holquist (ed.), trans. C. Emerson and M. Holquist, Austin, TX: University of Texas Press.

Ball, Douglas (1985) *Victorian Publishers' Bindings*, London: The Library Association.

Barker, Kathleen (1974) *The Theatre Royal, Bristol 1766–1966*, London: Society for Theatre Research.

Belsey, Catherine (1980) *Critical Practice*, London: Methuen.

Bhabha, Homi (1994) *The Location of Culture*, London: Routledge.

Billone, Amy (2007) *Little Songs: Women, Silence and the Nineteenth-Century Sonnet*, Columbus, OH: Ohio State University Press.

Bivona, Dan and Roger B. Henkle (2006) *The Imagination of Class: Masculinity and the Victorian Urban Poor*, Columbus, OH: Ohio State University Press.

Blain, Virginia (ed.) (2001) *Victorian Women Poets: A New Annotated Anthology*, Harlow: Longman.

Boos, Florence (ed.) (2001) 'The Poetics of the Working Classes', *Victorian Poetry*, 39, 2: 103–09.

Booth, Michael R. (1991) *Theatre in the Victorian Age*, Cambridge: Cambridge University Press.

——(1981) *Prefaces to English Nineteenth-Century Theatre*, Manchester: Manchester University Press.

Bowlby, Rachel (1985) *Just Looking: Consumer Culture in Dreiser, Gissing and Zola*, New York: Methuen.

Brake, Laurel (2001) *Print in Transition*, Basingstoke: Palgrave.

——(1994) *Subjugated Knowledges*, Basingstoke: Macmillan.

Brantlinger, Patrick (1998) *The Reading Lesson: The Threat of Mass Literacy in Nineteenth-Century British Fiction*, Bloomington, IN: Indiana University Press.

——(1988) *Rule of Darkness, British Literature and Imperialism: 1830–1914*, Ithaca, NY: Cornell University Press.

Bratton, Jackie (1981) *The Impact of Children's Fiction*, London: Croom Helm.

Bristow, Joseph (ed.) (2005) *Oscar Wilde, The Picture of Dorian Gray, The Complete Works of Oscar Wilde, Vol III*, Oxford: Oxford University Press.

——(1997) '"A Complex Multiform Creature": Wilde's Sexual Identities', Peter Raby (ed.), *The Cambridge Companion to Oscar Wilde*, Cambridge: Cambridge University Press, 195–218.

Broomfield, Andrea L. (2004) 'Eliza Lynn Linton, Sarah Grand and the Spectacle of the Woman Question: Catch Phrases, Buzz Words and Sound Bites', *English Literature in Transition*, 47, 3: 251–72.

——and Sally Mitchel (eds) (1996) *Prose by Victorian Women Writers*, New York and London: Garland.

Buckler, William E. (ed.) (1958) *Prose of the Victorian Period*, Boston, MA: Houghton Mifflin.

Buckton, Oliver S. (2007) *Cruising with Robert Louis Stevenson: Travel, Narrative and the Colonial Body*, Athens, OH: Ohio University Press.

Burnett, John (ed.) (1982) *Destiny Obscure: Autobiographies of Childhood, Education and Family from the 1820s to the 1920s*, London: Allen Lane.

——(ed.) (1974) *Annals of Labour: Autobiographies of British Working-Class People, 1820–1920*, Bloomington, IN: Indiana University Press.

Butler, Judith (1990) *Gender Trouble: Feminism and the Subversion of Identity*, New York and London: Routledge.

Byron, Glennis (2003) 'Rethinking the Dramatic Monologue', Alison Chapman (ed.), *Victorian Women Poets*, Cambridge: D. S. Brewer, 79–98.

Camlot, Jason (2008) *Style and the Nineteenth-Century British Critic*, Aldershot: Ashgate.

Carey, John (1992) *The Intellectual and the Masses*, London: Faber.

Cave, Richard Allen (1997) 'Wilde's Plays: Some Lines of Influence', Peter Raby (ed.), *The Cambridge Companion to Oscar Wilde*, Cambridge: Cambridge University Press, 219–48.

Chadwick, George F. (1996) *The Park and the Town: Public Landscape in the Nineteenth and Twentieth Centuries*, New York: Routledge.

Chapman, Alison (2007) '"Vulgar Needs": Elizabeth Barrett Browning, Profit and Literary Value', Francis O'Gorman (ed.), *Victorian Literature and Finance*, Oxford: Oxford University Press, 73–90.

Chase, Malcolm (1988) *'The People's Farm': English Radical Agrarianism: 1775–1840*, Oxford: Clarendon Press.

Christ, Carol T. (1984) *Victorian and Modern Poetics*, Chicago: University of Chicago Press.

Clery, E. J. (2000) *Women's Gothic: From Clara Reeve to Mary Shelley*, Tavistock: Northcote House.

Cohen, Ed (1996) 'Writing Gone Wilde: Homoerotic Desire in the Closet of Representation', Lyn Pykett (ed.), *Reading Fin de Siècle Fictions*, London and New York: Longman, 103–26.

——(1993) *Talk on the Wilde Side: Towards a Genealogy of Discourse on Male Sexualities*, New York: Routledge.

Cocks, H. G. (2003) *Nameless Offences: Homosexual Desire in the Nineteenth Century*, London: I. B. Tauris.

Codell, Julie F. (ed.) (2003) *Imperial Co-Histories: National Identities and the British and Colonial Press*, Teaneck, NJ: Fairleigh Dickinson University Press.

Colley, Ann C. (2004) *Robert Louis Stevenson and the Colonial Imagination*, Burlington: Ashgate.

Colley, Linda (1992) *Britons: Forging the Nation 1770–1837*, New Haven, CT: Yale University Press.

Collini, Stephan (1988) *Arnold*, Oxford: Oxford University Press.

Craft, Christopher (1994) *Another Kind of Love: Male Homosexual Desire in English Discourse, 1850–1920*, London: University of California Press.

——(1990) 'Alias Bunbury: Desire and Termination in *The Importance of Being Earnest*', *Representations*, 31: 19–56.

Crawford, Robert (2000) *Devolving English Literature*, 2nd edn, Edinburgh: Edinburgh University Press.

Crochunis, Thomas C. (ed.) (2010) *The Broadview Anthology of British Women Playwrights, 1777–1843*, Peterborough, Ontario: Broadview Press.

Cronin, Richard (2002) 'The Spasmodics', Richard Cronin, Alison Chapman and Antony Harrison (eds), *A Companion to Victorian Poetry*, Oxford: Blackwell, 291–304.

Crosby, Christina (2002) 'Financial', Herbert F. Tucker (ed.), *A Companion to Victorian Literature and Culture*, Oxford: Blackwell, 225–43.

Crouzet, François (1990) *The Victorian Economy*, trans. Anthony Forster, London: Routledge.

Cunningham, Gail (1978) *The New Woman and the Victorian Novel*, New York: Harper and Row.

Daley, Kenneth (2001) *The Rescue of Romanticism: Walter Pater and John Ruskin*, Athens, OH: Ohio University Press.

Davidoff, Leonore (1973) *The Best Circles: Society Etiquette and the Season*, London: Croom Helm.

Davis, Leith (1998) *Acts of Union: Scotland and the Literary Negotiation of the British Nation 1707–1830*, Stanford, CA: Stanford University Press.

——Ian Duncan and Janet Sorenson (eds) (2004) *Scotland and the Borders of Romanticism*, Cambridge: Cambridge University Press.

Davis, Tracy C. (2000) *The Economics of the British Stage 1800–1914*, Cambridge: Cambridge University Press.

——and Ellen Donkin (eds) (1999) *Women and Playwriting in Nineteenth-Century Britain*, Cambridge: Cambridge University Press.

——(1991) *Actresses as Working Women*, London: Routledge.

Dean, Bradley (2003) *The Making of the Victorian Novelist: Anxieties of Authorship in the Mass Market*, London and New York: Routledge.

Dellamora, Richard (1990) *Masculine Desire: The Sexual Politics of Victorian Aestheticism*, Chapel Hill: University of North Carolina Press.

Demoor, Marysa (ed.) (2004) *Marketing the Author: Authorial Personae, Narrative Selves and Self-Fashioning, 1880–1930*, New York: Palgrave Macmillan.

Denisoff, Denis (2006) *Aestheticism and Sexual Parody: 1840–1940*, Cambridge: Cambridge University Press.

Denvir, Benard (ed.) (1986) *The Late Nineteenth Century: Art, Design and Society: 1852–1910*, London: Longman.

Dickinson, H. T. (1985) *British Radicalism and the French Revolution: 1780–1815*, Oxford: Blackwell.

Dijkstra, Bram (1986) *Idols of Perversity: Fantasies of Female Evil in the Fin de Siècle*, New York: Oxford University Press.

Donohue, Joseph (1988) 'Recent Studies of Oscar Wilde', *Nineteenth-Century Theatre*, 16, 2: 123–36.

——with Ruth Beggren (eds) (1995) *Oscar Wilde's The Importance of Being Earnest*, Gerrards Cross, Bucks: Colin Smythe.

Dooley, Allan C. (1992) *Author and Printer in Victorian England*, Charlottesville and London: University Press of Virginia.

Dowling, Linda (1995) *Hellenism and Homosexuality in Victorian Oxford*, Ithaca, NY: Cornell University Press.

Ebbatson, Roger (2005) *An Imaginary England: Nation, Landscape and Literature 1840–1920*, Burlington: Ashgate.

Eliot, Simon (2007) 'From Few and Expensive to Many and Cheap: The British Book Market: 1800–890', Simon Eliot and Jonathan Rose (eds), *A Companion to the History of the Book*, Oxford: Blackwell.

——(1994) *Some Patterns and Trends in British Publishing 1800–1919*, Occasional Papers of the Bibliographical Society, 8, London: The Bibliographical Society.

Ellis, Kate Ferguson (1989) *The Contested Castle: Gothic Novels and the Subversion of Domestic Ideology*, Urbana, IL: University of Illinois Press.

Eltis, Sos (1996) *Revising Wilde*, Oxford: Clarendon Press.

Erickson, Lee (1996) *The Economy of Literary Form: English Literature and the Industrialization of Publishing: 1800–1850*, Baltimore and London: Johns Hopkins University Press.

Fay, Elizabeth (1998) *A Feminist Introduction to Romanticism*, Oxford: Blackwell.

Feather, John (2006) *A History of British Publishing*, 2nd edn, London and New York: Routledge.

Feltes, Norman (1993) *Literary Capital and the Late Victorian Novel*, London: University of Wisconsin Press.

——(1986) *Modes of Production of Victorian Novels*, Chicago and London: University of Chicago Press.

Ferguson, Moira (1992) *Subject to Others: British Women Writers and Colonial Slavery 1670–1934*, London and New York: Routledge.

Ferguson, Niall (2004) *Empire: How Britain Made the Modern World*, London: Penguin.

Fleishman, Avrom (1983) *Figures of Autobiography: The Language of Self-Writing in Victorian and Modern England*, Berkeley and Los Angeles, CA: University of California Press.

Flint, Kate (1996) 'Personal Identity and the Victorian Women Poet', Roy Porter (ed.), *Rewriting the Self: Histories of the Renaissance to the Present*, London: Routledge, 156–66.

——(1993) *The Woman Reader: 1837–1914*, Oxford: Clarendon Press.

Fortunado, Paul L. (2007) *Modernist Aesthetics and Consumer Culture in the Writings of Oscar Wilde*, London and New York: Routledge.

Foucault, Michel (1978) *History of Sexuality, Vol I, An Introduction*, trans. Robert Hurley, New York: Random House.

Foulkes, Richard (ed.) (1994) *Scenes from the Provincial Stage*, London: Society for Theatre Research.

Fox, Paul (ed.) (2006) *Decadence, Morality and Aesthetics in British Literature*, Stuttgart: Ibidem.

Frankel, Nicholas (2009) *Masking the Text: Essays on Literature and Mediation in the 1890s*, High Wycombe, Bucks: Rivendale Press.

——(2000) *Oscar Wilde's Decorated Books*, Ann Arbor, MI: University of Michigan Press.

Freedgood, Elaine (2000) *Victorians Writing About Risk: Imagining a Safe England in a Dangerous World*, Cambridge: Cambridge University Press.

Freedman, Jonathan (1990) *Professions of Taste: Henry James, British Aestheticism and Commodity Culture*, Stanford, CA: Stanford University Press.

Fulford, Tim and Peter J. Kitson (eds) (1998) *Romanticism and Colonialism*, Cambridge: Cambridge University Press.

Gagnier, Regenia (2000) *The Insatiability of Human Wants*, Chicago: University of Chicago Press.

——(1992) 'On the Insatiability of Human Wants: Economic and Aesthetic Man', *Victorian Studies*, 36: 125–53.

——(1991) *Subjectivities: A History of Self-Representation in Britain, 1832–1910*, New York: Oxford University Press.

Gallagher, Catherine (1985) *The Industrial Reformation of English Fiction*, London and Chicago: University of Chicago Press.

Gardner, Vivien and Susan Rutherford (eds) (1992) *The New Woman and Her Sister: Feminism and Theatre, 1850–1914*, Ann Arbor, MI: University of Michigan Press.

Genette, Gérard (1997) *Paratexts*, trans. Jane E. Lewin, Cambridge: Cambridge University Press.

Gere, Charlotte and Lesley Hoskins (2000) *The House Beautiful: Oscar Wilde and the Aesthetic Interior*, Aldershot: Lund Humphreys.

Gibson, James (ed.) (1993) *Thomas Hardy, Tess of the D'Urbervilles*, London: Methuen.

Gill, Stephen (ed.) (1984) *William Wordsworth, The Oxford Authors*, Oxford: Oxford University Press.

Gillies, Mary Ann (2007) *The Professional Literary Agent in Britain, 1880–1920*, Toronto: University of Toronto Press.

Glen, Heather (ed.) (1988) *Emily Brontë, Wuthering Heights*, London: Routledge.

Goodlad, Lauren M. E. (2003) *Victorian Literature and the Victorian State: Character and Governance in a Liberal Society*, Baltimore and London: Johns Hopkins University Press.

Guy, Josephine (1999) 'Aesthetics, Economics and Commodity Culture: Theorizing Value in Nineteenth-Century Britain', *English Literature in Transition*, 42: 143–71.

——(1996) *The Victorian Social-Problem Novel*, Houndmills, Basingstoke: Macmillan.

——(1991) *The British Avant-Garde: The Theory and Politics of Tradition*, Hemel Hempstead: Harvester Wheatsheaf.

——and Ian Small (2000) *Oscar Wilde's Profession: Writing and the Culture Industry in the Late Nineteenth Century*, Oxford: Oxford University Press.

Habermas, Jürgen (1989) *The Structural Transformation of the Public Sphere*, trans. Thomas Burger, Cambridge, MA: MIT Press.

Hadley, Elaine (1995) *Melodramatic Tactics: Theatricalized Dissent in the English Marketplace 1800–1885*, Stanford, CA: Stanford University Press.

Hammond, Mary (2006) *Reading, Publishing and the Formation of Literary Taste in England: 1880–1914*, Aldershot: Ashgate.

Hemmings, F. W. J. (1993) *The Theatre Industry in the Nineteenth Century*, Cambridge: Cambridge University Press.

Heywood, Christopher (ed.) (2004) *Emily Brontë, Wuthering Heights*, Peterborough Ontario: Broadview Press.

Higonnet, Margaret R. (1992) *The Sense of Sex: Feminist Perspectives on Thomas Hardy*, Urbana, IL: University of Illinois Press.

Hodnett, Edward (1982) *Image and Text: Studies in the Illustration of English Literature*, London: Scolar.

Holland, Merlin (2003) *Irish Peacock and Scarlet Marquess: The Real Trial of Oscar Wilde*, London: Fourth Estate.

——and Rupert Hart-Davis (eds) (2000) *The Complete Letters of Oscar Wilde*, London: Fourth Estate.

Holloway, John (1962) 'Hard Times: A History and a Criticism', John Gross and Gabriel Pearson (eds), *Dickens and the Twentieth Century*, London: Routledge, 159–74.

——(1953) *The Victorian Sage: Studies in Argument*, London: Macmillan.

Honnighausen, Lothar (1988) *The Symbolist Tradition in English Literature*, condensed and trans. Gisele Honnighausen, Cambridge: Cambridge University Press.

Houston, Natalie M. (2003) 'Towards a New History: Fin-de-Siècle Women Poets and the Sonnet', Alison Chapman (ed.), *Victorian Women Poets*, Cambridge: D. S. Brewer, 145–64.

Howe, Elisabeth A. (1996) *The Dramatic Monologue*, London: Prentice Hall International.

Hughes, Linda K. and Michael Lund (1995) *The Victorian Serial*, Charlottesville, VA: University Press of Virginia.

Irwin, Robert (2006) *The Lust for Knowing: The Orientalists and their Enemies*, London: Allen Lane.

Jack, Ian (ed.) (1986) *Emily Brontë, Wuthering Heights*, Oxford: Oxford University Press.

Jackson, Holbook (1913) *The Eighteen Nineties*, London: Grant Richards Ltd.

Johnson, R. V. (1969) *Aestheticism*, London: Methuen.

Jones, Anna Maria (2007) *Problem Novels: Victorian Fiction Theorizes the Sensational Self*, Columbus, OH: Ohio State University Press.

Jordan, John O. and Robert L. Patten (eds) (1995) *Literature in the Marketplace: Nineteenth-Century British Publishing and the Circulation of Books*, Cambridge: Cambridge University Press.

Jusovà, Iveta (2005) *The New Woman and the Empire*, Athens, OH: Ohio University Press.

Kaplan, Cora (2007) *Victoriana: Histories, Fictions, Criticisms*, Edinburgh: Edinburgh University Press.

Kaplan, Joel (1997) 'Wilde on the Stage', Peter Raby (ed.), *The Cambridge Companion to Oscar Wilde*, Cambridge: Cambridge University Press, 249–75.

Killeen, Jarlath (2007) *The Fairy Tales of Oscar Wilde*, Aldershot: Ashgate.

Knoepflmacher, U. C. (1998) *Ventures into Childland: Victorians, Fairytales and Femininity*, Chicago: University of Chicago Press.
Kooistra, Lorraine Janzten (2002) *Christina Rossetti and Illustration*, Athens, OH: Ohio University Press.
Ksinan, Catherine (1998) 'Wilde as Editor of Woman's World', *English Literature in Transition*, 41, 4: 408–26.
Kutzer, Daphne M. (2000) *Empire's Children: Empire and Imperialism in Classic Children's Books*, New York: Garland.
Landow, George (ed.) (1979) *Approaches to Victorian Autobiography*, Athens, OH: Ohio University Press.
Langbaum, Robert (1957) *The Poetry of Experience: The Dramatic Monologue in Literary Tradition*, London: Chatto and Windus.
Leask, Nigel (1992) *British Romantic Writers and the East: Anxieties of Empire*, Cambridge: Cambridge University Press.
Leavis, F. R. (1948) *The Great Tradition*, Harmondsworth: Penguin.
Lee, Debbie (2001) *Slavery and the Romantic Imagination*, Philadelphia, PA: University of Pennsylvania Press.
Leighton, Angela (2008) *On Form*, Oxford: Oxford University Press.
——and Margaret Reynolds (eds) (1995) *Victorian Women Poets: An Anthology*, Oxford: Blackwell.
——(1992) *Victorian Women Poets: Writing Against the Heart*, Hemel Hempstead: Harvester.
Levine, George (1981) *The Realistic Imagination: English Fiction from Frankenstein to Lady Chatterley*, Chicago: University of Chicago Press.
Levinson, Marjorie (1986) *Wordsworth's Great Period Poems*, Cambridge: Cambridge University Press.
Livesey, Ruth (2007) *Socialism, Sex, and the Culture of Aestheticism in Britain, 1880–1914*, Oxford: Oxford University Press.
Lodge, David (1977) *The Modes of Modern Writing*, London: Edward Arnold.
Lonsdale, Roger (ed.) (1989) *Eighteenth-Century Women Poets: An Anthology*, Oxford: Oxford University Press.
Lovejoy, Arthur O. (1924) 'On the Discrimination of Romanticism', *PMLA*, 39, 229–53.
Lucas, John (1966) 'Mrs Gaskell and Brotherhood', David Howard, John Lucas and John Goode (eds), *Tradition and Tolerance in Nineteenth-Century Fiction*, London: Routledge and Kegan Paul, 141–206.
McCabe, Colin (1985) *Tracking the Signifier. Theoretical Essays: Film, Literature, Linguistics*, Minneapolis, MN: University of Minneapolis Press.
——(1978) *James Joyce and the Revolution of the Word*, London: Macmillan.
McCalman, Iain (1993) *Radical Underworld: Prophets, Revolutionaries, and Pornographers in London, 1795–1840*, Oxford: Clarendon Press.
MacDonagh, Thomas (1996) *Literature in Ireland*, Nenagh: Relay.
McDonald, Peter D. (1997) *British Literary Culture and Publishing Practice: 1880–1914*, Cambridge: Cambridge University Press.
McEathron, Scott, John Goodridge and Kaye Kossick (eds) (2005) *Nineteenth-Century English Labouring-Class Poets, 1801–1900*, 3 vols, London: Pickering and Chatto.
Macfarlane, Robert (2007) *Original Copy*, Oxford: Oxford University Press.
McGann, Jerome J. (2000) *Dante Gabriel Rossetti and the Game that Must be Lost*, New Haven, CT: Yale University Press.
——(1991) *The Textual Condition*, Princeton, NJ: Princeton University Press.

——(1983) *The Romantic Ideology: A Critical Investigation*, Chicago: University of Chicago Press.

Machann, Clinton (1994) *The Genre of Autobiography in Victorian Fiction*, Ann Arbor, MI: University of Michigan Press.

Macheray, Pierre (1978) *A Theory of Literary Production*, trans. Geoffrey Wall, London: Routledge and Kegan Paul.

McKenzie, D. F. (1986) *Bibliography and the Sociology of Texts*, London: The British Library.

MacKenzie, John M. (1995) *Orientalism: History, Theory and the Arts*, Manchester: Manchester University Press.

Mackie, W. Craven (1998) 'Bunbury Pure and Simple', *Modern Drama*, 37: 327–30.

Mackinnon, Sir Frank (1960) 'Appendix II: Notes on the History of English Copyright', Paul Harvey, *The Oxford Companion to English Literature*, 3rd edn, Oxford: Clarendon Press, 881–90.

MacLeod, Kirsten (2006) *Fictions of British Decadence, High Art, Popular Writing and the Fin de Siècle*, New York: Palgrave.

Marcus, Stephen (1966) *The Other Victorians: A Study of Sexuality and Pornography in Mid-Nineteenth Century England*, New York: Basic Books.

Marsden, Hilda and Ian Jack (eds) (1976) *Emily Brontë: Wuthering Heights*, Oxford: Clarendon Press.

Marsh, Jan (1994) *Christina Rossetti: A Literary Biography*, London: Pimlico.

Mason, Michael (1994) *The Making of Victorian Sexuality*, Oxford: Oxford University Press.

Mathias, P. (1983) *The First Industrial Nation: An Economic History of Britain*, 2nd edn, London, Methuen.

Maxwell, Catherine and Patricia Pulham (eds) (2006) *Vernon Lee: Decadence, Ethics and Aesthetics*, New York: Palgrave Macmillan.

Maxwell, Richard (ed.) (2002) *The Victorian Illustrated Book*, Charlottesville, VA: University Press of Virginia.

Meisel, Martin (1983) *Realizations: Narrative, Pictorial and Theatrical Arts in Nineteenth-Century England*, Princeton, NJ: Princeton University Press.

Meisel, Perry (1980) *The Absent Father*, New Haven, CT: Yale University Press.

Mellor, Anne K. (1993) *Romanticism and Gender*, New York: Routledge.

——(ed.) (1988) *Romanticism and Feminism*, Bloomington, IN: Indiana University Press.

Mermin, Dorothy (1993) *Godiva's Ride: Women of Letters in England, 1830–1880*, Bloomington and Indianapolis: Indiana University Press.

——(1986) 'The Damsel, the Knight, and the Victorian Women Poet', *Critical Enquiry*, 13: 64–80.

Miller, Andrew H. (2003) 'Recent Studies in the Nineteenth Century', *Studies in English Literature 1500–1900*, 43, 4: 959–97.

——(1995) *Novels behind Glass: Commodity Culture and Victorian Narrative*, Cambridge: Cambridge University Press.

Miller, D. A. (1988) *The Novel and the Police*, Berkeley, CA: University of California Press.

Miller, J. Hillis (1963) *The Disappearance of God*, Cambridge, MA: Belknap Press of Harvard University Press.

Michie, Elsie B. (ed.) (2006) *Charlotte Brontë's Jane Eyre: A Casebook*, Oxford: Oxford University Press.

Moers, Ellen (1976) *Literary Women*, London: Women's Press.

Mole, Tom (2007) *Byron's Romantic Celebrity: Industrial Culture and the Hermeneutics of Intimacy*, Houndmills, Basingstoke: Palgrave Macmillan.

Monsman, Gerald (2006) *H. Rider Haggard on the Imperial Frontier: The Political and Literary Contexts of His African Romances*, Greensboro, NC: ELT Press.

Morgan, Charles (1943) *The House of Macmillan*, London: Macmillan.

Morgan, Thaïs (ed.) (1990) *Victorian Sages and Cultural Discourse: Renegotiating Gender and Power*, New Brunswick and London: Rutgers University Press.

Morris, R. J. and Richard Rogers (eds) (1993) *The Victorian City: A Reader in British Urban History, 1820–1914*, London: Longman.

Muir, Percy (1989) *Victorian Illustrated Books*, revd impression, London: Batsford.

Murphy, P. T. (1994) *Towards a Working-Class Canon: Literary Criticism in British Working-Class Periodicals, 1816–1858*, Columbus, OH: Ohio State University Press.

Nelson, James G. (1971) *The Early Nineties: A View from the Bodley Head*, Cambridge, MA: Harvard University Press.

Newlyn, Lucy (2000) *Reading, Writing, and Romanticism: The Anxiety of Reception*, Oxford: Clarendon Press.

Newton, K. M. (ed.) (1991) *George Eliot*, London: Longman.

Nord, Deborah (1995) *Walking the Victorian Streets: Women, Representation, and the City*, Ithaca, NY: Cornell University Press.

Nunokawa, Jeff (1996) 'The Importance of Being Bored: The Dividends of Enui in *The Picture of Dorian Gray*', *Studies in the Novel*, 28: 357–71.

——(1991) 'In Memoriam and the Extinction of the Homosexual', *English Literary History*, 58: 427–38.

O'Brien, Ellen L. (2008) *Crime in Verse: The Poetics of Murder in the Victorian Era*, Columbus, OH: Ohio State University Press.

Onslow, Barbara (2000) *Women of the Press in Nineteenth-Century Britain*, Houndmills, Basingstoke: Macmillan.

Orel, H. (1984) *Victorian Literary Critics*, London: Macmillan.

Perkins, David (1992) *Is Literary History Possible?*, Baltimore and London: Johns Hopkins University Press.

Peterson, Linda H. (1999) 'Anthologizing Women: Women Poets in Early Victorian Collections of Lyric', *Victorian Poetry*, 37: 193–209.

——(ed.) (1992) *Emily Brontë: Wuthering Heights*, New York: St. Martin's Press.

——(1986) *Victorian Autobiography*, New Haven, CT: Yale University Press.

Pettitt, Clare (2004) *Patent Inventions: Intellectual Property and the Victorian Novel*, Oxford: Oxford University Press.

Pick, Daniel (1989) *Faces of Degeneration: A European Disorder, c. 1848–c. 1914*, Cambridge: Cambridge University Press.

Pollock, Griselda (1988) *Vision and Difference: Femininity, Feminism, and Histories of Art*, New York: Routledge.

Poovey, Mary (1988) *Uneven Developments*, Chicago: University of Chicago Press.

Porter, Roy and Leslie Hall (1995) *The Facts of Life: The Creation of Sexual Knowledge in Britain, 1650–1950*, London: Yale University Press.

Powell, Kerry (1997) *Women and the Victorian Theatre*, Cambridge: Cambridge University Press.

——(1990) *Oscar Wilde and the Theatre of the 1890s*, Cambridge: Cambridge University Press.

Psomiades, Kathy (1997) *Beauty's Body: Femininity and Representation in British Aestheticism*, Stanford, CA: Stanford University Press.

——and Talia Schaffer (eds) (1999) *Women and British Aestheticism*, Stanford, CA: Stanford University Press.

Pratt, Mary Louise (2009) *Imperial Eyes*, 2nd edn, London: Routledge.

Prins, Yopie (1999) *Victorian Sappho*, Princeton, NJ: Princeton University Press.

Pulham, Patricia (2003) '"Jewels – Delights – Perfect Loves": Victorian Women Poets and the Annuals', Alison Chapman (ed.), *Victorian Women Poets*, Cambridge: D. S. Brewer, 9–32.

Pykett, Lyn (1992), *The 'Improper Feminine': The Women's Sensation Novel and the New Women Writing*, London: Routledge.

Raven, James (2005) 'The Promotion and Constraints of Knowledge: The Changing Structure of Publishing in Victorian Britain', Martin Daunton (ed.), *The Organisation of Knowledge in Victorian Britain,* Oxford: Oxford University Press, 263–86.

——(1992) *Judging New Wealth: Popular Publishing and Responses to Commerce in England, 1750–1800*, Oxford: Oxford University Press.

Ray, Gordon N. (1976) *The Illustrator and the Book in England, 1790–1914*, New York: Pierpont Morgan Library.

——(1955) *Thackeray: The Uses of Adversity 1811–1846*, London: Oxford University Press.

Rawlings, Peter (2004) 'Flirting with Literary Masculinities', *Times Higher Education Supplement*, 27 Feb: 29.

Reader, W. J. (1966) *Professional Men: The Rise of the Professional Classes in Nineteenth-Century England*, New York: Basic Books.

Reilly, Catherine (ed.) (1994) *Winged Words: Victorian Women's Poetry and Verse*, London: Enitharmon Press.

Reitz, Caroline (2004) *Detecting the Nation: Fictions of Detection and the Imperial Adventure*, Columbus, OH: Ohio State University Press.

Reynolds, Kimberly (1990) *Girls Only? Gender and Popular Children's Fiction in Britain, 1880–1910*, Philadelphia, PA: Temple University Press.

Reynolds, Margaret (2003) *The Sappho History*, Basingstoke: Macmillan.

Rich, Adrienne (1980) 'Compulsory Heterosexuality and Lesbian Existence' *Signs*, 5: 631–60.

Richards, Bernard (ed.) (1980) *English Verse 1830–1890*, London: Longman.

Richards, Thomas (1991) *The Commodity Culture of Victorian England*, London: Verso.

Richardson, Alan and Sonia Hofkosh (eds) (1996) *Romanticism, Race and Imperial Culture, 1780–1834*, Stanford, CA: Stanford University Press.

Richardson, Angelique and Chris Willis (eds) (2001) *The New Woman in Fiction and Fact: Fin-de-Siècle Feminisms*, Houndmills, Basingstoke: Palgrave.

Richardson, LeeAnne M. (2006) *New Woman and Colonial Adventure Fiction*, Gainsville, FL: University Press of Florida.

Rob, Graham (2007) *The Discovery of France*, London: Picador.

Robinson, Solveig C. (ed.) (2003) *A Serious Occupation: Literary Criticism by Victorian Women*, Peterborough, Ontario: Broadview Press.

Roden, Frederick (2002) *Same-Sex Desire in Victorian Religious Culture*, Houndmills, Basingstoke: Palgrave, Macmillan.

Roe, Nicholas (2002) *The Politics of Nature: William Wordsworth and Some Contemporaries*, Basingstoke: Palgrave.

Ross, Marlon (1989) *The Contours of Masculine Desire: Romanticism and the Rise of Women's Poetry*, Oxford: Oxford University Press.

Roth, Phyllis (1977) 'Suddenly Sexual Women in Bram Stoker's *Dracula*', *Literature and Psychology*, 27: 113–21.

Ruppel, Richard J. (2008) *Homosexuality in the Life and Work of Joseph Conrad: Love Between the Lines*, New York: Routledge.

Ruth, Jennifer (2006) *Novel Professions*, Columbus, OH: Ohio State University Press.

Rylance, Rick (2000) *Victorian Psychology and British Culture, 1850–1880*, Oxford: Oxford University Press.

Said, Edward (1993) *Culture and Imperialism*, London: Chatto and Windus.

——(1978) *Orientalism*, London: Pantheon Books.

Sanders, Mike (2009) *The Poetry of Chartism: Aesthetics, Politics, History*, Cambridge: Cambridge University Press.

Sanders, Valerie (1989) *The Private Lives of Victorian Women: Autobiography in Nineteenth-Century England*, New York: St. Martin's Press.

Saree, Makdisi (1992) *Romantic Imperialism: Universal Empire and the Culture of Modernity*, Cambridge: Cambridge University Press.

Schaffer, Talia (2000) *The Forgotten Female Aesthetes*, Charlottesville and London, University Press of Virginia.

Schwab, Ulrike (1993) *The Poetry of the Chartist Movement: A Literary and Historical Study*, Dordrecht: Kluwer Academic.

Scullion, Adrienne (ed.) (1996) *Female Playwrights of the Nineteenth Century*, London: J. M. Dent.

Sedgwick, Eve Kosofsky (1990) *The Epistemology of the Closet*, Berkeley, CA: University of California Press.

——(1985) *Between Men: English Literature and Male Homosocial Desire*, New York: Colombia University Press.

Seiler, Robert M. (1999) *The Book Beautiful: Walter Pater and the House of Macmillan*, London: Athlone Press.

Shattock, Joanne and Michael Wolff (eds) (1982) *The Victorian Periodical Press*, Toronto: University of Toronto Press.

Shaw, David W. (1999) *Origins of the Monologue: The Hidden God*, Toronto: University of Toronto Press.

Showalter, Elaine (1996) 'Syphilis, Sexuality, and the Fiction of the Fin de Siècle', Lyn Pykett (ed.), *Reading Fin de Siècle Fictions,* London and New York: Longman, 166–83.

——(1990) *Sexual Anarchy: Gender and Culture and the Fin de Siècle*, New York: Viking.

——(1977) *A Literature of their Own: British Women Novelists from Brontë to Lessing*, Princeton, NJ: Princeton University Press.

Sinfield, Alan (1994) *The Wilde Century: Effeminacy, Oscar Wilde and the Queer Moment*, London: Cassell.

Siskin, Clifford (1998) *The Work of Writing: Literature and Social Change, 1700–1830*, Baltimore and London: Johns Hopkins University Press.

Skilton, David (ed.) (1979) *Thomas Hardy, Tess of the D'Urbervilles*, Harmondsworth: Penguin.

Smail, Daniel Lord (2008) *On Deep History and the Brain*, London: University of California Press.

Small, Ian (ed.) (2005) *Oscar Wilde, De Profundis, 'Epistola: In Carcere et Vinculis', The Complete Works of Oscar Wilde, Vol II*, Oxford: Oxford University Press.

——(1991) *Conditions for Criticism: Authority, Knowledge, and Literature in the Late Nineteenth Century*, Oxford: Oxford University Press.

——(ed.) (1979) *The Aesthetes*, London: Routledge and Kegan Paul.

Spivak, Gayatri Chakravorty (1988) 'Can the Subaltern Speak?', Cary Nelson and Lawrence Grossberg (eds), *Marxism and the Interpretation of Cultures*, Urbana, IL: University of Illinois Press.

Stabler, Jane (2002) *Burke to Byron, Barbauld to Baillie 1789 1830*, Basingstoke: Palgrave.

Stape, J. H. (2004) 'Philip Holden and Richard J. Ruppel, (eds) *Imperial Desire: Dissident Sexualities and Colonial Literature*', *English Literature in Transition*, 47, 1: 339–42.

St Clair, William (2004) *The Reading Nation in the Romantic Period*, Cambridge: Cambridge University Press.

Stephens, John Russell (1992) *The Profession of the Playwright*, Cambridge: Cambridge University Press.

——(1980) *The Censorship of English Drama, 1824–1901*, Cambridge: Cambridge University Press.

Stern, Rebecca F. (2003) '"Adulterations Detected": Food and Fraud in Christina Rossetti's Goblin Market', *Nineteenth Century Literature*, 54, 4: 447–51.

Stowell, Sheila and Joel Kaplan (1994) *Theatre and Fashion: Oscar Wilde to the Suffragettes*, Cambridge: Cambridge University Press.

Sullivan, Jill (2011) *The Politics of the Pantomime: Regional Identity in the Theatre, 1860–1900*, Hertfordshire: University of Hertfordshire Press.

Sumpter, Caroline (2008) *The Victorian Press and the Fairy Tale*, Basingstoke: Palgrave Macmillan.

Sutherland, John (2009) *The Longman Companion to Victorian Fiction*, 2nd edn, Harlow: Pearson Longman.

——(1995) *Writers, Publishers, Readers*, New York: St. Martin's Press.

——(1976) *Victorian Novelists and Publishers*, Chicago: University of Chicago Press.

Sweet, Matthew (2001) *Inventing the Victorians*, London: Faber.

Temple, Ruth Z. (1974) 'Truth in Labelling: Pre-Raphaelitism, Aestheticism, Decadence, Fin-de-Siècle', *English Literature in Transition*, 17, 4: 201–22.

Thomas, Helen (2000) *Romanticism and Slave Narratives: Transatlantic Testimonies*, Cambridge: Cambridge University Press.

Thomas, Julia (2004) *Pictorial Victorians: The Inscription of Values in Word and Image*, Athens, OH: Ohio University Press.

Thompson, James (1996) *Models of Value: Eighteenth-Century Political Economy and the Novel*, London: Duke University Press.

Thornton, R.K.R. (1983) *The Decadent Dilemma*, London: Edward Arnold.

Tromp, Marlene (ed.) (2008) *Victorian Freaks*, Columbus, OH: Ohio State University Press.

——(2000) *The Private Rod: Marital Violence, Sensation, and the Law in Victorian Britain*, Charlottesville and London: University of Virginia Press.

Tucker, F. Herbert (1984) 'From Monomania to Monologue: "St Simeon Stylites" and the Rise of the Victorian Dramatic Monologue', *Victorian Poetry*, 22, 2: 121–37.

Van Ghent, Dorothy (1953) *The English Novel: Form and Function*, New York: Rinehart.

Vicinus, Martha (1974) *The Industrial Muse: A Study of Nineteenth-Century British Working-Class Literature*, London: Croom Helm.

Vincent, David (1981) *Bread, Knowledge and Freedom: A Study of Nineteenth-Century Working Class Autobiography*, New York and London: Methuen.

Walkowitz, Judith R. (1992) *The City of Dreadful Night: Narratives of Sexual Danger in Late Victorian London*, London: Virago.

Waller, Philip (2006) *Writers, Readers and Reputations: Literary Life in Britain, 1870–1918*, Oxford: Oxford University Press.

Warner, Eric and Graham Hough (eds) (1983) *Strangeness and Beauty: An Anthology of Aesthetic Criticism*, 2 vols, Cambridge: Cambridge University Press.

Weedon, Alexis (2003) *Victorian Publishing: The Economics of Book Production for a Mass Market, 1836–1916*, Aldershot: Ashgate.

Weeks, Jeffrey (1977) *Coming Out: Homosexual Politics in Britain, from the Nineteenth Century to the Present*, London: Quartet.

Weinstein, Mark A. (1968) *William Edmonstoune Aytoun and the Spasmodics Controversy*, New Haven and London: Yale University Press.

Wheeler, Michael (1985) *English Fiction of the Victorian Period 1830–1890*, London and New York: Longman.

White, Allon (1981) *The Uses of Obscurity*, London: Routledge and Kegan Paul.

White, Cynthia Leslie (1970) *Women's Magazines, 1693–1968*, London: Michael Joseph.

White, Hayden (1973) *Metahistory: The Historical Imagination in Nineteenth-Century Europe*, Baltimore, MD: Johns Hopkins University Press.

Williams, Anne (1995) *Art of Darkness: A Poetics of Gothic*, Chicago: University of Chicago Press.

Williams, Raymond (1973) *The Country and the City*, Oxford: Oxford University Press.

——(1963) *Culture and Society*, Harmondsworth: Penguin.

Wilson, A. N. (2002) *The Victorians*, London: Hutchinson.

Woodmansee, Martha (1994) *The Author, Art, and the Market*, New York: Columbia University Press.

Woolfson, Susan J. (ed.) (2000) *Felicia Hemans: Selected Poems, Letters, Reception Materials*, Princeton, NJ: Princeton University Press.

Worrall, David (1992) *Radical Culture: Discourse, Resistance and Surveillance, 1790–1820*, New York and London: Harvester Wheatsheaf.

Worth, Katherine (1983) *Oscar Wilde*, London: Macmillan.

——(1978) *The Irish Drama of Europe from Yeats to Beckett*, London: Athlone Press.

Wu, Duncan (ed.) (1997) *Women Romantic Poets: An Anthology*, Oxford: Blackwell.

Zlotnick, Susan (1998) *Women, Writing and the Industrial Revolution*, Baltimore and London: Johns Hopkins University Press.

Zorn, Christa (2003) *Vernon Lee: Aesthetics, History and the Female Intellectual*, Athens, OH: Ohio University Press.

Index